AF701104

The Forgotten Constitution

The Forgotten Constitution

The Origins, Realization, and Legacy of the French Constitution of 1791

MICHAEL P. FITZSIMMONS

OXFORD
UNIVERSITY PRESS

OXFORD
UNIVERSITY PRESS

Oxford University Press is a department of the University of Oxford. It furthers the University's objective of excellence in research, scholarship, and education by publishing worldwide. Oxford is a registered trade mark of Oxford University Press in the UK and in certain other countries.

Published in the United States of America by Oxford University Press
198 Madison Avenue, New York, NY 10016, United States of America.

© Oxford University Press 2025

All rights reserved. No part of this publication may be reproduced, stored in a retrieval system, transmitted, used for text and data mining, or used for training artificial intelligence, in any form or by any means, without the prior permission in writing of Oxford University Press, or as expressly permitted by law, by license or under terms agreed with the appropriate reprographics rights organization. Inquiries concerning reproduction outside the scope of the above should be sent to the Rights Department, Oxford University Press, at the address above.

You must not circulate this work in any other form
and you must impose this same condition on any acquirer

Library of Congress Cataloging-in-Publication Data
Names: Fitzsimmons, Michael P., 1949– author.
Title: The forgotten constitution : the origins, realization, and legacy of the French Constitution of 1791 / Michael P. Fitzsimmons.
Description: First edition. | New York : Oxford University Press, 2025.
Identifiers: LCCN 2024056208 (print) | LCCN 2024056209 (ebook) |
ISBN 9780197793947 (hardback) | ISBN 9780197793961 (epub)
Subjects: LCSH: France. Constitution (1791) | Constitutional law—France. |
Constitutional law—Europe. | Constitutional History—France. |
France—History—Revolution, 1789–1799.
Classification: LCC KJV4074.51791 .F58 2025 (print) | LCC KJV4074.51791
(ebook) | DDC 342.4402—dc23/eng/20241125
LC record available at https://lccn.loc.gov/2024056208
LC ebook record available at https://lccn.loc.gov/2024056209

DOI: 10.1093/9780197793978.001.0001

Printed by Marquis, Canada

MIX
Paper | Supporting responsible forestry
FSC® C103567

Contents

Contents

Acknowledgments

The completion of a project of this sort is never a singular accomplishment. One is invariably the beneficiary of courtesy, kindness, and generosity of spirit. That was even more the case with this study, which, during the research stage, encountered the COVID-19 pandemic, which limited travel, closed institutions and presented a host of difficulties. My gratitude is therefore all the deeper.

I would like to thank Timothy Perry, Special Collections Librarian at the University of Missouri Libraries, for making available to me what would otherwise have remained an inaccessible source, which turned out to be quite useful. The *Bibliothèque municipale* of Dijon kindly sent me digitized copies of two documents, for which I am deeply grateful. Karen Williams of Interlibrary Loan Services at Auburn University Montgomery was indefatigable in her efforts to procure items.

I owe an extraordinary debt of gratitude to Stephen Clay of the Institut d'études politiques de Paris. He enthusiastically encouraged me to pursue the topic and provided moral support throughout. This study may not be what he might have expected or perhaps wanted, but he was indispensable to its appearance. Crucially, he also engaged one of his students at Sciences Po, Stanislas Chagne, to photograph documents for me when travel was difficult because of the pandemic and surgeries. Stan was conscientious and meticulous in all he did. It is highly doubtful that this project would have seen the light of day without Steve and Stan and I cannot sufficiently express how grateful I am to them.

Kenneth Margerison, with whom I studied the French Revolution as an undergraduate and who has remained a lifelong friend, generously read the first draft of the manuscript in its entirety and offered useful criticisms and suggestions as well as insightful comments. The friendship and examples of William Doyle and Alan Forrest were a constant source of support and emulation. Theresa Fitzsimmons and Rochelle Ziskin both provided moral support during periods of discouragement and Rochelle was always helpful with material that might be of use—she referred me to the anecdote of the Duchesse de Tourzel with which this study opens. Mira Walker kindly offered logistical support.

I extend my deep thanks to the two anonymous readers for Oxford University Press. Their perceptive and useful comments, offered with a spirit of appreciation for the topic, encouraged me and, more importantly, improved the work. Thank you to both. It has been a privilege to work once again with Nancy Toff at Oxford University Press. I am also deeply appreciative for the helpful assistance of Rada Radojicic of Oxford University Press and the skillful copy-editing of Thomas Deva of Straive. Their courtesy and professionalism were exemplary.

It is a pleasure to acknowledge another act of support, but in this instance with a personal matter. Melissa Clark graciously took on responsibilities that would otherwise have fallen on me, taking me far away from my research, my computer, interlibrary loan service, and much more for a prolonged period. I am exceedingly grateful to her and, as is the case with Steve and Stan, it is difficult to envision that this study could have been completed without her help.

The illumination of the minds of the people of France, has been predictive of the great and glorious Revolution, of the forming of a new constitution, the enacting of new laws, and the abolishing of those things that were repugnant to the interest and prosperity of the kingdom. How pleasing must it be to see both the King and the National Assembly unite together in establishing the new constitution, and in promoting whatever may conduce to the good of the nation, and the benefit of mankind in general! May the flame of liberty, like the refulgent beams of the sun, be extended over the face of the whole globe; and may all nations partake of the great and glorious blessings of natural freedom!

Samuel Stearns
Dr. Stearns's Tour from London to Paris (1790)

And this, repeated I with exultation to myself, this is the National Assembly of France! Those men now before my eyes are the men who engross the attention, the astonishment of Europe; for the issue of whose decrees surrounding nations wait in suspense, and whose fame has already extended through every civilized region of the globe: the men whose magnanimity invested them with power to destroy the old constitution, and whose wisdom is erecting the new, on a principle of perfection which has hitherto been thought chimerical, and has served only to adorn the page of the philosopher; but which they believe may be reduced to practice, and have therefore the courage to attempt. My mind, with the sensation of elevated pleasure, passing through the interval of ages, anticipated the increasing renown of these legislators, and the period when, all the nations of Europe following the liberal system which France has adopted, the little crooked policy of the present times shall give place to the reign of reason, virtue and science.

Helen Maria Williams
Letters Written in France, in the Summer of 1790, to a Friend in England: Containing Various Anecdotes Relative to the French Revolution…

Introduction

In her memoirs, the duchesse de Tourzel recalled the inaugural meeting on October 1, 1791, of the Legislative Assembly—the successor to the National Assembly, which had disbanded the previous day—at which deputies discussed the protocols for their swearing in. They unanimously agreed to take their oath on the Constitution of 1791, which Tourzel claimed had "become the New Testament of the French."

When the constitution was carried into the chamber by six men, all those in attendance rose and remained standing with their head uncovered as the room resounded with shouts of "Long live the constitution!" Each deputy then took his oath with his hand on what Tourzel called "the sacred volume."[1] Although laced with sarcasm, the religious metaphors that Tourzel used to describe it reveal the stature that the new constitution, accepted by the king merely two and a half weeks earlier, had achieved in French consciousness and public life.

The Constitution of 1791 was the culmination of a decades-long response to the deficiencies and ultimate failure of the Bourbon dynasty and the distinctive mode of governance that it had forged. Under the Bourbons, the Crown sought to concentrate power within itself and to circumvent or debilitate representative institutions, especially the Estates General, which had the longest hiatus in its history under the Bourbons, but also provincial Estates, several of which became moribund during Bourbon rule. It also transformed administrative bodies, notably the *parlements*, particularly that of Paris, to make them more responsive to the Crown. One scholar regarded the new direction of the dynasty as so innovative that it created what he called a Bourbon style of government.[2]

A word often used to describe the Bourbon model is absolutism, but a wave of scholarship challenged that concept, making absolutism a term of dubious value and an object of debate.[3] Absolutism encompassed the theory that monarchical power was divine in origin and that, within the framework of Christian morality, the king could exercise it without challenge from other entities or bodies in the kingdom. In practice, this was not the case, as scholars have increasingly demonstrated during the past few decades.[4] Rather, French royal government was a process of negotiation, especially with the *parlement* of Paris and provincial Estates that might seek to limit it.[5]

Indeed, a British historian aptly characterized the polity crafted by Louis XIV as "a compromise state that resorted to a wide variety of ad hoc measures, bluff, negotiation, and intimidation..." and an American scholar who examined Crown dealings with Brittany, Dauphiné, and Provence declared that "absolutism never existed in these three provinces."[6] To use the term "absolutism" is to accept the premises underlying it, which are untenable.[7] This study therefore uses the phrase "monarchy-centered government" to denote the Bourbon model of governance. It signifies the Crown's goal of becoming the dominant source of authority in the kingdom but recognizes that there were limitations that the term "absolutism" conceals. The dynasty sought to place the Estates General in abeyance and to ignore or weaken other bodies as well, but the authority of the Crown had limits.

In the absence of a national institution, privilege became a main point of contact between the king and his subjects—a noteworthy feature of Bourbon governance was its expansive use of privilege as an instrument of government. Privilege emanated from the Crown and was guaranteed or could be revoked by it, which enhanced the authority of the king by providing him with leverage. A change of dynasty or opposing the Crown could entail loss of privilege. In the absence of the Estates General, the dynasty increasingly resorted to privilege to deal with the myriad corporate entities that comprised the kingdom. As rights and privileges became virtually synonymous, privileged corporatism in France became the "functional equivalent" of constitutionalism in England.[8]

The village of Saint-Jean-de-Losne in Burgundy is illustrative of the use of privilege and will be a recurring focus of this study. The privileges it received reveal its use by the Crown, but Saint-Jean-de-Losne, which made its privileges the focal point of its identity, would be influential in the breakdown of the acceptance of privilege and its ultimate suppression.

In addition, as the Estates General remained dormant well into the eighteenth century, the *parlements*, led by that of Paris, began to assert greater status for themselves. They contended that they were guardians of the law, which had an existence separate from the king, and were the intermediaries between the monarch and the kingdom. The Crown, not wanting to see the *parlements* fill the void created by the absence of the Estates General, resisted the claims. The conflict escalated and led Louis XV to suppress several *parlements*, most notably that of Paris, in 1771. The demand for a constitution in the 1780s grew out of a fear of despotism and the belief that the Bourbon model of government had failed.

This study begins with a brief overview outlining the foundation and crystallization of the Bourbon model of government that generated the crisis that produced the Constitution of 1791. Bourbon kings sought to achieve monarchy-centered government, unencumbered by other bodies, especially the Estates General, which met only once in the 200 years between 1589 and 1789—the previous longest hiatus had been seventy-six years. Under Louis XV, rising tensions between Crown and *parlements*, especially that of Paris, culminated with the suppression of the *parlement* of Paris, as well as others, by Louis XV in 1771.

Louis XVI restored the *parlement* of Paris soon after his succession, which led to a resumption of disputes over the extent of royal power. Crown management of relations with the *parlement* were generally successful until the 1780s, when a fiscal crisis precipitated by French aid to the American colonists during the War of American Independence emboldened the *parlements*. Crippling deficits made it apparent to the Crown that the system of fiscal privilege would have to be breached, which led the Controller-General of Finances, Charles Alexandre de Calonne, to convene an Assembly of Notables to address the fiscal crisis. Its failure in 1787 and Crown bankruptcy in 1788 led to the calling of an Estates General.

The elections to the Estates General and the drafting of *cahiers* raised political consciousness in the kingdom. Immediately after the opening of the Estates General a dispute over the procedures for verification of credentials produced a weeks-long stalemate that led to the Third Estate declaring itself the National Assembly. Three days later the Assembly proclaimed its intention to create a constitution. Originally envisaged as a task of weeks, the constitutional project expanded after the renunciation of privileges during the meeting of the night of August 4. It would take deputies two years to complete the constitution, which was promulgated in September 1791. Understanding the Constitution of 1791 is critical to understanding the course of the French Revolution and its legacy.

As contemporaries often noted, France was not a new country, but one with many centuries of history and tradition. It was a longstanding European power with an established system of government. The unique accomplishment of the National Assembly of repositioning a king to accommodate citizen sovereignty forged a new ideal of a constitution. Linda Colley, who examined constitutions globally, remarked that constitutions could be a vehicle of restriction and control or they could be an instrument that extends rights on a broader scale.[9] In his study of the United States Constitution, the only freely enacted constitution before the Constitution of 1791,[10] Eric Foner adopted this model and, using her words, posited constitutions as either "weapons of control" or "documents of liberation and rights." Because of its acceptance of slavery—at the time of the Constitutional Convention there were approximately 700,000 enslaved people, comprising about 40 percent of the population of the states from Maryland to Georgia and a majority in South Carolina—the former quality applied to what he called "the original Constitution."[11] Indeed, its institutionalization of slavery led Frederick Douglass to question how the United States Constitution could defend both freedom and slavery.[12]

The Constitution of 1791 was unequivocally a document of liberation and rights from the outset. In making a constitution a compact between monarch and people, in its written affirmation of civic and natural rights, by its assertion of legal equality as the essential element of political legitimacy, and its enactment of the greatest expression of popular sovereignty in the world, which gave birth to electoral democracy, the Constitution of 1791 was transformative and became the model for constitution making.[13] Its impact was immediate—by 1820, fifty constitutions were in existence in continental Europe.[14]

Its legacy was enduring. Despite the intent of the negotiators at the Congress of Vienna to stifle the principles of the French Revolution, the desire for constitutional government persisted. The revolutions in 1848 in Italy, Austria, Prussia, and elsewhere sought to create constitutions based on the French experience. In addition, because the Declaration of the Rights of Man and Citizen is part of the Constitution of 1791, it is associated with the concept of human rights proclaimed by the United Nations in the Universal Declaration of Human Rights in 1948, of which the Declaration of Rights was a foundation.

Today, with only a few exceptions, notably the United Kingdom, Canada, New Zealand, Israel, and Saudi Arabia, nearly every major country in the world has a written constitution. A codified constitution is generally regarded as a hallmark of modernity, legitimacy, and good order.[15] The Constitution of 1791 was the leader in this innovation. In view of the transformation it brought about in France and its leading role as an exemplar for Europe and the world, the origins and legacy of the Constitution of 1791 are well worth exploring.

The Forgotten Constitution: The Origins, Realization, and Legacy of the French Constitution of 1791.
Michael P. Fitzsimmons, Oxford University Press. © Oxford University Press 2025.
DOI: 10.1093/9780197793978.003.0001

I

THE CREATION OF A BOURBON STYLE OF GOVERNMENT

1

The Rebuilding of Royal Authority

On August 1, 1589, at St. Cloud, outside of Paris, Jacques Clément fatally stabbed the French king, Henri III. As he lay dying, Henri III, who was childless, designated Henri of Navarre as his heir. Navarre became Henri IV, marking the passage from the Valois to the Bourbon dynasty, but the transition occurred during the catastrophic Wars of Religion. Henri IV's first task was to retake the kingdom of which Henri III had lost control, but Henri IV was a Huguenot, which prevented him from assuming full power until he converted to Catholicism. He did so in 1593, which led to his coronation in 1594, although it was illustrative of the tenuous nature of Henri's situation that it occurred not in the traditional location of Reims, which was under the control of the Holy League—the Catholic alliance opposed to Henri—but at Chartres and with a different oil.[1] Paris, a League stronghold, acknowledged his rule soon after and its recognition led many other towns to accept Henri as well, although a few had to be subdued militarily.

Henri reached out to the Huguenots in France, many of whom had been alienated by his conversion. The resolution of their differences occurred with the Edict of Nantes, promulgated in April 1598, which recognized freedom of conscience and granted Huguenots the right to worship at designated sites. It encountered strong Catholic resistance and the *parlement* of Paris initially balked at registering it, although it subsequently did, with modifications. The edict ended the civil wars in France.

Henri was the monarch of a ruined kingdom.[2] The demographic consequences of the conflict were staggering, with war, famine, and disease producing a significant reduction in population. Over a thirty- to forty-year period, the loss may have been as great as two to four million people, with the high estimate representing perhaps nearly a quarter of the population.[3] During the first half of the sixteenth century the French monarchy had been the most powerful and developed in Europe.[4] By the time of Henri III's assassination, royal authority had been shattered and the new dynasty embarked upon a slow and difficult rebuilding of its power.

There was a desire for peace and strong rule by the monarch after the near disintegration of the kingdom.

The challenges confronting the new dynasty were daunting. It would have to resolve the religious conflict and reclaim territories lost to the Crown during the religious wars. State finances had to be rebuilt while keeping the Estates General in abeyance. Great nobles and princes of the blood had to be warded off and the *parlement* of Paris had to be prevented from becoming assertive. For most of its existence, the Bourbon dynasty generally succeeded in achieving all of these objectives except the last.[5] The *parlement* would contest royal power in the mid-seventeenth century with the first Fronde and disputed Crown claims of royal power during the eighteenth century.

In one of his most important actions, Henri appointed Maximilien de Béthune, duc de Sully, as superintendent of finances, one of several positions Sully held.[6] Although he is the best known, Sully was not the only capable administrator in Henri's service—Pomponne de Bellièvre as Chancellor and others were also effective in rebuilding the power of the Crown.[7]

Disaffection and even disloyalty by great nobles continued, with some princes of the blood and other relatives having dynastic ambitions of their own. One plot led to the execution of Charles Gontaut, maréchal de Biron, in 1602.[8] Ultimately, however, a reviving economy and, for the first time in decades, an effective central government centered on a royal council filled with loyal appointees of Henri, contributed to an improvement of conditions in France. The exclusion of great nobles from the council became a critical component of the "Bourbon style of government."[9]

Together Henri, with Sully and other ministers, created a prototype of governance that would, with some variation, be the model for his successors until the French Revolution. On May 14, 1610, however, Henri was assassinated by Jacques Ravaillac, a Catholic zealot embittered by Henri's toleration of Huguenots, whom Ravaillac wished to see forcibly converted.[10]

In a cruel irony, Henri strengthened the monarchy further in an entirely unanticipated fashion—through his assassination. In the aftermath of the assassination of two consecutive kings, there was a desire to elevate the position of the monarch to a degree that would make the idea of an attack upon his person or power unthinkable.[11] The *parlement* of Paris declared his widow, Marie de Medici, regent for Henri's eight-year-old son and heir, Louis XIII, which enhanced its power at the expense of the great nobles.[12]

The New Model of Governance in Jeopardy

However much he may have done to reinvigorate the monarchy and to begin to make it the primary center of power in France, following his assassination Henri's accomplishments and the model of government he had inaugurated were jeopardized. Although Marie quickly confirmed Sully as minister, rivalries and jealousies among princes of the blood and great nobles led to a deterioration in the position of the Crown. In an effort to placate them, Marie drew on the surplus that Sully had amassed and dissipated much of it in an ill-advised policy of largesse.[13] Marie's weakened authority, especially with respect to the great nobles, figured heavily in Sully's resignation as superintendent of finances in 1611.

In February 1614, encouraged by Marie's enfeebled position, a prince of the blood, Henri II of Condé, along with other great nobles, rebelled against her. Marie was able to negotiate a settlement with them during May by agreeing to convene an Estates General, which the nobles hoped would weaken royal authority.

The Estates General opened in late October 1614. The three orders held their meetings and discussions separately and communicated with each other only by messenger, a cumbersome process that made it difficult to achieve any sense of common purpose. Dissension and rancor among the three estates strengthened the position of the Crown by placing it in the position of arbiter. Contemporaries viewed the meeting as a failure because of an overriding concern with protocol, especially ceremonies and precedence, rather than with policy.[14] The Estates General failed and its lack of success allowed the accretion of power by the Crown begun by Henri IV to continue. Had the Estates General been able to enact a reform agenda, it would, in all probability, have stemmed the increase in strength of the monarchy.[15]

Indeed, the Crown recognized the threat that the Estates General posed to its authority. The circumstances that had allowed it to emerge unscathed had been fortuitous and could not reliably be expected to hold in the future. The Crown realized that an elected national body could have a standing equal to that of the king and could advance policies of its own, which would almost certainly weaken the monarchy. As a result, it became a fundamental tenet of Bourbon policy not to convene an Estates General.

The Crown was aided in that goal by the memory of the futility of its recent meetings. The Estates General of 1560 had been unable to prevent the drift toward civil war, another in 1588 had seen a political assassination and the renewal of conflict and that of 1614, meeting in extraordinary crisis conditions after the assassination of Henri IV and his predecessor, had descended into petty squabbling and accomplished nothing. Its unproductive record made the passing of the Estates General go unlamented.

In 1624 Louis XIII, Henri IV's son and successor, made Armand-Jean du Plessis de Richelieu a member of the royal council. It was the collaboration of Louis XIII and Richelieu that enabled the consolidation and growth of royal power begun by Louis's father to continue and lay the foundation for the establishment and refinement of monarchy-centered government. Only once after the reign of Louis XIII, during the Fronde, would the power of the Crown be challenged in a direct and fundamental manner, and that occurred during another transition of power with a regency under a foreign Queen Mother during the minority of Louis XIV.

The role of the *parlement* of Paris had to be addressed. Its right to register royal edicts had progressed to authorization to analyze them and ultimately to a right of remonstrance, which allowed the body to put forward objections, although it could not prevent an edict from becoming law. The magistrates of the *parlement* perceived their role as overseeing and protecting the rights and traditions of the kingdom and assisting the Crown in maintaining the safety and security of the kingdom even as they jealously guarded their own privileges.[16]

Henri IV had respected its traditional role but the *parlement* had little influence as he began to rebuild royal power. After it declared that Marie de Medici should be regent, the *parlement* gained a larger role under her regency and sought to supersede the Estates General as the primary guardian of the rights of subjects.[17] In an effort to diminish the role of the *parlement*, Richelieu established special tribunals, one in 1624 and another in 1641. In the latter instance the *parlement* refused to register the edict that established it, but the tribunal nevertheless convened and judged cases, with the *parlement* powerless to prevent it. Moreover, the Crown issued a provision that remonstrances had to be made within two months of the publication of the edict. If no remonstrance was forthcoming, the edict was registered automatically.[18]

Although Louis XIII and Richelieu did not create an orderly, stable structure of government, their achievement was nevertheless considerable—they were able in large measure to maintain the momentum begun by Henri IV in rebuilding and consolidating royal authority. Although the Crown would face another major threat to its power in 1649, Louis and Richelieu laid the foundation for Louis XIII's more illustrious son and successor, Louis XIV, to create secure and regular government and to establish French ascendancy in Europe.

Privilege as Constitutionalism

The gradual growth of the French state, with regions or provinces added over time, had created a structure riddled with myriad rights and customs that the Crown could override only at the risk of unrest or rebellion, which is how privilege came to suffuse the state and assume quasi-constitutional status. Burgundy offers an illustration of this process. After the death of Charles the Bold in battle in 1477, the French king, Louis XI, sent an army to Dijon, surrounding the city. As preparations for a siege were underway, Louis offered to recognize all existing liberties and privileges if Dijon accepted his rule. The city surrendered and French troops entered, even though many of its inhabitants had favored resistance.

The surrender of Dijon became the catalyst for a rebellion in favor of Mary of Burgundy, the unmarried nineteen-year-old daughter of Charles the Bold, with the town of Saint-Jean-de-Losne among those taking the lead in the uprising. Ultimately, however, due in part to Mary's announced engagement to Maximilian of Austria, which raised the unattractive prospect of Habsburg rule, Burgundy submitted to French rule.

Burgundy entered the French kingdom with its privileges and provincial estates intact and Louis XI granted the Estates of Burgundy the right to determine the levying of taxes in the province.[19] The Wars of Religion, however, led to a reemergence of Burgundian identity centered on strong loyalty to the Catholic faith and allegiance to the Crown was further strained by the assassination of Henri, duc de Guise, a leader of the Catholic forces, in 1588.[20] Burgundy held out against Henri IV until 1595, when it yielded and gave him a warm welcome when he visited Dijon in June of that year.

By 1635 Louis and Richelieu believed that they had consolidated the position of the Crown sufficiently to enter the Thirty Years War, which was moving in a direction detrimental to French interests. Although the French would ultimately emerge victorious, at the beginning of its participation in the war France was invaded by Imperial forces and in 1636 Burgundy was one of the areas that experienced the Habsburg onslaught.

Burgundy had been apprehensive about going to war with the Empire, so much so that after Louis XIII declared war in May 1635, the *parlement* of Dijon, in a bid to remain neutral, delayed registering the declaration until the following month. Saint-Jean-de-Losne became the site of a notable encounter. In anticipation of being within the theater of operations, it had begun defensive preparations, but the work was far from complete when Imperial forces under the command of Matthias Gallas arrived in late October 1636, to attack the town, intending to winter there. A French force of 150 men from the regiment of Conti was garrisoned in Saint-Jean-de-Losne and there were approximately 400 townsmen available to assist in the defense.

On October 26, 1636, after refusing an Imperial demand to surrender, Saint-Jean-de-Losne endured a heavy artillery bombardment.[21] After the inhabitants repulsed a sortie the following day, on October 28 Imperial forces began a larger assault, laying siege to the town. Despite a fearsome barrage on October 30, Saint-Jean-de-Losne held. Conditions were again difficult during the night of October 31 to November 1 as Imperial troops attempted to launch a heavy infantry assault, but they were hampered by continuing heavy rain that largely immobilized them.

On November 1, a religious holiday, Imperial artillery breached a portion of the fortifications on the west side of the town, leading Imperial forces to concentrate their attack there. Ultimately, however, the troops of the Conti regiment and the inhabitants held and repelled three attacks in close fighting. The battle resulted in the loss of hundreds of men and compelled a retreat, with Imperial officers taunting the troops for retreating from a defense by townsmen.[22] Relief came on November 3 with the arrival of a French force, which pursued Gallas after his withdrawal, inflicting additional losses of men and equipment on the Imperial forces. The victory at Saint-Jean-de-Losne was one of the few French successes in 1636.[23]

One of the inhabitants who had distinguished himself during the defense of the town, Martène, was chosen to go to the royal court to provide an account of the siege to Louis XIII. In December 1636 and March 1637, Louis XIII granted Saint-Jean-de-Losne exemption from all of the *tailles*, flood assessments, and any other grant or tax to which the rest of the kingdom or Burgundy might be subject.[24] For its valiant defense, Saint-Jean-de-Losne received the appellation of Belle Défense, a name that it briefly assumed during the Revolution.

The privileges of Saint-Jean-de-Losne thereby entered the patchwork of privileges between Crown and society that underpinned the Old Regime French state. As the Crown consolidated its position, it was necessary to cement loyalties and the awarding of privileges served to seal allegiance to the monarchy. Privileges of every variety were present throughout the kingdom and limited royal prerogative, but the bestowal on Saint-Jean-de-Losne by Louis XIII illustrates their underlying purpose—the immediate gain of loyalty outweighed future considerations.[25]

Richelieu died in December 1642 and Louis XIII in May 1643. With the most popular of French monarchs, Henri IV, as his predecessor and the best known of them, Louis XIV, as his successor, the reign of Louis XIII is somewhat overshadowed or treated in a cursory fashion.[26] The neglect is unfortunate because the legacy of Richelieu and Louis XIII—the preservation, consolidation, and advancement of the foundation begun by Henri IV, once again making the Crown the central component of the French state—is not insignificant. Their efforts ultimately crystallized under Louis XIV, although not without challenge.

Crown Preeminence Challenged

Louis XIV was a child, not yet five years old, when his father died. Louis XIII had preserved and strengthened the accomplishments of his father, Henri IV, but the political order was still nebulous at Louis XIII's death. The crystallization of the Bourbon model of monarchy would be the chief legacy of Louis XIV.

The beginning of his reign, however, was unpromising. The mother of Louis XIV, Anne of Austria, became regent, despite a provision in the will of her late husband banning her from being sole regent. Anne, however, succeeded in having the *parlement* of Paris annul the will. Spanish by birth at a time when France was at war with Spain, with little understanding of French politics and with the strained relationship with her late husband generally known, Anne's position as regent was not strong. Once she became sole regent the great nobles began seeking to reclaim power and prestige lost under Henri IV and Louis XIII.

Richelieu had recommended Cardinal Jules Raymond Mazarin as his successor and Anne made him first minister. They forged a close bond that provided stability, with Mazarin as devoted to the education and interests of the young monarch as Anne was.[27] Richelieu's endorsement helped Mazarin retain the services of Richelieu loyalists, providing additional stability and competency. The appointment of Mazarin appeared to signify the continuation of the Bourbon practice of using a chief minister for governance.

The reign of Louis XIV began at a difficult time. Although Louis XIII and Richelieu had turned the tide of the war in France's favor, its costs were ruinous. Their foreigner status made Anne and Mazarin, who was of Italian origin, unpopular. Furthermore, they compounded their unpopularity by ignoring traditional elites, both at the court and the *parlement* of Paris, which had invalidated Louis XIII's will in an effort to ingratiate itself with her. After several years of financial irregularities and manipulation and after being forced to register an unpopular edict through a *lit de justice* at which the young monarch was present, the *parlement* became restive.

Seeking to regain prestige and influence, magistrates drew up a series of demands that combined self-interest with a challenge to royal authority. They demanded an end to the creation of new venal offices, the regular payment of *gages*, the remuneration given to venal officeholders, as well as the suppression of intendants and the right of the *parlement* to consent to taxation.[28] After the Crown responded by arresting three leaders of the *parlement*, hundreds of barricades went up in the city, forcing the Crown to release them and making Anne and Mazarin aware that popular sentiment in Paris favored the *parlement* rather than the regency they led. The failed arrest attempt, in August 1648, is the conventional starting point for what has become known as the Frondes, reflecting its two different phases. The driving forces of the Frondes were rooted in selfish interests and devoid of any larger meaning, but they facilitated acquiescence to Louis XIV's model of monarchy-centered government.[29]

Despite its self-interested objectives, the perception that the Crown was thwarting attempts by the *parlement* to ameliorate difficult conditions made the *parlement* popular and increased the isolation and disapproval of Anne and Mazarin. Numerous anti-Mazarin pamphlets, ultimately numbering in the thousands and collectively known as Mazarinades, appeared, not only heightening animus toward Anne and Mazarin but also bringing favorable attention to the *parlement* because of what were perceived as efforts at reform.[30]

The Crown lost considerable authority to the *parlement* during the summer and fall of 1648. Beginning in early January 1649, the *parlement* began preparations usually employed when the city was under siege by foreign armies but in this instance clearly directed against the Crown, effectively initiating civil war.[31] The *parlement* received support from a number of great nobles, who were usually disdainful of the magistrates, but they shared a common antipathy for Mazarin. Weakened and unable to resist the *parlement*, Anne and Mazarin, along with the young monarch, left Paris for Saint-Germain-en-Laye on January 5, 1649.

Much now hinged on Condé, who, notwithstanding his participation in conspiracies to remove Mazarin, remained loyal to the Crown. With the Treaties of Westphalia having ended the war with the Empire in October, he had military forces to deploy against the capital that had not been available in August and he began a siege of the city. After several weeks of siege, the *parlement* had to yield. The Treaty of Reuil, concluded with the Crown in March 1649, included a provision granting amnesty to the *parlementaires* and their followers, ending the first Fronde.[32] The royal family returned to Paris in August and Mazarin remained in place.[33]

The settlement with the *parlement* inaugurated a second phase, sometimes called the "noble Fronde," which enlarged the scope of civil war. The greatest shortcoming of the Treaty of Reuil was that it had not addressed the grievances of the great nobles, who were angered that the *parlement* had made peace with the Crown and especially aggrieved that Mazarin remained chief minister. Condé was disappointed that his defeat of the *parlement* had not gained him political power and he entered into plots. Armed conflict began in January 1650, when the Crown arrested Condé, along with other princes, which led Condé loyalists to revolt.[34] The royal army could not be defeated by any single rebel force, but the revolt was spread widely throughout France, making it difficult to confront. The nobles, however, were divided into two contending factions. Although each shared the goal of removing Mazarin, each also sought to crush the other. For his part, Mazarin sought to drive a wedge between the *parlement* and the great nobles, which buttressed and even enhanced the position of the *parlement*.

The parties concluded a tentative peace accord in October 1650 but antipathy for Mazarin increased, fueled by Mazarinades and the continued imprisonment of Condé. Mazarin increasingly became the focal point for resentment amid a growing sense that royal power had been misused and that royal government had failed. Many looked to the *parlement* of Paris for direction.[35] In a remonstrance of February 1651, the *parlement* demanded the release of the princes and the dismissal of Mazarin, effectively realigning the interests of the two factions.

Realizing that to retain Parisian opinion in her favor Anne would have to agree to actions she had previously rejected, the *parlement* disingenuously sought to take advantage of that situation by issuing a statement thanking Anne for dismissing Mazarin—any disavowal would immediately have turned opinion against her. It also put forward a decree that prohibited foreigners from serving in royal councils, even those who had been naturalized. Furthermore, pressing its advantage to the fullest, the *parlement* stated that it could not ensure Mazarin's safety if he did not leave France.

In late April the *parlement* of Paris ordered the arrest of Mazarin. He went into exile in Cologne and Condé was freed from his imprisonment. Condé, however, left Paris in July 1651 for the provinces, leaving the *parlement* in the difficult position of having to deal with the consequences of its political interventions. If it supported Condé, it risked the renewal of civil war. If it sided with Anne, it would potentially clear the way for the return of Mazarin because she had the sole authority to appoint ministers. If it did nothing, it would forfeit the power that it had gained.

On September 7, 1651, in an elaborate and impressive ceremony, Louis XIV, two days after his thirteenth birthday, went before the *parlement* of Paris to assert his full powers as monarch.[36] Louis's assumption of full power placed the *parlement* in an uncomfortable position, wedged between two implacable parties whose dispute portended conflict and disorder for the kingdom. On one side, Anne, with the king's full authority and backing, could claim the prerogative to bring back Mazarin. Despite the decrees by the *parlement*, the magistrates could not plausibly enforce the exile of Mazarin if the fully empowered monarch desired his return.

When Condé took up arms against the Crown the same month, the conflict became greater and more destructive and lent credibility to Anne's assertion that the great nobles were destroying the kingdom. It had been plausible to view the earlier uprising as a stand against arbitrary power and imprisonment. In this instance, however, the lack of any discernible purpose strengthened the Crown. The perception arose that the young king and his mother were the only ones who could save the kingdom.[37]

Condé began his campaign in the fall of 1651 and fighting occurred throughout France, but the behavior of Condéan forces led the *parlement* of Paris to align itself with the Crown.[38] In October 1651 the *parlement* declared that the levying of taxes or conscription of soldiers required the approval of the monarch. It also rejected Condé's request that the monarch's power to conclude peace treaties be conferred upon him. By the spring of 1652, after months of war, the populace was war-weary, and that fatigue largely overwhelmed whatever ardor for one side or the other may have existed.

Condé marched on Paris and entered the city in April 1652. Royal and Condéan troops ravaged the countryside around Paris. During the summer of 1652 Paris experienced looting, rioting, and killing and the populace became largely indifferent toward whether Crown or Condéan forces triumphed if a victory by one side or the other would bring an end to destruction and disorder.

On July 2, 1652, Condé was defeated in a battle outside Paris, with his force suffering heavy losses, but he remained in control of the city. The Parisian populace felt a general revulsion for violence perpetrated by Condé supporters at the *Hôtel de Ville* on July 4, which included setting fire to the building and killing members of the municipal council. Some of his strongest allies in the *parlement* broke with him because of the bloodshed.[39] The royalism that took hold among Parisians was born of desperation and based on the recognition that royal rule was the lesser of two evils.[40]

In August 1652, with Condé's position becoming weaker, settlement talks began.[41] As Condé's position deteriorated further, he left Paris and continued his rebellion in Guyenne until 1653, after which he entered into the service of Spain, with which France was at war, as a general. In an arranged action, the municipal government asked the king to return to Paris, which led to a grand entry on October 21, 1652, without Mazarin.[42] Mazarin returned to Paris on February 3, 1653, with Louis XIV meeting him outside of the city. Mazarin entered Paris in the monarch's carriage and his return signified the affirmation of royal right.[43]

The brutality of the military campaigns and especially their effects on the civilian populace played a role in the political settlement that ensued.[44] Crown and parlementary forces moved throughout the area around Paris, engaging in conflict with peasants and villagers as they foraged for supplies. One provision of the Treaty of Reuil stipulated that the army of the *parlement* had to be disbanded, after which demobilized troops marauded the area around Paris, killing inhabitants and looting villages.[45]

The expanded fighting in the Condéan phase of the Frondes broadened the geographical extent of suffering as armies operating in different areas of

France lived off the land. Military encampments bred infectious diseases and the arrival of soldiers led to the devastation of villages, with confiscation of crops and livestock, raping of women, and burning of buildings and even entire towns.[46] The destruction was not confined to peasants and villagers. The country homes of magistrates of the *parlement* of Paris and other Parisians were razed and those of provincial parlementary judges were ransacked.[47] Many soldiers were of foreign origin and treated Frenchmen with the same degree of cruelty as they did foreigners on the frontiers.[48]

This was the manner in which many rural inhabitants experienced political conflict and they cared little, if at all, about court politics or the motives, respective rights, responsibilities, or institutional standing of *parlement* and Crown. To the degree that internal conflict represented the possibility of rampaging armies in one's region, the overwhelming majority of Frenchmen clearly desired stability. The degree of death or destruction could never be anticipated, making any outbreak of civil strife anathema. The devastation from the Frondes was not at the level of the Wars of Religion, but it was substantial.[49]

In the final analysis, the willingness of the French populace to accede to the system of government put in place by Louis XIV was primarily a resigned acceptance. Contemporaries did not believe that they were making a choice between strong or limited monarchy. Rather, they viewed the choice before them as one between effective monarchical rule and chaos, which must be recognized in order to understand the model of government established by Louis XIV.[50]

Mazarin's return in 1653 enabled a rebuilding of royal power to begin anew—one scholar termed it the restoration of the state.[51] The *parlement* had been unnerved by the violence unleashed by its dispute with the Crown. After the Treaty of Reuil it did not take a side for the remainder of the conflict, even as it sought to gain political advantage. In October 1652 the *parlement* of Paris had registered an edict that barred it from deliberating on matters of state or state finances and reverted to its royalist outlook in return for a recognized and defined role in the polity.

It was Louis's belief that Mazarin had not only saved the throne during the Frondes but had placed it in a dominant position, both domestically and in Europe. Mazarin's tutelage of his godson had been so exhaustive that Louis decided to assume the position of chief minister himself, a decision he announced the day after Mazarin's death in March 1661.[52]

It was almost certainly more than confidence inspired by Mazarin's training, however, that led to Louis's decision. The participants in the Frondes had uniformly proclaimed their loyalty to the monarch and had contended that they were opposing abuses or innovations by Mazarin. The assumption of the post of chief minister by Louis represented another means of consolidating his authority and subordinating French society to the Crown. In effacing the distinction between minister and king, Louis made any uprising by the princes of the blood or the *parlement* a revolt against him personally. This was, by definition, treason, and would make it difficult for any insurrection to acquire a broader following. Furthermore, to the degree that the exile of Mazarin had weakened and even threatened the Bourbon system of governance, Louis's action eliminated any such risk in the future.

The disestablishment of the chief minister post represented an alteration of the Bourbon style of government.[53] Louis XIV's two successors followed the precedent he established. Although there would be ministerial favorites, there would not be an officially recognized chief minister. In surveying the differences between France in 1661 and the traumatic period after Henri IV's assassination and the minority of Louis XIII, Richard Bonney stated that France in 1661 was scarcely recognizable in comparison with that traumatic era, which underscores the consolidation of Bourbon rule that occurred.[54]

Although the monarchy came out of the Frondes stronger and in a position to gain additional strength, the security and prestige of the Crown were based upon a consensus to which the elites of the sword and robe assented—this was the spirit of the compromise state.[55] They did so largely on their own terms and for their own benefit, which ultimately limited the degree of latitude available for fundamental reforms.[56] The institutional legacy of the Frondes was the retention of a societal structure based on corporations with their conflicting jurisdictions and privileges.[57]

The Expansion of Privilege

Louis built a standing army and used it not only to maintain order domestically but also to undertake an expansion of the territory of France, which extended the web of privilege and made it more complex. The first territorial gains came through the Treaty of Aix-la-Chapelle in 1668, in which France took possession of Lille, Douai, and other towns and territory in the north. It would have been counterproductive to do away with a system that had the support and cooperation of local elites, which meant that a key component of bringing Flanders into the French kingdom was to allow the region to retain its privileges.[58]

In Lille, Louis swore to recognize and honor the privileges of the city before its municipal officials swore their allegiance to him, a protocol that illustrated the quasi-constitutional nature of privilege. In addition, French administrators were told not to alter or infringe upon the privileges of the region. To be sure, there were limits to the respect shown for privileges if they were in conflict with the will of the Crown, but they were to be used to mold the region to conform to the customs and model of France. French rule proved unpopular until an Anglo-Dutch occupation of the area during the War of Spanish Succession turned sentiment in favor of France. The revocation of privileges, however, would have provoked deeper and more widespread disaffection, which meant they had to remain in place and be respected.[59]

In 1681, through a disingenuous process of using French-established courts, *Chambres des réunions*, to uncover putative historical links to the recently acquired territories in order to justify their annexation, France took Strasbourg and began a process of respecting and co-opting a variety of privileges and using them to absorb the city. The example of Strasbourg illuminates the degree to which privilege in France was kaleidoscopic, with varying models of privilege and its use in governance.

Strasbourg had been an imperial free city with its own currency and judiciary and had also been overlord to several rural communities. Its municipal government, which carried out all major responsibilities and determined local life, was configured through corporate, especially guild, bodies. The structure was widely admired for its balance of powers, although on the eve of it coming under French rule it had become increasingly oligarchic.[60]

Strasbourg came under French jurisdiction in September 1681 and French possession was subsequently affirmed in the Treaty of Ryswick in 1697. An intendant based in Breisach nominally administered the city, but it retained a considerable degree of its former independence. Its citizens, for example, were taxed only by the local government, which in turn negotiated with the Crown on its assessment. Its legal and judicial individuality led to its inhabitants being characterized by a historian of the city as "a rather special category of royal subjects."[61]

Gail Bossenga has argued that privilege was less a barrier to monarchical encroachment than it was a vehicle that was indispensable in the development of monarchical power and she dates its beginnings after the Frondes.[62] The Crown could circumvent representative institutions through the management and manipulation of corporate bodies. It could also create municipal offices, which often led local or regional officials, eager to protect urban or provincial privileges and to avoid the dilution of their own authority, to purchase them. Another mechanism used by Louis XIV was to have urban centers such as Lille, Lyon, and Toulouse directly pay to maintain urban privileges.

Under the Old Regime, beginning with Louis XIV, the Crown used closed corporate structures to align itself with whichever elements affirmed obedience to and secured revenues for it, irrespective of the social composition of the corporate institutions. There was, however, a fiscal contradiction in royal policy that would be a major precipitating factor in the French Revolution. Crown revenues, whether loans or subsidies, were premised on different forms of privilege, whereas the necessity of servicing loans and meeting other obligations led to efforts to expand the tax base, often by breaching privileges. The contradiction meant that the Crown could not create a more logical or equitable system of tax collection.[63]

For decades, however, the model was generally successful, which led to a situation in which "privilege and the state grew together."[64] The expansive use of privilege to cement loyalty to and strengthen the Crown by circumventing representative institutions was a defining characteristic of Bourbon rule.

The Fraying of Monarchical Rule

Louis left the *parlement* of Paris in place. Despite the fact that it was an agency of the Crown, in the absence of the Estates General and with the perception that the *parlement* had taken constitutional stands during the Fronde, it became generally viewed as the de facto representative of the kingdom.[65] In early 1673 Louis weakened its authority by requiring the *parlement* to register an edict upon presentation and to put forward any remonstrance within one week. At the end of that period, or six weeks for provincial *parlements*, the edict received the status of law.[66]

It is generally agreed that the measure was originally intended as a temporary wartime measure—it was promulgated during the Dutch War—but it held for the remainder of Louis's reign.[67] The action was an additional assertion of Louis's personal rule.[68] Just as the Estates General was consultative in nature, so, too, the *parlement* of Paris would not be included in any manner of partnership in governance.[69] Through this arrangement Louis succeeded in asserting his authority over the *parlements* and ensured that they could not put forward any claim to legislative authority.[70]

Personal rule, both without a chief minister and with a considerably reduced role for the *parlements*, became the model of governance under Louis XIV. Indeed, by the early eighteenth century, the belief existed, reflected particularly in Louis de Rouvroy, duc de Saint-Simon, that the French constitution was rooted in the royal blood.[71] The view of the constitution as consubstantial with the king would have rendered any notion of it as an entity separate from the monarch inconceivable. Louis's authority was more unfettered than that of his predecessors and it was buttressed by the standing army. Moreover, his personal control of patronage, the previous control of which by Richelieu and Mazarin had been a catalyst for revolts by aggrieved nobles, also strengthened monarchical authority.[72]

The War of Devolution had brought Lille and other towns under French control but Louis was angry that he had been denied Franche-Comté. After the Dutch War, which ended in 1678, Louis succeeded in gaining Franche-Comté and other territories in the Treaty of Nijmegen. Louis continued his territorial expansion thereafter through the *Chambres des réunions*, with the annexation of Strasbourg representing a notable triumph.

Louis's expansionism generated suspicion and alarm in Europe and his refusal to send aid against the Turkish threat increased antipathy toward him. His revocation of the Edict of Nantes in 1685 alienated Protestant monarchs and the Emperor formed the League of Augsburg in 1686 to oppose French expansion.[73] After French troops laid waste to the Palatinate, the Nine Years War began in 1688. Louis had not anticipated the war, for which France was unprepared, but he expected hostilities to be much shorter in duration than they were. The Treaty of Ryswick that ended the war in 1697 was a humiliation for him. France lost most of the territorial acquisitions it had made since the Treaty of Nijmegen and through the *Chambres des réunions*, although it did retain Strasbourg.

The war appeared to have chastened Louis. A failed harvest in 1693–94 caused considerable hardship. All regions of France saw an increase in death rates and a decline in birth rates—over one million people died in 1693–94. By the end of the famine the population of France had declined by 6.8 percent.[74] In the wake of the Nine Years War, Louis seemingly wished to avoid war and spare his subjects its privations.[75]

His intentions collapsed, however, when the issue of Spanish succession arose. In late 1700, after a long decline, Carlos II, the king of Spain, died without heirs and designated Philippe d'Anjou, the grandson of Louis XIV, as his successor. The succession was contingent upon two conditions—that there be no separation of Spain and its empire and that the monarchies of France and Spain never be merged. Louis accepted the provisions and Philippe became King Philippe V of Spain.

When Philippe ascended to the throne of Spain, Louis gratuitously remarked that the Pyrenees no longer existed. More significantly, the French Crown issued *lettres-patentes* that preserved Philippe's right to ascend to the French throne in the event of a disputed royal succession in France. Whether it was intended or not, the action gave rise to the perception that Louis was contemplating the possibility of combining the two monarchies, despite his acceptance of the condition that they not be merged.[76] Instead of clarifying the meaning of the *lettres-patentes* with an unambiguous statement, however, Louis did nothing to dispel the concerns of other powers.

The war that ensued, which could easily have been anticipated by Louis, was longer and more terrible than could possibly have been foreseen. The antipathy felt toward Louis by his opponents for his decades of arrogance led them to press their advantage to the fullest. Although France did not suffer a major invasion, the war was a defeat historic in scale that checked French preponderance in Europe.

Moreover, the suffering of the kingdom during the war was again horrific. The year 1709 saw a major famine and became known as the "year of sorrows." Marriage and birth rates dropped and the number of deaths exceeded births by more than 800,000. France lost about 3.5 percent of its population.[77] Although the 1709 crisis was not as severe as that of 1693–94, the battle for survival during 1709 "stripped the Old Regime to its essentials"—few were spared hardship.[78] Louis had recast the government of France to conform to his desire for personal rule, but he had used the personal rule he had achieved to pursue war and conquest, which had resulted in hardship. By the end of his reign, the longest in French history, the kingdom was exhausted by war and with the king himself.

In June 1709, after the catastrophic winter, Louis wrote a public letter to the royal governors that delineated the collapse of peace talks. Intended to encourage his demoralized subjects to continue the war effort, at which it succeeded, it acknowledged that the expectation of peace had been widespread throughout the kingdom and that he believed it his duty to explain the failure to secure it.[79] Louis claimed that he had both desired and sought peace and disclosed reasons for the collapse of the negotiations, particularly the demand of the allies that Louis wage war on his own grandson to remove him from the Spanish throne. The letter sought to associate the monarch with the kingdom in common cause, using it to link Louis with his subjects in an expression of national identity, but it was also an expression of the desperation of the Crown because Louis had never previously divulged such matters or sought to justify his position.[80]

By the end of his reign Louis was apprehensive about the future of his dynasty.[81] His son died in 1711 and his grandson Louis, duc de Bourgogne, in 1712. His oldest great-grandson died at the age of five in the same year. By 1713 the only two individuals left who were direct male descendants were his grandson, Philippe V, king of Spain, and a great-grandson, the three-year old son of Louis, duc de Bourgogne. To avert a general war in Europe once again if Philippe failed to yield the Spanish throne, it became necessary to turn to the sickly three-year-old, who was an unpromising choice because of his frail health.

Beyond Philippe and the three-year-old, the future Louis XV, the next closest in the line of succession were Philippe, duc d'Orléans, the nephew of Louis XIV, the prince de Condé, and the prince de Conti. The accession of any one of those from the collateral line would have been perceived as tantamount to an aristocratic reaction, which would have been compounded further if they died without a male heir. The vacuum created by the end of the Bourbon line would require the convening of an assembly to determine the next monarch, a development that would very likely have culminated by overturning the achievements of the Bourbon dynasty.

To prevent this potential outcome, Louis used his last will and testament to resort to an extraordinary action, which he justified by citing the need to prevent civil war. In contravention of all norms of royal succession, he made two of his illegitimate sons, the duc de Maine and the comte de Toulouse, eligible to take the throne after the princes of the blood. His will also dictated the establishment of a council during the regency, the intention of which was to limit the latitude of Orléans.[82]

Louis XIV appears to have recognized the difficulties that lay ahead for the system of government he had created and the stresses that had been placed on it by war. Indeed, among the many emotions swirling around him as he lay dying was a longing for change.[83] Louis XIV died on September 1, 1715, haunted, even on his death bed, by memories of the Frondes, especially that of the nobles.[84]

The Forgotten Constitution: The Origins, Realization, and Legacy of the French Constitution of 1791.
Michael P. Fitzsimmons, Oxford University Press. © Oxford University Press 2025.
DOI: 10.1093/9780197793978.003.0002

2

Louis XV

Transition and Discord over Monarchy-Centered Government

After the death of Louis XIV, the new king of an exhausted France was Louis's second great-grandson, a five-year-old, who was under a regency and who would not reach the age of majority until 1723. The day after Louis's death, the regent, Philippe, duc d' Orléans, went before the *parlement* of Paris to affirm his status as regent but also seemed implicitly to ask for its endorsement. Orléans had already agreed, with stipulations, to return the right of remonstrance prior to registration to the *parlement* and the *parlement*, by acclamation, proclaimed Orléans sole regent, ignoring Louis XIV's wishes in his last will and testament for a Regency council.[1] With its right of remonstrance restored, the *parlement* was favorably disposed toward Orléans.

Orléans's control at Louis XIV's death was not at all certain. Had he taken power arbitrarily as if the will did not exist, his authority would have been questioned and possibly put in jeopardy. Had he accepted the will unreservedly his power would have been limited. By enlisting the *parlement* in support of his course of action, Orléans secured a primacy that enabled him to achieve greater latitude to take on serious problems as well as public acknowledgment and parlementary support of his authority.[2] At the same time, however, to gain the support of the *parlement* he was ceding it a renewed political and increasingly quasi-constitutional role, which would have significant consequences as the century progressed. The idea of a French constitution emerged during the eighteenth century through a series of crises that led to claims and assertions by Crown and *parlement.* During these exchanges such terms as "absolute," "citizen," "law," "state" and others revealed the assumptions of the two parties and became indicative of the growing breach between them.

When the regent restored the pre-registration right of remonstrance, he stipulated that a remonstrance could only be put forward to make known legal objections to royal edicts.[3] Traditionally, in addition to remonstrances, there had been a less formal communication known as a *représentation*, which could address matters other than those conveyed in edicts. Acceptance of them was at the discretion of the monarch, as was his receiving of delegations of magistrates. From the time of the reestablishment of its pre-registration right, however, the *parlement* ignored the differentiation. A majority of its remonstrances under Louis XV were put forward independently of registration of edicts.[4] Moreover, in 1716 the *parlement* registered some portions of a royal edict and rejected others, a break with convention that exceeded the right of remonstrance given by Orléans, making it tantamount to a constitutional challenge. The body seemed to have expanded its power because its action led to the amending of the portions that had not been registered, giving the appearance that royal legislation required approval of the *parlement*.[5]

In early 1718 the *parlement*, shocked at the parlous state of finances, issued a remonstrance that concluded with a criticism of royal funds being placed in John Law's bank, putting them beyond proper oversight from the *Chambre des comptes*. It called for the practice to stop. The remonstrance created a gulf between the regent and the *parlement*, who had until this time worked relatively harmoniously with each other. Beginning in early 1718, however, Crown and *parlement* disagreed on the administration of royal finances, with Law as a central focus. Throughout 1718 the *parlement* sought to assert a greater role for itself in royal government.[6]

The actions of the *parlement* in the summer of 1718 represented a major effort to gain greater authority for itself, with Law's bank becoming a means to expand its power. The *parlement* moved beyond remonstrances to the issuing of orders, which led the regent to attempt to reduce its influence to what he thought it should be. In an order sent to the *parlement* in August 1718, Orléans accused it of abusing his confidence, seeking to reduce royal authority and attempting to assume control of state finances. He declared that it had violated the terms under which its right of remonstrance had been restored and had all but given up the administration of justice in favor of a political role. Its choice had reduced confidence in government and had made unwarranted intrusions into areas outside of its jurisdiction.[7]

Orléans preserved the right of remonstrance for the *parlement*, but any remonstrance had to be made within one week of submission of an edict, after which it would be regarded as registered. The *parlement* could not offer a remonstrance on an edict not submitted to it and it was also barred from deliberating on finances or any other matter of state unless specifically asked by the monarch. Furthermore, all parlementary decrees with respect to John Law were annulled.

Having previously been successful in extending its purview without a significant reaction from Orléans, the *parlement* ignored his order. The next day the magistrates convened and not only discussed finances but sent questions to the regent regarding them, stunning him with its blatant disregard of his will. The dispute culminated with a *lit de justice* in August 1718. The *lit de justice* did not reduce the powers of the *parlement* but only regulated their scope. Orléans, seeking to curtail the *parlement*, arrested three magistrates through *lettres de cachet* and exiled them from Paris. The *parlement* responded by suspending its judicial functions and stated that the suspension would continue until exiled magistrates were released. The Crown told the *parlement* that the suspension would displease the regent and not secure the release of the detained magistrates. The *parlement* resumed its judicial duties, which led to the magistrates being released.[8]

A Movement Away from Personal Rule

In February 1723, the *parlement* of Paris declared Louis XV's majority, although it took a somewhat assertive tone toward the young monarch. Near the conclusion of brief *pro forma* remarks, the first president of the *parlement* declared that the *parlement* was of little use unless it was heard. It was an early indication that the *parlement* did not view being reflexively submissive to royal will as an obligation, although it remained prudent and non-combative early in his reign.[9] Guillaume Dubois became chief minister but died in August. Louis named Orléans chief minister but he died in December 1723, after which the monarch named his cousin, Louis Henri, duc de Bourbon, to the post. The appointment appeared to signify a movement away from personal rule.

Bourbon's tenure was controversial and he was dismissed in June 1726, after only two and a half years, to be succeeded by André Hercule de Fleury. Fleury never assumed the title of chief minister but exercised the duties of the position and represented a continuation of the model of Richelieu and Mazarin. Like them, he served until his death, in 1743, but unlike them he degraded royal authority rather than enhancing it.

The two major points of contention between the regent and the *parlement* had been the financial actions of Law and the Papal bull *Unigenitus*. The quarrel over Law resolved itself with the collapse of Law's system and his flight in 1720. The dispute over *Unigenitus*, however, became the primary matter of dispute between Crown and *parlement* during Fleury's ministry.

Unigenitus had been issued by Pope Clement XI in 1713 and condemned theological tenets put forward by Pasquier Quesnel in a work titled *Réflexions morales* that expressed the beliefs of Jansenism. Jansenism was theological in origin, centered on how to reconcile the concepts of divine grace and human free will, but acquired political significance when it became intertwined with the relationship between the French Church and the Papacy as well as with monarchical power in France, especially under Louis XIV. Louis had, in fact, asked the pope to promulgate the bull because he wanted to suppress the Jansenist group.

The *parlement* of Paris, however, generally sympathized with the Jansenist outlook, especially the Gallican liberties achieved in the Concordat of Bologna.[10] Despite its Jansenist leanings, in 1720, apparently seeking a compromise, the *parlement* registered a royal declaration that attempted to reconcile the opposing sides, seeming to settle the matter, but Fleury resumed the dispute with the *parlement* soon after taking his position.[11]

Fleury believed that division in the Church could potentially undercut loyalty or obedience to the state, which meant that terminating the dispute was the greater national interest, despite the advantages of the Gallican tradition. The *parlement* believed that making *Unigenitus* the law of France could jeopardize the secular power of the monarchy, making it vulnerable to religious authority, both from within France and, in the institution of the Papacy, from abroad.

After the bishop of Senez published a pastoral letter in 1726 questioning the validity of *Unigenitus*, Fleury took advantage of the opportunity to act. He prohibited the bishop from carrying out his religious duties and exiled him internally to a monastery. More importantly, Fleury proclaimed *Unigenitus* to be an article of faith of the Church—a dogma. Both actions were affirmed by the pope.

Fleury used the papal confirmation as a cudgel against those elements that still resisted the bull and sought to prevent the *parlement* from acting on issues related to *Unigenitus*. In 1730 he presented a royal declaration to the *parlement* declaring *Unigenitus* the law of both the Church and the kingdom. The *parlement* was reluctant to register it, which led to a *lit de justice* at which several magistrates strongly expressed their opposition to the bull. Nevertheless, the registration occurred.

The episode united the *parlement* in anger against the Crown and led it effectively not to enforce the bull as dogma. Fleury chose to discard legal tradition by prohibiting the *parlement* from discussing *Unigenitus* and made clear that he viewed the body merely as a vehicle for the dispensation of royal justice. By ignoring traditional notions of French law and curtailing the rights of the *parlement*, Fleury was threatening to provoke a constitutional crisis centered on the question of whether the king should rule within the boundaries of the law or independently of it. Hostility toward *Unigenitus* grew and took hold with the public, weakening the Crown and strengthening the *parlement*. As the *Grand conseil* increasingly preempted cases from the *parlement*, the *parlement* issued a declaration in which it characterized itself as the perpetual defenders of the freedoms of the kingdom, a statement the Crown ordered to be removed from the registers of the *parlement*.

A major legacy of Fleury's tenure was to weaken the authority of the Crown. His struggle with the *parlement* over *Unigenitus* was unnecessary because it had been settled in 1720.[12] The future security of the monarchy depended upon whether respect for royal authority, based on the king's role as supreme executor and defender of the law, would continue to be affirmed. In this respect, the arbitrary policy of Fleury was damaging, revealing the fragility of law when faced with Crown authoritarianism.

The conduct of the Crown enabled the *parlement* to portray itself as the guardian and custodian of established law, upholding it against overbearing or arbitrary government. The *parlement* asserted that it protected the liberties of subjects and that this structural arrangement was comparable to a constitution. It did not contest or question the fundamental power of the monarch but the dispute allowed the magistrates to put forward publicly their notion of government, giving it greater articulation and authority than would otherwise have been possible.

Although the dispute over *Unigenitus* was nominally religious in nature, the conflict that ensued between Crown and *parlement*, which would continue for decades, was also a debate by proxy about the nature of government in France.[13] The *dévot* party symbolized monarchy-centered government whereas the Jansenists represented constitutional government in which the power of the monarch was tempered by representative bodies, particularly, in the absence of the Estates General, the *parlement*. The Jansenist critique of *Unigenitus* was a metaphorical debate on monarchy-centered government, as its arguments shifted to the secular sphere.[14]

Remonstrances were supposed to be private communications between the monarch and *parlement* and were therefore not published, leaving the public generally unaware of the claims made by the *parlement*.[15] Jansenist authors, however, published works that mirrored positions taken by the *parlement*. A particularly significant figure in this respect was Louis Adrien Le Paige, who published a two-volume work in the early 1750s. One scholar described Le Paige as perhaps more influential than Montesquieu, arguing that it was Le Paige who defined the strategy through which the *parlements* were able to contest claims of the Crown through historical references.[16] Le Paige contended that the *parlement* had an obligation to give priority to "fundamental laws," which outweighed obedience to the king's "momentary will" if there was a conflict between them. Fundamental laws were so intrinsic to the monarchy that they could not be abridged or modified without jeopardizing the monarchy itself. A multitude of "judicial Jansenism" books and pamphlets were effective in their criticism of hallowed institutions and their denunciations of "despotism."[17] These writings kept discussion and debate about the nature of government, particularly the extent of royal power, in the public eye.

Fleury's death occurred during the War of Austrian Succession and Louis had indicated that he would assume the role of chief minister upon Fleury's death. The political elements of the kingdom expected the monarch to take control of the government and assume the position of chief minister to reassure the nation in wartime.[18] Louis announced his intention to take the role of chief minister and rule personally, but without a capable chief minister, a situation that continued until the end of his reign, a void developed and the Crown fell victim to factionalism, dealing a blow to Louis's image as king.[19]

Louis XV and the *Parlements*

Although the death of Fleury lessened conflict with the *parlement*, during the following years discord continued.[20] Along with *Unigenitus*, taxation had been another issue that divided Crown and *parlement*. The medieval perception that the monarch should live off the resources of the royal domain continued to hold sway. A corollary of this belief was that taxes to meet the costs of war should be enacted on a temporary basis only.

The parlous fiscal situation of the Crown during the mid-eighteenth century meant that it relied on the ability of various controllers-general to prolong taxes that had been enacted on a temporary basis.

In December 1743, during the War of Austrian Succession, the Crown presented for registration more than a dozen edicts that established or revived a variety of taxes and duties. The *parlement* approved most of them but demurred on extra impositions on eggs, butter, wood, and coal, which would particularly affect the poorer elements of the populace. After some adjustments brought about through negotiations with the first president, the *parlement* registered the edicts, but the practice of resistance to fiscal measures by wringing concessions from the Crown would ultimately lead to friction.[21]

Moreover, in an illustration of the fact that even if *Unigenitus* did not remain as a point of contention religious issues continued to cause tension, a crisis arrived in the mid-1750s when the *parlement* took up denial of sacrament cases that had been sent to it by the *Châtelet*.[22] After the archbishop of Paris twice declined the *parlement*'s invitation to end the matter by administering the sacrament, the *parlement* took a stronger stand and ordered him to do so or possibly suffer the seizure of his temporalities. It also announced that it would hold a session that the peers would be asked to attend and, in an unusual and irregular act, to which the king would be invited.

Under ordinary circumstances, the usual occasion for the monarch to visit the *parlement* was to impose his will on it in a *lit de justice*. The invitation to the king had the potential to give rise to the perception that the *parlement* could summon the monarch and that it was virtually a co-equal with him, with perhaps even a share of sovereignty. The Crown, recognizing that for the same reasons the peers could also not be summoned, chose to denounce the archbishop's conduct to placate the *parlement*.

The issue of denial of sacraments culminated with a remonstrance by the *parlement* on April 9, 1753, that accused the clergy of seeking to free itself from all royal authority. The *parlement* proclaimed that it had as one of its responsibilities to bring truth to the monarch and lamented that the ordinary administration of justice had been disrupted. The most significant aspect of the remonstrance was its assertion of the "inseparable trinity" of the king, the state, and the law. The *parlement* maintained that there was no more important principle than that of the obedience of subjects to the monarch and the obedience of the monarch to the law.[23] This was a radical departure from the view propounded by Jean Bodin and elaborated by subsequent theorists that the king was above positive and customary law, a view that the Bourbon dynasty had regarded as axiomatic since its accession.[24] To accord law a co-equal status with the monarch rather than subordinate to him was strongly provocative.[25]

The remonstrance signified another divergence from generally held Crown views. Its distinction between the monarch, the state, and the law was at odds with the Bourbon notion of proprietary dynasticism, the belief that kings held the state as virtually their possession. Although Bourbon monarchs also subscribed to the "office" theory of kingship, which envisioned the king's purpose as governing the state, the proprietary dynasticism strand became particularly pronounced under Henri IV. In 1599, for example, as the *parlement* of Paris delayed registration of the Edict of Nantes, Henri asserted that the kingdom of France was his "by inheritance and acquisition." Although Louis XIV acknowledged the office theory of kingship, he also claimed that his only law was the well-being of his subjects and believed himself responsible for his people rather than accountable to them.[26]

The remonstrance suggested a contractual theory of government, a concept that had not been generally propounded since the Wars of Religion, when intimations of justifiable assassination had been associated with it. The views of the *parlement* expressed in the remonstrance would have been regarded by the Crown as adversarial and even hostile.

As the prospect of religious conflict or civil war, which had facilitated acceptance of monarchy-centered government, receded, a new ideal of government began to emerge from the *parlement* through its remonstrances. The Frondes were only two decades in the past when Louis XIV amended the right of remonstrance of the *parlement*, which itself, of course, had initially been involved in the Frondes. A century after the Frondes, however, the *parlement* used its remonstrances to advance a new model of government, premised on a model other than personal rule.

One should not, however, overestimate the impact of the remonstrance. On one hand, there was agreement between the Crown and *parlement* that monarchical sovereignty was unchallenged and that it should be used in accordance with law in order to demarcate the monarchy from despotism.[27] On the other hand, a factor that enhanced the significance of the remonstrance was that it was published.[28] The standard practice for remonstrances was that they were to be seen only by the monarch, which would enable him to alter an edict without loss of face or, more importantly, creating a perception of shared sovereignty. Its publication gave a constitutional matter wider dissemination than previously.[29] To have what was, in effect, a competing idea of governance and sovereignty emanating from an organ of the Crown and made public was extraordinary. The dismay of the Crown is easy to understand. In the wake of the remonstrance, Louis exiled the *parlement* in May 1753 and it remained in exile for more than a year, until September 1754.

The more aggressive posture of the *parlement* may, in part, have been driven by the publication of *The Spirit of Laws* by Charles-Louis de Secondat, baron de Brède et de Montesquieu in 1748. Montesquieu asserted that the *parlement* was the repository and historical memory of law, both fundamental and statutory. The April 1753 remonstrance replicated some of the language and vocabulary of Montesquieu's book and its discussion of the corporate distinctions of estates and orders yielded to a concept of society in which each individual had an equal relationship with the Crown. If taken to its logical conclusion, the new language of the *parlement* "risked undermining the juridical basis of the *ancien régime*" and foreshadowed the ideal of universal rights for mankind.[30]

There can be little doubt that the *parlement* became more assertive after the publication of Montesquieu's work. From 1716 through 1747, the *parlement* put forward twenty-five remonstrances. From 1748 until its suppression in 1771, it put forward forty-four remonstrances. The latter group also made greater reference to a constitution and to the rights of citizens.[31]

The exile of 1753 was a watershed moment in one critical respect. During their exile the magistrates devoted themselves to the study of public law and exchanged ideas in discussions among themselves. The exile lasted more than a year and from their study and discussions the idea that the nation is above the king developed. Their period of exile also led the magistrates to use historical arguments to rebut Crown claims.[32]

Neither Louis XIV nor any of his Bourbon predecessors had ever given thought to suppressing the *parlements* because of their ancient lineage, the support they enjoyed and the value they gave the Crown in appearing to accept disagreement and protest.[33] They attempted instead to manage the *parlements* by circumscribing their influence. Louis XIV did so by amending the right of remonstrance and in the 1750s Louis XV sought to lessen their influence by enhancing the authority of the *Grand conseil*, which was more responsive to royal will, by preempting cases from the *parlement* and sending them to the *Grand conseil* for resolution.[34]

In a speech to the king at the presentation of a remonstrance against the action in November 1755, the magistrates, in a direct rebuttal of the ideal of proprietary dynasticism, asserted that some of the power that they wielded in the monarch's name did not belong to them but to the state and they asserted that a common good existed. Emulating the argument of Le Paige, whose work had recently appeared and who contributed to the drafting of parlementary responses,[35] the remonstrance asserted that at the beginning stages of the monarchy the *parlement* had been the "general assembly of the nation" but that tradition had been lost because of conquests and the introduction of the feudal system. It maintained that all laws received their final form through the registration process.

Characterizing the preemption of cases to the *Grand conseil* as irregular, confused, and uncertain whereas the ordinary system of justice dispensed through existing tribunals was majestic, authentic, and invariable, the *parlement* asserted that the random preemption of cases suggested that one day the *Grand conseil* might aspire to a geographical jurisdiction of its own. The magistrates pointedly asked whether the *Grand conseil* had superseded the *parlement* through its interventions.[36] The implication of the remonstrance was that the *parlement* stood for the rule of law against the arbitrary and capricious interventions of the *Grand conseil.*

In a surprising statement, the *parlement* said that the action of the council had astonished Paris, an ominous assertion at a time when historical memory of the Frondes remained, as did, for the Bourbon dynasty, the knowledge that the city had for years prevented the accession to the throne of Henri IV. Furthermore, even more explicitly and perhaps disingenuously, the magistrates contended that the dealings of the council could potentially cause disorder and raised more than once the stability of the throne as a component of their argument. Alluding again to internal disorder, discord, and anarchy, the *parlement* asked Louis to adhere to the constitution and law of the state by assuring that lesser courts remained bound exclusively to it.

The concepts employed and the language used by the *parlement* in support of its claims were extraordinary. The word "constitution" or a variant of it, such as constitutional, was used nearly a dozen times in the remonstrance. The call by the *parlement* for the monarch to conform to the law implied that the monarchy was verging on despotism. By invoking a constitution and calling upon the monarch to abide by it, the *parlement* was suggesting a new ideal of governance, with the law at least as sovereign as the monarch.

In addition, the *parlement* used the word "citizen" more than the word "subject" in its remonstrance. In contemporary usage, "citizen" connoted association with a place, normally a town or city but also the state and was free of any direct affiliation with the monarch. By contrast, "subject" was explicitly connected to the king and signified submission and dependence.[37] The greater use of "citizen" served to emphasize the primacy of the state over the monarch and represented another rejoinder to proprietary dynasticism.

Finally, as it defended its jurisdiction to remain the sole agent of the Crown in the administration of justice, the *parlement* also sought to create a virtually co-equal role for itself with respect to the Crown. By characterizing itself in the remonstrance as the "Senate" or asserting that at its origin the *parlement* had been the "general assembly of the nation" it was portraying itself as the guardian of "the nation" against excessive exercise of royal power—despotism—rather than as an agency of royal authority.

The struggle between Crown and *parlements* was a struggle to win over public opinion, indicating the degree to which political culture had evolved since Louis XIV.[38] This is undeniably true, but remonstrances were generally not published, which meant that those that were represented an episodic attempt to curry public favor. More importantly, there was also an underlying, ongoing contest over competing ideas of governance, waged under "a stable political system working by well-understood, if sometimes tacit, rules,"[39] that was apparent in remonstrances in which words freighted with meaning were increasingly utilized. "Constitution" was the most overt rebuttal to personal rule. The use of "citizen" rather than subject was more subtle but it would not have gone unnoticed by the Crown.

There was a change in tone under Louis XV. The *parlement* of Paris conveyed "the confidence of an institution convinced of its right to exercise a constitutional role in the political life of the monarchy."[40] It was a stance that the Crown could not abide, particularly when the dynasty had worked assiduously to achieve monarchy-centered governance. Relations between Crown and *parlement* were deteriorating and the decline was so marked that a scholar of the remonstrances described the situation as "war with the *parlement*."[41]

The Escalation of the Conflict

With the prospect of war in 1756, for which the Crown would need the support of the *parlement* for fiscal measures, the Crown abandoned the enhancement of the authority of the *Grand conseil*, but hostility to the *Grand conseil*, which thought of itself as a supreme tribunal above the *parlements*, united the Parisian and provincial *parlements*. The claims of the *Grand conseil*, as well as the monarch's support of it, became the catalyst for parlementary questioning of monarchy-centered government. Indeed, in an outlook sometimes referred to as the "union of *parlements*," the Parisian and provincial *parlements* began to come together in an unprecedented fashion, united by a sense of common purpose.

In December 1756, the newly appointed chancellor, Jean-Baptiste de Machault d'Arnouville, drafted several restrictions on the *parlement*, which included limiting its remonstrances and prohibiting strikes.[42] The measures also strengthened the more pliant *Grand' chambre* and did away with two *Chambres des enquêtes*. All of the members of the suppressed chambers resigned as did nearly half of the magistrates of the *Grand' chambre*. The *parlements* of Bordeaux, Rennes, and Rouen cited the idea of a union of *parlements* to support their Parisian counterpart. The Crown retreated, suspending the measures, although the two *Chambres des enquêtes* remained suppressed, and Louis dismissed Machault.

The principle of the union of *parlements* was harmful to royal authority because of its implication that the *parlements* comprised a permanent institution national in scope that at a minimum exercised oversight on the monarchy or, more controversially, held a share of sovereign power. The repetitive use of the word "constitution" represented a suggestion of constitutional monarchy.[43] Indeed, although it approved new taxes for the Seven Years War after the Crown suspended its measures, the *parlement* of Paris became more resistant to subsequent requests and sought to use the leverage provided by registration to advance its arguments for limited monarchical government.

In a remonstrance in 1760, the magistrates opened with the observation that one of the most essential duties of the *parlement* was to speak truth to the king and it told him of the hardships caused by new edicts and asked for changes. Characterizing the current situation as a severe crisis, the *parlement* declared that the administration of the state had law as a foundation, with free registration buttressed by examination and verification as necessary preconditions. In another criticism of monarchy-centered government, the magistrates asserted that the supreme power, a reference to the king, however just it may be, could not by itself inspire. Rather, any judgment required an unfettered scrutiny by the *parlement* to determine the validity and motives as well as the need for its implementation.[44]

The Culmination of the Conflict between Crown and *Parlement*

Continuing advocacy of the union of *parlements*, heightened by tensions that arose in Brittany beginning in 1765 with the late-night arrest of the *procureur-général* of the *parlement* of Rennes, Louis-René de Caradeuc de La Chalotais, sharpened the conflict between Crown and *parlement* even further.[45] In 1763 the Estates of Brittany had refused to approve extraordinary taxes demanded on behalf of the monarch by the provincial governor, Emmanuel Armand de Richelieu, duc d'Aiguillon. The Crown viewed La Chalotais as a key figure in the opposition and he was arrested, along with his son and four other judges of the *parlement*. The arrest of La Chalotais generated accusations of despotism and led public opinion to turn against the Crown. The Crown established a special tribunal to try La Chalotais, who asserted that his trial was illegal. He contended that he should be tried by the *parlement* of Brittany or, if that was not possible, by the *parlement* of Bordeaux. The evidence against La Chalotais was so flimsy that the judges of the special tribunal did not want to issue a verdict.[46] With the case stalled, Louis revoked it to the *Grand conseil*, which, with little deliberation, peremptorily exiled La Chalotais to Saintes. The process increased anger against the Crown and opinion in both Brittany and France galvanized in support of La Chalotais.

In March 1765 the *parlement* of Rennes sent a letter to its Parisian counterpart relating what had occurred. After a second letter in June, the *parlement* of Paris decided to send a remonstrance to the king, which it did on September 6.[47] The remonstrance defended the *parlement* of Rennes and its protection of Brittany's privileges. It affirmed that no tax could be imposed in Brittany without the consent of the provincial Estates and put forward an extended defense of the *parlement* of Rennes, including the resignation of magistrates.

The remonstrance declared that the acts of the *Grand conseil* were arbitrary and absolute and it employed the term "absolute power" in a pejorative fashion. The *parlement* urged the king to return to an administrative routine more compatible with laws. It asserted that the *parlement* of Rennes belonged not to the monarch but to the state and that its actions were rooted in a general movement undertaken for the common good of the state by guarding against the violation of laws. The desires and efforts of Brittany were joined to those of the entire nation and, in the name of the entire magistracy, the *parlement* of Paris asked the king to act in accordance with the well-being of the state, to work for the restoration of public order, the rule of law and the honor of the magistracy.[48]

On February 2, 1766, the *parlement* put forward a remonstrance that once again included a pejorative use of the term "absolute power" as well as allusions to "subversion of laws" and "open infringement of the most sacred rights of the State." The magistrates urged the monarch to continue to respect laws necessary for proper monarchical authority.[49]

Eleven days later the *parlement* sent yet another remonstrance that opened with the contention that the *parlement* could no longer doubt that there was a widespread and powerfully driven plot underway seeking to subvert law and destroy the magistracy. The *parlement* suggested that the monarch was oblivious to the undertaking and urged him to return to respect for law and maintenance of the constitution. Although the remonstrance declared that the *parlement* recognized and would always recognize the person of the king as the plentitude of power, it argued that in their protestation the magistrates were acting in accordance with the constitution and in the royal interest by seeking to avoid an illegal action. The *parlement* concluded by asking for the prompt and complete reestablishment of the *parlement* of Rennes and the assurance that it would be allowed to judge its own members.[50]

The Crown ignored the remonstrances and the *parlement* of Rennes remained disbanded until July 1769. Of far greater concern to the Crown, however, was language in the remonstrances that implied that the magistrates of the *parlements* were a unified group national in scope rather than members of discrete provincial courts. The invocation of the stability of the state by the *parlement* as it also claimed to represent the wishes of the nation could only have dismayed Louis. Moreover, for the *parlement* to call upon the monarch to comply with the rule of law suggested that he was accountable to the magistrates.

The remonstrances led the Crown to respond in a meeting that has come to be known as the Session of the Scourging. The king opened his forceful statement by noting that what had happened in his *parlement* of

Rennes—with the possessive a clear rejoinder to the claim of the *parlement* of Paris that the *parlement* of Rennes belonged to the state rather than the monarch—was of no concern to any other *parlements.*[51] He had acted entirely on his own authority and he did not owe an explanation to anyone. After criticizing the impertinent tone of the remonstrances, Louis declared that the magistracy did not comprise a body nor a separate entity among the three estates of the realm. He denounced those who contended that all of the *parlements* comprised one body extending over different locales and stated that magistrates were officers of the monarch who carried out his duty of delivering justice to his subjects.

Louis observed that the *parlement* represented itself as responsible for the public welfare of the monarch and nation and that it was the arbiter between them. It was, he continued, as if the *parlement* had forgotten that sovereignty resided solely in his person. Indeed, to underscore his point the king reminded the magistrates that they derived their existence and authority from him alone and that the discharge of that authority, which they exercised only in his name, remained with him always and could never be used against him. Legislative power, Louis declared, belonged exclusively to him and magistrates took part only in the registration, publication, and execution of laws, but not their creation—the *parlement* had only a limited right to remonstrate in service to the king. Public order emanated from the monarch, as did the rights and interests of the nation. He added, again in an unmistakable refutation of the *parlement,* that there were those who dared to cast the nation as an entity separate from the king. The rights and interests of the nation were inseparable from those of the monarch, Louis asserted, and remained solely in his hands.

He warned that if the courts continued to disobey royal will instead of registering laws or edicts, he would, with regret, use all of his God-given power to safeguard his people from the consequences of the actions of the *parlement.* Louis cautioned the magistrates not to follow their own predilections and told them to reject any notion of association as well as other new ideas or "false and dangerous conceptions." He concluded by declaring that he would not tolerate the slightest infraction of all of which he had just spoken and that the *parlement* of Paris should set the standard for other courts of the kingdom.[52]

Louis's remarks have been described as a rejection all of the constitutional claims advanced by the *parlement* during the previous fifteen years and making clear that the *parlement* had no sovereign power.[53] It was a recapitulation of the Bourbon view of monarchy-centered government and an admonition to the *parlement* not to advance alternative articulations of the state or government beyond the king himself. The Crown printed and posted copies of Louis's remarks on March 3, and affixed them on the doors of the *Palais de Justice*.

On March 19 the *parlement* reminded Louis that obedience to the law was a duty and one of the commandments of a monarch. It contended that it spoke on behalf of magistrates of the different courts of law of the kingdom, thereby directly contravening the king's instructions at the Session of the Scourging. Although acknowledging that sovereign power resided exclusively in the person of the monarch, the magistrates again asserted that a law received its final form only when it had been verified by the *parlement*. The *parlement* reaffirmed its view of itself as the depository of laws and its obligation to examine new laws to assure public order and the rights of citizens.[54]

On November 22, 1766, Louis revoked the case to the *Grand conseil*, leading the *parlement* to issue a remonstrance that it presented on December 8. It denounced the arbitrary choice of court and stated that the revocation openly transgressed inalterable rules of law. To try the accused before the *parlement* of Rennes would preserve the sense of privilege the law granted to the accused magistrates. Louis responded that he recognized the importance of maintaining proper protocol in criminal law and to assign those accused the appropriate judge, but there were exceptional circumstances that regrettably caused him to depart from regular rules and the case of the Breton magistrates was one such instance.

After another exchange over the revocation of a case to the *Grand conseil* in late 1766, the *parlement* wrote the monarch of its increased misgivings. The rule of law, it contended, had always been above circumstances and it again complained about an administrative body carrying out judicial functions. The magistrates asked Louis to honor the traditional prerogatives of the magistracy and to observe legal norms. The king told the *parlement* to return the next day to hear his response and understand his intentions. In that meeting he informed the magistrates that he had decided not to pursue the matter any further, effectively removing the case from the *Grand conseil*. The charges would be dismissed but Louis imposed a strict silence on the matter. The accused would be released from prison but exiled from Brittany, which ultimately led to them being sent to Saintes.[55]

The *parlement* continued to pursue the matter, which led to a brusque response from Louis. He told the magistrates—apparently referring to the revocation of the case from the *Grand conseil*, the dismissal of the charges and the release of the accused from prison—that he was astonished that the *parlement* would raise new concerns when the honor of the magistrates had not been compromised. The *parlement* had misunderstood the spirit of justice and goodwill that he had shown and he expected it to drop the matter. The magistrates, however, sent another communication that clearly angered Louis, who gave a curt one-sentence reply.[56]

As preparations for the trial of La Chalotais and his colleagues began in March 1768, the *parlement* again put forward a lengthy remonstrance on the matter. To justify the action, the magistrates argued that if the *parlement* remained silent when the freedom of subjects was breached or the rights of the province violated, it would be betraying the duty it owed to the king. A simple distinction of territorial jurisdiction should not preclude it from acting. A dispute over privileges, the magistrates asserted, had become a fight about authority.[57]

The *parlement* also issued a remonstrance against the *Grand conseil*, particularly what it viewed as the attempt by the body to elevate itself above all courts of justice. After an extensive and dramatic argument against the *Grand conseil*, stating that it would result in trouble and disorder everywhere, the *parlement* asked Louis not to allow the *Grand conseil* to assume such status or supremacy of jurisdiction, which was contrary to the constitution.[58]

The latter remonstrance precipitated another harsh rebuke. Declaring that he could have ignored the remonstrances but wanted the *parlement* to know what he thought, Louis informed the magistrates that it was inexcusable for the *parlement* to pretend to misunderstand the facts and to raise doubts about the reality of a court recognized and authorized by ordinances and edicts registered by all of "his" *parlements*. He forbade the *parlement* from deliberating on any matter concerning the *Grand conseil* or its members, which contravened the respect owed to the king as well as the honor of the magistracy. The *parlement* persisted, however, and Louis criticized it again for its lack of respect toward him.[59]

Relations between the monarch and *parlement* had reached a critical juncture.[60] Louis viewed the *parlement* as insolent and the *parlement* had clearly lost respect for the authority of the Crown. After being told not to discuss the *Grand conseil*, it sent another remonstrance to the Crown in July 1768 complaining about it. The *parlement* contended that it was not demonstrating a lack of respect for the king when it was acting out of concern for the well-being of the state and public order.[61]

Louis responded that the *parlement* should recognize in his answer to its remonstrance that his decisions with respect to the *Grand conseil*, which had been established and maintained by his predecessors, were firm and fixed. In sending cases to the *Grand conseil*, the king, again pointedly using the possessive, was not seeking to diminish the dignity of his *parlements*, each of which had its own jurisdiction and was exclusively concerned with public order in the kingdom.[62]

Louis reinstated the *parlement* of Rennes in July 1769 but excluded La Chalotais and his colleagues from the restored body.[63] On August 12 he declared the accused officials to be completely innocent of the charges against them and ordered that all parties to the matter, and especially La Chalotais, maintain total silence on the case. It was an outcome that satisfied no one and the Breton *parlement* stated that a declaration of innocence by the monarch in lieu of a verdict produced by a trial was not acceptable.

When the *parlement* of Rennes returned to its duties, its members remained dismayed at the continued exclusion of their colleagues and sent a delegation to Versailles to ask Louis for their reinstatement. The king received the group but curtly denied the request and again stated that he did not owe an explanation to anyone. Learning of the presence of their Breton colleagues in Versailles, the *parlement* of Paris sent a letter of support, which also received a curt response from the monarch.

The Breton *parlement*, dissatisfied with the monarch's solution, drafted a remonstrance, which the Crown rejected. The *parlement* of Rennes wrote a letter to the chancellor, René Nicolas Charles Augustin de Maupeou, in which it accused d'Aiguillon, who had resigned his position in 1768, of "substantial abuse of power and an enormous crime." For his part, d'Aiguillon also wanted a trial to clear his name, which led the Crown to transfer the case to Paris for trial by the *parlement* with the princes and peers, although the trial would be held in Versailles.

Louis, however, quashed the trial, creating deep disaffection. La Chalotais and the magistracy did not have their honor restored and d'Aiguillon did not have his name cleared. The *parlement* sent a remonstrance that asked for a return to "order and justice" and suggested that the stability of the monarchy was at stake. The king remained unmoved and strongly rejected it.

The case ended with another strict admonition that all parties maintain complete silence on the matter.[64]

The *parlement* of Paris sent a remonstrance to which Louis responded by again reminding the *parlement* that its power and existence derived from him, who held the full plentitude of power in his person. The *parlements* were not tied to each other—each had its own territorial limits, which represented the extent of its jurisdiction and authority. The duty of the *parlements* was the application of laws and they had no right to expand or restrain the terms of a law. They should always be submissive, respectful, balance zeal with obedience and wisely advise authority without ever contesting it.[65]

The Suppression of the *Parlement* of Paris

The dispute continued to escalate, with the *parlement* in September 1770, denouncing what it called multiple acts of absolute power undertaken against the spirit and letter of constitutive laws, which led Maupeou to ask the magistrates if they were attaching themselves to new ideas.[66] Maupeou suspended it in January 1771.[67]

Maupeou, a former first president of the *parlement* who had left in 1768 to become chancellor, undertook a reorganization of the judiciary. The Crown seized the offices of incumbent magistrates and sent them into exile in different parts of France. In a reduction of its large geographic jurisdiction, Maupeou replaced the *parlement* of Paris with six *conseils supérieurs*, which expedited the administration of justice. In an elimination of venality of office, the new *conseils supérieurs* were staffed by judges whose salaries were paid by the Crown, ending judicial fees. The remaking of provincial *parlements* followed a similar model, although not all of them were suppressed.

Most significantly, the new courts did not have any political or constitutional responsibilities. They registered laws but had no authority to delay registration and no right of remonstrance. The transformation of the judiciary enacted by Maupeou and its constitutional implications did not provoke any significant resistance. After five hundred years, the *parlement* of Paris ceased to exist.

The measures enacted by Maupeou represented a fundamental alteration of the traditional understanding of the constitutional order in France.[68] J. H. Shennan pronounced the attack on the *parlement* as "nothing less than a reorientation of the monarch's function."[69] He also asserted that Maupeou's action was intended to break out of the "ideal of kingship enmeshed by traditional laws, customs, rights and privileges" by abolishing the sole body able to call upon the monarch to abide by these obligations.[70]

Traditional laws, customs, rights, and privileges comprised the notional definition of the constitution under the Old Regime and, without them or the *parlement* that was their putative overseer, there was only the will of the monarch.[71] It was this perception that gave rise to the sense of despotism.

The depth of concern is evident in a reworked version of the Lord's Prayer that appeared. It began with "Our Father, who art in Versailles," included "forgive your *parlements* that have upheld our interests" and concluded with "but deliver us from the devil of the Chancellor." By one account there were at least five hundred writings in circulation about Maupeou's suppression of the *parlement*, referred to as a *coup d'état*. Three-quarters were opposed to Maupeou and according to the observer, those that were favorable had been commissioned by him. The Crown also banned the entry of newspapers from Brussels and Bern, which had reported more freely on the government.[72]

In his exchanges with the *parlement*, Louis had strongly disputed its assertion of a distinction between the king and the state. The *parlement* had also posited the existence of a normative, uncodified constitution as the mediating instrument between monarch and state. Although Louis did not explicitly deny the existence of a constitution, his contention that the plentitude of power resided exclusively with him was tantamount to such a denial—there could be no limiting instrument.

In 1718, a few years after its pre-registration right of remonstrance had been restored, the *parlement*, in a message to the regent, had lamented that supplications and tears were the only means that subjects had at their disposal in dealing with the monarch.[73] Three decades later the *parlement* began to advance its belief in a constitution and the idea of law as independent of the king, both of which constrained royal power.

By the latter part of Louis XV's reign, the *parlement* was using such words as "despotism" and "citizens" in its remonstrances. The tacit position of the *parlement* was that the government of France was a constitutional monarchy rather than a product of the will of the king. It pushed its assumption so relentlessly and vigorously that in 1771 the Crown took the unprecedented step of suppressing the *parlement*, which had been in existence since the late thirteenth century. With the suppression of the *parlement* of Paris, the leading voice for the idea of a state governed by the king in accordance with an unwritten constitution had been extinguished.[74] There was no longer any catalyst around which national energy could mobilize or through which national opinion could express itself in opposition to royal will.[75]

Theories of a constitution in which power was shared between the monarch and the nation quickly developed after the suppression of the *parlement*.[76] The newly revealed fragility of the *parlement* led to a renewed focus on the Estates General and arguments for its exclusive right—rather than the *parlement*—to consent to taxation.[77]

During the quarrel with the Crown over the situation in Brittany, the *parlement* of Paris had stated that a dispute about privilege had become a struggle for power, a statement that underscores the role of privilege as a critical component in the normative constitutional structure of the Old Regime. Jean Egret contended that numerous historians had viewed parlementary opposition to the Crown as largely a clever defense of personal or corporate privilege under the guise of public good, an interpretation that had become accepted but was erroneous. The *parlements*, he argued, did not delude opinion but were the "faltering retainers" of opinion—opinion had supported the *parlements* only when they stood for the interest of all.[78]

In 1771, however, the organ of opinion that the *parlement* represented had disappeared. Despite his deep unpopularity, Louis XV had succeeded almost effortlessly in enacting an unprecedented alteration of the political and constitutional structure of the kingdom. In the aftermath of Maupeou's measures there was no institution through which national opinion could express itself. When Louis XV died on May 10, 1774, the judiciary of Maupeou remained in place.

The Legacy of Louis XV

At his death Louis XV was widely reviled. At the beginning of his reign, Orléans's uncertain standing as regent had led him to negotiate an agreement with the *parlement* of Paris to affirm his status as sole regent in return for which the *parlement* would regain its right of remonstrance prior to registration of a law. The *parlement*, stifled for decades, used its restored right to assert an alternate ideal of government during the reign of Louis XV, an effort aided in part by the absence of the Estates General. It advanced arguments for the existence of an uncodified constitution that placed limits on the power of the monarch and presented itself as the guardian of the constitution.

The claims by the *parlement* of a constitution or limits on royal power angered Louis and led to a conflict that culminated with the suppression of the *parlement* of Paris, ending its centuries-long existence. The attack on the *parlements* represented a major turning point in the political culture of the Old Regime, credibly opening the Crown to accusations of despotism. It made clear "that subjects of the French king had no rights, and no institutions, that the monarch was not able, and prepared, to violate."[79] Indeed, the suppression contributed to the revulsion felt toward Louis XV at his death.[80] The kingdom felt unsettled and the desire for balance and good order in governance became associated with the restoration of the *parlements* and the idea of a constitution.

The Forgotten Constitution: The Origins, Realization, and Legacy of the French Constitution of 1791.
Michael P. Fitzsimmons, Oxford University Press. © Oxford University Press 2025.
DOI: 10.1093/9780197793978.003.0003

II

THE TERMINAL CRISIS OF THE OLD REGIME

3

The Descent into Crisis

The new king of France, Louis XVI, the grandson of Louis XV, was nineteen years old when he ascended to the throne. His two immediate predecessors had reigned for a combined 131 years and each had been despised at his death. The new young monarch seemed to herald a fresh start for an unsettled kingdom.

During his education of Louis, one of his most influential tutors, Antoine de Quelen de Caussade, duc de la Vauguyon, had asked Jacob-Nicolas Moreau and the Jesuit Guillaume François Berthier to compile maxims about kingship, which la Vauguyon subsequently discussed with Louis over a period of years.[1] Another work by Moreau, however, *Les Dévoirs du prince*, would have a much greater influence. Much of it, including the idea that sovereignty consisted of full legislative power and was neither divided nor shared, was conventional and did not represent a significant departure.

Moreau, however, who had been tangentially involved in Maupeou's suppression of the *parlement*, took the concept of legislative authority even further, contending that royal power could override customary law or long-established fiscal privilege. Indeed, Moreau believed that all elements of society, irrespective of social privilege, should be subject to paying a defined proportional amount in taxes.[2] Moreau's view was a more expansive interpretation of royal power and was problematic because customary law and fiscal privilege were central components of the normative constitution.

The first major issue that would provide insight into the outlook of the new monarch, however, was whether he would continue the Maupeou judiciary or restore the *parlements*. Louis was divided in his outlook. On one hand, he appeared apprehensive about restoring the *parlement* of Paris because of his belief in his own authority. On the other hand, he did not like the chancellor, Maupeou.[3] He chose to dismiss Maupeou and restore the *parlement*, which he did in a *lit de justice* on November 12, 1774.

Although both the king and the *parlement* sought to maintain dignity and comity during an unprecedented reason for a *lit de justice*, each also used the occasion to advance an assertive position. The monarch opened the *lit de justice* by sternly telling the *parlement* that his predecessor had been forced to act because of its repeated defiance of his orders. He stated that he was recalling them to duties that they should never forsake, which was a warning against judicial strikes.

In his address to the monarch, the first president, Etienne François d'Aligre, who had spent the Maupeou years exiled from Paris, noted the public rejoicing at the recall of the *parlement*. He described the magistrates as men whose lives were a continual sacrifice to the law, of which the *parlement* was the repository, thereby demarcating law from the monarch and underscoring its autonomy.[4]

The reestablishment of the *parlement* was popular and seemed to signify the end of arbitrary royal rule and the restoration of a legal and constitutional balance that had been lost. After its reestablishment, the *parlement* of Paris did not pursue the ideal of the union of *parlements* and was generally pliant with respect to extending the *vingtième* and registering new loans. Although the *parlement* opposed Turgot's Six Edicts in March 1774, it did not lead to a confrontation with the Crown—the *parlement* raised the need to respect privilege but never accused the Crown of violating the constitution. Turgot fell and the edicts were withdrawn, not because of the opposition of the *parlement* but because of a rupture of ministerial harmony that the edicts precipitated.

The Growing Popularity of Louis XVI

The new king not only began to foster a sense of stability and relative harmony domestically but also enhanced his reputation in the area of foreign policy. In this crucial sphere of kingship Louis XVI also elevated his standing during the first decade of his reign. After British colonists in North America rebelled against the British government, the French government initially assisted the colonists surreptitiously with material aid, such as gunpowder, but by 1778, after the Battle of Saratoga, success for the colonists seemed possible. The foreign minister, Charles Gravier, comte de Vergennes, negotiated an alliance with the American envoy to France, Benjamin Franklin, which led to direct French entry into the war.[5]

French entry provided the colonists with the backing of a great power with a navy that could assure a reliable flow of supplies, especially weapons. This suited the French because their goal was to weaken the British through a prolonged conflict rather than to achieve an outright victory for the colonists.[6] Although French involvement seemed to enhance French prestige and advance French interests, there was a hidden underside to the apparent triumph because the war had been waged largely on credit rather than through a tax increase.

Turgot's successor was Jacques Necker, a Swiss banker who, following up on efforts by Terray and Turgot, sought to bring greater clarity to accounting methods and streamline the fiscal bureaucracy.[7] The significance of Necker's reforms is a matter of debate, but as important as the reforms themselves was the fact that they were seen to be made, which led to an increase in royal bond values. Over the following years, Necker was able to borrow hundreds of millions of *livres* and to rework existing loans.

Louis had almost certainly been unaware of the parlous state of royal finances when he agreed to go to war with Britain in support of the colonists. Turgot had told the monarch that there could be no more wars, no more borrowing of money and that taxes could not be increased because it would depress the economy. Necker had no such injunctions for Louis when he took office. In 1777 he floated a trial loan to gauge whether it would be possible to finance a war through credit. Issued with a high rate of interest, the loan succeeded handsomely. Necker's ability to meet the costs of war without a tax increase enhanced his image as a financial genius but the government was borrowing to finance a deficit, which meant that the costs of debt service would become greater in succeeding years.

In February 1781, in the face of mounting criticism as he sought to raise new loans to cover the expenses of the war, Necker put forward what he claimed was a statement on French finances, *Le Compte rendu au roi*. Because the reporting period was six to fifteen years behind, the *Compte rendu* was a composite of estimates provided by various departments and offices of revenues and expenditures for an "ordinary" year, which implied a peacetime year, enabling him to omit the costs of war. In this manner, calculating ordinary revenues against ordinary expenses, Necker was able to arrive at a surplus of 10.2 million *livres*.

Necker also stated, however, that there was additional ordinary income that came in, but he accounted for only a portion of it and did not stipulate how those funds were spent. As a result, even as an approximation of ordinary revenues and expenses of an "ordinary" year, the document was, in the words of one scholar, "incomplete, mysterious and infinitely controversial."[8] In 1781, the debt service on loans and annuities, which Necker omitted and the same scholar calculated at 16.3 million *livres*, exceeded the putative surplus of 10.2 million *livres*, producing a deficit.[9]

It was during the War of American Independence that the Crown began to finance its ordinary deficit by floating more loans, thereby increasing its long-term debt. Even after the conflict ended, after Necker was out of office, borrowing continued to cover the deficit, increasing debt service costs and the deficit for the next year. The practice led to a situation in which the French state was "locked into a self-generated drift toward insolvency" that would culminate in 1788 with a partial suspension of debt payments.[10] This trajectory of French finances was "the actual or potential situation that the *Compte rendu*, as published, conceals."[11]

Months after its publication, the *Compte rendu*, which sold tens of thousands of copies, brought an end to Necker's ministry, although it was not its duplicity that led to his fall. Rather, it was the fact that royal finances were a matter of great secrecy and to bring them into public view was a breach of protocol so egregious that it was described by one historian as unconstitutional.[12]

In addition, Vergennes, the foreign minister, contended that Necker's loans, dependent as they were on publicity, with the *Compte rendu* as an example, fundamentally changed not merely the nature of Crown finances but also the government of France by according a role to public opinion.[13] The notion that the French populace had any need to be informed about or especially that it had any right to have a role in royal financial affairs was contrary to the ideal of monarchy-centered government.

Descent toward Crisis

Although Necker's tenure ended, the structural crisis brought about by his borrowing continued. His successor, Jean-François Joly de Fleury, was not versed in financial matters and had difficulty grasping the complexity of Crown finances. Moreover, he reversed many of Necker's reforms. Public sentiment quickly turned against him and he enjoyed little standing.[14]

Joly de Fleury, who was in ill health, had been brought in primarily because he belonged to an established *parlementaire* family and enjoyed good relations with the body. He succeeded in securing a third *vingtième* in 1782, which the *parlement* grudgingly registered, but it added to his unpopularity. Furthermore, he continued the policy of borrowing heavily, ultimately accumulating hundreds of millions of *livres* in additional debt during his brief time in office, far in excess of revenue gained from the third *vingtième*. Joly de Fleury presented a *Compte rendu* to Louis that showed a deficit of eighty million *livres*.[15] Coming so soon after Necker's assertion of a surplus, the revelation met with incredulity and further eroded his standing at the Court, leading to his dismissal.

His successor was the youthful Henri Lefèvre d'Ormesson, a favorite of the king, who also resorted to loans, often at disadvantageous terms. He resigned after only seven months and his tenure has been described as "truly catastrophic."[16] The fiscal state of the Crown was becoming increasingly dire. Investor confidence had all but disappeared and it was apparent that a man of talent had to assume control of Crown finances. The choice fell upon Calonne, whom Louis named controller-general of finances in November 1783.

Calonne entered the post as a strong believer in monarchy-centered government. In 1766 he had helped to prepare Louis XV's remarks at the Session of the Scourging, at which Louis had asserted that sovereign power resided with the king alone and was not shared. Calonne's known role in this episode placed him at odds with the *parlement* from the outset of his tenure as controller-general and initiated a deterioration in Crown relations with the *parlement*.[17]

Calonne benefited from the end of the American War of Independence but, seeking to inspire confidence in the Crown, he undertook major public works projects. Lacking other investment opportunities, foreign capital poured in, lured by high rates of return. To understand fully the movement toward crisis, one must realize that the pace of borrowing, a critical component of the fiscal problem, did not subside after Necker's departure. To the contrary, it accelerated as both Joly de Fleury and Calonne borrowed more heavily than Necker did.[18] Floated at rates higher than elsewhere, the loans drove up the cost of servicing the debt, placing the Crown on a path to fiscal disaster.[19]

The level of borrowing became a catalyst for tension between Crown and *parlement*. Always eager to discredit Calonne, on December 29, 1784, the *parlement* issued a remonstrance against a loan of 125 million *livres*. The magistrates expressed astonishment that the Crown would cite the existence of war debt as justification for the loan—the war had ended more than a year earlier. There was reason to fear that war debts could serve as a continuing pretext for undefined expenses. It criticized the failure to liquidate war debt and asserted that such fiscal disorder was a road to "certain ruin" for a great power. The *parlement* urged Louis to correct all abuses that had thrown Crown finances into disarray, stating that he was the only one who could do so.

In his response, the king assured the *parlement* that he was seeking to restore order to Crown finances and to hasten liquidation of debt from the war, claiming that the yield from the previous loan had been devoted entirely to paying down war debt. He stated that the current request would largely be dedicated to the same end and that he anticipated making the final payments on the debt in 1786.

The *parlement* registered the edict on December 31, but it attached a resolution that exhorted the monarch to consider the importance of restoring good order to Crown finances, to verify that funds were directed to their stated purpose and to undertake other actions. The magistrates asked that he accelerate payments on the debt and meet ordinary expenses without resorting to new loans.[20]

The Monarchy Discredited

Crown finances were becoming a contentious matter between Crown and *parlement* but relations between them also worsened because of a development at Court. Louis René Edouard Cardinal Prince de Rohan, who was held in low regard by Marie-Antoinette, hoped to gain her favor to secure a ministerial post and in pursuit of this goal fell victim to an elaborate ruse. A Parisian jeweler had, on his own volition, created an extraordinary and expensive diamond necklace that he hoped to sell to Louis XV as a gift for his mistress, Madame du Barry, but Louis died before any sale could be completed. With enormous capital invested in the piece, the jeweler subsequently offered it to Louis XVI for him to give to Marie-Antoinette, but she declined it.

During the 1780s, Jeanne de Valois-Saint Rémy, comtesse de la Motte, an inveterate schemer recognized by the Crown as descended from a bastard branch of Henri II of the Valois line, launched an effort to secure a larger pension from the royal family. She sought to cultivate Marie-Antoinette in the belief that, as a woman, she would be more sympathetic and receptive to her request. Marie-Antoinette, however, aware of her questionable conduct, carefully avoided Jeanne.

In 1783, with her marriage in ruins, Jeanne met Rohan and became his mistress, through which she learned of his desire to gain support from Marie-Antoinette, whom he believed was blocking his path to ministerial office. Rohan found a place for Jeanne's estranged husband, Nicolas de la Motte, as a bodyguard for the comte d'Artois and provided her with some funds, but she aspired to greater status. Although Rohan was aware that Marie-Antoinette was avoiding her, Jeanne was able to convince him that she was, in fact, a secret confidante of the queen.

With the participation of both her estranged husband and her lover, Armand Gabriel Rétaux de Vilette, a skillful forger, Jeanne launched her scheme in 1784. She told Rohan that Marie-Antoinette wished to purchase the necklace but it could only be done surreptitiously because of the debilitated fiscal state of the Crown. She stated that the queen would assent to a full reconciliation if he would act as her intermediary with the jeweler. Vilette crafted letters, allegedly from Marie-Antoinette to the "comtesse," attesting to her interest in the necklace and noting the reluctance of the king to purchase it during a time of straitened fiscal circumstances. Jeanne convinced Rohan to make the purchase in order to achieve a reconciliation with the queen.

Before finally proceeding, however, Rohan asked for a meeting with the queen to receive her personal assurance of forgiveness and goodwill. Jeanne and her husband went to the Palais-Royal and succeeded in finding a prostitute who bore a physical resemblance to Marie-Antoinette. She was hired and brought to a nocturnal meeting with Rohan in the gardens of Versailles, where the impostor gave him the expression of friendship and support that he desired.

After providing the jeweler with a letter of credit from Rohan, allegedly countersigned by Marie-Antoinette, and after working out a plan to pay in installments, Jeanne and Rohan received the necklace in early 1785. They passed it to a man who claimed to be the valet for the queen but the plotters broke the necklace and Jeanne's husband sold the diamonds illicitly in London and Paris.

The plot went awry in August 1785, when Rohan could not muster sufficient funds to make the first payment. The jeweler wrote a letter to Marie-Antoinette obliquely inquiring about the necklace, which resulted in an investigation that quickly led to Rohan. Rather than concealing what had happened from the public, Louis XVI had Rohan arrested and imprisoned in the Bastille. Because Rohan was bishop of Strasbourg, the pope wanted his trial to be held in an ecclesiastical court, but Rohan, who was a prince of the blood, chose to be tried by the *parlement* of Paris.

The trial of Rohan, Jeanne, and several others began in May 1786, and its significance transcended the criminal actions underlying it. On one hand, there was the question of whether Rohan had committed a form of *lèse majesté* for assuming that Marie-Antoinette would be involved with such individuals as the other defendants or would have been a party to a surreptitious nocturnal meeting, both of which suggested a presumption of illicit activity or even criminal intent. On the other hand, there was the question of whether Rohan should be regarded as the victim of a fraud because it was plausible that Marie-Antoinette could be engaged in behavior of this sort.[21] In this respect, the trial effectively represented a judgment on the integrity of the monarchy.

The case against Rohan split the royal Court and the *parlement*—most educated observers generally viewed the cardinal as a victim of Court politics and arbitrary royal authority.[22] Ultimately, Jeanne de la Motte and Nicolas de la Motte, who was tried *in absentia* because he was in London, were found guilty and received harsh sentences. In the case of Rohan, however, there was dissension. The Crown had asked that Rohan be sentenced to exile for "criminal temerity" and for showing disrespect to the king and queen. Following a contentious deliberation, the magistrates, by a vote of thirty to twenty, found Rohan not guilty. Rohan exited the *Palais de Justice* to the acclaim of a crowd outside while at Versailles Marie-Antoinette, humiliated and angry, wept.[23] Although the episode has an almost comically absurd air about it, the Diamond Necklace Affair, as it has become known, had significant ramifications for the monarchy. The trial attracted considerable attention, and its outcome threw the monarchy into disrepute.[24]

The acquittal of Rohan irreparably harmed relations between Louis XVI and the *parlement* of Paris.[25] Having restored the body in 1774 after a years-long hiatus, in the aftermath of the verdict the king felt betrayed by it and was furious with it.[26] The decision shattered a decade of relative comity and was a major factor in the ensuing bitterness of the struggle between Louis and the *parlement* during 1787–88. One scholar contended that the trial destroyed the stability of Louis XVI's reign and another argued that in some respects it marked the "true unraveling of the *ancien régime*."[27]

The corrosive effects of the Diamond Necklace Affair are evident in the contrast in tone of two remonstrances from the *parlement* on Crown borrowing that were put forward a year apart. As noted earlier, on December

28, 1784, royal officials sought authorization for a twenty-five-year loan of 125 million *livres* at an interest rate of 5 percent, which led the *parlement* to issue a remonstrance at 6:00 p.m. the next day. The *parlement* registered the edict on December 31 but attached a resolution asking the monarch to undertake various actions.[28]

Although the *parlement* strongly disagreed with the policy of continued borrowing, the tone of its remonstrance was entirely respectful toward the monarch. The real target of the *parlement* was Calonne, and its statement that only Louis could restore order to finances was intended to show its antipathy for the controller-general. One year later, however, after the arrest of Rohan but before his trial, the tenor of a remonstrance and the comportment of the monarch were entirely different.

On December 13, 1785, Crown officials brought an edict for a ten-year loan in the amount of four million *livres* for registration. The *parlement* put forward a remonstrance on December 16 that began by pointing out that during the war it had registered all of the loans requested by the Crown. Even after the war ended it had approved two large loans, one for 100 million *livres* and the other for 125 million *livres*, but had done so on the basis of a promise from Louis that he would restore order to Crown finances. It was the duty of the *parlement*, the magistrates declared, to point out to the king the danger and consequences of repeated loans, with the reputation of the monarch and the well-being of his peoples dependent upon the reestablishment of good order in royal finances.

The *parlement* contended that the loan the Crown was currently requesting was really an annuity and was being disguised in an effort to avoid the contradiction arising from a statement by Louis that frequent resort to annuities was problematic, which had led him largely to renounce them. It was a remarkable act to accuse the monarch of duplicity and went far beyond earlier exchanges. To argue that a king was violating the constitution was to question his judgment. To accuse him of dishonesty was to question his character and it was all the more extraordinary for the fact that the amount in question was so small. After calling for greater austerity, the magistrates made a barbed allusion to the Diamond Necklace Affair when they stated that it was time for the monarch to set a personal example, as he had frequently assured the *parlement* he would, by, among other actions, curtailing "immodest gifts."

Louis tartly expressed his gratitude to the *parlement* for its solicitude for the happiness of his subjects and stated that he was much more concerned with their happiness than it was. He insisted that the edict be registered without delay and that a report be given to him by the following evening. On December 19 the first president, speaking for the *parlement*, urged the king once again to consider a course other than that of opening a new loan. Louis angrily responded that, after enlightening the *parlement* the previous day, he was quite astonished and displeased at the new delay but would listen to it the next afternoon.

The first president took the concerns of the *parlement* to the monarch the next day. He told Louis that the body felt itself caught between two conflicting imperatives. On one hand, it was obligated to defend the interests of peoples fundamentally bound to the king. On the other hand, the *parlement* wished to defer to the will of a sovereign to whom it devoted itself. Nevertheless, it was its solemn duty to speak important truths to the king. The first president asserted that the *parlement* was duty-bound to ask him again to consider that it was not always necessary to float a loan to pay off a debt and urged a policy of austerity instead.

Louis answered that the new observations of the *parlement* were not going to lead him to change course and that there was no one more devoted to the happiness of his people than he was. The *parlement* would be committing a wrong against him if it persisted in a long delay of the edict and Louis declared that he expected it to be registered the next day. On December 21 the *parlement* registered the edict, citing the express order of the monarch as the reason. Its registration decree urged the king to recognize the danger and consequences of excessive loans and to realize that the real path to healthy state finances lay in austerity by funding only necessary expenses.

The response clearly angered Louis. On December 23 royal officials brought a *lettre de cachet* to the *parlement* and ordered all of its members to appear the same evening at 6:00 and to bring the decree registering the loan. At the meeting, the king read the minutes of the *parlement* aloud and sternly told the magistrates that they were aware of the protocol for registration and should set an example by respecting it. The *parlement* should not insert into a registration that was to be posted and seen by the public matters that should remain within the boundaries of secrecy that was integral to the close relationship he allowed the *parlement* to have with him. He was, he said, removing extraneous material from the registration decree and, declaring that he was excising a hastily conceived and improperly edited decree, he did so with his own hand. Louis warned the magistrates that he would not tolerate abuse of his goodwill and confidence. In addition, shortly before concluding the meeting, the king specifically avowed his satisfaction with Calonne.[29]

The encounter brought into the open the bitter anger between Crown and *parlement*. The Diamond Necklace Affair dismayed the *parlement* because it seemed to represent reckless profligacy at the Court as the Crown was seeking large loans. To Louis, however, allusions to it by the *parlement*, given that the Court apparently had no culpability, seemed gratuitous, not only impugning the character of himself and Marie-Antoinette but also being used as a specious reason to block Crown requests for loans.

The Crown Attempts Reform

In August 1786, with international bankers becoming more wary of investing in French loans, even at high interest rates, Calonne was compelled to confront the state of French finances. The Crown was facing a deficit of staggering proportions, larger than the annual ordinary revenues of Spain or two-thirds of the budget of Austria.[30] Urging Louis to undertake a comprehensive reform of the tax structure of the kingdom, the centerpiece of the plan Calonne presented to him was a "territorial subvention," which was to be a proportional tax in kind to be paid by all landowners without exception. The measure would increase royal revenues but would also significantly breach the system of fiscal privilege.[31]

Because of the antipathy between Calonne and the *parlement*, as well as the clearly expressed view of the *parlement* that privilege should not be infringed, there was little prospect of Calonne's proposals gaining its support. In an effort to circumvent the *parlement*, Calonne recommended the convening of an Assembly of Notables, a body that had not been called since 1626. Calonne's intention was to gain its endorsement to reinforce his proposals when he presented them to the *parlement* and thereby virtually compel it to register them.

Louis considered the issue for several months before giving his approval and his thinking during those months is little known or understood.[32] One possible reason for his hesitation may have been that the Assembly of Notables had been moribund for nearly as long as the Estates General. Although the Crown appointed the membership of the body, it was a tenet of Bourbon rule not to cede any role in governance, even in an advisory or consultative capacity. In addition, Louis may have been cautious in undertaking a direct assault on privilege because of the resistance it could provoke and the destabilizing effects that could result—Calonne's program represented a repudiation of "the spirit and mechanism of the *ancien régime*."[33] Calonne subsequently claimed that he had warned Louis that taking on "the Hydra of privileges, exemptions and abuses" would draw a host of enemies.[34]

In 1786, however, Calonne, assured of the monarch's support, believed that he would have little difficulty in convincing the Notables of the necessity of his reforms. The Assembly of Notables, however, was not necessarily a pliant body.[35] Among its members were officers and senior members of the *parlements*, guardians and recipients of privilege, and officials of provincial Estates, major beneficiaries of it as well. The Crown chose 144 men, with members of the clergy and nobility dominant and few from the Third Estate, but there was a lack of clarity in the convening of the Assembly. Was it to be a body with a truly deliberative, albeit advisory, role, which would enable it to gain respect with the public? Or was it to be called simply to endorse a course of action already decided upon, in which case it would have little credibility? The issue was not addressed before the body met and would become its fatal flaw.[36]

A critical mistake made by Calonne and Louis XVI was their failure to use the appointments to pack the Assembly with supporters. Louis XIII had done this in 1626 and Calonne initially sought to have a core element of loyalists but their names were removed, almost certainly by Louis in an effort to keep the prestige of the body from being diminished. Even with known individual supporters removed, Calonne still had latitude with respect to institutional choices, but he miscalculated. He had two men from each provincial *parlement* appointed but *parlementaires* were hostile to him. Yet he named only eight, out of a possible thirty-three, royal council members, who could be reliably counted upon to support him. Calonne instead based his choices upon their importance, respect from the public and patriotism. He believed that patriotic men could easily be persuaded of the value of his reforms and that only selfish or narrow-minded men would oppose it.[37] Fortified by this belief and his abundant self-confidence, Calonne, despite a warning from the intendant of Brittany, for example, that the nobility of that province would not fully deliberate in the proceedings, forged ahead.[38]

The Assembly of Notables opened on February 22, 1787, with a brief speech by the king. He told them that he had brought them together to make them a part of his projects and that the proposals to be put before them were large and important. Because they were designed for the common good and because he knew that the Notables were driven by zeal for serving him, he had no apprehension about consulting them on their implementation. He concluded by saying that no particular interest should rise above the general interest.[39]

Louis's speech was followed by a longer one by Calonne, who began by recounting the dire fiscal situation that he had found when he came to office in late 1783 and what he had done since to restore confidence. After ruling out continued borrowing, a tax increase and after pledging economies, Calonne asserted that what remained was to take on what he called "abuses." It would be easy to take on minor abuses, Calonne asserted, but the greatest abuses were the pecuniary privileges and exceptions to laws common to all. These privileges exacerbated inequalities in tax assessment and created significant disparities between provinces and subjects of the same monarch. Calonne declared that what was required was a comprehensive solution.

Previous efforts had been blocked by the difficulty of reconciling a mass of local customs, claims and privileges as well as interests opposed to each other. After presenting a plan to establish provincial assemblies for those provinces that were not *pays d'états*, Calonne arrived at the centerpiece of his project. He stated that the king was committed to establishing a principle of uniformity—the exceptions currently in place were more tolerated than legitimate.

The monarch, Calonne declared, had concluded that the only means to resolve the problem was to replace the *vingtième* with a general tax that would not have any exceptions, including Church lands. In an effort to lessen the impact, Calonne added that the "first orders" of the State possessed honorable distinctions that Louis wished to maintain, leaving them exempt from any personal tax such as the *capitation*, which would be incompatible with their status, a remark that sought to make the idea acceptable by emphasizing that in theory the tax was on land rather than individuals.[40] Calonne adduced additional reform proposals and told the Notables that the matters before them were a question of the fate of the state.[41]

Calonne's speech, particularly its latter portion, made clear the purpose envisaged for the Assembly of Notables. It was to ratify a course of action already decided upon, as contemporaries quickly realized—one wrote that the Assembly had been convened to do away with any obstacles that could keep the program from being enacted.[42]

At the first full session after the opening of the Assembly, the comte d'Artois briefly addressed the body for only one purpose. He told the Notables that they should rely on their own judgment and not seek any outside advice. He advised them that he thought it would be preferable, even though the monarch had not mandated it, that all proceedings, both in plenary sessions and committee meetings, remain secret.[43]

Soon afterward, however, on the grounds that the French public needed to be informed, Calonne's opening speech was made public and became an object of intense public interest.[44] Its release discredited Calonne because it made clear that he regarded his plan as the only possible solution. Moreover, its disclosure came to be perceived as a mistake for making known publicly the dire condition of state finances and that Calonne was equally misguided in expecting that the Notables would blindly comply with what was asked of them.[45]

Angered by the pliant role to which they had been consigned, the Notables responded by rejecting the tax proposal immediately and almost unanimously. They contended that, to ascertain whether the deficit was as great as Calonne had announced in his opening speech, they needed to have access to the royal financial accounts to determine the fiscal condition for 1786 by comparing them with Necker's *Compte rendu* of 1781.[46] With the memory of the controversy surrounding Necker's disclosure still fresh, it was a request that the Notables did not expect to be granted and served as a useful excuse for inaction.

Their resistance was aided by an unusual procedure that Calonne put in place for the meeting. Instead of a unified body, as had been done in 1626, Calonne divided the Notables into seven committees, each headed by a prince of the blood. Questions were to be decided not by a majority of individuals but by a majority of committees, which Calonne had almost certainly designed to facilitate the passage of his proposals. It would be theoretically possible for a measure to be approved with as few as forty-four votes instead of seventy-three in a unified body.[47]

Although it may have been designed to serve Calonne's purposes, the committee system provided an added layer of secrecy and enabled the Notables to avoid pitfalls in which Calonne had hoped to trap them. In order not to alienate public opinion, for example, the Notables endorsed the principle of fiscal equality and renounced their exemption from the *capitation*.

In committee, however, a distinctly different attitude prevailed. The Estates of Brittany had sent its representatives to the Assembly of Notables without any instructions or mandate, which they sought to conceal by omitting it from the minutes of the meeting. After the arrival of its delegation in Versailles, the Estates continued to remind its members that they did not have a mandate to negotiate the matters under consideration. On March 20 the Breton Notables claimed that the privileges of Brittany could not be discussed or negotiated. They asserted that any modification of the tax system in the province was the exclusive prerogative of the province itself. Likewise, a Notable from Burgundy vigorously defended the privileges of the province in his committee, pointedly noting that Louis XVI had confirmed them when he took the throne.[48] One contemporary noted that little was expected from the Notables in either patriotism or energy and that when the Notables were not contentious they were indifferent, often skipping meetings to spend time at various clubs.[49]

As his project failed to make progress and rumors began to circulate that the Assembly would be dismissed and a *lit de justice* used to implement his program, Calonne addressed a plenary session of the Notables on March 12. He told them that the issues before them demanded their full attention and all of the proposals needed to be approved, but he emphasized that the territorial subvention was its most important component and offered uniform taxation.[50]

The Notables took offense at Calonne's remarks, which they believed misrepresented their position, especially a statement in which he declared that they agreed with the substance of the program and differed only on its form. Except for the proposals on the *corvée* and the provincial assemblies, this was untrue—its other components had been rejected in form and substance. When Calonne submitted his speech for the minutes, the offending passage had been removed and other changes had been made. Nevertheless, all seven committees inserted statements into the minutes declaring their disagreement with Calonne's characterization of their position.[51]

Trust between Calonne and the Notables was all but broken but he met with them in another plenary session on March 29. It lasted only thirteen minutes, with the brevity of the meeting indicating how strained relations had become. Indeed, that day the portion of Calonne's March 12 speech in which he had indicated that the Notables accepted the reform program in substance but not in form appeared in the *Journal de Paris*, assumed to have been inserted by Calonne himself. Angered again, the Notables demanded a retraction. Calonne extricated himself by claiming that the text had not been properly printed.[52]

Louis was frustrated with the detailed examinations conducted by the Notables and Calonne was exasperated. Calonne commissioned a pamphlet directed against the Notables, provocatively titled *Avertissement* (warning). It asserted that the reestablishment of financial equilibrium was in the interest of all and that the burden of the Crown's proposals would not fall on the people. After presenting an outline of the reforms, the pamphlet noted the equivocal attitude of the Notables toward the proposals and speculated on possible reasons for their stance.

It conceded that the tax burden would be heavier but asserted that it would fall only on those who currently did not pay enough. Stating that privileges would be sacrificed, the pamphlet asked if the Notables instead preferred to overburden the non-privileged—the people. It then appeared to defend the Notables by observing that they had already agreed to sacrifice their fiscal privileges and had also agreed to the idea that the land tax should be extended to all land without exception. It contended that it would be wrong to believe that reasonable doubts on the part of the Notables represented malevolent opposition because that perception would be harmful to the nation.[53]

Calonne's disingenuous defense of the Notables was, of course, a veiled threat, suggesting that the time for "reasonable doubts" was coming to an end and that continued opposition to the proposed measures, especially the territorial subvention, would be viewed as harmful to the nation. Left unsaid was that the Notables, in the midst of a severe fiscal crisis, were resisting a more equitable tax distribution and that the burden would continue to fall on "the people." To underscore its argument, the pamphlet was accompanied by Calonne's proposal for the land tax.

Calonne went to great lengths to disseminate the pamphlet. He took the extraordinary step of having it distributed free of charge in both Paris and provincial towns and clergy were encouraged to read it from the pulpit.[54] Its publication and remarkable diffusion poisoned relations between Calonne and the Notables and on April 8, soon after its appearance, Louis dismissed Calonne, a move that the public welcomed.[55] Although he dismissed Calonne, Louis still wanted to enact the program that Calonne had devised.[56] He also realized that the objections of the Notables could not simply be ignored or overridden. The proposals would have to be amended.

Louis addressed the Notables in a plenary session on April 23. He reiterated his determination to eradicate the deficit and reaffirmed his support of the land tax, which he believed was the critical component in resolving the fiscal crisis. He offered several concessions that met nearly all of the objections raised by the Notables, including making the tax proportional to the amount of the deficit and limiting its duration, as they had asked.[57] In another significant gesture, the *Garde des sceaux* informed the Notables that they would be given access to the royal accounts to demonstrate the reality of the deficit. He also stated that the monarch had announced economies that would amount to fifteen million *livres*.[58] Although the Notables regarded the economies as insufficient, Louis's address was well received.[59]

As the accounts were in the process of being communicated to the Notables, Louis made another concession to them. When Louis dismissed Calonne he had replaced him with Michel Bouvard de Fourqueux, who reluctantly accepted but resigned only three weeks later. Soon after, Louis named Etienne Charles Loménie de Brienne, archbishop of Toulouse and a member of the Notables who had been one of the leaders of the opposition to Calonne, as head of the Royal Council of Finances. It was anticipated that Brienne would choose a new controller-general and would himself serve as a virtual chief minister.[60] On May 5 the monarch named Pierre Charles Laurent de Villedeuil, also a member of the Notables, to replace Fourqueux, which meant that the two highest-ranking financial officials had come from the Assembly of Notables.

The Crown clearly believed that with one of their own in charge of royal finances, the Notables would believe him and accept the existence of the deficit, particularly after the transmission of the royal accounts. It was widely expected that the territorial subvention would pass, an expectation reinforced by the fact that the Crown had given preponderance to the clergy and nobility in the provincial assemblies, which would administer the land tax.[61]

After receiving them, the Notables began to examine the royal accounts, which were difficult to understand. Although the committees could not agree on the amount of the deficit, they were in agreement that it was considerable. Their response, however, was to urge the monarch to pursue greater economies than those mentioned at the plenary session. They also suggested administrative measures to prevent future deficits.[62]

Brienne struggled to focus the attention of the Notables on the current deficit and stressed the need to address it immediately. He told them that there would be a further reduction in state expenditures of approximately forty million *livres* but warned that no additional reductions could be expected. Brienne asked them to enact the land tax but they instead asked for greater economies from the Crown in the amount of sixty-five million *livres.* On May 10 the Notables rejected the land tax and instead recommended the formation of a financial council to oversee revenues and approve or reject all financial operations.[63]

The committees put forward different reasons for their unwillingness to approve the tax. Some cited the complexity of the royal accounts, which they claimed prevented them from establishing the size of the deficit, meaning that they could not estimate the amount of the revenue that the tax should produce, how long it should be in effect or even whether it was needed at all. Other committees contended that they should not anticipate the decision of the *parlement.* All but one of the committees asserted that because the Assembly was not a representative body it could not legitimately consent to it.[64]

In the face of such intransigence, Brienne knew that he had little choice but to dismiss the Notables. Rumors that the Assembly was about to be dissolved began to circulate, generating alarm because nothing had been enacted. Brienne was excoriated for his change of stance after becoming a minister and there were calls for his dismissal. Any lingering satisfaction with the fall of Calonne quickly evaporated.[65] In a plenary session on May 25 Louis dismissed the Notables and his brief concluding remarks were gracious, praising them for their efforts although he reminded them that the deficit remained unresolved. Brienne was less generous in his speech and emphasized the deficit and the failure to achieve a solution.[66]

Several members of the Notables responded. Most of the responses were unremarkable, but a brief speech by the abbé de la Fare, who spoke in his capacity as an official of the provincial Estates of Burgundy, was revealing. After professing his love and loyalty to the king, he said that deputies of the *pays d'états* were going to take back to their fellow citizens the "assurance that the privileges of corporate bodies and provinces, these ancient remains and precious conventions of the national constitution were to be religiously preserved and maintained." Although he added that the *pays d'états* would jointly combine to enhance the stature of the monarch and the prosperity of the kingdom, his remarks made clear that those goals would not be at the expense of provincial privileges.[67] His speech, as brief as it was, provides insight into the manner in which, however much they may have sought to disguise it, the defense of privilege was a primary motivation for many of the Notables.[68]

What was apparent to contemporaries, particularly after the appearance of Calonne's pamphlet, was that after three months the Assembly of Notables had done nothing to resolve the fiscal crisis that had been the reason for its convocation and the existence of which the Notables acknowledged.[69] Because they had, in fact, negotiated with the Crown on the land tax and requested modifications during those three months, the statement that they could not assent to the tax because the Assembly was not a representative body rang hollow.[70] Rather, their abrupt abdication of responsibility, especially after the Crown met most of their objections and adopted nearly all of their recommendations, gave rise to the perception that they were unwilling to give up pecuniary privileges in order to achieve fiscal solvency for the kingdom. To many it appeared that privilege had triumphed over the well-being of the polity.[71]

Although they failed to address the fiscal crisis, the Notables did approve the Crown plan to establish provincial assemblies in *pays d'élections*, the provinces without provincial estates. They were to be an instrument of local government for the Crown and, one scholar has argued, a means to bring greater fairness to taxation. Originally, their composition was to have been based on tax assessments on land, but the Notables asked that the assemblies be divided into the three estates and led by a nobleman. Brienne acquiesced but amended the structure to allow them to be led by a clergyman or a noble. Most significantly, however, half of the places were designated for the Third Estate and vote was to be by head in general session.

Notwithstanding their brief existence—Necker did not summon them in 1788—the assemblies served as a means to learn collective political procedures and represented the beginning of a transition from the old to the new. They prepared the way for the National Assembly to create a state in which officials did not owe obedience to the king but instead to a clearly defined hierarchy of governmental functions.[72]

The Aftermath of the Assembly of Notables

After the Notables had received the royal accounts, each committee had put forward an estimate of the deficit. The mean amount of the estimate was 140 million *livres*, which was accepted and made public. In his closing speech to the Notables, Brienne, dripping with sarcasm, complimented them for making known this important truth and lauded them for the great service that they had performed for the state in doing so.[73]

Observers realized that the Notables had disbanded leaving matters in the same state as they had been, except that there was broader awareness of the catastrophic condition of state finances.[74] Some found the revelations made at the meeting deeply unsettling.[75] In an age when economic matters were generally only imperfectly understood, the deficit and its ramifications were not entirely comprehended, but there was a pervasive sense that it was injurious to the kingdom, a perception that launched a fundamental and unprecedented reconsideration of the French state. Was France primarily a conglomeration of privileged individuals, corporations and provinces or was it a grander entity defined by common bonds and ideals? Calonne was a powerful royal official who had advocated the breaching of fiscal privilege as royal policy. Although his pamphlet had not produced the immediate effect that he had hoped of putting pressure on the Notables to approve his program, it did have an unanticipated result that endured. His contention that there was perhaps a fundamental conflict between the fiscal privileges enjoyed by entities within the kingdom and the general well-being of the state legitimized the questioning of privilege.

A distinctive characteristic of the period following the dismissal of the Notables was the degree to which the traditional concept of the state underwent a fundamental reexamination, with privilege as a central focus. It was after the dismissal of the Notables that the term "privileged orders" as a pejorative term gained greater usage. Although it would not fully crystallize until 1788, the core element of the reevaluation was a movement away from acceptance of privilege as a valid instrument of government to rejection of it as inimical to the common weal.

In addition to initiating a reconsideration of the nature of the French state, the failure of the Assembly of Notables altered the political situation in France. The only course available to the Crown after the Assembly of Notables was the convening of the Estates General, which it was loath to do. The calling of the Assembly of Notables had seemed to indicate, beyond its tactical use, an implicit recognition of the need for public affirmation of policy, however limited the representation of 144 Notables as "the public" may have been.[76] The appearance and dissemination of Calonne's pamphlet considerably broadened the concept as well as the role of the public as he sought to enlist opinion against the Notables. His pamphlet, *Avertissement*, had quickly become referred to in Versailles as "appeal to the people."[77] Public opinion would increasingly become a force and consideration in policy to a degree unprecedented under the Bourbon dynasty. In one single act, not only had Calonne legitimized the questioning of privilege but had also accorded a role to public opinion in policymaking.[78]

The fiscal crisis that led to the convening of the Assembly of Notables and the failure of the Notables to address it were the catalyst for the terminal crisis of the Old Regime. Never again would the Crown be in control of events to the degree that it was when the Assembly of Notables opened. It had chosen the members of the body and had devised a voting procedure highly advantageous to the Crown, but Calonne could not gain its assent to his reform program, even with the full support of the monarch behind him.

In declaring that the financial well-being of the kingdom was in the interest of all and stating that the burden of the proposed reforms would fall only on those who did not pay enough rather than the people, Calonne discredited fiscal privileges without explicitly taking that position. His pamphlet legitimized public discussion and criticism of privilege.

To be sure, the Crown had previously hired writers to influence public opinion, but its purpose had been chiefly to counter criticism, as when the Maupeou courts were put in place, for example.[79] Similarly, Necker's *Compte rendu* had been directed toward public opinion, but its purpose had been to maintain his reputation and popularity. By contrast, Calonne sought to enlist public opinion for the purpose of enacting a royal program against the resistance of recalcitrant elites. In monarchy-centered government, royal will was supposed to be sufficient—to appeal to the public to achieve a Crown goal was a major departure from the Bourbon style of government.

At the end of 1787, the Crown appeared ineffectual and arbitrary, the elites selfish, and the kingdom weak. Louis had changed the political landscape by having convened the Assembly of Notables, revealed the deficit to them and established provincial assemblies.[80] Frustration over the failure of the Assembly of Notables to address a domestic crisis was compounded by a recession and a perception of national weakness in foreign affairs.[81] Indeed, Guillaume Chrétien de Lamoignon de Malesherbes, regarded as one of the king's more perceptive ministers, wrote that the situation of France in 1787 bore little resemblance to the situation of France in 1786 because the Assembly of Notables had led to events that had no parallel in French history.[82] The sense of decline was palpable and would form a backdrop to the fiscal and political crises that followed.

The Forgotten Constitution: The Origins, Realization, and Legacy of the French Constitution of 1791.
Michael P. Fitzsimmons, Oxford University Press. © Oxford University Press 2025.
DOI: 10.1093/9780197793978.003.0004

4

The Erosion of Monarchy-Centered Government

The failure of the Assembly of Notables left the Crown in a difficult situation. Denied the endorsement that it had hoped would strengthen its prospects before the *parlement*, the Crown, unwilling to call the Estates General, had to present its program from a position of weakness. It sent its proposals for a stamp tax and land tax on June 22 but the *parlement* took them up only on July 2. The dilatory response of the *parlement* and its questioning of the existence of a deficit and request for access to royal accounts exasperated Louis. On July 29 he ordered it to give him a decision on the land tax the next day, declaring that he had structured it solely to meet the needs of the state and that the account he would publish each year would leave no doubt on that issue.[1]

On August 2 the *parlement* replied that in light of the difficult financial situation of state finances and the commitment of the *parlement* to maintaining the rights of the nation, only the Estates General, which represented the nation, could assent to a new tax. Avoiding any euphemism such as "assembled nation," the *parlement* asked the king to convene the Estates General prior to imposing any new tax, to which the monarch curtly replied that he would make his intentions known.[2]

On August 4 Louis withdrew the stamp and land tax edicts and the following day sent the *parlement* orders to assemble for a *lit de justice.* At the session the *Garde des sceaux* offered a lengthy presentation that concluded with the statement that the monarch did not distrust the *parlement* but that under the constitution of the kingdom he was its sole administrator. He asserted that the current circumstances were too urgent to brook any further delay because the needs of the state were beyond doubt and could soon be calamitous.[3]

The first president responded by imploring the king to take under consideration the crisis in which the state now found itself, a crisis announced, admitted, and acknowledged at the Assembly of Notables. The *parlement* had given its assent for twelve years on various taxes amounting to 200 million *livres* but it could no longer accede. The magistrates declared that it was a constitutional principle of the French monarchy that taxes could be consented to only by those who paid them, which guaranteed obedience. The *parlement* denounced the stamp tax and the territorial subvention and again called for the convening of the Estates General. If, despite the supplications and representations of the *parlement*, the monarch chose to deploy his "absolute power," the *parlement* would continue to protest what it regarded as the imposition of illegal taxes.[4] The *Garde des sceaux* ordered the registration of the edict for the land tax but the *parlement* instead restated its objections. From the formal platform used for a *lit de justice*, Louis ordered the registration of the stamp tax as well.[5]

In a remonstrance of August 6, 1787, directed against the stamp and land taxes, the *parlement*, emulating the Notables, professed that it was unable to verify the existence of the deficit and asked that accounts of revenues and expenditures be given to it along with a list of cuts and other economies that Louis had announced. Incredulous, the king noted that the accounts had been given to the Assembly of Notables, which had included several parlementary magistrates. The Notables had verified the existence of a deficit and he, Louis, had announced the sum of the cuts he intended to make. A new examination of accounts would not only not produce any additional information, but examination of accounts was not a duty of the *parlement.*

The *parlement* suggested that the deficit might be exaggerated and asserted that it was justified in asking for certitude. Citing five years of peace and the burden it would impose, the *parlement* asked Louis to withdraw the stamp tax. The magistrates again claimed that only the "assembled nation" could assent to new taxes.[6]

A clearly angered king held a *lit de justice* in which he ordered the *parlement* to register the edicts.[7] The next day, August 7, in an extraordinary act, the *parlement* protested the registration and declared the edicts null and void. On August 13 the *parlement* denounced the publication of the land tax and stamp tax registrations in the *Journal de Paris* and reaffirmed its protest of August 7.[8]

Louis prohibited the publication and circulation of the *parlement*'s statement to lower courts and on August 15 exiled the *parlement* to Troyes. On August 27 the *parlement* issued a defiant proclamation asserting that only the Estates General could heal the wounds of the state. If ministers continued to abuse the authority of the monarch, the French monarchy would be reduced to a state of despotism. The *parlement* asked that its statement be circulated to lower courts, but it was not.[9]

Communications between Crown and *parlement* were closely held and their content unknown to the public, but the remonstrances were indicative of a breakdown in governance. Louis claimed full authority in the kingdom whereas the *parlement* asserted a limited role for the nation through the Estates General. Aware of the unwillingness of the Crown to summon it, the *parlement* was assuming a maximalist position—never during the entire century had the *parlement* called for a meeting of the Estates General. In 1718 the magistrates had claimed that the *parlement* was the voice of the people in the absence of the Estates General, which at that time had been inactive for more than a century.[10] The 1718 statement was a rare acknowledgment that the status of the *parlement* was in large measure dependent upon the absence of the Estates General, making the decision to call for its convocation a surprising and somewhat puzzling one.

One explanation is that it was a purposeful plan by the *parlement* intended to solidify its position. On one hand, the calling of the Estates General by itself weakened the Crown and, if the Estates General met with success, it would further weaken it. The *parlement* was a permanent body whereas the Estates General was periodic, so the *parlement* would presumably gain strength in its dealings with a potentially politically debilitated monarch. On the other hand, if the Estates General failed, there would be no institution left that could rival the *parlement* and the Crown would not be able to circumvent it.[11] If these were the calculations of the magistrates, there was little to be lost in calling for the convocation of the Estates General.[12]

The decision has also been attributed to a recognition by the *parlement* of its own weakness. Over the years from 1774 to 1787, Louis had usually been able to avoid ministerial disunity that the *parlement* could exploit. The *parlement* realized that only the Estates General could place limitations on royal power that the *parlement* could not.[13]

Although the public would not have been fully aware of it, the government of France was at a complete impasse. The *parlement* was accusing the king of illegal registration and suggesting that obedience to him might be called into question while urging an action that it knew was anathema to the Crown. The Crown was effectively claiming that the monarch alone ruled, creating the perception of despotism. One informed observer noted that the Crown believed that compromise on the stamp tax would weaken royal authority whereas the *parlement* seemed determined to resist all financial reforms.[14]

With the functioning of the French state in question, the two sides entered into secret negotiations that achieved a compromise. The Crown withdrew the stamp and land taxes and the *parlement* registered the first and second *vingtième* on September 19. A few days later the Crown recalled the *parlement* to Paris.[15] Although Paris had been disconcerted by the "transfer" of the *parlement* to Troyes—the Crown had prohibited use of the word "exile"—the outcome was not entirely a victory for the *parlement*.[16]

The settlement raised questions about the sincerity of the *parlement* in demanding the convocation of the Estates General, especially because the demand had not been made public. Its argument had been that only the Estates General could consent to taxation but the *parlement* had acquiesced to taxation without the convening of the Estates General. Although the two *vingtièmes* were a continuation of an existing tax, it was a tax that had traditionally been levied only during wartime, so its prolongation represented a departure from past practice, further weakening the argument of the *parlement*.[17] Moreover, although there was strong opposition to the stamp tax, opinion was more divided on the land tax, which would have eased the burden of lesser landholders and brought the clergy and nobility into the tax net. The fact that members of the *parlement* had a personal interest at stake with the land tax did not escape notice.[18]

Even as it ended the political crisis, the settlement left the Crown short of the additional revenues that the stamp and land taxes would have generated—the land tax alone had been projected to generate 25 million *livres* more than the *vingtièmes*.[19] In mid-November the *parlement* had seemed amenable to approving the loan request but it stipulated that the preamble to the loan approval edict would promise that the Estates General would be convened by April 1788.[20]

The Deterioration of Relations between Crown and *Parlement*

On November 19, 1787, the Crown, in a marathon meeting that lasted many hours, resorted to what was effectively a preemptive *lit de justice* to register loans that totaled over 400 million *livres* while promising to call the Estates General within five years. Louis arrived at the *Palais de Justice* and presented the edict for the loans. It was read aloud and magistrates discussed it but before they could vote the *Garde des sceaux* took orders from the monarch and pronounced the edict registered. Louis then left. As he was leaving, the duc d'Orléans told Louis that what he had done went against norms and protocol, to which the king replied that he did not care and it was permissible because he wished it.

In a remonstrance that took nearly five months to complete, the deepening political crisis was apparent. It opened with the declaration that the principle of freedom had been attacked at its core and that despotism had superseded law, with the magistracy having been reduced to being an instrument of arbitrary power. The magistrates objected to the November 19 meeting with the king because it represented an act of absolute power that eradicated essential principles, historic truths, and positive laws on which the rights of subjects had rested for thirteen centuries.

Noting that Louis had suppressed the decree of the *parlement* after the meeting, the magistrates asserted that the register of the *parlement* was an inviolable record that preserved the rights of subjects and monarchs alike. Precluding a vote meant that the deliberation was not complete, but the Crown had sent out a decree indicating approval by the *parlement*, leaving the body feeling betrayed. The will of the monarch, the *parlement* asserted, was not law. In order for royal will to be made legal, it had to be legally published and its underlying premises freely verified. These were the bases of the French constitution that had been born with the French monarchy and the magistrates traced the rights of the people and the monarch back to the year 803. They asked the king if he was willing to eradicate the constitution by subsuming the *parlement* to his person.[21]

The remonstrance contained harsh criticisms, but Louis was unapologetic. He brusquely told the *parlement* that it was superfluous for the king to speak of registration of a law or freedom of votes. When he went to the *parlement*, it was to hear discussion of the law and to allow him to determine with greater knowledge whether it should be registered. He contended that this was what he had done on November 19 and that everything done that day was legal. The king claimed that he was correcting an error rather than altering the register of the *parlement*.[22]

The magistrates professed surprise at Louis's statement that his will alone sufficed in matters of administration and legislation. They also observed that the monarch did not rule to the same degree in all provinces. In Béarn, the first article of its covenant was an oath of the king to respect its privileges, an oath that was renewed in each reign in person at the assembled provincial Estates. Each province asked for a *parlement* for the defense of its particular rights. Without these rights and the *parlements*, the monarch could overturn the rights and privileges of the provinces, making his will uniform but, the *parlement* asked, would the action be prudent or just?[23]

The *parlement* issued a decree denouncing *lettres de cachet* and lamenting the descent of the monarchy to despotism.[24] Rumors swirled that magistrates would be abducted by royal forces and imprisoned and those not incarcerated would be sent to Tours or Poitiers. Only a direct intervention by Brienne, it was believed, had averted the action.[25]

There had been a sense of political crisis present even before the November 19 session, but the April 11 remonstrance seemed to affirm it. Louis was clearly angered by it because on the day it was presented Brienne reportedly met with the first president of the *parlement* and made it known that the *parlement* was putting itself at risk of retaliation if it continued to push the king to his limit.[26]

The threat could not have come as a surprise to the first president. There had been rumors for weeks of action to be taken against the *parlement* and the *parlement* was said to be preparing a "national revolution" in secrecy. According to one informed observer, as Anglomania increased in France there was a fascination with a constitution that made men free, in stark contrast to the despotic machinations of ministers in France. The *parlements*, perceived as representatives of the nation, gained favor as concern grew that the Crown would seek to subject or even suppress the *parlements* altogether, giving the monarch untrammeled power.[27]

Based on a rumor that the *parlement* of Paris was on the verge of suspension, on May 3, 1788, it issued a decree that circulated widely and gained notice in the city. The brief declaration emphasized the rights of the people and stated that any tax that did not have prior approval of the Estates General was illegal, which may have been one of the first public statements demanding the convocation of the Estates General by the *parlement*.

The *parlement* never used the word "constitution" in its May 3 declaration, claiming instead that the statement consisted of "maxims" that it was obligated to uphold. The declaration included "customs and capitulations" of provinces, which encompassed their privileges, among the maxims. It stated that it was placing these principles in the hands of the Estates General and each of the three orders that "together or separately" comprised the nation.

Although the *parlement* clearly regarded the tenets it advanced as fundamental principles and therefore effectively constitutional in nature, the word "constitution," which it had used in remonstrances, was not utilized in the public statement. It would have implied a limitation upon the sovereign will of the king that he would have found objectionable, even inflammatory. At the same time, however, there can be little doubt that the *parlement*, using euphemisms, was putting forward the notion of a constitution in May 1788.

Seeking to avoid its interception by royal authorities, the decree was registered at the Châtelet and sent by special delivery rather than ordinary mail to every court of justice in the kingdom. In a disinformation campaign, according to the *parlement*, the Crown created a false version of the statement, altering it so that criticisms of ministers in the original appeared to be directed against the king personally. The *parlement* responded with a condemnation of the counterfeit. Days later the Crown annulled the May 3 pronouncement and sent criers into the street to announce the annulment, even as a similar declaration by the *parlement* of Rouen arrived in Paris.[28]

On May 5 the Crown sought to arrest two of the more vocal magistrates, Jean Jacques Duval d'Eprémesnil and Anne Louis Goislard de Montsabert, but when police arrived at their residences late at night both men were able to evade them and seek shelter in the *Palais de Justice*. The *parlement*, along with the ducs and peers, assembled to denounce the attempt "to kidnap them from their homes" and to substitute despotism for the rule of law.

After completion of the statement, the first president and some colleagues left for Versailles to present it to the monarch. Around midnight the still-assembled *parlement*, expecting the return of the first president, saw instead a detachment of the royal bodyguard, which surrounded the *Palais de Justice* with the peers and magistrates inside. The commander, Agoust, said that he had orders from the king to arrest Duval and Goislard de Montsabert but the *parlement* refused to hand them over and Agoust left.

The first president returned at 3:00 a.m. on May 6 with the news that Louis had refused to see him. At 11:00 a.m. Agoust returned with orders from his superiors and commanded the two magistrates, on orders of the king, to follow him. When the *parlement* remained silent and no one stepped forward, Agoust designated a lesser judicial official to tell him if Duval and Goislard were present. The official, Larchier, looked over the benches and told Agoust he did not see them. Agoust asked Larchier to swear to him that he did not see them, which he did. Agoust then asked the *parlement* and the first president if the two magistrates were present but was met with total silence. Agoust stated that he would leave to report what happened and that Larchier would be in his custody. In order to prevent Larchier from being taken away, Duval handed himself over and hours later Goislard did the same. Agoust left, declaring that the *parlement* was free but that Louis had ordered its doors closed and that it be placed under guard.

The magistrates, before ending a session that had continued for thirty hours, denounced the action as a kidnapping that violated the sanctuary of justice. They asked the king to restore the two magistrates to their duties but Louis responded instead by calling for a *lit de justice* to be held on May 8.[29] There was a sense of unease in Paris with the use of force against the *parlement*. Parisians remained passive, although later in the day of the arrests Agoust was recognized as he crossed the Pont Neuf and narrowly escaped being lynched.[30]

The *lit de justice* delivered the expected action against the *parlement* of Paris as well as provincial ones, with the monarch denouncing all of them. He accused the *parlement* of Paris of elevating the opinion of each of its members to the same level as his will and added that the provincial *parlements* were guilty of the same pretentions and undertakings. The king said he wanted to convert a moment of crisis into a salutary epoch for his subjects by carrying out a reform of the judiciary.

The *Garde des sceaux* Chrétien François de Lamoignon de Basville then put forward an edict that suspended the *parlements*. The task of registration of edicts formerly carried out by the *parlement* would be fulfilled by a plenary court. The right of registration for provincial *parlements* would be denied to their successor body but one magistrate from each provincial *parlement* would be named to the plenary court. *Bailliage* courts were to be empowered to hear cases involving up to four thousand *livres*. There would be *grands bailliages*, forty-seven in total, to hear criminal cases and civil cases that did not exceed twenty thousand *livres*. The former jurisdictions of the *parlements* were to be retained but subdivided into smaller jurisdictions, which would make the administration of justice more efficient and less costly.

Lamoignon sought to generate support for the action by including a measure that abolished the use of torture as well as other provisions, including the free administration of justice. Nevertheless, the edicts immediately recalled the actions of Maupeou and renewed fears of despotism.[31] The Crown offered magistrates of the *Grand' chambre* seats in the plenary court, but all of them declined and were exiled. The *parlement* objected to the judicial reorganization but the king brushed all comments aside and ordered the doors of the *Palais de Justice* opened so that the ordinance could be read, which was done.[32] The *parlement* of Paris complied with its suspension.

The Politicization of the Provinces

The acquiescence of the *parlement* of Paris to its suspension led to a shift in political momentum from Paris to the provinces, where the reaction to the edicts was much more vigorous, fueled by a fear of despotism.[33] A remarkable reaction came from Dauphiné. On May 20 the *parlement* of Grenoble issued a decree stating that if the monarch persisted in his actions, he would break all bonds and abolish all treaties that bound Dauphiné to France. The province would regard itself as detached from its oath of loyalty to the monarch. In addition, Agoust, the leader of the action against the *parlement* of Paris, had his name stricken from the register of the nobility of Dauphiné.[34]

The Crown exiled the *parlement* of Grenoble but in what became known as the "day of the tiles," because of the raining down of roof tiles on royal troops, citizens protested the dismissal of the *parlement*. Despite orders to the contrary, some of the royal forces opened fire, which led to fatalities. Subsequently, led by younger magistrates of the *parlement*, inhabitants of Dauphiné sought to reorganize the provincial Estates, which had not met since 1628.[35]

In Rouen, where the *parlement* had issued a statement that echoed that of May 3 by the *parlement* of Paris, there was unrest among citizens who wanted the *parlement* to be more forceful. The Rouen magistrates put forward a declaration denouncing ministers as traitors, especially Lamoignon, who was described as a defender of despotic principles. The vehemence of the pronouncement jolted contemporaries. One called it "truly terrible" and a Parisian barrister wrote to a friend in Dijon that it was the most vigorous he had ever seen.[36] There was also discontent in Dijon and Pau and concern that Burgundy, Franche-Comté, and Languedoc could see unrest on the scale of Dauphiné and other areas. As troops in Paris continued to surround the *Palais de Justice*, the city became more restive and some feared a general rebellion in the kingdom.[37]

On July 5, 1788, the Crown issued a decree calling for information on the procedures used for the convening of the Estates General. The decree authorized the printing of pamphlets without prior approval and led to an extraordinary increase in the number published.[38] It has been argued that the solicitation of ideas about the Estates General and the inconclusive stance that the Crown maintained until its opening was a calculated effort designed to sow division in society. Having agreed on November 19 to convene the body, the Crown wished to generate controversy over its composition and procedure in order to weaken it as an institution and render its deliberations unobjectionable.[39] Within two weeks of the announcement, however, the Crown was considering a much earlier meeting date—May 1, 1789, rather than 1792, as originally announced—as the only means to restore calm.[40]

Military forces had been deployed in both Brittany and Dauphiné to quell rioting and these two regions became focal points during the summer of 1788 and offered contrasting responses that formed a frame of reference for the Estates General.[41] In Brittany, the nobility, the dominant political group in the province, led the opposition and sought above all to preserve its historic privileges. The nobles attempted to gain the support of the clergy and the Third Estate but had limited success, especially with the Third Estate. It was only with great difficulty that the nobles in Brittany were able to put together a deputation of all three orders to present a memorandum to the king. Its overriding concern was privilege and the monarch mollified them by assuring the Bretons that the privileges of the province would be preserved in return for loyalty and submission.[42]

The restoration of the *parlement* of Rennes represented a victory for noble resistance but in mobilizing against the Lamoignon edicts the Third Estate began to articulate its own political grievances. The politicization of the Third Estate would lead to a movement to reform the Breton constitution by reducing the dominant position of the nobility in the Estates of Brittany, pitting the two groups against each other in a bitter dispute.[43]

In Dauphiné, events took a course that provided a sharp contrast to Brittany. A broad coalition of all three orders came together in a sense of common purpose driven by concern for the welfare of the kingdom. Days after the "day of the tiles," leading members of all three orders in Grenoble gathered and called for restoration of the *parlement* and the convocation of the Estates General. In addition, in a significant claim, they asserted the right of citizens to assemble and deliberate on matters of importance to the nation and invited all three orders of the cities and towns of the province to send deputies to Grenoble to form a new assembly, signifying a revival of the Estates of Dauphiné.[44] The leaders of the meeting were summoned to Versailles and taken before the king, who was gracious to them. He authorized them to gather, stating that Estates were never disagreeable to him whereas *parlements* that wanted to be masters always would be.[45]

The general assembly of all orders of 145 communities met at the *château* of Vizille, outside of Grenoble as a precaution against a recurrence of violence.[46] Because of its large size, the Third Estate of Grenoble elected ten delegates to represent it at the assembly. The meeting at Vizille had a number of aspects that captured the attention of much of the rest of the kingdom. The Third Estate was numerically dominant, with 391 representatives whereas the clergy had forty-nine and the nobility 233. The three orders met in common rather than separately and questions were decided through vote by head rather than by order.

At the same time, the assembly decreed that its president must be a member of the clergy or nobility, with the secretary from the Third Estate. It elected René François de Sales de Roux-Deagent, comte de Morges, as president and Jean-Joseph Mounier as secretary. Morges addressed the assembly, telling its members that the public good had brought them together and that they were deliberating on the means to maintain the constitution of the state. Asserting that the suspension of the *parlement* violated the privileges of the province, the assembly stated that the edicts had been "registered militarily" and would not be obeyed because they were contrary to the constitution. The assembly also called for the convening of the Estates General.

Having noted that it was in the interest of ministers to sow division among provinces and different groups of citizens, especially through privileges, the delegates proclaimed that their glory was to be found in being French and announced their willingness to give up the province's privileges. As the assembly closed on July 22 the members of the Third Estate conveyed their compliments to the clergy and nobility for forgetting their former claims and maintaining union among the three orders. Morges replied on behalf of the nobility and clergy that they were always ready to join with their fellow citizens for the good of the nation.[47]

The invocation of a constitution by the Dauphinois assembly was a clear indication that the concept of a constitution as an instrument independent of the king had moved beyond the veiled remonstrances of the *parlement* of Paris and had begun to take hold more broadly in the kingdom. In addition, the declaration by Dauphiné that citizens had the right to assemble in pursuit of the well-being of the kingdom was a novel claim contrary to the Crown ideal of monarchy-centered government.

As late as early August 1788, Brienne continued to promise the king that he would be able to avoid holding the Estates General. On August 8, however, the Crown unexpectedly announced that the Estates General would meet in May 1789, advancing the date by three years. It also suspended the plenary courts, although tensions with remaining provincial *parlements* had not eased.[48] As the accounts of royal fund managers became depleted, just over a week later, on August 16, the Crown, in a declaration of bankruptcy, suspended payment on the debt. It also mandated that creditors accept 40 percent of their payment in paper tender. Bond payments also slowed, leading one contemporary to note that there was no longer any money or confidence.[49]

The Emergence of Privilege as a Political Focus

The calling of the Estates General and bankruptcy dealt major blows to royal authority and have tended to overshadow the fear of despotism that had been present.[50] Moreover, the calling of the Estates General set in motion a rapid and intense sequence of events that has obscured much of that which preceded it. From provincial parlementary cities and towns, however, the specter of despotism was disconcertingly real.[51]

The setting of a date for the Estates General and bankruptcy served to clarify concerns and provide greater focus to the political energy that had mobilized. Until August 1788, there had been two issues competing for attention in the public consciousness—a compound of fear of despotism and ambivalence about privilege. On one hand, privilege was regarded as a barrier to despotism, with the sanctity of privilege giving it quasi-constitutional status. On the other hand, privilege was recognized as divisive and injurious to the common weal,[52] especially the fiscal privileges of the clergy and nobility but in other ways as well.

The events of August 1788, disentangled the issues of despotism and privilege and provided greater clarity with respect to the latter. The calling of the Estates General and bankruptcy significantly reduced despotism as a leading concern. Privilege emerged as the primary issue because suspension of debt payments dissipated whatever doubts may have remained about the magnitude of the fiscal crisis.

The suspension of interest payments in August 1788, was the catalyst for a comprehensive reconsideration of privilege that expanded beyond the fiscal dimension in which it was rooted. In view of the fiscal state in which France found itself, the pecuniary privileges of the clergy and nobility were a critical issue. The contrast between the dire need of the state for revenue and fiscal privilege served to create a clear antithesis between them. Privilege and the nation became mutually exclusive categories.[53]

It is illustrative of the role that the events of August 1788 played in making privilege a focal point that a man who would emerge as a pivotal figure, abbé Emmanuel Joseph Sieyès, began to put some of his emerging political thoughts on paper during that month. He wrote *Essai sur les privilèges*, although it was not released until later. In his private notes he denounced exceptions to laws common to all and drew a distinction between the "*privilegiés*" and the Third Estate.[54] The pamphlet expressed his initial doubts much more strongly. He condemned all privileges as by nature unjust, odious, and contrary to the supreme goal of political society and concluded by describing privileges as the most dangerous of prejudices that had appeared on earth.[55]

As the larger debate over privilege began, the weakening of monarchy-centered government gained momentum. Brienne resigned on August 25 and as he left Versailles a hostile crowd jeered farewell to him as "the bankrupter."[56] The same day, Louis appointed Necker as director-general of finances and two days later allowed him to enter the royal council as a *ministre d'état*.

The *Parlement* Marginalizes Itself

The *parlement* continued to gain in popularity as well. On September 12 a contemporary wrote that the magistrates were stronger than ever because they were supported by the entire nation.[57] As Lamoignon's *grands bailliages* foundered, the *parlements* demanded their abolition, and on September 14 Lamoignon resigned, with his reforms suspended until the opening of the Estates General. Goislard de Montsabert and d'Eprémesnil were recalled, the *parlement* of Paris was to be restored, and the requirement that state creditors accept a portion of their payment in paper was overturned, which increased confidence.[58] On September 23 Louis reestablished the *parlements* to their previous duties and set the meeting date for the Estates General for January 1, 1789. Amid joyous public demonstrations, the *parlement* of Paris resumed its functions on September 24, with its first act the registration of the appointment of Charles de Paule de Barentin as *Garde des sceaux.*

Louis's desire to rule exclusively was now not only limited by the popularity of Necker but also by that of the *parlement.* The *parlement*, with a monarch declining in authority, had greater latitude to pursue its constitutional vision and ideals, which quickly led to a disastrous result. On September 25 the *parlement* issued a strong condemnation of Brienne and Lamoignon for destroying the constitutional rights of the nation and denounced Agoust for his actions. It attacked the overturning of constitutional principles through the *lit de justice* on May 8 and the violation of the rights and privileges of provinces granted at their annexation.[59]

More importantly, however, also on September 25 the *parlement* registered the decree for the convening of the Estates General and asked that the procedures of 1614 be followed, which meant separate deliberations and vote by order. Almost immediately after its acclaimed return to Paris, the popularity of the *parlement* immediately vanished.[60]

Dale Van Kley asserted that the ruling was defensive in nature rather than a self-interested attack against the Third Estate. According to his argument, the *parlement* feared that the Crown would be able to dupe the Third Estate into working with it.[61] This is consonant with the view of William Doyle that the *parlement* was aware of its own weakness and with the contention of John Hardman that the monarch had virtually called the Third Estate into existence as a political force, but the *parlement* wanted a weak Estates General dominated by the nobility. Kenneth Margerison characterized the decision as an effort by the *parlement* to counter the July 5 call for inquiry into the organizational history of the Estates General, arguing that the *parlement* believed the call was a ruse that would allow the Crown to arrange the meeting to its advantage.[62]

Had the *parlement* of Paris cited the form recently promulgated for the Estates of Dauphiné, with representation of the Third Estate equal to that of the First and Second Estates combined, its popularity would unquestionably have soared to even greater heights and placed it in a strong position to influence events. Instead, by stipulating the usages of 1614, it marginalized itself and led much of the public to put its faith in Necker and the Estates General. Necker's popularity continued to rise as that of the *parlement* sank.[63]

The Venetian ambassador put forward one explanation for the disastrous pronouncement. He believed that because the *parlement* had succeeded in having several of its members elected to the Third Estate delegation in 1614, which had given the *parlement* a major influence, it wanted to replicate that situation. He thought that the magistrates saw a similar opportunity in the upcoming Estates General if the protocols of 1614 were followed once again—it would enable the *parlement* to master the deliberations.[64] Undoubtedly the ambassador understood that the bid for influence in 1789 would be through the Second Estate delegation rather than that of the Third, but ultimately only five magistrates from the *parlement* of Paris were elected to the Estates General. If the intent of the decision was to maximize the influence of the magistrates, its effect was precisely the opposite—it minimized their ability to affect events.

Necker sought to calm the anger caused by the declaration by reconvening the Assembly of Notables to ask it about the forms to be used at the Estates General. The decision was welcomed, although for those expecting the Notables to overturn the decree of the *parlement* it is difficult to understand why it would have been.[65] A major criticism that the Notables had raised about the provincial assemblies that Calonne had proposed was what they termed the "confusion of orders." They extracted a concession that ensured that the president of each assembly would be a member of the First or Second Estate.

The Assembly of Notables convened again on November 6, 1788. Louis, in his opening speech, told the Notables that before holding the Estates General he wanted to consult them on the forms he should specify for the meeting, once again using the Notables to diminish the *parlement*.[66] The first president of the *parlement* of Paris, Louis-François de Paule Le Fèvre d'Ormesson, spoke to the Notables and reaffirmed its endorsement of the forms of 1614.[67] Many among the Notables viewed his speech as pretentious and an intrusion into a matter that had been placed before the Notables for resolution.[68]

The Notables divided themselves into six committees to consider four aspects of the Estates General, the most significant of which were the number of deputies for each order and the form of deliberation. To judge by public comment, sometimes quite detailed, the proceedings of the second Assembly of Notables were more accessible than those of the first—the opening speeches were quickly printed and committee decisions were soon known to the public.[69]

As the meeting went on, the Notables moved in the direction of the *parlement* of Paris, favoring the forms of 1614, which led to discontent among the Third Estate in provincial cities of the kingdom.[70] One contemporary noted that the cause of the people was losing ground because the meeting was dominated by the interest of the privileged.[71] Even as the outcome became increasingly clear hope lingered that the force of public opinion would prevail or the Crown might intervene on the side of the Third Estate.[72]

As the Assembly of Notables was in session the *parlement* of Paris attempted to regain influence with a statement it issued on December 5. With the meeting of the Estates General ostensibly scheduled for January 1, the magistrates expressed concern that letters of convocation had not yet been sent and that there was unrest in the kingdom in both urban and rural areas. The *parlement* also complained that there had been views attributed to it after its September 25 declaration that it had never held—the magistrates claimed to be equally devoted to all three orders of the nation. The *parlement* did not rescind its decree of September 25 and declared its deference to the wisdom of the monarch on the necessary modifications that reason, liberty, justice and the general view might demand.[73]

The *parlement* sent the statement to Versailles but Louis took his revenge when he completely dismissed any further policy role for it. In a two-sentence reply on December 9 he declared that he had nothing to say in response to the *parlement* and that he would be dealing with "the assembled nation" to take all necessary actions to achieve order and prosperity in the state.[74] The displacement of the *parlement* by both the public and the king was complete. A leading voice during the eighteenth century arguing for the existence of a constitution had effectively been silenced, but, as events in Dauphiné demonstrated, the concept of a constitution was beginning to take hold in the kingdom itself.

As the second Assembly of Notables was meeting, there was extensive political activity in the kingdom, with Brittany and Dauphiné as continuing focal points. In Brittany there was unrest within the Third Estate because it felt "subjugated" by the nobility. It was asking for a more equal distribution of the tax burden and changes in the constitution of the provincial Estates.[75]

In Dauphiné the three orders of the province, meeting at Romans in November, wrote a long letter to the monarch that drew favorable attention.

Stating that they believed it necessary to put forward principles that would serve as the only acceptable bases for the Estates General, the letter called for the representation of the Third Estate to be equal to that of the combined First and Second Estate delegations. The attendees also asked that all deliberations be held jointly and that voting be by head.

The letter concluded by asserting that the king would gain a constitution that would respect his rights and protect those of his subjects. The representatives of the province expressed the hope that one day the Estates General would be established on stable principles and formed to the satisfaction of the entire kingdom. Comprised of a large number of freely elected deputies, the provinces could sacrifice some of their particular privileges in order to assure the enjoyment of national rights and Dauphiné hastened to offer itself as an example. It was the quality of being French that joined all of the orders of all provinces, which would enable them to deliberate on behalf of all of France. They would never forget that they were French and that the French nation always associated its glory with that of the monarch.[76]

The second Assembly of Notables ended on December 12 with a recommendation that each of the three orders have the same number of deputies and that deliberations be held by order, which led to considerable anger. There had been some divergence among the committees, but it was not substantial. The first committee was the outlier, voting narrowly, thirteen to twelve, against the same number of deputies for each order and declining, by a vote of twenty-one to four, to decide on the manner of deliberation, asserting that it should be left to the Estates General to decide. In the other five committees the decision was for each order to have an equal number of deputies and to deliberate by order, although the third committee was open to allowing the Estates General to change the form.[77]

The second Assembly of Notables radically transformed the dimensions of the political crisis. Until the second meeting, there had been competing conceptions of power. One argued for unshared monarchical power and the other advocated respect for legal protocols to prevent ministerial abuses of power. That debate continued and placed France on the road to constitutional monarchy, but it was overtaken by a larger dispute in which an antithetical dichotomy between the nation and "the privileged" formed.[78]

Indeed, an anonymous pamphlet that appeared illustrates both the anger toward the Notables and the focus of the debate on privilege. It noted that the monarch had twice convened the Notables to consult them on the interests of the throne and the nation. In 1787, he wrote, they had defended their privileges against the throne and in 1788 they had defended their privileges against the nation.[79]

One result of the decisions by the *parlement* of Paris and the second Assembly of Notables was to expand the range of concern about privilege beyond its fiscal component—the debate on privilege now came to encompass the composition of the Estates General as well. The year 1788 completed a movement away from acceptance of privilege as a legitimate instrument of governance to rejection of it as inimical to the common good.

Privilege and Governance in a Provincial Town

As the reaction against privilege began to crystallize in 1787 and 1788, hostility toward it moved beyond royal administration and pamphlet debates. In some cases, provincial administrators also accorded privilege less legitimacy and became more assertive in their determination to move against it.

In the 1780s the Estates of Burgundy committed itself to building the Canal de Bourgogne, an extensive project encompassing three separate waterway legs. One of the arteries would benefit the town of Saint-Jean-de-Losne, as would another project, the repair of a bridge in the town. Beginning in November and December 1786, the *élus*, the officials for the Estates of Burgundy, assessed Saint-Jean-de-Losne a charge of 1940 *livres* as its portion of the cost of the projects.[80]

The town resisted the assessment, citing the *lettres-patentes* of 1636 and the decree of 1638 that exempted it from royal taxes for its stand during the Thirty Years War. The residents contended that their privileges derived from the same source as those of the nobility, military service, and argued that the view of the Estates that the royal acts did not exempt them from provincial assessments or common municipal charges for the province was mistaken. In response to the observation of the *élus* that the inhabitants paid the *capitation* and the *vingtième*, the town replied that in doing so it followed the policy of the nobility and other privileged entities. Saint-Jean-de-Losne also disputed the charge levied for the bridge. It asserted that the province would gain the most from the bridge, which was a continuation of the primary route from Dijon to Franche-Comté, Seurre, and Auxonne.[81]

Despite its pleas, the Estates persisted in its efforts to collect the charges for the year 1787.[82] In March 1788, after the *élus* asked the town to pay, it again protested the charges that had been levied upon it.[83] The mayor and municipal officers asked the Estates to delay its decision until the question had been settled by the Crown, to which the town had appealed. One could not blame the town, the officials wrote, for wanting to maintain its hard-earned and richly deserved privileges. They had been granted for services rendered to the state under various circumstances in which the inhabitants of the town had spared neither their lives nor property and the passage of 150 years had not repaired the losses. Contending that Saint-Jean-de-Losne was the most impoverished town of the province, they asked that the matter be sent to the royal council for resolution.[84]

The town's behavior exasperated royal and provincial officials. The intendant of Burgundy, Antoine Léon Amelot de Chaillou, sided with the Estates and opposed the claim of Saint-Jean-de-Losne. He wrote to the secretary of the Estates of Burgundy complaining of the town's "disobedience" and stated that he would not tolerate its claims. He had, he wrote, sent Saint-Jean-de-Losne an order to remit the assessed amount and told the Estates that if the town continued to present more difficulties he would feel obligated to do everything he could to make the town cease its behavior.[85]

As the Estates of Burgundy continued to pursue the assessment, on January 29, 1789, the citizens of Saint-Jean-de-Losne held a general assembly in which they restated their belief in the extent and validity of the town's exemptions. They declared that its privileges had been confirmed by eleven different monarchs and most recently by Louis XVI. They noted that the town's assessment for 1788 was nearly double that of the preceding year and contended that their stance did not contradict the current general view, an apparent allusion to the critique of privilege. The nation was seeking reform but could not reasonably expect reforms to be applied retroactively—in this respect, the inhabitants of Saint-Jean-de-Losne were objecting to assessments being demanded for preceding years. The assembly concluded with the residents of the town reserving the right to determine the future fate of its privileges.[86] In February 1789, the Crown ruled against Saint-Jean-de-Losne, annulling the claims made in the January 29 meeting as detrimental to the authority of the king.[87]

The Intensification of the Debate

In late December 1788, five of the seven princes of the blood sent a communication to Louis under the title *Mémoire des princes*.[88] Implying the irrelevance of the Third Estate, they declared that the state was in danger, with the rights of "the two orders of the State" dividing opinion. The document criticized the effrontery that had led elements of the Third Estate to demand representation equal to that of the first two orders combined at the Estates General. This arrangement, they contended, would compromise the interests of the Third Estate, which would be better served under the current constitution.

It was important that the only form of convening the Estates General be the constitutional one, affirmed, they contended, by law and tradition—the distinction of orders, the right of deliberating separately, the same representation for each order, which were inalterable foundations of the French monarchy. To capitulate to the demand of the Third Estate for double representation would only increase its pretentiousness and lead to other pointless concessions.

After additional observations, the princes commanded the Third Estate to cease its attacks on the rights of the first two orders, rights that were as old as the monarchy itself and that should be as inalterable as the constitution. The Third Estate, they declared, should limit itself to reducing its tax burden. When it did confine itself to this endeavor, the first two orders, recognizing in the Third Estate citizens dear to them, would be able, through the generosity of their sentiments, to renounce their pecuniary interests and support equality of taxation.[89]

In its decree of September 25, the *parlement*, which considered itself the guardian of the constitution, had cited precedent—the forms of 1614, the immediately preceding Estates General. During the second Assembly of Notables, however, the nobility had begun to attribute constitutional status to deliberation and vote by order.[90] The princes of the blood had taken a lead role in the second Assembly of Notables and the *Mémoire des princes* amplified their view that deliberation and vote by order were constitutional in nature.[91]

If the princes thought that their offer to consider consenting to equal taxation, an action that the Assembly of Notables had refused to countenance only weeks earlier, would calm the situation, they were mistaken. To the contrary, the imperious and patronizing tone of their declaration inflamed opinion instead.[92] Many pamphlets appeared in response to it.[93]

Without question, the most significant response was *Qu'est-ce que le Tiers-état?* by Sieyès. It appeared quickly after the publication of the *Mémoire des princes* and Sieyès alluded to it in his pamphlet—he also referred to his work as his "*mémoire sur le tiers-état.*" It is by no means unreasonable to conclude that his striking opening, in which he stated that the Third Estate is everything, had until this time been nothing in the political order and wanted to be something, was an angry riposte to the outlook expressed in the *Mémoire des princes*.[94]

Intended by the princes to impose a solution through what they regarded as a major concession, the *Mémoire des princes* polarized opinion to an even greater extent.[95] The princes did not earn any gratitude for the ostensible concession they had advanced, not only because of its conditional nature but especially because of the paternalistic and condescending manner in which it was offered. Furthermore, by proposing to yield their fiscal privileges, even conditionally, the princes effectively delegitimized them and breached the sanctity of privilege.

The *Mémoire des princes* intensified and expanded the debate on privilege. Its allusion to "the two orders of the state" provided insight into their point of view, in which the Third Estate had no meaningful role. It strengthened the conviction of many in the Third Estate that double representation and vote by head were necessary conditions for the Estates General. The rejection of both by the *Mémoire des princes* was a factor in the enlargement of the debate on fiscal privilege to encompass political privilege as well.

Defense of privilege had served as a bulwark against despotism but with despotism removed as a major concern it took on a different character. Defense of privilege after the bankruptcy of the Crown, particularly political privilege symbolized in vote by order, signified the hijacking of the Estates General by the clergy and the nobility.[96] The *Mémoire des princes* seemed to confirm the belief that defense of privilege represented an effort to co-opt the constitution, which is why it inflamed public opinion as much as it did.[97] The denial of the existence of a constitution by the Third Estate in 1788 and 1789 stemmed from its association with clerical and noble privilege. It was for this reason that the ripostes by Sieyès focused on privilege. The association also produced a backlash against the ideas of Montesquieu.[98]

Soon after the appearance of the *Mémoire des princes*, the Crown announced some of the arrangements for the Estates General. Necker had been meeting with Louis for more than a week and it was anticipated that the regulations would be favorable to the Third Estate. When the plans were announced on December 27, they seemed to meet many of its expectations. The Estates General would be held in Versailles and would be comprised of

1,200 deputies, with representation for the Third Estate being equal to the First and Second Estates combined.[99]

Necker was trying to defuse tension and achieve an outcome that would not lead to a boycott by any of the orders. The nobility had made clear its insistence on the same number of deputies for each order and deliberation and vote by order. The Third Estate in some areas was threatening not to participate in the Estates General unless the Third Estate received double representation.[100] Necker's equivocation—offering double representation but with no statement on voting procedures—was sufficiently artful to avoid any boycott.[101]

Initial exhilaration within the Third Estate was quickly tempered when it became evident that the decision was more ambiguous than it appeared. It was widely assumed that vote would be by head but this had not been specified.[102] Although concern about fiscal privileges of the nobility remained, uncertainty surrounding the manner of voting at the Estates General intensified the debate on political privilege and led to the political atmosphere becoming more charged and contentious.[103]

The Bourbon Style of Government Degraded

The meeting of the Assembly of Notables in 1787 was a watershed moment for the Bourbon dynasty. Only fifteen months after its dismissal, the concept of a constitution independent of the will of the monarch had advanced from confidential communications between Crown and *parlement* to the kingdom at large and had begun to gain acceptance.

With the traditional notion of a constitution premised in part on the idea that the *parlement* protected the liberties of subjects, the exile and suppression of *parlements* left the standing of those liberties open to doubt. A major factor driving the desire for a constitution was not only to rein in despotism but also to bring an end to chaos and conflict in royal government and restore order and stability by enumerating the role of the institutions of government. The *parlement* of Paris had irreversibly damaged itself with its September 1788 ruling, which led to the idea of a constitution that would establish a continuing role for the Estates General in the future through regular convocations.

In addition, Calonne's attempt to mobilize public opinion to pressure the Notables to pass his program legitimized public opinion as a factor in domestic policy, a sphere previously regarded as an exclusively royal purview. Furthermore, Calonne's implicit critique of privilege made public criticism of it permissible. The debate on privilege melded with the inchoate sense of the constitution, enlarging the controversy beyond its original fiscal dimensions.

The Forgotten Constitution: The Origins, Realization, and Legacy of the French Constitution of 1791.
Michael P. Fitzsimmons, Oxford University Press. © Oxford University Press 2025.
DOI: 10.1093/9780197793978.003.0005

5
Toward the Estates General

In the aftermath of the December 27 announcement, the year 1789 began in a tense political atmosphere as the strong backlash against the *Mémoire des princes* continued and *Qu'est-ce que le tiers état?* appeared in January. After a 175-year hiatus, expectations for the Estates General were considerable, but they were further elevated by the discrediting of the *parlement* of Paris, which led many to believe that only the Estates General could represent the nation. After a hiatus of 175 years, however, there was uncertainty and unease. The voting procedure remained unresolved and sharpened tensions, but many in the Third Estate remained hopeful that the Estates General could bring beneficial change.

On the Eve of the Estates General: Brittany and Dauphiné as Contrasting Models

As 1789 began France was in an unsettled state. In early 1789 one handbill observed that the end of 1788 had been memorable for the vigorous clash of opinions and contradictory opposing interests on the great issue of the Estates General. Each province, each order, each *corps*, and each individual seemed to be in a war over rights, claims, usages, and forms to the detriment of reason, justice, and equity. It noted that the history of France comprised a vast arsenal of arguments but the great variety of historical precedents on the current question provided little guidance for the regeneration of the state mandated by the overwhelming imperative of earlier events.[1]

The December 27 decision to double the representation of the Third Estate had initially met with exhilaration but it had been assumed that the decision entailed vote by head.[2] The enthusiasm generated by the ruling quickly waned when the public recognized that the doubling of the Third Estate was a discrete decision and that the voting method remained undetermined. Without vote by head, of course, the doubling of the Third Estate's representation would be meaningless. Far from calming passions, Necker's action served to intensify them and to make the issue of vote by head more important than ever, especially as the backlash against the *Mémoire des princes* continued unabated.[3] The degree of anticipation was extraordinary.

One contemporary noted that writers and speakers were concerned only with the constitution to the exclusion of other considerations.[4] Taxation remained an issue, with one demand being fair and proportional assessment of taxes shared among the three orders.[5] In the fall of 1788 the Third Estate of towns in Brittany had requested the suppression of the *corvée* and other taxes and the establishment of a general tax payable by all three orders.[6] It appears that the Crown, perhaps encouraged by the offer of the princes to consider yielding their fiscal privileges, began to weigh the creation of a general tax to replace the *corvée* and the *taille*. One consideration was that the tax had to be given a name that nobles or those newly ennobled would not find offensive.[7]

Tensions were acute in Brittany, where the perception within the Third Estate of being oppressed by the nobility was perhaps greater than anywhere else in France.[8] The intendant of Brittany believed that it was the province in which taxation was the most inequitable and in an earlier observation he had stated that the nobility of Rennes thought of itself as in charge of the province.[9] The assessment and collection of taxes were overseen by the Estates of Brittany, which the nobility dominated. With the burden of taxation falling most heavily on the poor, the Crown found the administration of the Estates wanting.[10]

The Estates opposed any change in the tax structure and its Intermediate Commission had praised the resistance of the *parlements* to taxation and agreed with the proposition that only the Estates General could approve taxes proportional to the needs of the state. The members of the commission stated that Brittany had a particular constitution and asked if it would be violated. After complaining about Rennes being overrun with royal troops the commissioners declared that when it united with France, Brittany had consented to becoming an integral part of a kingdom governed by fundamental laws. To attack those laws damaged the principle of association that had been concluded.[11]

With the bankruptcy of the Crown in August 1788 what had until that time been a regional grievance acquired national import and gave greater validity to the concerns of the Third Estate in Brittany. In late 1788, as the biannual opening of the Estates of Brittany approached, the Third Estate of various towns in Brittany began to agitate against the existing level of representation in the Estates.[12] Led primarily by Nantes and Rennes, the Third Estate began to seek approval for sending additional deputies to the Estates and declared that if its demands were not met its representatives would withdraw, which would paralyze the Estates. It amended its position to reassure the Crown by agreeing to vote on the *don gratuit* before presenting its demands, but it would not deliberate on any other issue unless its demands for equal taxation, greater representation in both the Estates and the intermediary commission and the right of the Third Estate to choose its deputies for the Estates General were accepted.[13]

Both the nobility, which was caught off guard by the activism of the Third Estate, and the Third Estate were firm in their resolve, the former to maintaining the structure of the Estates and the latter to amending it. The nobility was also angry about the December 27 decree that doubled the representation of the Third Estate, which they regarded as a threat to their privileges and the special status of the province.[14] As the scheduled opening of the Estates approached, delegates of the Third Estate arrived more than a week early to formulate strategy and goals. Members of the nobility, determined to resist the efforts of the Third Estate and to intimidate it, came to Rennes in unprecedented numbers—between 1,200 and 1,300, including many who had never previously attended. Alarmed, the Third Estate sent additional individuals to assist and protect its deputies.[15]

The Estates opened on December 29 and the following day approved the *don gratuit* at the amount requested by the Crown for the years 1789 and 1790.[16] The day after that, however, on December 31, the clergy put forward a routine measure to renew the authority of the intermediary commissioners. The Third Estate opposed it, but the clergy and the nobility approved it over the opposition of the Third Estate and proceeded to name their intermediary commissioners. The Third Estate refused to name its commissioners until its demands had been heard. The clergy and nobility refused to allow them to be presented, after which the meeting adjourned.

The rules of the Estates required the participation of all three orders so the refusal of the Third Estate to choose its intermediary commissioners threw the body into a stalemate that continued for days. In early January the Crown suspended the Estates until February 3 and instructed representatives of the Third Estate to return to their communities to receive new powers to deliberate on all matters.[17]

Tensions were running high. Even before the opening of the Estates a member of the Third Estate had been concerned about the actions that the anger and spite of the nobility might lead them to take.[18] Law students in Rennes took responsibility for protecting the representatives of the Third Estate because of the large numbers of nobles in attendance.[19] They also sought to form a confederation that had as its goal to become "free men under the authority of laws" and asked their counterparts in the Third Estate of Nantes to disseminate their manifesto to different towns of the province.[20]

The day after the suspension of the Estates the nobility reassembled to denounce an article in the decree suspending the Estates that seemed to suggest a greater level of taxation for the province. Believing that the pause was intended to abolish the Estates, they swore an oath to defend the Breton constitution and pledged that they would never enter into any form of administration contrary to that of the Estates of the province.[21] Despite the suspension of the Estates, the nobility and clergy continued to meet for the remainder of the month. They drew up a protest against the Crown's December 27 decree doubling the representation of the Third Estate and declared that they would not send deputies to an Estates General convened under this new form. They also protested against a royal decree issued on January 20 that they viewed as destructive of the Breton constitution.[22]

The bitterness exploded in violence on the morning of January 26, 1789, with an unrestrained rampage by hundreds of liveried servants in Rennes. They gathered initially at the *Champs de Montmorin*, where they heard a speech demanding that their masters maintain their privileges and a lowering of the price of bread. Many of those in attendance were inebriated and, armed with clubs allegedly supplied by a nobleman and led by four noblemen, the crowd made its way to the *Palais de Justice* shouting "vive la Noblesse" and praising the Breton constitution. They swarmed through the streets of Rennes for hours, beating many of those they encountered, even in cafés. They especially denounced the law students, claiming that they wanted to abolish the privileges of their masters.

A city guard who apprehended and sought to disarm one of the rioters had a pistol held to his throat by a nobleman who threatened to kill him if he did not release the culprit. Henri Charles Gabriel de Thiard de Bissy, comte de Thiard, the military commander, brought the situation under control the next day, but before it ended there were a handful of fatalities—the numbers vary from two to four—and many more wounded. In the aftermath, a number of noblemen locked themselves in the meeting room of the Estates for days and would not venture out.[23] The *parlement* of Rennes refused to conduct an investigation of the event.[24]

On January 30 a contingent of young men from Nantes arrived in Rennes to aid their counterparts, and young men from Caen, Angers, and Poitiers were poised to send assistance to the patriots in Rennes as well.[25] The Crown cancelled the scheduled reopening of the Estates. A number of nobles ventured out to speak with a group of young men of Rennes and Nantes to ask that they sign a petition in support of the Breton constitution, promising them that their rights in the Estates would be discussed but offering no more. When the young men ascertained that the nobles were acting on their own accord and not on behalf of the Estates, their request received no reply.[26] Clearly concerned about their safety, the nobility asked for help from the comte de Thiard, who had been attempting to defuse tensions and restore calm. He arranged the departure of the representatives of the clergy and nobility from Rennes on February 1.

The emotional power of events in Brittany is apparent in a statement in which the law students of Angers pledged their assistance to their counterparts in Rennes. In a February 3 general meeting they denounced what they called the "privileged class" trying to undercut reforms offered by the king in his wisdom. They proclaimed that it was in their interest and honor to come to the aid of the Breton law students as the cause that they were defending was that of all French.[27]

The perceived complicity of the magistrates of the *parlement* in the riot compounded the bitterness of the Third Estate in Rennes.[28] The violence led to a perception that the nobility of Brittany would stop at nothing to defend their privileges and the inaction of the *parlement* of Rennes undermined confidence in the rule of law. Although there were other areas of France in which the nobility was in strong opposition to the doubling of the Third Estate delegation for the Estates General, it was Brittany that became the leading symbol of privilege in 1789.[29]

Avoiding Rennes or Nantes, on April 16 the clergy and nobility of Brittany met in St. Brieuc to elect deputies to the Estates General. Thiard was bemused as he observed the proceedings, which had disputes that he described as extreme. He opined that they might refuse to elect any deputies because competing groups would prefer to have no deputies at the Estates General than any from a group other than its own.[30] His prediction proved correct. In a meeting that he described as "more tumultuous and less legal" than any meeting he had ever seen, the nobility intimidated those in the clergy who favored electing deputies. Thiard believed a primary reason for its opposition was concern about decisions that the Estates General might make, especially with respect to a general constitution that could cover all provinces of the kingdom. The Breton nobility, he stated, wanted Brittany to be a state within the state.[31]

Dauphiné projected an antithetical example, although developments there did not proceed as smoothly as the Dauphinois sought to portray them. Aware of the attention they were receiving, the Dauphinois attempted to make their deliberations appear to be an object of greater consensus than they actually were.

In September 1788 an organizational meeting to suggest to the Crown the structure of the three orders in the revived Estates of the province took place. On September 15 the nobility presented an offer agreed to by 219 noblemen as well as some clergy in which they agreed to abolish the *corvée* and replace it with a tax paid by all three orders. The clergy in the meeting unanimously endorsed the measure and it passed. After a brief meeting, the Third Estate effusively thanked the clergy and nobility.[32]

Days later, however, there was a split between the clergy and nobility on one side, concerned about the dominating influence of the Third Estate, and the Third Estate on the other. The clergy and nobility left the meeting and went to a nearby church. The Third Estate sent representatives who apologized for some ill-considered remarks, but the meetings were suspended for three days.[33] The quarrel was glossed over in the minutes and by the end of the month the deliberations concluded in a seemingly harmonious fashion.[34]

The Crown decreed the organization of the Estates late in October 1788, modifying the plan of the province that cleared the way for the Estates to meet. The Estates consisted of 144 members, with twenty-four for the clergy, forty-eight for the nobility, and seventy-two for the Third Estate and all votes were by head. In his opening remarks the president of the Estates, the archbishop of Vienne, told its members that the deliberations in Dauphiné could serve as a model both for other provinces and the nation at the Estates General. The president of the nobility, the comte de Morges, was more reserved in his speech, acknowledging public opinion but also noting the need for balance among the three orders in the Estates.[35]

The Estates opened in December 1788 in Romans. Because the Estates were newly reconstituted, there was no old business, which allowed its members to focus on the Estates General. The archbishop of Vienne had written

Necker asking that the province be allowed to elect its deputies to the Estates General during the session. Necker's reply was guarded, stating that the request seemed reasonable but the province had not informed him of the number of deputies it wished to send. This was followed by a second letter from Necker in which he stated that the king recognized the inconvenience of reconvening the Estates a second time to elect deputies. Therefore, even though the second Assembly of Notables was still meeting and had not yet given its advice, he was allowing the 144 members of the Estates to elect deputies to the Estates General. The Estates formed a committee to consider the question of the number of deputies for Dauphiné at the Estates General.[36]

The committee presented its report on December 9, again seeking a national audience with its rhetoric. The report opened with the statement that it was time for the sacred title of citizen to be earned and that all French should come together as if they were members of the same family. It set the appropriate number of deputies for Dauphiné at thirty, with five from the clergy, ten from the nobility, and fifteen for the Third Estate. It proposed that the provinces deliberate in common and vote by head at the Estates General, which itself would have the Third Estate delegation be equal in number to those of the First and Second Estates combined. The report declared that love of the nation should guide all deliberations and noted that Dauphiné was sacrificing its particular interests and asked other provinces not to engage in rivalries with each other and look instead to the interests of the nation and the throne.[37] The proceedings in Dauphiné inspired much of France.[38]

After the Crown announced the doubling of the Third Estate representation in late December, the Estates, undoubtedly encouraged by the seeming approval given earlier by Necker, moved ahead with the election of its deputies to the Estates General even though the electoral regulations had not yet been issued.[39] A magistrate in the *parlement* of Paris believed the Dauphinois were seeking to dictate the process for elections to all of France.[40] Others saw events in Dauphiné in more benign terms, which was that the province was leading the way or setting an example.[41]

Lending some credence to the magistrate's view that Dauphiné was seeking to influence or even impose the rules for the Estates General, on January 2 the Dauphinois declared that they could not take part in the meeting unless the number of Third Estate deputies was equal to that of the other two orders, that the three orders deliberated in common and that vote was by head. The approval of the resolution precipitated an emotional reaction in the Estates that led to its author, Mounier, being proclaimed as a deputy to the Estates General. Moreover, as other deputies were elected, each one pledged loyalty to these principles.[42] The mandate was printed and circulated in late January.[43]

Even as the province sought to project a sense of common purpose among the three orders, however, there was underlying discord, with growing unease among both the clergy and nobility about the dominant role of the Third Estate. The intendant wrote to the *Garde des sceaux* that the primary reason for unrest among the clergy and nobility was the great influence of the Third Estate in the deliberations of the three orders, particularly with respect to the election of deputies to the Third Estate from Grenoble.[44] A number of members of the clergy and nobility had not supported Mounier's resolution and in the following days, hoping to preserve their rights and privileges, they began an effort to amend its terms.[45] On one occasion, members of the clergy and nobility met apart from the general assembly.[46] There were continuing rumors that clergy and noblemen continued to protest against the mandate, but their efforts failed to gain support and the Dauphinois were able to resolve their differences.[47]

Despite the dissension, the Dauphinois held together.[48] In a letter to Necker in late January the archbishop of Vienne stated that the Estates of Dauphiné had not been seeking to make the law for other provinces with respect to its mandate for the Estates General. At the same time, he wrote, they were firmly convinced that for the Estates General to use protocols different from those used by the Estates of Dauphiné would be fruitless. He assured Necker that the Dauphinois regulation applied only to what the archbishop called "definitive deliberations," meaning full meetings of the body itself, but that preparatory meetings could be held by the orders separately.[49]

By maintaining its cohesion, Dauphiné emerged as the counterpoint to Brittany, with the Breton constitution the example of privilege and subordination of the Third Estate and Dauphiné the model for the ideal of the three orders joined together in a sense of common purpose.[50] Conscious of their new national stature, the Dauphinois urged other provinces to view the Estates General in terms of the good of the nation rather than to advance particular interests.

They also wrote pamphlets seeking to persuade other provinces to accept their outlook. In October 1788, before the Estates of Dauphiné had been reconstituted, a group comprised of all three orders replied to an inquiry from the *syndics-généraux* of the Estates of Béarn. They told the Béarnais that provinces, orders, and individuals were too isolated and had not realized that the isolation had been intended to weaken them. One component of division and isolation was commitment to the defense of privileges and the Dauphinois contended that to enjoy national rights, provinces should retain only those privileges that were not injurious to the happiness of their fellow citizens.[51]

Although the Dauphinois were aware of the national attention they had garnered, it would be a mistake to view their efforts merely as public posturing.[52] They sincerely believed in what the businessmen of Grenoble called the "principles of Dauphiné."[53] Private correspondence conveyed the same sentiments. In his letter to Necker, the archbishop of Vienne told him that if the Estates General was held in a form different from that of Dauphiné it would be "useless and pernicious," both to the monarch and the kingdom.[54]

The Breton path of confrontation and the Dauphinois model of conciliation presented a contrast and effectively a choice as to which method should be emulated at the Estates General. The heightened political activity in the two provinces meant that their delegations were the most politically experienced when the Estates General opened, enabling them to gain early influence.[55]

Preparations for the Estates General

A primary reason that Brittany and Dauphiné received the attention that they did was because they mirrored the varied expectations of change that gripped much of France. Observations by the Venetian ambassador on the situation reveal how critically important the voting procedure had become. He opined that if the Third Estate achieved vote by head France would become a virtual "democratic republic." He worried that animus and discord among the three orders could become permanent and cited Dauphiné as the good example and Brittany as the bad example of conditions in France.[56]

The September 25 opinion of the *parlement* and the decision of the second Assembly of Notables conveyed the impression that the nobility sought to retain its privileges. It was in this setting that a movement known as the union of orders began, seeking to reverse the image of the nobility as clinging to its privileges and to ally with the Third Estate against the ministry.

Most members of the nobility appear to have believed that yielding their fiscal privileges would be sufficient to win over the Third Estate. The more politically astute, however, recognized that more would be necessary. Dauphiné had responded to the attack on its *parlement* with a movement to reestablish its provincial Estates but organized them with a doubled Third Estate and vote by head. Despite some friction, the Dauphinois innovation became the model for the more politically sophisticated members of the nobility through the Society of Thirty.

It has been argued that the most important feature of the Dauphinois program was not the increased representation for the Third Estate, which was based upon the provincial assemblies established by the Crown, but its insistence on the political union of the three orders of the kingdom. Events in Dauphiné served as the inspiration for the movement for a union of orders, which was rooted in the belief that royal despotism could be overcome by national unity in the form of a union of the three orders that would make possible the establishment of liberty. The union of orders movement began in the autumn of 1788, based on the creation of a political program that could win the support of all three estates of the kingdom. An important component of the program was that the nobility would yield its tax privileges to gain the confidence of the Third Estate, which would enable the latter to work with the nobility, assuring the status and political influence of the latter. Honorific privileges would be retained.[57]

The agency of the campaign for a union of orders was the Society of Thirty and its model was Dauphiné, although that model required more accommodation from the First and Second Estates than yielding their fiscal privileges. A member of the nobility in Dauphiné, François-Henri, comte de Virieu, wrote a pamphlet attributing the course of events in Dauphiné to the remarkable generosity of the clergy and nobility of the province. The two orders had agreed to yield their fiscal privileges and had accepted the doubling of the Third Estate and vote by head. In this manner, according to Virieu, Dauphiné had overcome despotism and established a constitution that could be a model for the entire nation.

There was nothing in the program of a union of orders that suggested any willingness to allow the Third Estate to determine the political agenda for the nation or to create a new conception of society or political organization. The Society of Thirty simply sought a reform of the extant constitutional system, driven by the belief that without the interference of ministerial intrigue or particular privilege, the monarch would come to see the will of the nation.[58]

The movement for a union of orders appeared to suffer a devastating setback when the second Assembly of Notables refused to give up fiscal privileges and the princes of the blood demeaned the Third Estate.[59] In late December 1788, however, the nobility of Burgundy, meeting in Dijon, revived its prospects when it agreed to yield its fiscal privileges and endorsed equality of taxation for all taxes approved by the Estates General.[60] By February 1789 both domestic and foreign observers agreed that the nobility was acquiescing to the principle of equality of taxation.[61]

The nobility viewed the relinquishment of its tax privileges as a major concession and did not envision any significant weakening of its other privileges. Indeed, the union of orders ideal, the most advanced position among the nobility prior to the opening of the Estates General, had as a premise that the first two orders would retain privileges that did not infringe upon the rights of the nation. Among those to be maintained were property rights, specifically seigneurial rights, which meant that it was not possible to attain legal equality through the union of orders.[62]

Without question, the surrender of fiscal privileges by the nobility was a major concession and one that the Assembly of Notables had refused to make. It neutralized one of the major components of the grievances of the Third Estate about privilege and the "privileged classes." Except for the noble membership of the Society of Thirty or those with a similar political outlook, however, the nobility was generally unwilling to give up the political privilege that aggrieved the Third Estate—deliberations and votes by order at the Estates General.

The doubling of the Third Estate delegation in late December 1788 complicated the situation. Margerison, the leading scholar of the union of orders movement, tentatively concluded that, with the doubling of the Third, the Crown was seeking to ally itself with the goals of the union of orders. Necker's course, however, was unclear, particularly because the electoral regulations discouraged the ideal of the union of orders by disallowing the three orders meeting together in electoral assemblies.[63] It is certainly possible that the Crown feared a boycott of elections by the nobility or a refusal to elect deputies if it pronounced vote by head in advance. An inability to convene an Estates General would have been a disastrous outcome for the Crown but to have the body fail through internal divisions, as in 1614, might benefit it. To announce the doubling of the Third Estate delegation at the Estates General without stipulating a voting procedure was unusual and certain to provoke controversy, as it did.[64] If the Crown had specified vote by head, it would have cemented a strong alliance with the Third Estate and strengthened the Crown against the nobility, its chief antagonist.

Instead, the Crown left matters unresolved with months to go until the meeting. By March 1789 the majority of the nobility felt that it had not received anything in return for the renunciation of fiscal privileges, especially the assurance of vote by order. The members of the nobility in the union of orders movement were committed to the Dauphiné model of joint deliberation and vote by head, but their efforts were hamstrung by the uncertainty. Much of the nobility was left feeling betrayed or uncertain, with a majority holding tenaciously to vote by order to avoid being relegated to insignificance.[65]

The desire of the nobility to retain its privileges and distinctiveness is evident in a study of noble *cahiers*. Nearly 89 percent of them endorsed fiscal equality, but with respect to their own order the greatest single demand, found in 40 percent of *cahiers*, was the preservation of its honorific rights and prerogatives. The next most requested provision was to prohibit nonnobles from carrying arms. Only 6.6 percent of noble *cahiers* called for equality between nobility and Third Estate and fewer than 3 percent favored opening military careers to the Third Estate.[66]

The outlook of the majority of the nobility can be seen in electoral proceedings at Bar-sur-Seine in Burgundy. As elections of deputies were underway, a delegation of the electoral assembly for the nobility went to the electoral assembly of the Third Estate and announced that its members regarded being citizens as above being nobles. The delegation declared that it wished to convey to its fellow citizens the desire of the nobility to solidify union among all the orders and announced its support for equal taxation.[67] Days later, however, it enjoined its deputy to participate only in vote by order and not by head.[68] It may be reflective of the sense of betrayal among the majority of the nobility that as the opening of the Estates General approached, a conservative backlash against the Society of Thirty gained momentum.[69]

By early 1789, a sense of the momentousness of the occasion was taking hold, but the irreconcilable positions of the nobility and Third Estate produced deep uncertainty. In mid-February, a Parisian wrote to a friend that France was on the eve of the most fortunate or most unfortunate outcome that could ever occur. He added that there had not been, and perhaps would not be for another thousand years, a crisis similar to the one they were experiencing that before the end of the year would either carry France to the height of power and greatness or reduce it to the depths of catastrophe and destruction. After some additional musings, he closed by stating that the only way for the Third Estate to have freedom and power was to have double representation and vote by head at the Estates General.[70]

There was no basis for compromise because both the nobility and the Third Estate believed that if its view did not prevail it would be consigned to insignificance at the Estates General. This realization led the Third Estate to reassure the nobility of the respect in which the Third Estate held it and to declare that the nobility would retain its honorific privileges. In Saintonge, for example, the *cahier* of the Third Estate stated that the nobility, having honorably given up its pecuniary privileges, should retain all of its ancient prerogatives.[71] Similarly, the Third Estate of Châlons-sur-Marne declared that the nobility, a considerable portion of which had already renounced its pecuniary privileges, would continue to enjoy all of the honorific distinctions to which it was entitled.[72]

The terms of the controversy and debate have sometimes been misunderstood. The goals of the Third Estate were limited and two of the three major ones had been attained by early 1789—the doubling of the Third Estate delegation and acceptance of fiscal equality. The doubling of the Third Estate was meaningless, of course, without vote by head, which is why the Third Estate was determined to achieve it and the recent precedent of the provincial assemblies lent support to the demand. Moreover, a prevalent belief within the Third Estate was that vote by order undermined any sense of national will because each order would vote in its own interest.[73]

For its part, as a protest by the nobility of Burgundy makes clear, the nobility believed that its recognition of fiscal equality was evidence of its good faith and was not only insufficiently acknowledged or appreciated but also not met with a reciprocal action. The nobility further believed that it would be marginalized if vote by head was the procedure used at the Estates General.[74]

The suppression of orders and privilege were not objectives for the Third Estate. Indeed, a comprehensive study of *cahiers* revealed that complaints about deferential privileges to which the nobility was entitled—wearing of swords and the like—appeared in only 8.3 percent of *cahiers* and grievances against judicial privileges were rare.[75] The Third of Estate in Dijon, meeting in January 1789, stated in a message to the monarch:

> We will always respect distinctions founded on social order and necessary to the glory and security of the state. The ministers of the altars will always

> have our respect; the heads of armies will always have our gratitude and consideration; the Clergy and the Nobility will not cease to be distinct and separate orders. Honorific privileges, more worthy of them than pecuniary privileges, will forever class them in a rank properly superior to that of the Third Estate.[76]

Similarly, in an address to the king, the Third Estate of Alençon praised the renunciation of pecuniary privileges by the clergy and nobility and said that the action should prevent division among the three orders. The Third Estate of Alençon stated that it would respect the differences that should continue to exist among the different groups of citizens and that it would be neither jealous nor humiliated by honorific prerogatives, knowing how essential they are in a monarchy.[77]

Even in tense and highly polarized Brittany, similar sentiments could be found.[78] In a brief prepared for its deputies at the Estates General, residents of Rennes denounced the usage of the term Third Estate, which they contended comprised 99 percent of the nation. They asked that the term Third Estate be replaced by "the people" or "the nation," which would be more accurate and dignified. At the same time, however, they also professed their respect for the nobility.[79]

The goals of the Third Estate were the doubling of its representation and vote by head at the Estates General.[80] Most members of the Third Estate were willing to recognize the distinction of orders but not to allow it as a basis for voting at the Estates General—vote by order at the Estates General was the only form of its opposition to orders.[81] The refusal by the nobility to renounce vote by order meant that the resentment of the Third Estate continued and the antithetical stances increased the tensions between them.

Opposition to privilege was not comprehensive. The citizens of Dauphiné defined the outlook of much of the Third Estate when they stated that they opposed only those privileges that affected the well-being of their fellow citizens.[82] Dauphiné itself, in fact, after offering to yield its privileges, reserved the right to retain them if the Estates General could not come to an agreement on reform.[83]

The privileges most deeply opposed by the Third Estate were tax privileges,[84] but the nobility had renounced its fiscal privileges, defusing the issue. The major difference between nobility and Third Estate, with each side taking an unyielding position, was on procedures for the

Estates General. In most other respects, especially in *pays d'élections*, their views were generally aligned.[85]

The Elections to the Estates General

The elections to the Estates General were eventful, as was the drafting of the *cahiers* associated with them. The drawing up of *cahiers* compelled participants to enumerate the issues that they wished to see treated at the Estates General and the citizenry took the task seriously.[86] Likewise, the choice of deputies to be sent to the Estates General forced electors from each order to make clear the strategy and goals they hoped to achieve at the meeting. The political nation became fixated with the Estates General.[87]

The *cahiers* were drawn up in electoral assemblies from February to April 1789, beginning at the *bailliage* level. The *cahiers* from the *bailliage* electoral assemblies, numbering in the thousands, were distilled and collated by committees of electors into larger and more comprehensive general *cahiers*. In the process, the more local concerns of *bailliage cahiers* were excised which, through a process of consensus, allowed the general *cahiers* to reflect more national issues.[88]

The general *cahiers* confirm the polarization that developed around the issue of vote by order or head. Although approximately 20 percent of *cahiers* avoided the issue, 212 *cahiers* specified that vote by order be used at the Estates General. Of those that specified vote by order, 60 percent came from the nobility whereas only two *cahiers* from the Third Estate requested vote by order. As small as it is, the latter number requires qualification because one of them mandated consent by all three orders, which would effectively have given the Third Estate a co-equal status. Conversely, 219 *cahiers* favored vote by head and nearly 80 percent of those came from the Third Estate, with only 6 percent from the nobility.[89] Moreover, a number of clerical and noble electoral assemblies, particularly the latter, sought to assure vote by order at the Estates General by binding their deputies with imperative mandates. The vesting of deputies with imperative mandates precluded them from participating in deliberations if the protocol used at the Estates General was anything other than vote by order.[90]

Insight into the inchoate notion of a constitution and the general idea of it that was beginning to crystallize as the Estates General approached is found in a pamphlet attributed to Guy-Jean-Baptiste Target, who would become a member on the Committee on the Constitution in the National Assembly. He wrote that he heard the word "constitution" repeated endlessly but was concerned that many of those using it had only a vague and confused idea of its meaning. He contended that a constitution was a consistent form of conduct that operated in an unvarying manner, like a machine.[91]

Many traditional notions of the king had been cast off during the spring of 1789, marking the debilitation of the Bourbon style of government, and "constitution" was effectively a catchword for the redefinition of governance, from monarchy-centered government to a new model that included regular meetings of the Estates General.[92] The Estates General would, at a minimum, have a veto on taxation and perhaps a larger role, particularly because the *cahiers* indicated a belief that legislative power belonged to the nation.[93]

The desire for a constitution was widespread but, as an examination of a rural and urban *cahier* from the region of Rouen reveals, it was amorphous and undeveloped. In an indication that the perception of systemic failure extended even deep into the countryside, the village of Duclair opened its *cahier* with the observation that abuses were innumerable and could not be corrected in one session of the Estates General. In its initial section on the constitution, the village asked that the Estates General concern itself above all with the constitution of the state. It asked that the body enact one by putting in place a small number of defined laws and determine the demarcation between legislative and executive power. This accorded with numerous *cahiers* that associated the idea of a constitution with stability.[94]

The *cahier* of the Third Estate of Rouen also began with a request for a constitution. Convinced that the major source of error and abuse by administration was the lack of a clear fundamental law, the *cahier* asked the Estates General to create a constitution that would delineate the terms of governance. It offered fifteen suggestions, beginning with the tenet that France was a hereditary monarchy and that the king alone possessed the power to govern in conformity with the law. The nation held legislative power through the Estates General in conjunction with the monarch.[95]

The prevailing outlook of emphasizing a few clear and precise laws on fundamental principles seemed to indicate a preference for a customary constitution in which the Estates General had a defined role. The Estates General would establish a brief but comprehensive set of foundational principles for the governance of the kingdom that in concept would be analogous to the British constitution.[96]

The drafting of *cahiers*, beginning at the *bailliage* level, politicized the citizenry by requiring members of electoral assemblies to formulate goals and envision change. Because their creation was national in scope and graduated, it had a cascading effect—as *bailliage cahiers* were collated into the larger general *cahiers*, political consciousness increased. Furthermore, in hundreds of instances electoral assemblies ordered the printing of the general *cahier*. The largest number of printed *cahiers* came from the nobility, but their printing also served to expand political consciousness and enabled goals or ideas to move far beyond the assemblies that initiated them.[97]

The election of deputies drew considerable attention. The content of *cahiers* was going to be merged or collated and could therefore be viewed as provisional, but the choice of deputies was a decision that would bring back the local focus of the *cahier*. Each electoral assembly had to choose a deputy or deputies who would best represent it in the pursuit of the objectives put forward in its *cahier*.[98] The elections garnered attention throughout France.[99]

At the local level, relations among the three orders were often amicable.[100] In Amiens, for example, on March 20 there was a general meeting of the three orders in advance of the separate electoral assemblies that took place in early April. In its assembly on April 2 the first act of the nobility was to renounce its fiscal privileges. It sent a deputation to the assembly of the Third Estate to notify the Third Estate of its action and the Third Estate expressed its gratitude.[101] At the local level there seems to have been a recognition that the problem of vote by order or head could not be settled locally but could only be resolved once the Estates General met.

Although the *cahiers* of the nobility indicated a strong preference for vote by order, underlying that stance were variations in instructions if vote by order came into question. The most prevalent position was simply to charge a deputy with an imperative mandate to follow vote by order, which precluded participation if vote by head was the protocol.[102] Several noble assemblies, however, placed additional guidelines in their *cahier* to advise deputies on the matter. In Nemours, the nobility charged its representative to pursue vote by order but, if that was not possible, he could participate in vote by head, with the provision that vote by head be conducted separately by order rather than in a general assembly.[103] The nobility of Angoumois specified vote by order but stated that if a plurality of the nobility chose to vote by head its deputies were to protest but not break away from the Estates General.[104] The nobility of Troyes authorized its deputies to vote by head if two-thirds of the nobility agreed.[105]

Giving its deputy greater latitude, the nobility of Beauvais advised him to seek vote by order but also instructed him that if unanimity was lacking among the three orders, the three orders, in the interest of the nation, should then meet in common and vote by head.[106] Similarly, although recommending that he follow vote by order, the nobility of Dôle, Ornans, and Quingely gave their deputy broad discretion to decide on the form of deliberation.[107]

The matter of deliberation and vote by order or by head was unquestionably the most contentious and divisive question in advance of the Estates General.[108] Apart from that question, however, there were shared concerns, including bringing regularity and stability to the political life of the nation. The city of Nantes asked for a codification of the respective rights of the king and the nation. What was envisaged was an agreed-upon set of conventions to be set forth in a document—the word used was charter—that would be registered in tribunals and municipalities.[109]

The desire for a delineation of the rights of the nation was shared by the nobility as well.[110] The nobility of Lauragais began its *cahier* with the demand that no proceedings on taxation could begin until the rights of the nation had been recognized and assured.[111] Similarly, the nobility of Beauvais stated that no discussion on taxes could be held until a constitution was drawn up and registered in all courts of the kingdom.[112]

The Third Estate of Clermont-Ferrand also used the word "constitution" in its *cahier*. It asked that fundamental principles be stipulated in precise articles and recognized as basic precepts of French government. A copy of what it also called the "code" would be placed in all of the courts and tribunals of the kingdom.[113] It is important to understand, however, as the synonymous use of "constitution," "charter," and "code" demonstrate, that what was sought was not necessarily a written governing document but a set of agreed-upon protocols.

The fourth edition of the *Dictionnaire de l'Académie française*, which was the edition current in 1789, equated a constitution with an ordinance, law or regulation, and it was in this sense that the Third Estate of Clermont-Ferrand employed the term.[114] Just as statutory or administrative law in the form of ordinances, laws, or regulations brought order to society, a delineation of rights between the monarch and the nation would bring order to the state. The struggles with the *parlements* under Louis XV and Louis XVI had led to concern about the extent of royal power and a yearning for stable government. The requests reflect a desire for order and balance in the state.[115] They also represented a rebuff of sweeping claims of royal power and a rejection of the *parlement* as the guardian of constitutional norms.[116]

The ideal of a constitution embodied the aspiration of a new political edifice that would be stable, predictable and devoid of the crises of preceding years.[117] It also encompassed the belief that the monarchy needed consent to impose new taxes.[118] It did not, however, envision a legislative power divided from executive power. The conception remained of a traditional Estates General convened for consultation and consent to new taxation. The kingdom had gone 175 years without consultation, which the demand for the periodicity of the Estates General would correct. The king would be guided by his subjects rather than treacherous ministers.

Anticipating the Estates General

The emotions that engulfed France as the opening of the Estates General approached were varied. On one hand, there was a sense of hope and high expectations—hope that the fiscal and political crises could be resolved and that good order and stability could be achieved through a constitution that would include regular meetings of the Estates General. On the other hand, there was uncertainty and even apprehension, in which the antithetical positions of the nobility and Third Estate on vote by order or head played a significant role. There was an awareness that since the authorization of publication of pamphlets on the Estates General in July 1788 it had become clear that France was divided against itself, with cleavages between Crown and society, between orders, between provinces as well as other divides.[119]

The mixed sentiments are evident in the *cahier* of the Third Estate of Château-Thierry. Demonstrating both the sense of momentousness and the hopes it held for the meeting of the Estates General, it instructed its deputies that:

> …they bring to this august assembly the good sense that will overcome obstacles that initially seem insurmountable; that they carefully avoid extreme opinions, impetuous parties, overly prompt assents or overly opinionated opposition on questions immaterial to its rights and interests.

Reflecting the misgivings brought about by the diametrically opposed positions of the nobility and Third Estate and the doubts they created, the Third Estate of Château-Thierry also gave its deputies the following admonition:

> The Third Estate desires and demands that its deputies remember that they are not dispatched toward enemies whom they should face audaciously and proudly, but toward citizens with whom they are going to address the peace and happiness of the nation; that in the conflict of opinions necessary to the search for truth, that in the zeal inseparable from love of the public good, wisdom and moderation should be the companions of boldness and steadfastness.[120]

By the late winter and early spring of 1789 most of France, with the exception of Paris, had drafted *cahiers* and elected deputies.[121] Having offered guidance and chosen representatives, the kingdom felt itself engaged in some fashion with public policy. It was a heady experience beyond the realm of living memory.

At the same time, there were troubling undercurrents. There was increasing distrust of the nobility because of its adherence to vote by order. The stance served to raise doubts about the appearance of generosity made in several localities, an allusion to the offer to give up tax privileges.[122] There were also rumors that dozens of judges in the *parlement* of Paris were plotting to thwart the opening of the Estates General.[123] According to the Venetian ambassador, the *parlement* had demanded the convocation of the Estates General in the belief that it would never occur. It had done so simply to gain the favor of the nation and was beginning to make its real intentions known.[124]

The Crown was aware that the convening of the Estates General had ended the Bourbon style of government. On the eve of its opening, Louis reportedly asked Necker if the monarch was to present a constitution to the Estates General or if the Estates General was to present one to him. Later in the day and even more pointedly, Marie-Antoinette allegedly asked Necker if the Estates General would be the master of the king or if the king would be master of the nation.[125] The questions of Louis and Marie-Antoinette underscore internal contradictions within the Crown. Louis had doubts about monarchy-centered government, as did many of those around him—indeed, one close associate of the monarch, Louis-Charles le Tonnelier, baron de Bretueil, had been advocating for a written constitution.[126]

On the eve of the opening of the Estates General, Bretueil was reportedly under consideration as chief minister.[127]

There was also a larger crisis beyond the political one. The harvest of 1788 had been poor and had led to a subsistence problem reflected particularly in the price of bread. The confluence of bankruptcy, a political breakdown, and a poor harvest created a sense of systemic failure that formed as the Estates General opened.

The Forgotten Constitution: The Origins, Realization, and Legacy of the French Constitution of 1791.
Michael P. Fitzsimmons, Oxford University Press. © Oxford University Press 2025.
DOI: 10.1093/9780197793978.003.0006

III

THE REALIZATION OF THE CONSTITUTION

6

The Pledge of a Constitution

Amid high hopes, the Estates General opened in Versailles on May 5, 1789. From the outset it went badly. Deputies of the clergy and nobility were attired in resplendent garb whereas the Third Estate was relegated to solemn black clothing, which suggested inferiority rather than a co-equal status with each of the other two orders and almost certainly reminded deputies of the assertion by the princes of the blood that there were two orders in society. The first sentence spoken by Louis XVI struck a discordant note. After declaring that the day he had long awaited had arrived, he observed that he was surrounded by representatives of the nation that he had the distinction "to command." The verb was jarring—it was felt that he should have said "to govern."[1]

Louis implied that he would convene the Estates General regularly and recognized the debt. He acknowledged the general unease present in the kingdom but denounced the "exaggerated desire for innovations" that had taken hold. He also expressed appreciation that the first two orders had renounced their fiscal privileges and said that he would not be disappointed in his hope that the three orders could work together for the good of the state. At this juncture, however, rather than indicate the form to be used at the meeting, he announced that he had ordered a major reduction in expenses and regretted that he could not relieve the burden of his subjects as quickly as he would like. He stated that he would make available to deputies the exact state of finances and told deputies that addressing the fiscal crisis would be their primary task. Although the kingdom was in turmoil, the king stated, he did not doubt that the body would conduct itself wisely and prudently. The judgment by the deputy Adrien Duquesnoy, a member of the Third Estate, that Louis's opening remarks were graceless and brusque reflected the disappointment in them.[2]

Necker offered a three-hour speech that was a dry financial analysis. He was unable to continue and handed it to the secretary of the Society of Agriculture, who completed the reading of it. Although Necker presented a list of primary and secondary topics for the Estates General to consider and urged deputies to be united, he did not address the form of deliberation and voting to be followed at the meeting. Necker did say that he would allow the two privileged orders to renounce their fiscal exemptions and that they could meet separately to make the renunciation. By the conclusion of Necker's speech, deputies were tired.[3]

Whereas Louis's speech had struck a discordant note, there was disappointment and discontent with that of Necker.[4] It led to the perception that he had compromised his standing as a man of the nation that he had previously symbolized.[5] The belief took hold that out of fear of dismissal he was unwilling to follow his convictions, a development that had been anticipated, and ultimately had contradicted himself.[6] The speeches were particularly disappointing because many *cahiers* had stipulated that deputies were to deal with the fiscal crisis only after the constitution had been established.[7]

The failure to resolve the forms to be used at the Estates General is puzzling, particularly because it was widely recognized as the most pressing concern. Robert Blackman noted the contradiction in the fact that representatives elected under an absolute monarchy were implicitly given the latitude to determine the extent of their own powers.[8]

The deputy Duquesnoy criticized Louis for not addressing "the constitutions, etc."[9] The reference to constitution or constitutions centered on restoring order to governance rather than writing a document, which, until two months prior to the opening of the Estates General, was unprecedented at a national level and in May 1789 was still an unproven experiment in the one country in which it existed, the United States. It was understood more in the British sense of agreed-upon conventions in the structure and operation of government.[10] It was in the same sense that one contemporary observer recalled that at the opening of the Estates General all groups sought to give France a constitution.[11]

With regular future meetings of the Estates General anticipated to be a part of the constitution in the future, the most fundamental question was the procedure it should use for deliberations and voting. For much of the nobility, France had a constitution and vote by order was one of its basic tenets. For the Third Estate regular meetings of the Estates General was the means to enable it to have a more meaningful role in governance, but this was possible only if vote by head was the protocol followed. It was the need to settle these and other issues that led Duquesnoy to write of "constitutions, etc." at the time that the meeting opened.

Once again, the possibility that Louis wanted to weaken the Estates General should be considered. If it failed in the manner of 1614, it would once again discredit the body and leave the authority of the Crown unaffected and perhaps even stronger after the collapse of support for the *parlement* of Paris. A primary cause of the failure of the Estates General in 1614 had been the inability of the three orders to cooperate. A functioning Estates General that could potentially infringe upon the power of the Crown was not what Louis wanted and to have a disagreement over procedures at the very beginning could serve Crown interests. Although he had been heavily applauded by the Third Estate, Necker, fearful of jeopardizing his position, was unwilling to fill the vacuum created by the absence of a decision.

The Crown could also have used the Estates General to its advantage. The Estates General was initially envisaged as a means to strengthen the monarch by ensuring that he received good counsel from elected representatives rather than insidious ministers. The involvement of the Estates General in decision-making would facilitate acceptance of royal decisions, in contrast to the *parlements*.[12] The opening of the Estates General offered the Crown an opening to take the initiative, but it did not.

Whatever the reason may have been for not stipulating the protocols to be used, it was a grave error. Louis's authority was at its zenith when the Estates General opened. Although there was disapproval of and disappointment with his speech, he was repeatedly applauded and cheered during it. As a Swiss observer later noted, no one would have begun the Estates General by directly disobeying the monarch. Had Louis ordered common deliberations and vote by head, he would have won the Third Estate to his side. Conversely, if he had decreed deliberations and votes by order, he would have had the support of the clergy and nobility.[13]

The failure by the Crown to establish the procedure to be followed for deliberations and voting or to offer a specific reform program deprived it of the ability to control the agenda of the Estates General. The next day the clergy and nobility convened in separate meeting rooms to verify the credentials of their members.

The Beginning of a Stalemate

Despite a plea that the nobility delay the verification of powers until all deputies were present—Paris was still holding its elections and not all of the delegations from the provinces had arrived in Versailles—the nobility voted to proceed. Having decided to verify powers, the nobility opened discussion on whether verification should be done separately or jointly with the other two orders. By a plurality it chose not only to verify powers separately but also, despite the knowledge that it would introduce discord, to seal itself off from all communication with the Third Estate. After naming twelve commissioners to carry out the task of verification, the nobility adjourned for five days, allegedly to give the commissioners time to complete it.[14]

Whatever the reason for it may have been, the adjournment made the nobility inaccessible to the other two orders and precluded any discussion or negotiations with them on verification of powers. A Third Estate delegation led by Mounier presented itself to the chamber of the nobility on May 7 only to discover that it was not in session and the delegation was referred to the commissioners verifying the credentials. The purpose of the visit was to inform the nobility that the Third Estate was delaying verification and awaiting the arrival of the clergy and nobility in the general meeting room so that the three orders could undertake it together. The commissioners told Mounier that they would relay the news of the visit and its purpose to the nobility when the order reconvened.[15]

When the nobility met again on May 11 Paris had still not sent deputies to the Estates General and there were areas in which the election of deputies was regarded as problematic because the electoral assemblies had included members of other orders. The problematic delegation, of course, was that of Dauphiné, but there were others as well. The commissioners verified the powers of 237 deputies.[16]

The nobility voted that the verified powers of the 237 deputies sufficed to allow it to constitute itself legally as an order. It then named two deputations of eight members each to offer its compliments to the clergy and the Third Estate.[17] The next day, it decided to accept an invitation from the clergy to name commissioners to negotiate with the other two orders.

It is clear that in acting so quickly the nobility was seeking to impose vote by order as the method to be followed at the Estates General—as one noble deputy noted, the vote to verify powers separately was the first motion.[18] Its consistent use of the word "legally" constituted to describe its position was intended to strengthen it against any alternate arrangement, implying that any other form would be irregular. Although it named commissioners to take part in the conferences initiated by the clergy, the chamber also made clear that they had no latitude and that all decisions would have to be made by the chamber as a whole.[19]

In addition, over the following days the nobility did not take up the renunciation of fiscal privileges, even though it was for this reason that Necker had said that they should meet separately.[20] The nobility occupied itself with the verification of credentials of deputies and the issue of pecuniary privileges arose only briefly, in its eleventh meeting. One of the men named as a commissioner to the meetings sponsored by the clergy scheduled to begin that day, May 22, stated that it would enhance the prospects for success if the commissioners could announce at their opening that the nobility would renounce its fiscal privileges and accept equal taxation. He reassured his colleagues that the renunciation would stipulate that the apportionment of taxes could only be done by an Estates General deliberating and voting by order.

The chamber acknowledged that almost all *cahiers* of members contained a renunciation of pecuniary privileges and equal apportionment of taxation. Many deputies argued, however, that the time to inform the other two orders of the renunciation had not yet arrived. They contended that the *cahiers* also strictly mandated that they could not discuss in any manner the question of taxes before "the bases of the constitution had been assured in a positive manner by precise standing laws," which meant vote by order. They argued against allowing the commissioners of their order making this aspect of their *cahiers* known to the other two orders. Several delegations protested against any renunciation without first addressing constitutional matters. The nobility adjourned without making a decision.[21]

The chamber returned to the question the next day and voted to renounce all pecuniary privileges but only after each order, meeting freely, had established the bases of the constitution. The decision prompted protests and reservations by nearly two dozen delegations.[22]

The nobility believed that the offer was a propitious one that would be well received. In part this may have been because of the experiences some had had at the local level when they renounced their pecuniary privileges. The announcement had often met with thanks or gratitude on the part of the Third Estate and any linkage to vote by order that had accompanied it had been ignored in the interest of comity. The nobility underestimated or misunderstood the desire of the Third Estate for a larger role in governance of the kingdom, which could only be attained through vote by head and therefore made the Third Estate unwilling to yield or compromise on the matter.

On May 6 the Third Estate met in the general meeting room, the *Salle des États-Généraux*, often referred to as the *Salle des États*, to verify the powers of all deputies of the body. It quickly discovered that the clergy and nobility were in separate meeting rooms to undertake verification of their members. The breaking away of the other two orders unleashed a "general murmur" in the room but the Third Estate sought to organize itself. One of its early actions was to reject the term "Third Estate" and to designate itself instead as the "commons."[23] Third Estate lent itself to vote by order, which the commons sought to quash, but the term "commons" preserved social distinctions, which it was not seeking to overturn.

The commons began discussing how to respond to the withdrawal of the clergy and nobility and distilled several motions down to two. One motion called for sending deputations to the "privileged orders" to advise them that the commons was awaiting them before beginning the verification of powers. The other opposed sending any deputations to give the clergy and nobility time to reflect on the thoughtlessness of provisional separation, which was made all the more repugnant because each order had an equal interest in the verification of the powers of all. The latter motion won the approval of the commons.[24]

The next day, however, the commons reconsidered its stance after a deputy from Auvergne urged sending deputations to the other two orders to advance the work of the Estates General. It would not pose any inconvenience to send delegations, which would make known to the clergy and nobility that the commons could verify powers only with them present. He added that the gesture would demonstrate the strong desire to fulfill the purpose for which the Estates General had been summoned and place the clergy and nobility in an untenable position.

Many deputies opposed sending any delegations because the commons had not verified powers and therefore could not send any deputation. Opponents also argued that the greatest success for the commons could be achieved through inertia. The debate was spirited and led a deputy to propose that if the commons as a body could not send deputations it could at least allow those who believed that there should be a gesture to go to the rooms in which the clergy and the nobility were meeting to invite them to meet in the common room.

A deputy from Dauphiné, almost certainly Mounier, praised the idea and expressed his belief, on the basis of a speech by the archbishop of Vienne, that the clergy was inclined to join the commons for verification of powers and that in any case the clerical deputies from Dauphiné would, for this verification, enter the *Salle des États*. Following this observation, the question of allowing those deputies who wished to form a deputation to do so was voted upon and passed handily.[25]

As the reversal of a decision from the preceding day reveals, the proceedings—recorded in a "*récit des séances*" rather than "*procès-verbaux*"—were uncertain and much more chaotic than the written record indicates.[26] As a contemporary observing the disarray noted, it was not surprising because one had 1,200 men arriving from all corners of France who did not know each other and they were unable to agree on the first step.[27] Indeed, two deputies from Angers wrote on May 8 that deputies were fatigued from the disorder of the first two days of meetings.[28] The greatest advantage that the commons had was their complete unity of purpose in achieving vote by head.

The commons sent a delegation of twelve to the clergy and nobility to invite them to come to the *Salle des États* to form a joint assembly to verify powers of all deputies. It was through this initiative that the commons learned that the nobility had adjourned after naming its commissioners to verify the powers of its deputies. The clergy was meeting and promised the delegation from the commons an answer within fifteen minutes. Nearly an hour later the clergy delivered its reply, which was that the clergy would name commissioners to negotiate with those of the nobility and the Third Estate on the verification of powers and seek to establish harmony among the orders.

Many in the commons believed that inaction was the most advantageous course, which led it to defer any decision and to organize itself into a body without verifying powers. The sense of disorganization and chaos remained great, however, and when two members of the Dauphinois deputation, which commanded great respect, put forward an idea to bring about order in the deliberations it was eagerly embraced.[29]

On May 13 a delegation of noble deputies arrived at the *Salle des États*. They were seated in the section that the nobility had occupied on the day the Estates General opened, signaling that the commons would preserve distinction of orders even if it would not accept vote by order.[30] The spokesman for the nobility declared that it desired to maintain "fraternal union" among the orders and then read two decrees that the nobility had approved. The first was that in which the nobility named commissioners to verify the powers of its deputies and the second rejecting verification with the other two orders and constituting itself as an order. The spokesman notified the commons that the nobility had accepted the invitation of the clergy to negotiate with the other two orders.

After the noble deputation left the commons began its discussion by noting the hypocrisy of the address by the noble delegation in expressing the desire of the nobility for fraternal union while sending commissioners to negotiate the verification of powers, which the commons had disallowed and the nobility had already completed. Some in the commons argued that the insincerity presented an insurmountable obstacle to union and that under the circumstances the naming of commissioners to confer with the other two orders was pointless.

The next morning, May 14, Jean-Paul Rabaut de Saint-Etienne spoke to the commons and pointed out the advantages to be gained by participating in the conferences and the disadvantages of not participating.[31] He asked that sixteen or a proximate number of members of the commons be named to confer with the clergy and the nobility. The goal of those named would be to reunite the deputies of the nation in the *Salle des États* without ever yielding on vote by head or the indivisibility of the Estates General.

Isaac René Guy Le Chapelier, from Rennes, opposed Rabaut and argued vigorously against participation with a harsh denunciation of the clergy and nobility. He contended that all avenues of conciliation were useless and dangerous and that the commons should order the clergy and nobility to cease their separate meetings and summon them to the *Salle des États*. If they failed to respond, the members of the Third, the term he apparently used, would declare themselves as representatives of the nation, a stance that another deputy believed had been orchestrated by the Breton delegation as a whole, especially when many among them spoke in support of it. Nearly all of the Breton deputies spoke passionately against any course of conciliation and the vehemence with which they argued against it offended many in the commons, with one observing that they had an implacable hatred for the nobility and were not alarmed by the prospect of civil war.[32]

On May 18 the commons voted in favor of Rabaut's motion. The commons would name commissioners to confer with those chosen by the clergy and nobility on the means to bring all deputies together to verify powers in common and the commissioners would provide a written report on the conferences. After overwhelmingly approving Rabaut's measure the meeting adjourned. The following day the commons elected sixteen commissioners, including Rabaut, Le Chapelier, and Mounier.[33]

The Beginning of Conferences

As it started to elect its commissioners to the conciliatory conferences, the nobility began with a statement that it was the duty, interest, and dignity of the chamber to hold firm to verification and vote by order as it sought to establish "amiable communication" among the three orders. It decided to elect eight commissioners but during the voting a deputation from the commons arrived. The spokesman for the deputation, Target, announced that the "deputies of the commons" had elected commissioners for conferences proposed by the clergy and that they would be present on the day the clergy and the nobility deemed most convenient.

The president of the nobility informed the group that the nobility was at that moment choosing its commissioners and the results would be known, after which the delegation of the commons left. After its departure, a member of the nobility, Duval d'Eprémesnil, the magistrate of the Paris *parlement*, spoke out against the appellation of "commons" that the Third Estate had adopted for itself and characterized it as very anti-constitutional. Several other members spoke in support of his observation.[34]

The nobility did not complete the election of its commissioners until May 22 and the conferences began on May 23. Despite opposition from Duval d'Eprémesnil, the nobility authorized its commissioners to offer the renunciation of pecuniary privileges but linked it to separation of orders.[35]

The first conference began at 5:00 p.m. with mutual expressions of goodwill and sincerity, leading the archbishop of Arles to announce that it was in this spirit that the clergy regarded it as a duty, at a time when "everything was gaining a new existence," to consent to equal taxation. Anne Charles Sigismond de Montmorency, duc de Luxembourg, the spokesman for the nobility, declared that the same desire had been expressed in a majority of its *cahiers* and had led the nobility assembled in different jurisdictions to renounce tax privileges. At the same time, however, to remain faithful to their mandates, he declared that, before any renunciation could be offered, the nobility had to resolve issues related to the bases of the constitution.

The nobility insisted on the respect to be given to precedent and cited the previous Estates General in 1614 at which verification had been undertaken separately, claiming that joint verification would lead to vote by head in the general assembly.[36] The commons, which the minutes of the nobility consistently refer to as the Third Estate, responded through its spokesman, Target, that the questions related to the verification of powers were the only reason that it was present, that verification was the sole matter it was authorized to negotiate and was independent of the forms to be used in the Estates General. The archbishop of Arles said that the clergy would abstain from taking a stance on the issue. A debate on historical precedents extending back to 1356 ensued between the nobility and the commons.[37]

The commissioners of the commons stated that members of the previous Estates General, overly occupied with narrow interests, had not elevated themselves to the dignity of "legislators."[38] The minutes of the commons record that the nobility recognized that the Estates General of 1614 had, in fact, made a mistake by sending questions of contested powers for resolution to the *Conseil du Roi*. The commons used that statement to argue that if one accepted that there had been one error in former usages there could be two and that separate verification of powers could be another one.

The minutes of the nobility state that the commons asserted that France did not have a constitution, an assertion not mentioned in the minutes of the commons. The commissioner for the nobility reported to his chamber that its commissioners had proven that there was a constitution. It was, the nobility claimed, not necessary to create a new one, which would destroy the one that had existed for centuries, but only to repair it.

When the clergy averred that verification of powers could not be decided simply on the basis of historical precedent and that justice and reason would have to be factors as well, the commissioners for the nobility responded that their imperative mandates precluded any deliberation by head, even for the verification of powers. It again contended that the question of verification of powers in common was a means to predispose the issue of vote by head or by order in favor of the commons. It also denounced the use of the term "national assembly" by the commons as prejudicial. The meeting concluded after four and a half hours with the commons inviting the nobility to join them for verification of powers and assuring its commissioners that the action would not prejudge the question of vote by head or by order. The commissioners for the nobility did not respond.[39]

It was an inauspicious start to the conciliatory conferences, with no common ground to serve as a starting point for negotiations. The nobility had already verified the powers of its deputies, which was the sole purpose of the conferences for the commons, and it asserted that meetings and vote by order had constitutional status that could not be amended. Moreover, both the nobility and the commons, with each expecting support for its position, were unhappy with the passivity of the clergy in its role as intermediary.[40]

The atmosphere surrounding the negotiations did not improve. The second meeting, on May 25, began with observations by the commons on the uncertainty of facts, the variation of forms from epoch to epoch, the obvious errors that had blended into former protocols and the differences between 1614 and 1789. The commons argued vigorously about the differences between previous meetings of the Estates General and the trajectory of what they called "the National Assembly of 1789."

After additional discussion the commissioners for the nobility asked that the Third Estate put forward a project for conciliation. The commons responded that this was not their mission. A long argument followed until the conference ended after three and a half hours with no date set for the next one, although the parties agreed they should be resumed.

It was clear that the negotiations were at an impasse. Obviously frustrated, the commissioners for the commons gave a report to their colleagues and then effectively resigned when they said that they believed their mission to have been completed but that they considered it worthwhile to resume negotiations.[41]

The negotiations collapsed the next day, however, when the nobility passed a resolution decreeing that for the current meeting of the Estates General powers should be verified separately.[42] After learning of the resolution, the commons declared that the nobility had repelled all efforts at conciliation and decided that the only remaining course for the commons was to make a new approach to the clergy and invite them to join the commons.[43]

The 1614 Estates General had been unable to resolve differences between the orders during deliberations and had discredited the body, but in 1789 the inability to begin deliberations redounded to the discredit of the Crown and especially the monarch. The issue paralyzing the Estates General had been known long in advance and could have been resolved at the opening but was not. Moreover, the *Garde des sceaux* kept Louis informed of developments on a regular basis so Louis could have intervened to settle the matter but did not.[44]

Indeed, at this juncture the Crown still had sufficient authority to impose a settlement. Each of the three orders was still tentative in its course of action and a royal intervention would almost certainly have been decisive. Instead, however, in the aftermath of the collapse of the conciliatory conferences the Crown merely sought to take them over to continue them. On May 28 Louis wrote to the head of each of the three orders asking for their continued participation with the same commissioners. The letter was carefully crafted to appeal to the nobility and the commons by using both "Estates General" and "National Assembly," which the monarch said he had called to assist him in the regeneration of the kingdom. The conferences would be held under the auspices of the *Garde des sceaux* and commissioners chosen by the king and would begin at 6:00 p.m. the next evening.[45]

The commons only learned of the letter from a deputation of the clergy that the commons had hoped was there to respond to its invitation to join it. The delegation of the clergy announced that the clergy had accepted the monarch's invitation and had suspended consideration of the offer of the Third Estate. The head of the commons responded that the commons could make no determination until the king's letter arrived.

The news of the letter disconcerted the commons, which after a brief discussion decided not to act in any manner until it had seen the letter. Moments later a royal representative arrived with the unsealed letter and read it to the chamber. The discussion of the letter was regarded as so important that the deputy Pierre Victor Malouet proposed that the meeting room be closed to non-deputies. The commons rejected his proposal but the head of the commons enjoined spectators from expressing approval or disapproval of motions or opinions. Spectators were also forbidden to seat themselves among the deputies.[46]

The debate was animated, with members of the commons especially angered by a motion adopted by the nobility declaring that, because it was its duty to support the constitution, the nobility would follow vote by order, thereby predetermining the ostensible object of the negotiations.[47] After six and a half hours of discussion, with some deputies opining that the declaration made resumption of the conferences useless and conciliation with the nobility impossible, the commons adjourned at 11:00 p.m. without making a decision. The commons resumed debate the next morning, May 29, and after a long discussion voted to participate in the conferences.[48]

The conferences began on May 30 at 6:00 p.m. with the *Garde des sceaux* presiding and Necker among the commissioners present for the Crown.

The clergy, citing its desire to preserve its position as mediator, declined to put forward any views or proposals. Discussions began with a noble commissioner reading a long memorandum arguing that the verification of powers should be undertaken separately by order.

At the completion of the reading a member of the commons, referred to as the Third Estate in the minutes, told the meeting that its delegation had been charged to keep official minutes of the conferences that would be recognized and signed by all participants. The nobility and clergy immediately objected that they should not be bound by a resolution taken by the Third Estate.

The commons responded that they were not imposing an obligation but seeking to establish an accurate historical record of the conferences. One of the commissioners for the nobility noted that the resolution used the word "commons" to denote the Third Estate and that this innovation in words could bring about an innovation in principles. He protested the use of the word and stated that he could not allow it. He was overruled, however, and the conferences continued. Long and contentious arguments followed without any resolution until the meeting adjourned at 9:45 p.m.[49]

The opening session set the tone for the following meetings. When the conferences resumed on June 3 with a reading of the minutes of the previous meeting, the discussions bogged down over the use of the designation of commons rather than Third Estate.[50] The commons concluded its arguments in favor of the term with the observation that in the ministerial report submitted to and approved by the king in council the previous December 27, in which the doubling of the Third Estate representation had been approved, the title of commons had again been given to the people of France.[51] A commissioner of the nobility took issue with the interpretation of the word.

The bickering went on at length and when the meeting did begin it became an exchange of historical precedents that each side believed supported its stance. A member of the commons delegation restated that justice and reason should prevail over previous usages and protocols. He told the noble commissioners that they should not be persuaded that the facts were on their side and criticized the interpretation that the nobility attached to them.

Disagreements about historical precedent extending back to the 1483 meeting continued and in one exchange went back to 1355, 1356, and 1467. The commons disputed the validity of any reference to the 1560 meeting because no records existed for its verification of powers and dismissed any allusion to the 1588 meeting because it had been held under the influence of the Holy League.

Another historical precedent raised by the nobility once again led to an argument over the use of the word "commons" instead of Third Estate. The nobility refused to recognize the minutes, to which they otherwise had no objections, if they employed the term "commons."[52] Even at this early stage a noble deputy believed that any reconciliation among the orders was more remote than ever but that the conferences would continue.[53]

The *Garde des sceaux* attempted to arrange a compromise after the clergy, to the chagrin of the commons, also refused to sign them, but his suggestions were not well received by the clergy or the nobility. Ultimately, on the invitation of the three orders, the *Garde des sceaux* appointed a clerk in the chancellery to oversee the minutes and serve as secretary for the conferences.[54]

The trajectory of the conferences was clearly not promising and on June 4 the royal commissioners offered observations to the three orders that they hoped would advance the proceedings. The commissioners of the three orders agreed to present the proposal to their respective chambers.[55]

The royal conferences resumed on June 6 but again became mired in disagreement when the nobility reiterated its refusal to sign any minutes that employed the word "commons."[56] The stance of the nobility seemed to exasperate the *Garde des sceaux*, who asserted that their recorded protest should remove all difficulties. The nobility, he contended, could have no interest in refusing to sign the minutes. The nobility responded that there was a considerable difference between protesting a word and suppressing it and they wanted the word "commons" suppressed. After a long discussion some commissioners for the clergy agreed to sign as witnesses but disagreements between the nobility and commons continued until the meeting ended at 10:00 p.m.[57]

Like the preceding clergy-sponsored conciliatory conferences, the Crown conferences were at a complete impasse. The commissioners met once more, on June 9, but the session was brief. The clergy announced that it would sign the minutes once they had been recognized as precise by the commissioners of the three orders. A commissioner for the nobility stated that although he and his colleagues fully recognized the exactitude of the minutes, they were required not to give approval in the name of their order because of the use of the word "commons," a new term, they contended, to designate the Third Estate. The nobility was protesting all innovation in usages, principles, and words. The commons replied that it had presented the basis for its use of the word and that the protest of the nobility seemed entirely without merit. At 10:15 p.m. the commissioners of the clergy and the commons, as well as the royal official appointed secretary, signed the minutes, ending the conferences.[58]

The Aftermath of the Failures of the Conferences

The failure of the negotiations effaced virtually all vestiges of goodwill that may have been brought to the Estates General from the local level prior to the meeting.[59] The commons concluded that the nobility was not a good-faith interlocutor, illustrated particularly by a heated exchange between Mounier, the personification of seeking harmony with the other orders, and the noble commissioner Bouthilliers.[60] In addition, the equivocation of the clergy during the conferences also made them a more doubtful partner than had originally been envisaged.

The collapse of the second set of conferences frustrated the commons—one deputy wrote that they had not come much further than where they were on the first day—and led to a more independent and emphatic course of action by the commons. On June 10 it decided that inaction was no longer advantageous and that it would become more assertive. It concluded that it was futile to seek the support of the king, whom it believed was under the influence of interests opposed to the commons—the princes, the great nobles, bishops, the *parlements*, and ministers, except for Necker, although it was losing faith in him because of his weakness and timidity.[61] The change of course on June 10 began when Sieyès, a member of the Paris delegation that had arrived after the Estates General opened, received the opportunity to speak.[62] Because the Bretons had alienated many deputies through their aggressiveness, they did not want to put themselves forward but it was widely suspected that Sieyès was working in concert with them.[63]

Sieyès began by retracing the conduct of the commons since the opening of the Estates General and its dealings with what he called "the two privileged orders." He argued that the commons could not remain long in a state of inertia without betraying its duties and the interests of its constituents. Sieyès contended that because the nobility had spurned the path of conciliation, the only option for the commons was to summon the members of the "two privileged chambers" to come to the *Salle des États* for the common verification of powers. He offered a motion stating that it was the duty of representatives of whatever class to which he might belong—he appears to have been avoiding the word order—to come together to form an active assembly capable of beginning and fulfilling its mission. If the "two classes" of deputies persisted in their refusal, the commons would issue a final invitation, after which it would act on its own. Sieyès asked the commons to take a definitive role in the verification of powers, which would be necessary for the validity of any future actions. He also suggested that the announcement of default against the non-compliant did not constitute a schism because the default would last only as long as the clergy and nobility wished. It could be overcome if they joined the commons, which would happily receive them.

The members of the commons enthusiastically applauded Sieyès's observations. There was some opposition to them but, after modifications to which Sieyès consented and despite some procedural difficulties brought about by inexperience, his proposal ultimately passed with only three dissenting votes.[64]

For its part, after the collapse of the conferences the nobility undertook the election of a president, vice-president, and five secretaries. Their terms were to be fixed and limited rather than for the duration of the Estates General. The nobility narrowly defeated a proposal that set a term of one month and approved a second motion specifying a duration of two months for their duties. It elected the duc de Luxembourg, who had been one of the commissioners for the nobility during the conferences, as president.

On June 12 the nobility received a visit from a delegation of the commons, which it admitted to the chamber. In an exchange laden with dueling vocabulary, the spokesman for the delegation said that the commons wished to end the absence of deputies of the "privileged classes" and extended its final invitation to join the commons in the *Salle des États* to begin work in the national interest. The president of the nobility replied that the "order of the nobility" would consider the invitation of the "order of the Third Estate" and give a reply. After the deputation departed from the chamber the nobility named a committee to draft its response. The next day the nobility narrowly approved, by a vote of 116–110, its reply to the "order of the Third Estate."

Pursuing its consistent line of argument, the nobility stated that it was following the usages of previous Estates Generals for the verification of powers and again cited the constitutive law of separation and mutual independence of orders. "The Order of the Third Estate," it declared, had not followed the same course and the "Order of the Nobility" had offered its reasons for proceeding separately during the conciliatory conferences. The nobility had believed that the renunciation of its fiscal privileges prior to the conferences would immediately resolve many difficulties and open deliberations for the Estates General, leaving unsaid, of course, that the renunciation had been conditional upon deliberation and vote by order. After offering justifications for its actions, the nobility declared that the nation would now judge whether the nobility was responsible for the stalemate at the Estates General.[65] The head of the commons tersely responded that the commons hoped that the nobility would join the commons to work together.[66]

In the *Salle des États*, the commons elected Jean-Sylvain Bailly as president and undertook a full roll-call of all deputies—clerical, noble, and commons—before beginning deliberations. It also sent a letter to the monarch explaining its conduct and provisionally approved subdividing its membership into subcommittees for examining the minutes of elections of deputies to begin the verification of powers.[67]

On June 13 three clerical deputies from Poitou entered the *Salle des États* and the commons warmly welcomed them. The next evening several more *curés* joined and their spokesman, Dominique Dillon, explained that they had come to have their credentials verified in common because all other possibilities for harmony and patience had been exhausted. They sought, he said, to bring an end to the unfortunate situation.[68]

The entry of the *curés* was a major advance for the commons. It revealed a split among the clergy that favored the commons and the commons was better positioned to contend with the stalemate. Whereas the commons was overwhelmingly united on the questions of deliberation in common and vote by head, the nobility was less unified in its position of separate deliberation and vote by order because some noble deputies carried secondary instructions in their *cahier* that authorized them to depart from those positions.[69]

Moreover, members of the commons were more committed to the meeting of the Estates General than the nobility. The question of the duration of powers had not arisen in the internal discussions of the commons but a substantial minority of noble deputies—118 out of 244—had voted to limit their powers to one month. The entry of the clerical deputies was the first movement after five and a half weeks of stalemate and it worked entirely in favor of the commons.

Because the nobility had been operating in isolation and had been almost exclusively focused on deliberation and vote by order, it had not considered any larger agenda.[70] During discussions on June 17 some members of the chamber argued that it should undertake a work plan for a constitution whereas others sought to find a path of conciliation among the three orders. The nobility voted overwhelmingly to devote itself to a work plan for a constitution.[71]

The chamber of the nobility elected to divide itself into ten subcommittees to consult *cahiers* on constitutional matters only.[72] There was little additional discussion of the project but it appears that its purpose was to compile, based on the *cahiers*, principles that should be given constitutional status to clarify the current constitution. The final product of the project would unquestionably stipulate deliberation and vote by order as well as other tenets that would almost certainly be unacceptable to the commons.

The same day that the nobility committed itself to producing a constitution saw the culmination of the most important debate to date for the commons. After the initial entry of *curés* on June 13 many others had joined the commons in the following days. At the beginning of the meeting on June 15 Claude Marolles, a *curé* from Saint-Quentin, entered to have his credentials verified. He told deputies that he had been sympathetic to the cause of the commons from the opening of the Estates General because it was tied to those of the clergy and the entire nation. He had come, he declared, because he recognized the indispensable necessity of the common verification of powers of a "National Assembly."[73]

Almost certainly influenced by Marolles's speech, Jérôme Le Grand put forward a motion that the commons take for itself the title of "National Assembly."[74] The "constitution of the assembly," which referred to the name to be taken, became an object of competing motions, with some of the proposed appellations cumbersome or partisan.[75]

The debate was extensive but a critical turning point came during the evening session of June 16 when Sieyès abandoned his suggestion of "Known and Verified Representatives of the French Nation" and, in the words of one deputy, "unscrupulously appropriated" the term initially put forward by Le Grand.[76] As discussion on the question was in progress during the evening session of June 16, a delegation of noble deputies presented itself to the chamber. It read a measure approved by the nobility stating that it would name commissioners to meet with the other orders to consider proposals made by the clergy and to discuss means to address the high cost of grain and public misery. The initiative was abruptly dismissed.[77] The meeting concluded with the introduction of a new motion, almost certainly Sieyès's appropriation of the term "National Assembly," and a delay on voting until the next day.[78]

Deliberations resumed on June 17 and began with the reading of five competing motions. According to one eyewitness account, after the reading a profound silence fell over the body as the magnitude of its undertaking became apparent. Out of 583 deputies who voted, 491 voted for the appellation of National Assembly and ninety voted against it, with two votes lost.[79]

The new name had much to recommend it, beginning of course with its brevity but also because it gave primacy to the idea of the nation and made no mention of the schism. Perhaps most importantly, it also had the advantage of the Crown having previously used it in its letter of invitation to the three orders for the Crown-sponsored conciliatory conferences. It had used the words Estates General and National Assembly in a virtually synonymous fashion, which conceivably made it possible that the term National Assembly could supersede Estates General. It would have been hypocritical for the Crown to raise objections to it after it had used it.[80]

The entry of clerical deputies into the chamber of the commons had fundamentally altered the traditional composition of the Estates General, thereby necessitating, in the view of the commons, a new designation. Moreover, by eliminating the term Estates General and creating a new name, the commons may have been seeking to put an end to disagreements about historical precedent with respect to deliberation and voting. As a new body it would not be bound to any past procedures and could move forward unencumbered. The nobility clearly recognized this aspect because in a letter to the monarch on June 19 it stated that the spirit of innovation threatened the constitution.[81]

The newly-proclaimed National Assembly of the commons and *curés* put forward a justification for their action that provides insight into the many crosscurrents present during the opening weeks of the Estates General. Its declaration that after verification of powers the Assembly recognized that it included representatives sent by 96 percent of the nation was a concession to competing motions on the constitution of the assembly that had referred to numerical strength. Such a massive deputation, the statement proclaimed, could not remain paralyzed by the absence of deputies of *bailliages* or classes of citizens, a clear allusion to the nobility. Such absences could not prevent the Assembly from exercising the plentitude of its rights, especially because it was an overwhelming and pressing duty. The Assembly stated that the work of national restoration could and should begin without delay by those deputies who were present—a declaration that there were to be no more conferences on deliberations and voting—and that the task should be pursued with single-minded determination and without interruption.

The term National Assembly was the most appropriate in the current state of affairs, deputies asserted, both because the members who comprised it were the only ones legitimately and publicly known to be verified, an effort to delegitimize the verification carried out by the nobility, whose proceedings were closed. The legitimacy of the Assembly was rooted in the fact that its members had been sent by the near totality of the nation. No deputy, irrespective of the order, a rare use of the word and directed at the nobility, or class that had chosen him had the right to exercise his duties outside of the Assembly.

The statement announced that the Assembly would never lose hope of reuniting all deputies who were currently absent and would never cease to call them to fulfill the duty imposed on them to participate in holding the Estates General. The use of the term Estates General by the newly-proclaimed National Assembly, which was seeking to draw remaining deputies and supersede the Estates General, perhaps indicates that the speed of events was outpacing the ability of deputies to absorb them. The linguistic confusion would continue in the weeks ahead.

The statement assured deputies currently outside of the Assembly that they would be welcomed and that, after the verification of powers, they would be able to participate in the great undertaking that should ensure the regeneration of France. It was going to write up its statement in order to send it to the king and the nation.[82]

Later in the afternoon the Assembly unanimously adopted two motions. It claimed that taxes could be legal only if they were authorized by the nation but provisionally authorized the continued collection of all existing taxes despite their illegal origin. It pledged to work closely with the monarch to determine the principles for national regeneration and declared it would devote itself to consolidating the public debt and placing creditors under the honor and loyalty of the French nation, which was essentially the task that Louis had presented to deputies at the opening of the Estates General.

The Assembly also committed itself to investigate means to alleviate the food shortage in the quickest and most effective manner. It decreed that it would create a committee that would take up the matter and asked the king to provide the committee with all the information it might need.[83]

During the evening session the Assembly received a letter from Louis that conveyed his disapproval of the actions of the commons during the week since the breakdown of the conciliatory conferences. It opened with a statement that he would never refuse to receive any of the presidents of the three orders who were sent to see him, which perhaps implicitly represented an endorsement of orders meeting separately. Louis strongly condemned the repeated use of the phrase "privileged orders" that the "Third Estate" used to refer to the first two orders. The expression, he wrote, only encouraged division, was inimical to the well-being of the state, which could only come about through the cooperation of the three orders that comprised the Estates General, whether they deliberated separately or in common.[84]

The letter, addressed to Bailly as dean of the Third Estate, had been written from Marly on June 16, the day before the commons declared itself the National Assembly, but its tone and content made clear that he would disapprove of that action as well. It may have been driven by a report from Barentin that the commons had raised the question of whether the approval of the monarch was necessary to the operations of the Estates General, although it decided that the royal veto was generally recognized.[85] Nevertheless, Louis may have been angered by the questioning of his authority.

The proclamation of the National Assembly by the commons was an action that converted a traditionally consultative body, the Estates General, into a more active one. It presaged the appropriation of sovereignty and marks the beginning of what we have come to think of as the French Revolution, which led an early scholar of the Revolution to call it "the first Revolutionary step."[86]

At the same time, however, it is in some respects less far-reaching than it initially appears and can be viewed as much as a tactical measure as a momentous act. The commons decided to adopt the new appellation of National Assembly because the entry of the clergy into its chamber changed the traditional structure of the Estates General. It was a term that was neither bold nor confrontational, as Louis recognized. His initial reaction had been to observe that the new name was only a phrase. Furthermore, not only had the Crown itself used it but it had also been present in many *cahiers*.

In assuming the title National Assembly, the Third Estate/commons was not demarcating a constitutional role. Rather, the name change was undertaken to break the stalemate, to thwart any rival effort and to allow the Estates General to begin meeting as a union of orders, replacing vote by order with majority rule in a single body.[87]

The boldest claim was the assertion that the Assembly had the right to authorize taxation, but the idea that the Estates General should consent to taxation was in many *cahiers*. It was not only a bid to make the body permanent but also an effort to prevent the potential appearance of a resolution of the fiscal situation by having the Crown accept the renunciation of tax privileges by the clergy and nobility and then dissolve the Estates General. Just as the National Assembly had taken on the task of alleviating public misery, so, too, it had to be seen as solving the fiscal crisis. Its assurance of protection to creditors sought to win the financial class to its side.

The conservative aspects of the statement and the degree to which it was intended to attract the clergy and nobility are often overlooked. The statement that no deputy "in whatever order or rank he may be chosen"—rather than the simpler "no deputy"—could exercise his powers outside of the Assembly reflected its willingness to maintain distinction of orders as long as deliberation was in common and vote was by head. Every delegation of the clergy and nobility that had been admitted to the chamber for visits had been seated in the section reserved for its order at the opening of the Estates General and the *curés* who had entered the chamber and become part of the National Assembly had been seated in the section reserved for their order.[88] The Assembly was following the model of the union of orders.

Another reason that the Assembly was seeking permanence is that the *curés* who had entered the commons had done so to end the stalemate. For most of them the idea of a permanent national chamber was an open question—they remained loyal to their order and to the Church and were not seeking to merge their order with the commons.[89]

Louis's letter, with its use of the term Third Estate, its reproach of the commons for its intemperate language, its reference to presidents of each order and potential legitimization of vote by order, confirmed the Assembly's wariness of the king that had emerged after the collapse of the second set of conciliatory conferences. At Marly grieving the recent death of his son, Louis was removed from Necker and susceptible to the influence of more reactionary elements at the Court, although Necker was also annoyed by the proclamation of the National Assembly.[90] Louis returned to Versailles on June 17 and called for a royal session to be held on June 22.

At 9:00 a.m. on June 20 deputies of the Assembly arrived at the *Salle des États* and found it guarded by royal troops who prohibited them from entering. Bailly and two secretaries went to the main entrance of the room and asked to see the commanding officer of the detachment. The officer, the comte de Vassan, told Bailly that he had orders to prohibit anyone from entering the *Salle* because it was being prepared for the royal session.

Bailly protested the prevention of the opening of the meeting, which was scheduled for the current hour. Vassan told Bailly that he had been authorized to allow the officers of the Assembly to gather any papers that they might need. As they entered they saw that almost all of the seating areas for deputies had been covered and that all of the aisles were guarded by a large number of soldiers. In the courtyard and on the exterior door were posters announcing that the three Salles were being prepared for the royal session, which was unusual because the royal session was going to be held in the *Salle des États*. The announcement also asserted that the monarch demanded the suspension of the "assemblies of the orders" until the royal session.

The officers left the *Salle des États* and went to a nearby tennis court, where they convened the Assembly. At 10:30 a.m. the president, Bailly, read two letters from Henri Evrard, marquis de Deux-Brézé, the master of ceremonies for Louis. The first announced the suspension of the meetings of the three orders that had been proclaimed in the posters seen by the officers of the Assembly and the order denying deputies the right to enter the meeting hall. Bailly told his fellow deputies that his response to Brézé was that Bailly had not received any instruction from the monarch about a royal session or the suspension of meetings and that it was his duty to appear for the scheduled meeting. After receiving Bailly's letter Brézé wrote a second letter affirming that his first letter to Bailly had been written on a direct order from Louis and reiterating the suspension of the meetings of the different orders until after the royal session.

The various developments—the covering of the benches in the meeting rooms, the heavy troop presence, the suspension of meetings without prior notification—led the Assembly to believe that the Crown was preparing to dissolve it. Because of this perception, deputies, with only one dissenting vote, approved a decree designed to counter any such effort. It stated that the Assembly had been called to determine the constitution, secure a return of public order and maintain the principles of the monarchy.

Nothing could prevent it from continuing its deliberations wherever it might be forced to convene. Anywhere its members met, it declared, there was the National Assembly.[91]

The statement declared that all members of the Assembly swore never to disband and that they would reassemble anywhere that circumstances might demand until the constitution of the kingdom was established and consolidated on solid foundations. All members would confirm this unshakeable resolution with their signature. They then swore an oath to the decree and signed it.[92] After all deputies signed the decree, those whose verification was not yet complete and alternate deputies asked to sign also and the Assembly agreed to their request. After announcing that the committee appointed to alleviate misery would meet the next day, Bailly adjourned the Assembly for two days, until June 22.[93]

The action has become known as the Tennis Court Oath and marks the genesis of a written constitution in France, although the statement did not stipulate that the constitution would be written. The Tennis Court Oath was in many respects a tactical measure that sought to achieve two objectives. The first was to avoid dissolution by the Crown, both by announcing a task of fundamental significance and by authorizing itself to reassemble to complete it.

The secondary purpose was to coopt the agenda of the nobility, which had adopted the forging of constitutional principles as its primary undertaking. The Assembly did not want to leave the task solely to the nobility, which was the reason it asserted the right to reassemble anywhere to continue it. Moreover, if Louis dismissed the Assembly, a self-proclaimed *sui generis* body, and left the drafting of constitutional principles to a rump nobility and clerical Estates General or dissolved the entire body and delegated the codification to the *parlement* of Paris, the Assembly could reassemble to contest the effort.[94]

In the final analysis, the Tennis Court Oath was intended more to forestall possible dismissal than it was a call for a written constitution. The decree said only that the principles of the constitution would be established but it did not specify a written format. Indeed, given that the only written national constitution in the world, that of the United States, had been in force only three and a half months, the more probable model was a statement of principles to become the anchor for an unwritten constitution in emulation of the more widely known British example.

In whatever manner the constitution was envisaged, the National Assembly had now defined and committed itself to a primordial mission. The nature and contours of the constitution remained entirely uncertain, but the momentousness of the decree and the scope of its task would increase exponentially six weeks later and become a landmark in the history of Western constitutionalism.

The Forgotten Constitution: The Origins, Realization, and Legacy of the French Constitution of 1791.
Michael P. Fitzsimmons, Oxford University Press. © Oxford University Press 2025.
DOI: 10.1093/9780197793978.003.0007

7

The Collapse of Monarchy-Centered Government

The days between the Tennis Court Oath and the royal session saw much political maneuvering. Although the nobility heeded the Crown request to suspend meetings until after the royal session, it did not remain inactive. It drew up a strident letter to the king and a large delegation presented it to him on June 21. The letter contended that innovation threatened the constitution and that the nobility had followed law and custom. It accused what it called "the deputies of the order of the Third Estate" of believing that they could arrogate to themselves the authority of the other two orders and the sanction of the monarch. The statement also accused the Third Estate of believing itself able to turn its decrees into laws, which had been printed and sent to the provinces. The letter was so confrontational that many noble deputies refused to sign it and asked that their refusal be included in the minutes, which it was.[1]

The Assembly disregarded the order not to meet and, with its usual meeting room still heavily guarded by royal troops, convened in a parish church in Versailles, Saint-Louis, on June 22.[2] The meeting began with Bailly reading a letter from Louis, dated June 21 and addressed to Bailly as "president of the Third Estate," informing him that the royal session had been delayed until June 23 and that the meeting room would be open only for that moment, which again suggested the possibility of dissolution.

As the meeting was beginning, a deputation of the clergy presented itself to the Assembly. When the delegation entered, deputies rose to greet it and, even in the small confines of the parish, seated them in a section designated for the clergy. Its spokesman, the bishop of Chartres, informed the Assembly that the order of the clergy had chosen to join it for the purpose of joint verification of powers. Obviously pleased, Bailly assured the delegation that the "deputies of the order of the clergy" would be received warmly and with the respect owed them. He also pledged that the section designated for the clergy would be available to them. Several dozen members of the clergy—150 in the estimate of one deputy, including five bishops—entered the Assembly to hearty applause.[3] The archbishop of Vienne, of the Dauphinois delegation, conveyed the happiness of the clergy at the beginning of the achievement of the union of orders and stated that the clergy was particularly pleased that the union was with the deputies of the commons.

Shortly afterward two members of the nobility, Henri François Lucretius, marquis de Blacons, and Jean Antoine, comte d'Agoult, both elected by the assembly of the three orders in Dauphiné, entered the Assembly and were also heavily applauded. They submitted their credentials, which were sent to the Committee on Verification.[4] The entry of a large number of clergy and two members of the nobility could only have fortified the resolve of the Assembly as the royal session approached. However small the noble representation may have been, for the first time the Assembly had members of all three orders within it and could plausibly claim to represent the nation better than either of the other two orders. Moreover, not only was the numeric strength of the Assembly overwhelming, but the clergy had fractured, with a majority siding with the Assembly. The unity of the nobility was also beginning to break, as the refusal of many to sign the letter to the king indicated.

On the day of the royal session, as had occurred at the opening of the Estates General, the clergy and the nobility entered through the main door whereas the commons, after being made to wait so long that it threatened to leave, had to enter through a side door. The clergy and nobility were seated to the right and left of the monarch but the commons had to stand along the sides and in the aisle of the chamber.[5]

In a display of force clearly intended to overawe, there was a heavy presence of armed guards inside and outside the meeting room. There were thousands of troops throughout Versailles through which deputies had to pass to attend the session.[6] When Louis entered, he was accompanied by the princes of the blood, dukes and peers, and the royal bodyguard. At the first meeting on May 5, one observer noted, the room had reverberated with cries of "Long live the king," but at the June 23 session the hall was completely silent.[7]

The king began with a short speech in which he professed his goodwill and pointed out the freedom that he had given to the Estates General. After he finished, the *Garde des sceaux* read a declaration nullifying all that had transpired, a reference to the assumption of the title of National Assembly, tacitly reasserting separation of the three orders. Louis resumed speaking and declared that in the future there would be no tax assessed or loan issued without the consent of the nation. To secure such consent there would be future meetings of the Estates General without fixed intervals. Its meetings would be held in closed session with voting by head on questions of taxation but with all other issues to be decided through vote by order. After sternly gazing at the Assembly, he decreed that tomorrow the three orders would meet separately and brusquely ordered deputies to separate immediately, after which he left.[8]

Most bishops, a number of *cures*, and all of the nobility left the room. The members of the Assembly, however, refused to leave, which led Louis to send his master of ceremonies to tell Bailly that the Assembly must depart. Its members not only refused, but some shouted that there was no force that could make them leave. Moreover, in direct defiance of the monarch, the Assembly decided that it would continue with all of the deliberations that it had taken to that point.[9]

The royal session represented Louis's first direct involvement since the opening of the Estates General seven weeks earlier, but, after seven weeks of growing trust and confidence among the commons, his intervention was too late. One deputy of the commons later wrote in his diary that Louis had sought to use the royal session as a kind of *lit de justice* in the heart of the Estates General.[10] The same deputy also wrote that one had to have been a witness to the royal session to feel the full force of public opinion.[11] He had awakened that morning filled with anxiety and sinister thoughts, but he was going to bed that night calm, believing that the session had worked against the Crown.[12]

The Assembly opened at 9:00 a.m. on June 24 but once again found itself under a heavy armed presence on all sides and anyone who was not a deputy was prohibited from entering. Deputies were forced to enter the *Salle des États* through a side door. The actions upset deputies, who felt themselves under siege, believed the freedom of the Assembly threatened and its right to control its own security compromised.[13]

In a surprising action from men steeped in a culture of hierarchy and obedience, the day after the royal session a majority of the clergy disobeyed the monarch and left their chamber to enter the Assembly for verification of credentials. One deputy noted that the entry of the clergy had occurred despite the heavy armed presence around the Assembly, that it marked the failure of the royal session and demonstrated that those in authority had made a major miscalculation.[14] As it prepared to adjourn for the day, the morale of the Assembly was buoyed further when Stanislas Marie Adélaïde, comte de Clermont-Tonnerre appeared to announce that a part of the nobility would enter the next day.

One hour after the opening of the meeting on June 25 many nobles joined the Assembly and took their places in the benches reserved for their order. Their entry followed a spirited meeting of the nobility, which is barely mentioned in its minutes, the day after the royal session. According to one noble deputy who entered that day, in the June 24 meeting of the nobility, Clermont-Tonnerre had offered a motion pointing out the risks of continued opposition to efforts to unite the orders. His motion had provoked murmurs of disapproval and led to an animated discussion about whether or not it would be placed in deliberation. Ultimately, it was not.[15] It was after the decision not to discuss his proposal that Clermont-Tonnerre made his way to the Assembly to announce that members of the nobility would be entering it the next day.

As they joined the Assembly, Clermont-Tonnerre, their spokesman, told deputies that the members of the nobility who were joining were yielding to the dictates of their conscience and fulfilling a duty. Those who had come were ready to work with the Assembly on the great task of regeneration, although each of them reserved the right to make known to the Assembly the degree of activity allowed. Bailly warmly welcomed them. The entry of dozens of members of the nobility buoyed the Assembly and signaled that the Crown effort had failed. The Assembly had approximately two-thirds of the deputies originally elected to the Estates General within it.

Resuming discussion from the previous day, the Assembly decided to send a delegation to the king to protest its meeting place being surrounded by armed guards, an action made even more pressing by the fact that the Crown had increased the military presence around it, bringing in additional troops from other garrisons, including hussars. The troops were also continuing to prohibit the public from attending its meetings. Deputies learned that a crowd outside was preparing to force its way into the meeting room and, in an indication of the manner in which the Assembly continued to aspire to the union of orders, asked the archbishop of Vienne, Clermont-Tonnerre, and Bailly to address those gathered outside to restore calm. They promised the crowd that the Assembly would work to provide accounts of its meetings and urged it to disperse to restore peace.[16]

The Assembly Moves Forward

From its chaotic beginnings it had taken weeks for deputies to formulate internal rules of order and forge itself into a working body. It had taken longer to form bonds of trust and confidence, but those ties had enabled them to withstand the intimidation tactics of the Crown. In the days after the royal session, however, the chemistry of the Assembly was altered by the addition of scores of new men, many of whom were unlike themselves, particularly with the arrival of noble deputies on June 25. The Assembly had to begin again to build trust, confidence and a sense of identity.

Whereas the men of the commons had been able to mingle freely with each other, the deputies of the clergy and nobility were seated in separate sections reserved for each order, making access inconvenient. Members of the different orders would interact or become acquainted only in the subcommittees into which the Assembly divided itself or in official committees.

To meld the three orders into a cohesive functioning institution was difficult under any circumstance, which was one reason that the Estates General had historically been an imperfect and sometimes failed body. The occasional nature of its convening, often with long intervals that hampered the formation of institutional memory, was an additional structural deficiency. The process of coming together was more challenging after weeks of bitter division.

An advantageous factor was that the clerical and noble deputies who entered wanted to take action. This aspect, however, was offset by the fact that those joining the Assembly may or may not have agreed on the need for a constitution, the task to which the Assembly had committed itself. The success of the Assembly would require it to surmount significant challenges, particularly with respect to the project of the constitution.

Clermont-Tonnerre spoke about the constitution and his imperative mandate. His mandate stipulated that he should codify a constitution and elucidate the principles on which it is based. It also specified vote by order and dictated that the delegation conform to that provision. At the same time, however, his mandate had a clause stating that the veto of one of the orders should not prevent the drafting of laws for the public good. This, Clermont-Tonnerre declared, was the reason that he and others had entered the Assembly. Even if the Assembly did not allow them to vote he asked that they be allowed to speak in debates.

Shortly after Clermont-Tonnerre spoke, a deputation of noble deputies who had remained in their chamber presented itself to the Assembly. The Assembly initially refused to admit them because their credentials were unknown and unverified but relented when their former noble colleagues in the Assembly received them.[17] François Alexandre Frédéric, duc de la Rochefoucauld-Liancourt read a resolution approved by the chamber of the nobility declaring that it adhered purely and simply to the propositions outlined by the monarch in the royal session on June 23. Bailly replied that the Assembly could regard the noble chamber only as absent deputies and that it continued to hope that the members of the noble chamber would join it.[18] Bailly's remarks angered the nobility, many of whom demanded that the chamber offer a response immediately, but it voted to defer a response until the next day.[19]

The two presentations revealed the deep divide in both tone and outlook between the noble deputies who entered the Assembly and those who remained in the noble chamber. Clermont-Tonnerre signaled an openness to the project of a constitution and initially asked only for the right to participate in debates. The nobility who had remained in their chamber offered a proposal that the Assembly would never accept because the most significant declarations by the monarch during the royal session had been his mandate that deliberations and voting be by order and his nullification of the National Assembly.

Indeed, the minutes of the noble chamber make clear that the motion had been adopted because it committed the nobility to nothing.[20] It was a ploy to counter the criticism of their erstwhile colleagues that they were doing nothing other than rejecting compromise. The offer by the nobility represented a reversion to the *status quo ante* and had no chance of being accepted by the Assembly, which had broken the stalemate and held the overwhelming majority of men originally elected to the Estates General.

Before the noble deputation had arrived, the Assembly had received a delegation of electors of Paris, which conveyed their allegiance to its decrees, particularly that in which it had adopted the name National Assembly. The electors promised to support its principles at all times and under any circumstances. A second Parisian delegation also expressed its unconditional support.[21] The support of Paris encouraged deputies, with one presciently observing that Parisian opinion could tip the balance and enable the Assembly to triumph if the Crown moved against it.[22]

The Crown Appears to Yield

Soon after the Assembly opened on June 27 additional deputies from the clergy and nobility joined it, taking a place with their respective orders.[23] It was becoming increasingly apparent that the royal session had failed and that the Assembly was in a dominant position with respect to the other two orders. With defections certain to continue, the Crown appeared to yield.

Louis summoned the presidents of the clergy and nobility to ask those remaining in their respective chambers to join the Assembly. Each president returned to his chamber with a letter written in Louis's own hand asking those deputies remaining to join with the other two orders. The king wrote that those who felt bound by their imperative mandates could enter but not participate until they received new powers from their constituents. To accede to his request would be to give him a sign of attachment.[24]

The letter was an effort to gain time to continue preparations to dissolve the Assembly by force, a task made all the more urgent by the increasing unreliability of some of the troops in Versailles, including the royal bodyguard.[25] Louis's letter never used the term National Assembly and he did not ask the clerical and noble deputies to accept vote by head. In a reversal of the royal session on June 23, at which the king had disallowed imperative mandates for the current and future meetings of the Estates General, he restored them and authorized deputies who believed they needed new powers from their constituents to seek them. At the same time, he ordered them to remain in the "Estates General" and to participate in deliberations, even if it was only in a consultative fashion.

Late in the afternoon of June 27 the recalcitrant clerical and noble deputies sullenly entered the Assembly. Each president delivered a terse one-sentence statement offering the reason for entering, both of which stressed obedience to the monarch and their lack of allegiance to the Assembly.[26]

Bailly welcomed them graciously, expressing happiness that the three orders were united and noting the lively joy that their entry had precipitated. To reassure them, Bailly declared that they would be recognized as noble deputies but not as deputies of the noble order.[27] Deputies of the commons were elated—Duquesnoy wrote in his diary that finally it was possible to hope and praised the nobility for its magnanimity. The deputy Charles Jean Marie Alquier wrote to the municipal officers of La Rochelle of the happiness in Versailles and Paris and asked them to disseminate the news throughout the province.[28] To celebrate the event, the Assembly adjourned until June 30.[29]

Although genuinely celebrated and felt, the festivities and joy were misplaced because many of the clerical and noble deputies were not acting in good faith.[30] The sense of defeat that the recalcitrant deputies felt when they entered the Assembly is evident in a June 29 letter written by Jean Joseph de Châteauneuf-Randon, marquis d'Apchier. He asserted that in the centuries to come no one would believe that a revolution of this kind had occurred in so little time and with so little resistance from the clergy and nobility. He also criticized the Crown. He said his correspondent knew of the resistance the nobility had put up to the verification of powers in common and denounced the exaggerated claims of the Third Estate. Apchier mentioned that they had entered the Assembly silently, with a sense of sorrow and regret, had stayed only briefly and declared that he would oppose any measure enacted through vote by head. He further stated that he was going to request the convocation of a new electoral assembly and seek permission to leave the Assembly when the nobility of Gévaudan elected a new deputy.[31]

To be sure, the recalcitrant deputies had obeyed the king and entered the Assembly, but they had also taken note of his authorization to refrain from participating in its deliberations until they received new powers. Reversing his earlier invalidation of imperative mandates would mire the Assembly in procedural issues for an extended period, suggesting that the Crown was deliberately seeking to undermine the body to give itself more time to bring in additional troops.

During the hiatus a majority of the recalcitrant nobility gathered at the residence of the duc de Luxembourg.[32] Whether the effort originated with the meeting cannot be determined, but several noble deputies began to prepare plans to impede the deliberations of the Assembly by asking to have their electoral assemblies reconvened to receive new instructions.[33] Many among them planned to leave the Assembly, return to their *bailliage*, ostensibly to receive new powers, but not return.[34]

Prior to the opening of the meeting on June 30 there was an indication of how difficult the melding of the three orders would be. There were three presidents in a single body and they met shortly before the Assembly opened.[35] Cardinal Dominique de la Rochefoucauld, who had entered the Assembly only after Louis's request, announced his intention to run for the presidency of the Assembly. His bid was decisively defeated, however, and Bailly remained president.[36] Bailly's presidency led one member of the commons to observe that it was a unique event in the annals of French history when a member of the commons presided over cardinals, princes of the blood and nobles.[37]

Also prior to the meeting of June 30 many members of the nobility discussed whether to return to the Assembly before deciding, out of obedience to the monarch, that they should.[38] They arrived two hours after the meeting had begun and Bailly invited them, along with the clergy who had entered on June 27, to submit their credentials. Although some did, others demurred. Scores of deputies, both clerical and noble, included with their credentials a declaration asserting that they could not deliberate in common until they received new powers from their constituents. Some went further and protested against the Assembly and its acts.[39] After listening for several hours to the reading of dozens of protestations, a deputy argued that those whose credentials were not yet verified could not be considered members and therefore did not have the right to make any protests.[40]

The protests, as well as their general comportment, made it apparent that the newly-entered deputies were not acting in good faith and that they could not be reliable partners.[41] The deputy Duquesnoy, who had been hopeful after the initial entry on June 27, was disgusted and viewed the consolidation of the Assembly as a Pyrrhic victory. The entry of the clergy and nobility had redoubled the bitterness and the commons had mishandled its victory by reciprocating it. He opined that there were men among all three orders who were inimical to the common good and who wanted to see the Assembly fail.[42]

The animus ran deep on both sides. In many instances the protestations of noble deputies expressed their contempt for the Assembly, with some feeling humiliated by their presence in it.[43] One asserted that his *cahier* prohibited him from approving of any innovation and declared that he would await new instructions from his constituents, but until they arrived he would protest any proceedings of the three orders together.[44] Another contended that to enter the Assembly would betray his oath and do away with the dignity of being a deputy of the nobility.[45]

One deputy of the commons doubted that many of the recalcitrant deputies who were going to write to ask for new powers would present the request to their constituents in a manner that would lend itself to unlimited powers being given.[46] For many deputies of the commons, who believed that the achievement of the formation of the Assembly had come at great personal risk to themselves, the contempt exhibited was an intolerable affront.[47]

The clerical and noble deputies who entered on June 27 were aggrieved that a body formed only ten days earlier to break the stalemate was implicitly claiming that it superseded the Estates General, which had hundreds of years of history. They were angry at entering an entity that not only had never previously existed but had also established procedures that they believed were without precedent.[48] One noble deputy wrote that they had been elected to an Estates General and felt adrift in a National Assembly.[49]

The purpose of the Assembly—to establish a constitution on firm foundations—also generated anger. It was a direct affront to the professed belief among the majority of the nobility that distinction of orders was rooted in the constitution.[50] The commons attempted to accommodate their view by preserving separation of orders in the seating arrangements of the Assembly but it would not allow it for voting or deliberations. The newly-entered clerical and noble deputies were in a body they despised and that was committed to a goal that they regarded as illegitimate.

On July 1 the Assembly heard a report from its Rules Committee proposing that the Assembly divide itself into thirty subcommittees of forty members each. Members would be assigned by following a list of *bailliages* in alphabetical order without distinction among deputies. The subcommittees would consider issues presented to them, which subsequently might be brought to the Assembly to be discussed and decided, and membership would be reconstituted every month.[51]

The next morning the assignments of members to the subcommittees were announced but again there were developments that underscored the challenges facing the Assembly in achieving an identity. During the meeting cardinal de la Rochefoucauld read a statement claiming reservations on behalf of the minority of the clergy, including the right to deliberate separately as an order on certain issues. The declaration provoked an uproar in the Assembly and led the archbishop of Vienne to say that the reservation made by the minority of the clergy, which had met before they entered the Assembly that morning, had been taken while the majority of the clergy was meeting in the Assembly.[52] Another deputy declared that the Assembly could neither listen to nor accept any protest that contravened its rights.[53]

The reservation threatened to undermine the formation of the Assembly and provoke a new schism.[54] Its founding statement on June 17 had stated that all verified representatives must be in the Assembly and the matters over which the minority of the clergy might see fit to assert its claim were not specified. The Assembly disallowed the reservation by declaring that it viewed the statement by Rochefoucauld as a specific, individual view and deferred any resolution until after the verification of powers.[55]

The attempt by the clergy to reserve the right to deliberate separately apparently influenced the nobility. Without advising the Assembly, the majority of the nobility, claiming that it had not renounced the right of assembling itself, met informally that evening to discuss the issue of imperative mandates for those deputies who held them.[56] Some of the protests submitted by noble deputies specifically linked the imperative mandate of vote by order to the protection of privilege.[57] The reemergence of separate deliberations forced the Assembly to confront imperative mandates.

Having learned that the majority of the nobility was planning to meet late in the afternoon, toward the end of the meeting on July 3 the Assembly heard a proposal to affirm that all mandates held by deputies that prevented them from voting in the Assembly be declared invalid, with proponents arguing that the lack of participation by deputies could not be permitted to deter the work of the Assembly. The proposal led to an uproar and the advancement of several other resolutions. The new president of the Assembly, the archbishop of Vienne, referred the motions to the subcommittees, which were to meet that evening, for consideration.[58]

During the evening of July 3, however, the majority of the nobility did not attend the meeting of their assigned subcommittee but instead met as an order in their former chamber.[59] The nobility used the meeting to appeal to the king to revert to his stance at the June 23 session by protesting against the "reunion and confusion" of orders in a single meeting room, against the name National Assembly and against vote by head. The nobility claimed that it was seeking to save the essential principles of the French monarchy as well as the rights of their order and declared that they would submit a statement of principles to the monarch. It named a committee to begin drafting it.[60]

The hostility of the recalcitrant deputies toward the Assembly became even more apparent the next day. The Assembly had been discussing whether to give Saint-Domingue a delegation but when the vote to decide the issue began—the first voice vote of the full Assembly—a large number of deputies, both clerical and noble, refused to participate. Some left the meeting room just before their name was called whereas others remained silent when called.[61] Their outlook is captured in a letter of Joseph-Louis Robert de Lignerac, duc de Caylus, who wrote to his constituents on July 4 that his presence in the Assembly was "absolutely useless."[62] Another noble deputy likewise characterized the presence of many noble deputies as useless and noted that a substantial number had left and returned to their *bailliages.* On July 7 he noted that not one member of the majority of the nobility had spoken in the Assembly.[63] Many left the Assembly altogether.[64]

The Divergence between Noble Deputies and Their Constituents

In their adhesion to deliberation and vote by order and hostility toward the Assembly, the noble deputies were unaware of a sharp evolution in outlook that had occurred among their constituents. When they had been elected as deputies and sent to Versailles with imperative mandates, the question of deliberations and vote by order had been paramount. In Versailles the noble deputies isolated themselves, closing their chamber to the public and sealing themselves off from the other two orders, which meant that they were in contact primarily with others who thought as they did.

They were oblivious to the perception of disaster that the stalemate at the Estates General had created in the provinces. In many *bailliages* a desire to address problems had superseded earlier concerns with forms of deliberations and voting. Cloistered in Versailles, however, many noble deputies failed to detect the change in opinion.

The encounter of a noble Norman deputy with his constituents revealed to him the shift in sentiment among the nobility produced by the deadlock. Marie François Henri de Franquetot, duc de Coigny, a member of the nobility who had entered only on June 27, left Versailles and returned to Caen to reconvene his electoral assembly. Unrest in the province led the nobility not to gather, but during his stay in Caen he met with a large number of his constituents. He learned that they had every intention of annulling the imperative mandate of their deputies and to direct them specifically to do all that they could to foster goodwill and to cooperate in bringing about the well-being of the nation. Coigny pledged to the Assembly that the delegation would participate fully in its deliberations and recognize and accept all that had been enacted during their absence. He added, as a personal reflection, that, with the provinces in turmoil, he believed the best way to proceed was for the Assembly to work on the constitution, which was the only means to restore calm in the kingdom.[65]

Another example of the divergence in perspective between noble deputies in Versailles and their constituents in the provinces is found in the duc de Caylus, who represented the nobility of the *bailliage* of St. Flour in Auvergne. He had written to his constituents on June 28 to request the convening of the nobility to grant him new powers to replace the imperative mandate with which he had originally been sent to the Estates General. In his letter he told his constituents that he was prepared to resign because his views were utterly opposed to the new order of things that was coming into existence.[66]

The nobility of St. Flour met in late July and conveyed to Caylus the joy that they had felt at receiving the news of the union of orders that had occurred on June 27. The assembly rebuked him by pointedly noting that it was only by general agreement among the different orders that made up the Estates General that it could function in a useful, satisfying, and advantageous manner for the nation, the task with which he had been charged.

The electors annulled his imperative mandate and the limited powers with which he had restricted himself and voted unanimously to give Caylus all necessary and sufficient powers to work with the assembled nation toward the well-being of the common fatherland. In order to leave no doubt about the purity of their intentions and the disinterested sentiments motivating them, the nobility decided that its resolution would be printed and include the name of every member in attendance. Furthermore, the cover letter that accompanied the new powers had a sentence reiterating the charge to work for the common good.[67] Caylus would not have seen the statement and conferral of new powers until early August. Nevertheless, the tone and content of the new instructions demonstrates the gulf that existed between the majority of the nobility in the Assembly and their constituents in the provinces, especially with respect to the project of a constitution.

One of the central premises of noble deputies at the Estates General for their refusal to compromise was the assertion that the separation of orders was a fundamental constitutional principle of the French monarchy, but its purported constitutional status was never fully established. Although the nobility strongly preferred vote by order, a number of noble deputies arrived with instructions authorizing them under certain circumstances to deviate from vote by order. Perhaps intimidated by the vehemence of the arguments for its constitutional status, especially by Duval d'Eprémesnil, few, if any, exercised the latitude they had been given.

Rather, the assertion of deliberation and vote by order became a device to unify the nobility in its negotiations with the commons and to seek to maintain influence in the Estates General. The stance increasingly hardened over time—after the king asked them to join the other two orders, some noble deputies dramatically professed a preference to die for the sake of preserving the separation of orders.[68] It was indicative of how isolation in their chamber at Versailles had trapped them in a self-reinforcing rigidity of thought.

The perspective in the provinces was entirely different. The alacrity with which the nobility in the provinces altered mandates demonstrated that they did not ascribe constitutional status or even priority to the separation of orders.[69] The expressions of happiness at seeing the consolidation of the Assembly in late June supports the view that the nobility outside of the Estates General was committed to working in common toward the establishment of the constitution upon sound principles.

The nobility of Bar-sur-Seine, for example, annulled its earlier imperative mandate for vote by order, replacing it with an injunction to its deputy to use his judgment to contribute to the Assembly and to advance the strength and well-being of the state.[70] Similarly, the nobility of Condom, which had previously been adamant on vote by order, annulled its imperative mandate and provided its deputy with unlimited powers as circumstances demanded and enjoined him to regard the interests of the nobility as inseparable from those of the nation.[71] Likewise, an assembly of the nobility of the province of Maine convened in Le Mans on July 20. When they had elected deputies in March, its members had expressed a strong preference for vote by order, but in July the eighty-four members in attendance voted unanimously to give their deputies unlimited powers, with no reservations or limitations, and ordered them to enter the Assembly and work for the common good.[72]

The stalemate at the Estates General led much of the provincial nobility to reject the importance they had formerly attached to vote by order. Moreover, whereas noble deputies at the Estates General emphasized constitutional principles of the French monarchy, their constituents in the provinces increasingly professed their dedication to the more impersonal concept of state, nation, or fatherland. Provincial nobles were prepared to accept new constitutional principles that reflected greater concern with the French state rather than tenets rooted in the society of orders and premised on privilege associated with the French monarchy.[73] Their loyalty to the Crown was no less than it had been but their focus had changed.

The Assembly represented inchoate new values and sought to establish a constitution that a significant portion of the provincial nobility was prepared to welcome.

Caylus was not the only noble deputy to be upbraided by his constituents. Maximilien-Auguste Bleickard d'Helmstatt, comte de Helmstatt and Louis Gabriel, comte de Gomer, who represented the *bailliage* of Sarreguemines, received a similar reprimand. When Helmstatt wrote to request new powers from his constituents, he informed them that because of his mandate and his personal opposition to the Assembly, he intended to use the hiatus until the arrival of his new powers to leave Versailles to take the baths to restore his health.[74] Gomer left Versailles and returned to his residence in Dieuze.[75]

When the nobility of Sarreguemines met, its members noted the serious troubles afflicting their province. They stated that the two deputies had never held imperative mandates and unanimously declared their dismay that their deputies had used a pretext of illness to leave Versailles. The members of the assembly saw themselves forced to implore the deputies of the order of the nobility at the National Assembly—the term they used even after Helmstatt's statement of personal opposition to it—to return to Versailles, join the Assembly, and carry out the duties with which they had been entrusted. The view of the nobility of Sarreguemines, they declared, was that in naming its deputies it had not conferred an honorific title upon them. It expected them to work for the well-being of the state and of the part of the province that they represented.[76]

The overwhelming majority of noble deputies to the Estates General came from a military background—four out of five, according to one calculation, with most of them having served in the infantry or cavalry. In many cases their early entry into military service, often during adolescence, had stunted their education. Most had only a secondary education and not infrequently it was barely adequate. They felt themselves culturally and educationally apart from the Third Estate.[77] Furthermore, only forty-five of approximately three hundred noble deputies had taken part in provincial assemblies before their arrival at the Estates General.[78]

The narrow strata from which the noble deputies were drawn was not representative of their counterparts in *bailliages*. Many of them would have served in provincial assemblies, in which a doubling of the Third Estate and vote by head had been the protocol. The involvement of nobles in the assemblies increased the awareness of a number of them to administrative problems and led to the development of a greater civic-mindedness and a concomitant weakening of loyalty to traditional hierarchy. The assemblies offered a new logic and institutionalized manner of political action that led to a focus on the needs of provincial inhabitants. The emergence of a reform constituency led to the change of perspective brought about by participation in the assemblies.[79]

To many nobles in the *bailliages*, a stalemate of such duration over a questionable constitutional principle, a principle that had not been observed in the structure of the provincial assemblies, was unacceptable. They were committed to resolving the crisis that had led to the convening of the Estates General and viewed bringing the body to a standstill as folly. To the nobles in the *bailliages*, the task of deputies was to improve the functioning of the state and pursue its well-being.

By early July, with one deputy expressing cautious optimism that the threat of intrigue and internal subversion by noble and clerical deputies was beginning to recede, the Assembly sought to move ahead.[80] On July 6 several deputies argued that it was necessary to begin work as quickly as possible on the constitution.[81] Subsistence issues were of importance but they asserted that the responsibility for them fell within the administrative realm. Constituents had not sent deputies to Versailles to procure subsistence but to assure their freedom and to place the constitution of the state on solid foundations. To this end, they contended, the Assembly should exclude all motions that did not advance the goal of the constitution after all of the time that had been spent on the interminable difficulties of verification of powers, imperative mandates, and other matters. They maintained that the Assembly should name a committee that would be given the responsibility of creating a work plan to begin the task. The Assembly approved the proposal and each of the Assembly's subcommittees named one member to establish the committee.[82]

Addressing Imperative Mandates

On July 7, aware of the threat that the issue posed to its functioning, the Assembly took up the question of imperative mandates. After they had joined the Assembly, many of the recalcitrant deputies had asserted that they were rigidly bound by an imperative mandate to carry out the wishes of their electors as expressed in the *cahiers*, which often stipulated vote by order. Until they received new powers to give them greater latitude, they asserted, they should abstain from all deliberations.[83]

Many deputies awaiting new mandates would not bring the Assembly to a halt, but it had the potential to weaken its status. The abstention of scores of deputies for a prolonged period would undermine the union of orders and possibly call into question the standing of the Assembly. The Crown and nobility had shown a readiness to use the issue to their own ends. Louis had told the recalcitrant deputies that they could enter but did not have to participate until they received new mandates and they had used that authorization to inundate the Assembly with protests until the Assembly put an end to it. The deputy Jean-François Gaultier de Biauzat believed that the Crown was deliberately using the issue of imperative mandates to impede the Assembly.[84]

The conduct of noble deputies from Bourg-en-Bresse, Claude Jean Baptiste Garron de la Bevière and Joseph Folch de Cardon de Sandrans, illustrates both the schism and the manipulation of imperative mandates to undermine the Assembly. In late March 1789, in its electoral assembly the nobility of Bourg-en-Bresse proclaimed its commitment to strengthening the union, fellowship, and concord essential to bring about the well-being of all three orders and the happiness of all.[85] The next day, convinced, it stated, of the importance that the three orders of the province have only a single view on matters of importance to the province, the nobility agreed to draft *cahiers* in common with the clergy and the Third Estate.[86] The nobility of Bresse gave full powers to its deputies to demand a "charter" laying out fundamental and inviolable principles. It recommended that its deputies act in concert with the other two orders to achieve the union of orders, of which, they claimed, Bresse was currently a model. They were given the right to act on the basis of their honor and conscience.[87]

In Versailles, however, both deputies remained in the chamber of the nobility and claimed that they carried imperative mandates, which they did not. Garron de la Bevière was hostile to the Third Estate, characterizing one proposal made during the conciliatory conferences as not conciliatory but an act of war.[88] Both men were among the recalcitrant deputies who entered only on June 27. They took advantage of the monarch's authorization to seek new powers from their constituents. They suggested that they be given no more powers than they currently held, which led nineteen noblemen to send a letter to the deputies telling them that their mandates on vote by order were not imperative and apparently telling them to improve their conduct. The chamber of the nobility at Versailles, however, deemed their mandate the most imperative of all.[89]

Garron de la Bevière claimed on July 2, after three days, that deliberations in common were so onerous that he was not sure he could sustain it. He added that he could not and did not want to cooperate with what was being done and eagerly awaited his new powers.[90] Both deputies asked to be recalled and replaced because of the state of their health, which required their resignation. The nobility of Bourg-en-Bresse refused to accept their resignations and asked them to remain in their duties. With both deputies apparently unwilling to accept the letter stating that their original mandate was not imperative, the nobility of Bourg-en-Bresse reconvened in an assembly on July 14. Declaring that its deputies believed themselves hindered by their original mandate, the nobility gave them full and complete powers to work for the happiness of the nation and of each and every subject of the king. After the letter arrived from the deputies asking that they be recalled because of the poor state of their health, the assembly stated that it had no authority to receive the resignations and undertake election of new deputies and asked them to continue their duties.[91] The nobility of Bourg-en-Bresse regarded the reconvening in July as unnecessary and the exchange demonstrates that the chamber of the nobility sought to use imperative mandates to impede the Assembly.

It was the anticipation of such use of imperative mandates that led the Assembly to move against them directly. On July 3 Charles Maurice de Talleyrand-Périgord put forward a motion that annulled any imperative mandate instruction that prohibited deputies from voting in the Assembly or ordering them to withdraw from it.[92] Reports on subsistence and other matters delayed further consideration until July 7 and the discussion that day was an extended one because many deputies wanted to speak. Defenders of imperative mandates sought to use them to hinder the Assembly by asserting that the Assembly should not undertake any important deliberations until the deputies with imperative mandates received new powers, which would have stalled progress on the constitution.

One deputy privately noted that the need to work quickly was more apparent because of the presence of armed troops around Versailles that posed a threat to the Assembly. He wrote that the sense of defiance among deputies was extreme and that anything that tended to stretch out the proceedings of the Assembly was viewed as suspect. He believed that imperative mandates had been invalidated by the formation of the Assembly and that the issue should not be debated. A discussion offered the opportunity to give holders of imperative mandates all the time they needed to reconvene local assemblies, which would stall work on the constitution. He foresaw completing important preliminary tasks by the end of July, which was the deadline that that the holders of imperative mandates were requesting to receive their new powers.

He observed that it would be inconvenient to take up what he called a "*code national*" before all interested parties could take part. Otherwise, it would give rise to many plausible pretexts for complaints in the future. At the same time, it was beneficial for those who held imperative mandates for vote by order to see the unyielding attachment to the principles of the Assembly by its members and to realize that prolonged resistance would result only in being deprived of the right to be represented.[93]

The debate continued into the next day, July 8, when the Assembly settled the issue. After several motions failed to pass, the Assembly voted by a wide margin, almost unanimously in the words of one member, 731–28, far less than the number of deputies in the body, that there was nothing to deliberate. The question had effectively been decided earlier, especially by the decrees of June 10 and June 17.[94]

The near unanimity of the vote resulted in part from a misunderstanding of the meaning of "nothing to deliberate." For the commons, a majority of the clergy and a portion of the minority of the nobility, the initial decree of the National Assembly on June 17 had resolved the issue of vote by order and it was pointless to reconsider it. The majority of the nobility, most of whom were absent, and the minority of the clergy, many of whom were also absent, believed that their imperative mandates remained valid and that "nothing to deliberate" meant that their validity continued, but they were quickly disillusioned when the meaning of the vote became clear.[95]

That evening, in response to an invitation from its president, the nobility met again as an order, much to the dismay of the commons.[96] It devoted the meeting to a consideration of "the current situation of the different orders that comprise the Estates General," almost certainly a reaction to the vote that day, with the use of the term "Estates General" seeking to de-legitimize the Assembly. Because many members were back in their respective *baillages*, the nobility decided to reconvene the next evening to discuss the matter further.[97]

As the debate on imperative mandates was underway, the Assembly heard a message from Saint-Jean-de-Losne announcing a decision to yield its privileges. At its general meeting in January, the citizens of the town had restated their claim that they were exempt from provincial and common charges and had reserved the right to determine the future fate of the town's privileges.[98] Although the Crown had denied the town's claim with respect to provincial assessments, its exemptions from royal taxation granted by Louis XIII remained valid and recognized but the town, in the summer of 1789, chose to give them up.

The deputy Charles Hernoux, a native of Saint-Jean-de-Losne, told his colleagues that the town was one of the first to give the Assembly proof of patriotism and of disinterestedness that should inspire all French. For six centuries, he stated, Saint-Jean-de-Losne had enjoyed immunities and prerogatives worthy of the most elevated groups. Its privileges were rooted in its courage and loyalty and had been reconfirmed at the beginning of each reign. At a moment in which the fatherland was in a deplorable situation and in need, however, the town now valued its privileges only for the satisfaction it provided to relinquish them. Hernoux told the Assembly that the town had ordered him—not merely authorized him—to make the declaration that Saint-Jean-de-Losne was renouncing all of its fiscal privileges.

He read the town's announcement, which stated that the relinquishment would take effect as soon as the Assembly had determined the bases of the constitution through a stipulation of the rights of the nation and those of the monarch and when it had established a more equitable tax system. The Assembly enthusiastically and universally applauded the announcement, which was included in the minutes of the meeting.[99]

The reading occurred as the Assembly was debating imperative mandates. The renunciation of privileges by Saint-Jean-de-Losne caught the attention of the Assembly and almost certainly figured in the relinquishment of seigneurial dues a few weeks later.[100]

The Crown Threat to the Assembly

After settling the question of imperative mandates, the Assembly sought to address the perceived threat posed by the presence of armed troops around Paris and Versailles.[101] It sent a deputation to the king asking him to withdraw the troops encamped in the area. Louis met with the delegation that evening and assured its members of his good intentions, declaring that the troops posed no threat to the "Estates General." Their presence, he told the deputies, had no other goal than to restore calm and they would remain only as long as necessary to guarantee public safety.[102]

The Assembly found the monarch's response less than reassuring. His use of the term Estates General would not have escaped notice because deputies were attentive to the use of the term National Assembly—the deputy Gaultier de Biauzat wrote that the difference between the two was not a question of words but of the grand design.[103] Louis had said that he was receptive to being presented with a written address on the matter so that he could make an open public response. Honoré Gabriel Riqueti, comte de Mirabeau prepared an address and the Assembly named a deputation of twenty-four deputies to present it to the monarch.[104]

Évelyne Lever and Munro Price contended that the goal of the Crown was to persuade the Assembly to accept some form of Louis's declaration of June 23.[105] It was an unattainable objective because necessary components would almost certainly have been deliberations and vote by order as well as a reversion to the Estates General. In this context, the monarch's use of the term was significant.

Underscoring the concerns of Gaultier de Biauzat, during a reading of Mirabeau's speech for approval by the Assembly, a reactionary noble deputy asked why the term National Assembly was being used when the monarch had not approved the appellation.[106] His implication was that the Assembly was an unauthorized body, which could potentially justify its dissolution. Many members of the majority of the nobility were hostile to the address and, when the nobility met as an order that evening, it considered a proposal to send a message to Louis stating that the address by the Assembly requesting that he withdraw troops had been made without the participation of the nobility. It was effectively a tacit approval to dissolve the Assembly but the nobility declined to assent to the message.[107]

Despite their disquiet about the troops surrounding them, deputies sought to move ahead with their primary task and were encouraged on July 9 by the reading of a letter from the nobility of Agen.[108] The letter modified the limited powers originally given to its deputies and praised the "spirit of peace of the members of the National Assembly." It strongly endorsed the project of a constitution and declared that the constitution should be determined in advance of any subsidies or loans guaranteed to the Crown. Calling the constitution the sole guarantee of public happiness, the Agennois nobles ordered their deputies to enter the Assembly and work for its establishment.[109]

The letter was one of the first indications the Assembly had of the schism that was opening between much of the provincial nobility and their deputies in Versailles and heartened deputies.[110] One deputy wrote in his newspaper that the spirit of conciliation and justice that prevailed in the provinces would be viewed with interest. He also expressed admiration for the speed with which the nobility of Agen had revoked the original limited powers of its deputies.[111]

After approving the address to the monarch, the Assembly heard the first report of the committee formed to determine the preliminary questions associated with the constitution.[112] Revealing once again the uncertainty surrounding the project, its spokesman, Mounier, began by stating that the committee had to make a precise determination of the word "constitution," illustrating how novel the idea was, and, once that had been done, to consider it in a manner that could be appropriate for a large kingdom and grasped by constituents.[113] Mounier told deputies that the committee thought that a constitution was a fixed and established order in the manner of governing. A constitution, he declared, is a precise and constant form of government—the expression of the rights and obligations of the different components that comprised it.[114]

Although France had valued political norms, it did not have a complete and consistent system of government. It also did not have a constitution because powers were confused—judicial power was not separate from legislative power and powers were in contradiction, which resulted in a constant struggle. Mounier outlined ten principles that the committee believed should be used for drafting the constitution. It recommended the formulation of a declaration of the rights of man, from which the rules would follow. The committee recommended that all work related to the constitution be discussed in the subcommittees and that there be only three meetings per week of the Assembly to consider and determine the projects prepared by the subcommittees.[115]

Although some deputies expressed reservations about the proposed declaration of rights, the report was well received.[116] One deputy was surprised that the committee had been able to prepare the report so quickly and praised it as "clear, methodical and full of good plans." Another judged it to be an excellent outline for a constitution.[117]

Gilbert du Motier, marquis de Lafayette submitted a proposed declaration of rights on July 11 but the idea proved problematic to deputies. Trophime-Gérard, comte de Lally-Tollendal defended the recommendation by the committee to put forward a declaration of rights only with the constitution. Despite the defense by Lally-Tollendal, one deputy wrote that some of his colleagues disliked the idea, saying that their constituents had not sent them to Versailles to produce a philosophical treatise. Those who favored a declaration of rights thought that it should be short and offer only the most incontestable principles and ridiculed Lafayette's project.[118]

That evening Louis dismissed Necker and other ministers perceived to be sympathetic to the Assembly and ordered Necker to leave the country. His action appeared to presage the dissolution of the Assembly and precipitated a popular uprising in Paris. There were many motives underlying the insurrection in Paris, especially the subsistence crisis, and the sense among Parisians that Necker was indispensable to its resolution. Another significant factor, however, was that the Assembly had captured the loyalty of much of the populace, which some deputies had sensed.[119] The insurrection saved the Assembly from dissolution.

It is reflective of the expectation that the Assembly would be forcibly dissolved that the wife of the deputy François Ménard de la Groye had expressed her fears to her husband in a letter. In his reply, a private letter not intended for public consumption, Ménard told his wife that her concerns were groundless because he did not believe it possible to dissolve the body or to reduce it to inaction. The nation, he wrote, was fully aware of its rights, much energy had been expended, and the needs of the state were too pressing.[120]

The uprising in Paris led deputies to conclude that it was imperative to hasten the completion of the constitution.[121] They debated whether it should have each of the thirty subcommittees submit a draft of a constitution to be given to a committee that would condense them into a single project or whether to form a committee that would act as a steering committee. It would produce projects that would be submitted to the subcommittees for consideration before being given final approval by the entire Assembly.

The Assembly voted overwhelmingly to form a committee, which would be comprised of eight members.[122] One deputy complained that the subcommittees were organized in a manner that simply fostered conversations and were nearly useless to press forward with matters.[123] In accordance with the distinction of orders under which the Assembly continued to operate, the committee was to have two members from the clergy, two from the nobility and four from the commons. Those elected were Jean Baptiste Marie Champion de Cicé, the archbishop of Bordeaux and Talleyrand, the bishop of Autun, for the clergy, the comte de Clermont-Tonnerre and the comte de Lally-Tollendal for the nobility and Mounier, Le Chapelier, Sieyès, and Nicolas Bergasse for the commons.[124]

On July 15 a chastened monarch entered the Assembly without pomp, without bodyguards and accompanied only by his two brothers. Speaking at times in a low and breaking voice he asked the Assembly to aid him in restoring order and calm in Paris. He also announced that he had ordered the troops around Paris and Versailles to withdraw. In a sign of his awareness of both his weakness and the lack of trust in him, Louis asked the Assembly to make his intentions known in Paris.

The president of the Assembly, the archbishop of Vienne, thanked the monarch for the withdrawal of troops, adding, in an indication of lingering mistrust, that he assumed they were returning to their original garrison rather than simply being posted at a greater distance from Paris and Versailles. He also asked Louis to restore immediately unfettered communication between Paris and Versailles, which had been blocked.[125] Furthermore, he requested that the king assure deputies that there would be open communication between the Assembly and himself at all times.

The president also asked the monarch to approve the sending of a delegation by the Assembly to Paris in the hope of restoring order. Finally, attributing the insurrection to the dismissal of Necker, the archbishop requested that he reconsider the changes in his council. Louis replied that with respect to the delegation the Assembly knew his intentions and wishes and that he would never refuse to communicate with the Assembly any time it believed it necessary. He then left, with many deputies accompanying him back to the *château*.[126]

It was a humiliating encounter for Louis to be questioned on troop movements and members of his council, both of which had traditionally been unchallenged royal prerogatives. He also had had to ask for the assistance of the Assembly in calming Paris. His visit to the Assembly marked the end of monarchy-centered government. The American ambassador, Thomas Jefferson, described the visit in letters to John Mason and Thomas Paine as the monarch surrendering at discretion.[127]

A deputation prepared to leave for Paris to publicize Louis's announcements.[128] When they entered Paris, the deputies encountered the discordant sight of tens of thousands of men armed as if they were in a civil war but behaving with all of the gaiety of a holiday.[129] Protected by the newly formed municipal militia, the delegation made its way to the *Hôtel de Ville*. Lafayette informed the crowd of Louis's announcement of the withdrawal of troops and read it the speech he had given to the Assembly. Other deputies also spoke to the multitude and calm was restored.[130]

As humbling as his visit to the Assembly had been, Louis had to endure an even more humiliating experience two days later when he visited Paris with a delegation of fifty deputies to give his approval to the new municipal government established during the insurrection. A British observer described the abject state of the monarch. He noted that Louis looked deeply depressed and that he appeared to be more of a captive than a "patriot king." He also passed along a letter from Paris that characterized the monarch as being "led in triumph like a tame bear by deputies and the city militia."[131]

It was not only the monarch who capitulated. On July 16 a noble deputy notified the Assembly that noble members who had absented themselves from the body while awaiting new mandates from their constituents would return before receiving their new powers to work for the common good. They would fully participate despite their imperative mandates and vote by head.[132]

The majority of the nobility, after meeting that morning prior to the opening of the Assembly, announced that it would end its separate deliberations and join its aspirations to those of the entire Assembly.[133] Deputies who had previously declared themselves constrained by imperative mandates and who had refused to participate in the Assembly now did, even without receiving new powers from their constituents.[134] The announcement was of little consequence because the number of those attending the separate sessions had steadily dwindled, from 158 on July 3, the first meeting, to approximately 88 on July 9.[135] Cardinal de la Rochefoucauld made a similar declaration on behalf of the minority of the clergy.[136] The developments led Thomas Jefferson, in a July 17 letter to Thomas Paine, to opine that the Assembly had "a carte blanche."[137]

July 1789 marked the end of the Bourbon style of monarchy-centered government in France. The format and contours of the constitution the Assembly had pledged to create were unclear, but the uprising in Paris, which was replicated in municipalities across France, meant that the process would not be a purely abstract legal procedure. The Assembly would engage the attention of much of France, which had mobilized to defend it. Deputies were aware of the power and responsibility suddenly thrust upon them—a clerical deputy wrote to his nephew in late July that the nation seemed to have placed not only confidence but the assurance of rescue in the National Assembly.[138]

A letter from Châlons-sur-Marne is illustrative of the degree to which the kingdom looked to the Assembly. It praised the eminent position deputies had given to the constitution because the troubles in France were pressing and required prompt and powerful solutions. The town expressed confidence that the nation would benefit from the wisdom and strength of purpose of deputies. It declared its full trust in the Assembly to achieve its goals and stated that Châlons-sur-Marne gained its assuredness from the talents and virtues of men in the body, which they expected to reinforce the good intentions of the monarch.[139] The Assembly received many such messages.

The balance of government in July 1789 was uncertain, but the Bourbon style of government was over. The future political structure of the kingdom would be determined by the National Assembly under the aegis of its Committee on the Constitution, but the undertaking would soon take an unexpected turn.

The Forgotten Constitution: The Origins, Realization, and Legacy of the French Constitution of 1791.
Michael P. Fitzsimmons, Oxford University Press. © Oxford University Press 2025.
DOI: 10.1093/9780197793978.003.0008

8

The Expansion of the Constitution

The insurrection in Paris gave the Assembly a position of dominance over the Crown but it was strengthened even further in following days and weeks because of popular uprisings in provincial cities across France.[1] In many instances the new municipal officials declared that they would accept orders only from the Assembly. The king had lost control of the kingdom.[2]

The situation distressed deputies because their objective had been to restore political stability. In his diary, Duquesnoy lamented the collapse of authority in France and wrote that the Assembly should act quickly to restore the king to his throne, a description that underscored Louis's weakness. The most overriding task and only goal for the Assembly, he claimed, should be the constitution.[3]

Although the rising in Paris had saved and strengthened it, the Assembly remained fractured. When the majority of the nobility entered the Assembly after agreeing to terminate its separate meetings, it met with a skeptical and even hostile reception.[4] When a member of the majority of the nobility rose, apparently with the intent of speaking, the uproar it generated led him to remain silent and sit down.[5]

Reports of anarchy and violence gave the constitutional project added urgency. It was a daunting task because it was virtually unprecedented. The only written national constitution in existence was that of the United States, a new country of a few million people on the fringes of the Atlantic world. Moreover, its constitution had been in force for only four and a half months and was a second effort after the failure of the Articles of Confederation. With the American constitution the only extant example, the Committee on the Constitution reached out to Jefferson, asking him to meet with it to offer any insights he might have.[6]

Deputies were eager for the Committee on the Constitution to present its report. The Assembly viewed the constitution as a means to consolidate the debt and resolve the fiscal crisis that had been a major catalyst in the calling of the Estates General.[7] At the end of its meeting on July 21, only a week after the formation of the committee, the Assembly exhorted the committee to conclude as quickly as possible the responsibility with which it had been charged.[8]

By late July reports of rural violence, the early stages of what would become known as "the Great Fear," were beginning to reach the Assembly. Deputies found the reports of unrest increasingly disconcerting.[9] Moreover, there had been renewed unrest in Paris where Joseph-François Foullon de Doué was beheaded by an angry crowd at the *Place de Grève.* Soon afterward his son-in-law, Louis Bénigne François Bertier de Sauvigny, the intendant of Paris, was lynched at the *Hôtel de Ville.*

With the resurgence of violence in Paris, as well as reports coming in from the provinces, the Assembly decided to push the committee into action.[10] On Friday, July 24, during its evening session, it ordered the committee to present an account of its work on the following Monday, July 27. It also told the committee to put its report in a form that would allow at least some parts of it to be sent immediately to the subcommittees for discussion.[11]

After the vote by the Assembly, the committee, fewer than two weeks after its formation, put forward a report on the constitution.[12] The committee offered its report in separate presentations. Champion de Cicé, the archbishop of Bordeaux, began by noting that only a constitution could secure the happiness of future generations. He told his colleagues that the committee believed its obligation was to find the desires of the populace through the *cahiers* that it had been able to consult, which would be the object of the second report by Clermont-Tonnerre. He acknowledged the desire of the Assembly to have a declaration of rights precede the constitution. The committee, he said, was working on the declaration but there was a difference of opinion within it over expression and form.

Champion de Cicé informed deputies that along with the two competing projects for a declaration of rights the committee was presenting the first chapter of the constitution on the principles of French government. The committee believed that there were two critical issues to be addressed concerning legislative power. The first was whether what he called the "*Corps législatif*" would be periodic or permanent. Champion de Cicé acknowledged a divergence between the *cahiers* and the committee. Whereas the *cahiers* indicated a preference for periodic meetings, the committee unanimously believed the legislature should be permanent.

The second question was whether the *Corps législatif* should be comprised of a single chamber or multiple chambers. Champion de Cicé explained the arguments for each position but asserted that if there were two chambers they should be structured without any distinctions by order. He concluded with the observation that he had given the Assembly an overview of the issues of concern to the committee and said all were susceptible to improvement, which the Assembly would do.

Clermont-Tonnerre followed with a second report, which consisted of a summary of the *cahiers* on the question of a constitution. Constituents, he stated, were in agreement on one point, which was that they desired the regeneration of the state. Some expected only a reform of abuses and the reestablishment of a fourteen-century old constitution whereas others viewed the existing social regime as discredited and asked for a new constitution, which would retain monarchy and monarchical forms of government.

Clermont-Tonnerre outlined the ideas of monarchical government and said that the greatest number of *cahiers* recognized the necessity of royal sanction for the promulgation of laws. He summarized other aspects, including legislative power, during which he observed that a greater number of *cahiers* favored periodic meetings of the Estates General over a permanent body.

After dealing with other matters in the *cahiers*, Clermont-Tonnerre presented the results of the examination of them, which was divided into two sections—avowed principles, on which the *cahiers* were in agreement, and questions, on which they were not. There were eleven avowed principles and eighteen questions. Among the former, incontestable issues that the Assembly could settle quickly, were that the French government was monarchical, that the monarch held executive power, that royal sanction was required for the promulgation of laws, that the nation made the law with royal sanction and that national consent was required for loans and taxes.

The eighteen questions to be decided by the Assembly largely dealt with the exercise of power and the making of laws. The first was whether the monarch had legislative power "limited by the constitutional laws of the kingdom." The following questions asked whether the monarch alone had the right to make provisional laws for police and administration and whether such laws would be submitted to sovereign courts for registration. The next eleven treated the meetings, composition and procedure of the Estates General. The final three asked whether taxes would be valid until the national debt was liquidated, whether *lettres de cachet* would be abolished or modified and whether freedom of the press would be undefined or modified.

Deputies were not seeking to reduce the powers of the monarch, but instead sought to ensure that he received better counsel through the Estates General rather than from questionable or corrupt ministers, enabling him to exercise power more effectively. Deputies of the Estates General were accountable to the nation whereas ministers were not.[13] It is in this context that the report of the Committee on the Constitution should be considered, particularly the preponderance of concern with the Estates General.

The presentations provide insight into the limited objectives of the Assembly in its early stages.[14] The reports had been delivered by members of the First, Second and Third Estates in a body in which seating was still by order.[15] The member of the commons, which comprised half the committee, spoke last and most briefly. The structure of the presentations in this manner may have been an effort to reassure recalcitrant deputies, especially among the nobility, who were receiving new instructions from their constituents to participate in the Assembly and to work on drafting a constitution. The committee wished to make known that the Assembly was carrying out its role as representatives of the nation by using the *cahiers* as the basis of its deliberations.

The *cahiers* represented a snapshot in time during the winter and spring of 1789. Events had moved quickly since that time and the political landscape in July 1789 was markedly different from what it had been in March and April. In this respect, in view of the sensitivity to terminology by deputies and some of the public, it is unclear why the committee used the term "Estates General" in its report. Parisians had not rallied to the defense of the Estates General but to the National Assembly and the new municipal authorities that had sent messages had stated that they would take orders only from the National Assembly.

Blackman contended that the assumption of the title of National Assembly was rooted in the politics of the moment rather than in a grand design for a constitutional role beyond what *cahiers* had requested and the language of the report supports this assertion.[16] Another explanation is that the committee was using the language of the *cahiers* as it summarized them and it may also have been that the committee sought to calm apprehension at the rapid pace of political change. Nevertheless, whereas the Estates General had been a consultative body, the Assembly envisaged a larger role in the future, which makes the use of what was already an anachronistic term difficult to understand.

The report, hewing entirely to prescriptive tradition, was cautious. This was most apparent in the article that asked whether *lettres de cachet* would be reformed or abolished. In both the Maupeou edicts in 1771 and in the more recent exile of the *parlement* to Troyes in 1787, *lettres de cachet* had been the mechanism for dismantling or exiling the *parlement*. After the return of the *parlement* of Paris two magistrates had been imprisoned in November 1787 through them. The exile and subsequent arrest of the two magistrates made the king appear despotic and *lettres de cachet* his instrument for despotism, making them a constitutional issue. *Lettres de cachet* became a focus of sharp grievance and gave rise to a conviction that no subject could be secure until fundamental laws were written down.[17] The idea of a declaration of rights as a precursor to a constitution was almost certainly driven in large measure by the reaction against *lettres de cachet*. *Lettres de cachet* were incompatible with a declaration of rights, which makes it difficult to see how they could be "reformed."

The article is all the more puzzling because the nobility had proposed their abolition and at the royal session of June 23 the king, claiming to want to assure the personal freedom of all citizens, had asked the Estates General to find the most convenient means to abolish *lettres de cachet* while balancing the needs of public safety and necessary precautions.[18] The emphasis was clearly on abolition. With its allusion to possible "reform" of them, the report seemed timid and demonstrates the cautious nature of the Assembly in July 1789.

Indeed, rather than envisioning a significant role for the Estates General, the primary responsibility of which was approving taxes, the report seemed more concerned with the powers of the monarch in a manner that gave him considerable latitude. The deferential tenor of the report is apparent in the first question posed, which was whether the king had legislative power "limited by the constitutional laws of the kingdom." Based on the *cahiers*, it implied that the Assembly was open to vesting legislative power to the monarch with only vague limits.

The next article effectively confirmed that there would be a body but still potentially gave the king wide discretionary power. It asked whether the monarch alone could make provisional laws for police and administration in the intervals between convening of the Estates General. The only limit was whether laws of this sort would be freely registered by sovereign courts. It is clear that the Committee on the Constitution did not envision any major change in the fundamental political structure of the kingdom. The overriding goal was to make the Estates General the preeminent voice of the kingdom, supplanting the *parlement*, which would act as guardian of the rights and interests of the Estates General in the intervals between its meetings.[19]

The next several questions centered on the Estates General but were generally framed in relation to royal power. Article four asked if the Estates General could be dissolved only of its own volition, but the following two asked whether the king alone could convene, adjourn, and dissolve the Estates General and whether in the event of dissolution he was obligated to call a new one immediately.

Several articles dealt with the composition of the Estates General, beginning with the question of whether the first two orders would be joined in the same chamber and followed by asking whether the two chambers would be comprised without distinction of order. Article fourteen asked whether individuals associated with the Court could serve as deputies in the Estates General. The fifteenth article was the sole one centered on procedure, asking whether a two-thirds majority would be necessary to constitute a resolution.

The final three questions focused on policy. Article sixteen framed the issue of taxes by asking if, because they were intended to liquidate the national debt, would they be collected until its total elimination? Articles seventeen and eighteen were those concerned with *lettres de cachet* and freedom of the press.

The report lacked any larger vision. It may have been a faithful summary of the *cahiers*, but the political outlook of the kingdom had shifted significantly since their formulation.[20] It did not outline any positive role for the Assembly or a successor body. Letters written after the presentation of the report reveal the disappointment over how little change the report offered. In Dijon, an observer wrote that it was scarcely innovative in its proposals and would leave the king in a strong position. Jefferson likewise noted the advantageous position given to the monarch.[21] Nevertheless, in the aftermath of the report, the Assembly was impatient to begin moving forward with the constitution and excited at the prospect of it.[22]

The Unexpected Expansion of the Constitutional Project

Reports of violence and lawlessness in the countryside continued to pour into the Assembly. To address the unrest, a number of deputies began meeting at the Breton Club to devise a course of action to stem the turmoil. To pacify the peasantry by dealing with one of its major grievances, those involved worked out an arrangement in which Armand Désiré Vignerot Duplessis Richelieu, duc d'Aiguillon, one of the largest landowners in France, would propose the elimination of seigneurial dues through a long-term redemption.[23]

During the evening session of August 4, in a setting fraught with fear and tension,[24] the Assembly greeted Aiguillon's proposals with enthusiasm and ardent applause. The fervor of the ovation sparked a wave of intense emotion that set the Assembly on an entirely unanticipated course. Caught in the emotion of the moment, other deputies advanced to the podium to renounce privileges in a process that continued for hours. Members from all three orders and different parts of the kingdom stood in line at the podium to yield an array of privileges. The relinquishments cascaded in an extraordinary fashion, with each seeming more stunning than those that had preceded it.[25] Before the meeting concluded at approximately 2:00 a.m. a wide variety of privileges had been given up.[26]

Deep into the proceedings, the marquis de Blacons proposed that all provinces should follow the example of Dauphiné and give up their privileges and franchises.[27] The president of the Assembly, Le Chapelier, a Breton, surrounded by the Breton delegation, declared that because the imperative mandate for Rennes required that decisions of the Assembly be submitted for consideration to the provincial Estates, he wanted to make certain reservations of particular rights, but he had no doubt that after such a patriotic act Brittany would overwhelmingly consent to a generous abandonment of all of its privileges.[28]

Another Breton deputy stepped forward to declare that these reservations did not hold for a large portion of the province and that those areas renounced all particular privileges, franchises and rights. Brittany would form a "federative pact" with the other provinces that would have the king at its center. It was a moment of political theater for the delegations of Brittany and Dauphiné to act together to yield the privileges of their respective provinces, aware that each had represented the antithetical position to the other. One deputy wrote that after the two delegations came together the enthusiasm knew no limits.[29]

Indeed, the joining of the Breton and Dauphinois delegations precipitated a reaction by other *pays d'états* and provinces, the deputies of which proceeded to relinquish the privileges of their respective provinces and consent to the same level of taxation for all.[30] Those constrained by imperative mandates assured the Assembly of the compliance of their constituents.[31] Following the renunciations made by the provinces, deputies for a number of cities of the kingdom, including Paris, Lyon, Marseille, Clermont-Ferrand, and others, renounced their rights and privileges.[32] One observer noted that it was the first time that all the provinces formed their act of union with each other.[33]

In describing the situation of France before the Revolution, one contemporary, noting their privileges, characterized the various provinces as forming "small republics in the state."[34] It was particularly the renunciation of the privileges of provinces, cities, and towns that became the structural foundation for the Constitution of 1791.[35] A noble deputy said of the meeting that it was a question of striking down all privileges of every sort, clearing all obstacles, and he especially noted the renunciation of privileges by provinces and cities.[36]

With the repudiation of privilege, an entirely new compact had to be forged.[37] Privilege had formerly been mediated by the king, which is the reason that the Breton deputy who had proposed the "federative pact" had been careful to stipulate that the monarch would be at the head of it—it was to reassure Louis that his role would not be diminished by the abolition of privilege.

The session was also striking to outsiders. One observer wrote that the Assembly suddenly changed because of the meeting. Previously occupied with "metaphysical declarations," an allusion to the Declaration of Rights, it had moved to more useful ideas and tangible results by striking down privilege and addressing the misery of the countryside.[38] Handbills that circulated immediately after the meeting listing the renunciations defined them as bases for the constitution.[39]

As individuals who had attended the meeting of August 4 returned to Paris and brought news of it, crowds of Parisians gathered to share the joy of the news. One newspaper reported that the renunciations surpassed all hopes and led to a gentle fraternity among citizens.[40] A visiting German student described Paris as in a state of joyful delirium after the news of August 4 became known and compared it to the emotion that had gripped the Assembly during the meeting. He also noted the sentiment of fraternity, observing that he was using a new word to describe a new situation.[41] The association of the constitution with the meeting of August 4 enabled the constitution to capture the imagination of the public and gain a strong loyalty.[42]

For a few weeks the meeting infused the Assembly with a sense of common purpose and mission. The influence that the meeting had is evident in a letter sent by a conservative noble deputy who had been in the majority that reluctantly joined the Assembly on June 27, Charles-Elie, marquis de Ferrières. In a letter to a constituent on August 7 Ferrières declared that the meeting had produced a result that twelve centuries of the same religion, the same language and the habits of common manners had not accomplished—the reconciliation of interests and the unity of France in the sole objective of the common good of all.[43]

The meeting of the night of August 4 enabled the Assembly to forge a functional consensus based on the ideals it had conceived that night—one deputy wrote that there would be only one view in the Assembly.[44] The deputy Alquier wrote on August 8 that privilege no longer existed in France and "this great decision is the preliminary for the French constitution."[45] The political outlook of deputies was utterly transformed. The abolition of privilege resulted in a new ideal of the polity based on freedom, equality, and fraternity under the benevolent authority of the nation.[46] The guiding principles that came into existence that evening—to do away with privilege and to bring all French together—provided an unambiguous agenda, one far clearer than the varying and sometimes conflicting instructions contained in the mass of *cahiers*.

It was, in fact, no longer possible to use the standard of prescriptive tradition because tradition had been swept aside during the meeting. To the degree that a written constitution generally comes into existence with the creation of a new state or a revolutionary rupture with the earlier constitutional system, the decision in favor of a written constitution for the Assembly resulted from the night of August 4, which saw the creation of a "new state" based on legal equality rather than privilege.[47] Indeed, one Provençal deputy wrote to his constituents that one should not see in the new constitution any materials from the old one and the deputy Michel René Maupetit wrote that the old edifice had been destroyed and it was now necessary to construct a new one. The Assembly, he declared, had the materials and all that was needed to build the new structure was calm.[48]

Much of the public similarly understood that the meeting had created a new constitutional framework.[49] The Assembly had formulated a new ideal of the polity and would be looking forward rather than to the past. After August 4 the Assembly would lead the way rather than adhere to past practices, justifying its new role with the assertion that the national will had changed.[50]

The fact that the Assembly was aware that it had created an entirely new foundation for governance and was prepared to defend it against any possible reaction from the king is evident in a deliberately obscure, little-known agreement forged on August 4, the pact of association. During the meeting the privileges of all of the provinces had been renounced, which was publicly known and codified in the articles promulgated by the Assembly on August 11. Because privilege had been a defining attribute of the Old Regime and a primary instrument of governance, its abolition weakened the monarch, who had granted it and been its guarantor and arbiter. The Assembly, in its final measure during the meeting of the night of August 4, added an article designed to associate Louis with the redefinition of the polity by naming him "Restorer of French Liberties."

At the same time, to prevent any attempt by the king to reimpose privilege, deputies concluded, in a furtive fashion because of its seditious implications, a pact of association through which they vowed to resist any such effort.[51] Had a pledge to resist royal authority become publicly known, it would not have been possible for the monarch to associate himself with the decrees. Moreover, it could have alienated a large portion of the populace because the *cahiers* were in strong agreement that the government of France was monarchical. Nevertheless, forging the unwritten compact revealed the depth of conviction by the Assembly of the validity of its new ideals as well as its resolve to realize them through the constitution.[52]

From August 5 until August 11 deputies codified the renunciations into a document known as the August decrees, which became the basis of the functional consensus forged around the new conception of the polity devised by the Assembly. The decrees conveyed the foundational premise for the constitution and encapsulated the pact of association in article ten. It proclaimed the permanent abolition of privileges of every kind of provinces, principalities, *pays*, cantons, cities, and communities of inhabitants, all of which were to be merged into rights common to all French. Unlike most of the articles, it passed without any modification.[53]

Functional consensus is not philosophical consensus—the renunciations and their codification in the August decrees merely provided the point of departure for reform and the constitution.[54] Years later a deputy wrote that the night of August 4 was as important to the constitution as the Parisian insurrection of July 14 had been to the Revolution.[55] The qualifier of functional is also apposite because the consensus began to break down within weeks. Despite its deterioration, the Assembly never deviated or drew back from its ideal of a kingdom devoid of privilege and governed by laws common to all. The dissolution of the consensus resulted from disagreement over the degree to which the reforms should be realized.

After finishing the August decrees, the Assembly declared that after completing the constitution it would determine the laws deemed necessary to realize the principles derived from the night of August 4 and that they would be sent to all the provinces.[56] They were to be disseminated across the kingdom along with an appeal for the reestablishment of public calm approved on August 10.[57]

Although unrest continued and had unnerved deputies in the days prior to the meeting of August 4, the confidence and sense of mission that the meeting had imparted left them almost imperturbable in its aftermath.[58] In a letter to constituents on August 17 the deputy Charles François Bouche used the metaphor of a climber high upon a mountain to describe the situation of the Assembly. The climber, he wrote, rests on a high mountaintop with a calm breeze around him while he is gazing at a clear, calm sky but can hear beneath him wind blowing through valleys and caverns.[59]

The importance that the Assembly attached to the constitution and the sense of mission that it instilled in the Assembly is also evident in a letter by the deputy Ménard de la Groye to his wife on August 21:

> It is a great and arduous undertaking, that of reforming the outdated laws of a great empire and changing its constitution almost in its entirety. It is necessary to battle a multitude of particular interests and to compel to give into reason prejudices sanctified by the course of centuries that have acquired the most imposing authority.... Undoubtedly great objections will be raised against us and our proceedings will be harshly criticized, but we would scarcely be worthy of the exalted duties we have to fulfill if this consideration was capable of weakening our fortitude and diminishing our efforts. The sublime quality of legislator that is entrusted to us should make us cast our glance to a distant future and we should prepare

for future races the happiness that it will perhaps not be possible for us to allow the current generation to enjoy.[60]

Bouche and Ménard de la Groye are illustrative of the critical mass of deputies who produced the Constitution of 1791—it was largely nameless members who forged it. Edmond Louis Alexis Dubois-Crancé, a noble deputy, asserted that the driving force of the Assembly was made up of 500 deputies of the commons, 250 clerical deputies, almost all of whom were *curés*, and the former minority of the nobility, 20 percent of the noble delegation, for approximately 800 out of 1,200 deputies. They worked harmoniously in the public interest until June 1791, when the monarch fled Paris, and were the core of what he called "this immortal assembly."[61]

The Monarch Equivocates

Two days after the distillation of the renunciations into decrees, on August 13 the entire Assembly presented them to the monarch. Louis gratefully accepted the title of "Restorer of French Liberties," but said nothing about the other articles. He simply told the deputies that his goal was to work with the Assembly to assure public freedom and declared that the wisdom and intentions of the Assembly would inspire great confidence.[62] After the presentation, the Assembly and the king went to the chapel for a *Te Deum*.[63]

What Louis did not say, apart from accepting the title accorded to him personally, was that he assented to the decrees, the blueprint for the constitution. The expectation of the Assembly had been that the king would immediately accept and promulgate them. It was almost certainly for this reason that the entire body had presented them to symbolize a sense of common purpose.[64] It is not surprising, then, that the next day the question of a royal veto arose for the first time. On August 14 a deputy inquired about the influence of the king on legislation and asked whether he would have the right of a veto. If so, would it be limited or unlimited, suspensive or absolute?[65] The unnamed deputy's questions, however, were tabled.

As the month went on without the decrees being promulgated, deputies became increasingly uneasy about Louis's intentions, which led them to return to the question of royal influence.[66] As time went on, there was also growing disquietude among the public. Reporting on the outlook of the public on September 8, one newspaper asserted that it remained astonished at what it had seen and all that it was reading and could scarcely believe that the new ideals would endure. The public spoke endlessly, the paper claimed, of whether the constitution would really change matters and realize the ideals advanced on August 4 and in the Declaration of the Rights of Man.[67]

Ostensibly to accelerate work on the constitution, deputies decided to begin discussion of a royal sanction and other issues.[68] The debate was protracted and passionate and concluded on September 11 with the monarch being vested with a suspensive veto rather than an absolute one.[69] In an apposite description, Blackman characterized the suspensive veto given to Louis as a "defensive measure."[70] It was an outcome thrust upon the Assembly by Louis's refusal to promulgate the August decrees, which deputies saw as the base of the constitution. Operating under the norm of prescriptive tradition, the Committee on the Constitution report on July 27 had simply stated that the sanction of the monarch was necessary for laws to be promulgated. There had been no mention of a veto and certainly no consideration of overturning the will of the monarch.

The decision on the veto shattered the functional consensus forged after the meeting of August 4. Louis's recalcitrance led to the enactment of a measure that stripped him of sovereignty, which made the debate heated.[71] It was effectively an invocation of the pledge of resistance in the pact of association by preemptively striking at a presumptive effort to reclaim privilege.[72] The passage of the suspensive veto represented the transfer of sovereignty from the monarch to the nation and the transition from monarchy-centered government to constitutional monarchy.[73]

The vote on the veto, as well as well as another creating a unicameral rather than bicameral legislature, dismayed those who were sympathetic to monarchical power. The Crown had desired an absolute veto and a bicameral legislature—an absolute veto would strengthen the king and a bicameral structure would weaken the legislature.[74] It provoked a schism in the Committee on the Constitution and necessitated the election of a new committee.[75]

Through his passive resistance, which continued after the decision on the veto and legislature as he refused to promulgate the August decrees, Louis excluded himself from exercising any influence in the drafting of the constitution. The Assembly would bring into existence a constitution "created de novo by an act of sovereign will."[76] The belief took hold that the nation could design a constitution free of restraints, historical or political, and it would ultimately consign the monarch to the role of primary functionary.[77]

The Assembly ensured that the veto would come into force only with its successor body, which meant that the king could not veto the August decrees or the constitution.[78] It had not been considered and was, in fact, almost inconceivable that the monarch would resist the national will through inaction. The suspensive veto was the means to prevent the will of the nation from being undermined and grew out of his resistance to the August decrees.[79]

The breach over royal power did not extend to the attack on privilege—after the vote on the veto the Assembly pressed the king to approve the August decrees but he remained evasive.[80] On September 14 Antoine Barnave proposed that discussion of the length of the suspensive veto be postponed until Louis promulgated the decrees. The Assembly tabled his motion but did send its president to meet with the monarch to request that he sanction them.[81] Louis prevaricated and provided written comments to the Assembly rather than promulgating or approving them—one deputy characterized his response as almost equivalent to a refusal and another believed that elements of the clergy and nobility were prevailing upon him not to sanction them.[82] Their concerns were not misplaced. According to one scholar, as early as August 5 Louis had written to the archbishop of Arles that he would never allow the spoliation of the clergy and nobility and would not give his approval to the decrees.[83]

Deputies were chagrined, particularly because they had felt it was urgent to have them widely disseminated throughout the kingdom.[84] There was dismay in the public as well. One contemporary noted that Louis had given neither a sanction nor a refusal and characterized the response as a victory for the aristocracy.[85] Many in the Assembly believed that the monarch was seeking to enter into a negotiation with them and that he had already assented to the decrees with his acceptance of the title "Restorer of French Liberties."[86] In addition, because the decrees were regarded as constitutional, it was simply a question of their promulgation rather than observations.[87]

On September 21 Louis informed the Assembly that he would consent to the publication but not the promulgation of the decrees, which one conservative noble deputy described as "a little Jesuitical."[88] A resident of Bourges noted that the king had finally given an answer, but it had been obtained only with difficulty and even then what an answer it was.[89]

Eager to believe and to work with the monarch, the Assembly accepted a casual, almost insouciant, concurrence by Louis and set the term of the suspensive veto.[90]

Louis was aggrieved at the dismissive attitude exhibited toward him by the Assembly.[91] Whereas deputies had viewed the king's reaction as obstruction or evasion, he saw his statements as pertinent and nuanced, especially his observations on the foreign policy ramifications of the decrees. His response that he would publish rather than promulgate them was rooted in the fact that he saw the August decrees as a declaration of intent rather than completed legislation.[92]

Believing it had lost valuable time in seeking to gain the monarch's assent to the decrees, the Assembly felt great urgency to work on the constitution.[93] In late August a clerical deputy had lamented the loss of time in working on the constitution, noting that the Assembly was not dealing with the primary issue in the *cahiers*.[94] Deputies decided to devote four days each week to the constitution and Friday and Saturday to finances.[95]

Louis's continuing refusal to promulgate the August decrees raised tensions, which were exacerbated in Paris when a new provisioning crisis arose.[96] A large crowd of women marched to Versailles and gathered at the royal residence. Louis met with a group of them and promised that Paris would receive supplies. Later, a second delegation of women arrived along with the president of the Assembly, Mounier. The Assembly had agreed to present the grievances of the women and sent its president to press Louis to approve the August decrees and the Declaration of Rights. Louis was offended by what seemed to him intimidation and considered leaving Versailles. Ultimately, however, amid much confusion on the grounds, he announced in the evening that he would approve both measures.

The next morning some members of the crowd found an entrance that was not guarded and entered the grounds of the royal residence. A clash ensued that led to the death of two bodyguards as well as members of the crowd. In an effort to calm the situation, the king appeared on the balcony. The crowd shouted for the royal family to go to Paris, to which Louis reluctantly agreed.[97]

A critical catalyst in the unrest that culminated in the removal of the royal family from Versailles to Paris had been a rumor about the Flanders regiment, which had recently been moved to Versailles. It was rumored that at a banquet given on October 1 by the royal bodyguard for the officers of the regiment that the latter drank toasts to the royal couple and deliberately did not offer toasts to the nation. Even worse, it was alleged that officers had stomped on the tricolor cockade.

The Flanders regiment was royalist in its sympathies and it had been brought to Versailles in September, as the monarch equivocated on the August decrees—indeed, Louis may have moved the regiment to Versailles to give himself greater latitude with the August decrees.[98] It is plausible and lends credence to suspicions among deputies of prevarication by the monarch. Aware of the degree to which the ideals would diminish the power of the Crown, Louis sought to evade approval of them. Although they had not yet been officially circulated, the provisions of the decrees were widely known and were popular and admired. It was symbolic that the king's last official act in Versailles was to sanction the decrees that would dismantle the society that Versailles represented.[99]

Gaining Acceptance for the New Ideal

Some areas of France saw an immediate and enthusiastic embrace of the new values of the Assembly. In Périgueux, for example, in what was called an "act of union," citizens of Périgueux and the province of Périgord gathered without distinction of rank or order. The attendees unanimously renounced all exclusive claims, particular interests, and distinctions that they had heretofore enjoyed but were now antithetical to the public interest. Furthermore, those present solemnly promised not to seek to reclaim them and to be good citizens.[100]

In other areas the reaction was not as effusive and, after the initial elation produced by the August decrees had waned, provinces wrestled with the loss of their privileges, refusing to accept some of the renunciations that had been offered.[101] As much as the meeting of August 4 provided the Assembly with a sense of direction and purpose, the renunciations also placed many deputies in a difficult position. They had to persuade constituents to give up valued, often centuries-old privileges in exchange for a document based on diametrically opposed principles that was not yet in existence.

The deputies of Provence, a *pays d'états* in which privileges were a major component of provincial identity, approached the issue cautiously.[102] In an initial letter to his constituents on August 5, the deputy Bouche told them that, had they been in the Assembly during the meeting, they would have renounced the privileges of the province, especially because deputies of other provinces were yielding those of their provinces. He minimized their significance, asserting that they consisted mostly of titles and words rather than tangible benefits.

Bouche claimed that the deputies of Provence had reserved the right to give the province time to convene at the local level and perhaps even in the Estates to deliberate on the renunciation of privileges. It could choose whether to join with the other provinces or to cling to privileges rather than unite with them in bonds of gratitude and reciprocity. It was a binary decision that could not be adjusted and would determine the happiness or unhappiness of Provence. He asserted that he had no advice to give and would leave the matter to each of the localities to decide.[103]

In an illustration of the various political crosscurrents that the Assembly had to navigate, the issue was all the more delicate because Provence had created a constitution for itself and had sent it to the deputies in the Assembly.[104] The deputy Jacques Verdolin commended its authors for their efforts and told them that if the Assembly had given each province a constitution based on its privileges, it would have been valid. Privileges, however, had been discarded during the meeting of the night of August 4 and replaced by uniform governance.

The deputies of Provence had put forward reserves but, Verdolin stated, when the deputies of the first two orders had given up all of their privileges it was difficult to maintain those of the provinces. It was imperative that there be only one king, one nation, and one law. Because every province was giving them up, Provence would lose nothing by renouncing its privileges. Ultimately, Verdolin declared, he believed Provence would not be making any sacrifices because the bases of the national constitution would be the same as the provincial one. He closed, however, by emphasizing the reservations that the Provençal deputies had made with respect to provincial rights and its particular constitution.[105]

The reservations mentioned by the Provençal deputies were a polite fiction designed to avoid offending the province and affording it an opportunity to concur in the renunciations.[106] The pact of association forbade reservations by any province and was secondarily directed against provinces that might seek to reclaim or retain their privileges through an appeal to their traditional guarantor, the king.[107]

On August 16 Verdolin wrote to ask communities in Provence to give their prompt approval to the August 4 decrees. He stated that the city of

Rennes and all of the municipalities of Brittany, which had a far greater number of privileges than Provence and had clung more strongly to them than any other province in the kingdom, were sending their adhesions to the Assembly daily.[108] Opposition of any province would only slow the work of the Assembly and the constitution of Provence could not have any standing in the current circumstances because, he repeated, there was only one king, one law, and one nation, which made necessary one uniform constitution that would apply to the entire kingdom.[109]

The inhabitants of Provence were receptive to the decrees of the Assembly—the commissioners for the communities of Provence wrote to deputies that they were greeted with astonishment, admiration, and surprise and that the Assembly had surpassed the hopes of the nation. The commissioners stated that they would investigate the legal and regular means to undertake a renunciation of the privileges of the province and indicated that they believed the renunciations would not encounter any problems.[110]

On August 27 the commissioners for the commons of Provence began to solicit the organization of village assemblies. A village renunciation of privilege offered inhabitants the opportunity to take part in the advantages of a constitution and the confederation of all of the provinces. The commissioners offered a template to be used in renouncing privileges and urged immediate action. They asked that a copy of the renunciations be sent to the commissioners so that they could send them to the Provençal delegation in Versailles.[111]

In this manner Provence abandoned pursuit of its own constitution, renounced its special sovereign status and declared that it would accept all decrees of the Assembly.[112] The commissioners of the commons of the province organized scripted village meetings in which the inhabitants renounced their privileges and sent extracts from eighty-five of them to the Assembly.[113] The sense of enthusiasm was also evident in the city of Aix, where a municipal officer told assembled citizens that the meeting of August 4 would become as celebrated for them as the year 1689 was in England.[114]

The mention by the Provençal deputies of Brittany accepting the new ideals was generally accurate. Rennes acted expeditiously to renounce its privileges. In a wide-ranging meeting on September 7 that also opined on the royal veto and the structure of the legislature, the city declared that it adhered unconditionally to the decrees of the Assembly and renounced its rights, franchises, and immunities. It declared its inviolable attachment to the principles just established by the Assembly.[115]

On August 9 the nobility of Nantes gathered to proclaim that its loyalty to the fatherland superseded its loyalty to the province. The nobility regarded it as their duty to renounce all of their prior protests and declarations and announced that they were yielding all privileges and exemptions that contravened the August decrees. They reaffirmed their pledge on August 27 and many made individual announcements.[116]

The deputies for Nantes in the Assembly cautiously wrote to the *sénéchaussée* of Nantes asking it to assemble constituents to express their intent regarding the destruction of privileges by the Assembly, especially the proscription of those of provinces and cities. The officials of the *sénéchaussée* wrote to the mayor and municipal officers asking them to convene the "*corps et corporations*" of the city to ascertain the general view of the residents.[117] The provisional municipal government of Nantes nullified the imperative mandate of its deputies that specified the protection of the privileges of the city.[118] It replaced it with unlimited powers to act freely for the good of the province and asked that the declaration be made known to the Assembly.[119] On September 14 Nantes also had a general meeting in the *Hôtel de Ville* to grant unlimited powers to its deputies and adhere formally to the pact of association.[120]

As the letter indicated, the voting had been conducted in a manner antithetical to the spirit of the night of August 4—by corporation, which had been the protocol for the elections to the Estates General. Thirty-seven corporations voted in favor of giving deputies unlimited powers whereas fifteen voted to maintain the imperative mandate. Outside the city ninety-seven parishes voted for unlimited powers and fifty-eight for retaining the imperative mandates. The results were sent to the deputies in the Assembly and to the Crown.[121] As time went on, Brittany became less enthusiastic than its deputies had led the Assembly to believe, and the level of opposition led to concern about future divisions. Brittany, however, remained calm during the autumn of 1789.[122]

As Brittany accepted the new ideals advanced by the Assembly, Dauphiné, in contrast, was experiencing unrest and seeking to reconvene its provincial Estates. A particularly unsettling aspect for the Assembly was that Mounier, who had left the Assembly after the October Days and returned to Dauphiné, was suspected of involvement in the effort.[123] In many respects, during the autumn of 1789 Brittany and Dauphiné effectively reversed positions. In the spring of 1789 Dauphiné had symbolized a new ideal and Brittany had represented adherence to an old order. In the autumn 1789 it was Brittany that symbolized commitment to a new vision of France and Dauphiné that represented clinging to an outdated ideal.

To be sure, the transition in Brittany was by no means seamless. At the end of the year there was a campaign in the province to discredit the Assembly, which led its deputies to publish a pamphlet countering the criticisms levelled against the Assembly and to have it distributed in the province.[124]

Some noble and clerical deputies on the Intermediate Commission of the Estates of Brittany sought to resist the new administrative structure enacted by the Assembly. They attempted to make reservations and protest against the decree of the Assembly establishing the new departmental administrative structure. Other commissioners of the provincial Estates, however, denounced their action as attachment to old values and far removed from submitting to the decrees of the Assembly and contributing to the regeneration of the kingdom.[125]

In an apparent effort to counter the perception of remaining attached to the old administration, in late January 1790, as municipal elections approached, a group of sixty noblemen in Rennes convened to denounce the old administrative structure and to proclaim their loyalty to the new constitution. They renounced their former oath as Breton nobles and proclaimed that they were choosing the rule of law and denouncing any resistance to the desires, will, or well-being of their fellow citizens.[126]

The actions by the nobility in the Estates and the *parlement* led to a response by the young men of Rennes. They sent a letter to Nantes suggesting that for the well-being of Brittany they combine to mount a defense against the machinations of the nobility.[127] Ultimately, however, the efforts by the nobility in Brittany were fruitless. Indeed, the degree to which the new ideals had taken hold in Rennes is evident in a primary assembly there on May 17, 1790. In that assembly former magistrates of the *parlement* of Rennes mingled on an equal basis with tanners, grocers, and bakers—a situation that would have been inconceivable a year earlier.[128]

Resisting the New Ideals

A very different reaction came from Alsace and especially Strasbourg. When they arrived in Versailles the two deputies of the city of Strasbourg,

Jean de Turckheim and Etienne François Joseph Schwendt, had pledged that they would energetically defend all the privileges of the city.[129] During the meeting of August 4 they had been extremely circumspect in their renunciation. In a letter to municipal officials written the next day, the deputies opened by pronouncing themselves somewhat embarrassed by the proceedings. After recounting some of the renunciations initially offered, they wrote that they were only precursors in the patriotic delirium that took hold of the Assembly—there were more inconceivable ones to come.

After describing the coming together of the delegations of Brittany and Dauphiné and the frenzy of renunciations that followed, they wrote that when Alsace was called the embarrassment of the deputies was extreme. They had offered the privileges contingent upon the ratification of the city, effectively seeking to retain the privileges of the city and province.[130] Schwendt and Turckheim observed that their slowness in offering them and the reservation they had attached had already generated reproaches. They warned that it would be exceedingly difficult to defend Strasbourg's privileges against the national view of laws common to all and added that Strasbourg should not set itself against the national will by seeking to retain its privileges. They noted the generosity of spirit of other provinces in renouncing their privileges and, like their colleagues from Provence, cited the example of Brittany.[131]

In another letter the deputies announced that the Assembly had determined that all orders, provinces, cities, and individuals were to give up their privileges for the sake of the nation and submit to the common regime that the Assembly was going to establish. They expressed regret over their inability to present any homage to the Assembly from the city but they had conformed to their *cahier* and offered only a conditional declaration.[132] They enclosed a copy of the declaration they had given to the Assembly, which expressed their belief that the city would make all sacrifices necessary for the common fatherland of which it had been a part for one hundred years.[133] Turckheim and Schwendt asserted that it was absolutely necessary for the city to renounce its privileges. They cautioned that, because of the relinquishments that had been offered, it would be nearly impossible for the city and the province of Alsace to stand alone against the rest of the kingdom by seeking to preserve their privileges.[134]

Turckheim and Schwendt's confidence that the city would yield its privileges was misplaced. Despite the pleas of its deputies, Strasbourg stood firm in defense of its rights and privileges. On August 19 it agreed to equal taxation but refused to give up its structure of municipal government. It praised the principles put forward by the Assembly but stated that it hoped the Assembly would be wise enough to preserve the structure of the government of Strasbourg because it was indispensable.[135] The request by Turckheim and Schwendt for the city to renounce its privileges precipitated the resignation of the municipal government but the resignations did not dissuade the city from seeking to maintain its privileges. On September 19 Strasbourg notified its deputies of its unwillingness to yield its privileges and in support of its stance it began to prepare a lengthy defense of them.[136]

As the extent of the changes became clear, along with the resolve of the Assembly to achieve them, the city and the province became more combative in their reservations.[137] The unyielding adhesion to its privileges by Strasbourg led Turckheim to resign from the Assembly in late September. His resignation letter warned the city that continuing the defense of its privileges could have adverse consequences.[138] His warning went unheeded—by late September Strasbourg was aligning itself with the clergy and nobility of Alsace in an effort to retain privileges.[139] In early October Strasbourg sent a letter to its deputies asserting that the August decrees failed to make a distinction between simple privileges and concessions that were a product of territorial superiority that Strasbourg and Alsace had before its voluntary reunion to France. It enclosed a long memorandum in which it advanced its reservations with respect to the August decrees.

The document began by acknowledging that the patriotic fervor of its deputies had been constrained by their imperative mandate, even though the deputies agreed with the new ideals of August 4 and had invited the city to deliberate on relinquishing its privileges. The request had led to the resignation of its municipal officials but Strasbourg had sent its own homage to the Assembly praising the new ideals it had put forward.[140] It was willing to yield pecuniary privileges but expressed reservations about Strasbourg and Alsace giving up other privileges. The city declared that commitments made by monarchs must be honored and asserted that its status as a frontier province made the preservation of its special arrangements imperative.

Perhaps most provocatively, the city contested article ten of the August decrees, which codified the pact of association. It declared that the province of Alsace and the city of Strasbourg could not purely and simply adopt the article nor consent to the destruction of their privileges. The *mémoire* declared that Strasbourg was resigned to its fiscal sacrifices but did not believe that more should be asked of it. Quoting their mandate, the brief declared that its deputies could never consent to the destruction of the city's privileges. Strasbourg concluded its arguments with the observation that if there were no exceptions made for Alsace, there would be incalculable trouble in the province as a result of people having felt misled by exaggerated and false promises.[141]

The impasse continued throughout the fall, with the city clinging to its privileges and Schwendt attempting to tell it that its position was untenable. To complicate matters further, Turckheim, disillusioned by the transfer of the royal family to Paris in October 1789, reverted to a defense of Strasbourg's privileges after his resignation from the Assembly. He wrote that he had been honored by the city's confidence to allow him to represent it in the Estates General and that he had fulfilled his duties with enthusiasm and faithfulness. But, he wrote, although principles had changed, he did not believe it was his duty to change his to meet them.[142] He published a pamphlet in which he asserted that Strasbourg had more to fear than to hope from other French provinces, which sought uniform government.[143] On November 1 Schwendt informed Strasbourg that it would be nearly impossible not to yield to the imperative of uniform administration for France, which would not be as unsettling as they might believe.[144]

On November 25 Schwendt informed the city that the Committee on the Constitution had announced its report on the new structure of municipal government and two days later wrote that he was powerless to prevent it from moving forward and that it applied without exception to all cities of the kingdom.[145] On December 1, in response to observations sent to him by the city, he stated that he had done all he could to counter the new municipal administrative structure but in vain. Its objections had gone unanswered by the Assembly, which refused to consider them.[146]

In a blunt letter on December 7 Schwendt wrote that it was necessary for Strasbourg to cast aside old ideas and former principles and to submit to "the Empire of the new constitution." He did not see any legal means to escape it because the Assembly was aggressively resolved not to allow any exceptions.[147] On December 10, with the legislation completed, Schwendt told the city that he would no longer be recognized in the Assembly to voice his objections. Enclosing a copy of the legislation, he invited them to use it to judge the intentions of the Assembly and reminded Strasbourg that the Assembly had made every specific consideration yield to the principle of uniformity of structure for new bodies and in the application of law.[148]

Strasbourg persisted and asked that the establishment of the new municipal structure be delayed until the new judiciary had been put in place. Schwendt responded that their request was impossible and added that the Assembly would not listen to him because the request was "absolutely contrary to the spirit and moral obligations of the Assembly."[149]

Tensions sharpened as the inevitability of a new municipal administration became clear. The city acknowledged that it was the lone holdout and that its citizenry was divided on whether to sacrifice its privileges. One former municipal official argued that under the circumstances it was the duty of Strasbourg to conform. A newly-founded newspaper in the city advocated acceptance of the constitution, stating that by bringing citizens together and making representation more equal it would correct deficiencies in the constitution of Strasbourg.[150]

On January 2, 1790, baron Philippe Frédéric de Dietrich, the royal commissioner for mines, spoke to the municipal officers and chided them for their efforts to maintain the rights and prerogatives of the city after the Assembly had made clear that it was its duty not to make an exception for Strasbourg. Dietrich told them that Schwendt had told him that he had been the only representative in the entire kingdom against the reorganization of municipal government. Telling the officials that they had exhausted all avenues of fulfilling the wishes of their constituents, he added that they should not allow any citizen to ignore the decrees of the Assembly.[151]

Strasbourg yielded. A month later, on February 3, the city gathered for the election of a mayor and municipal officers under the procedures and structure decreed by the Assembly. Dietrich was elected mayor.[152] Two months later, on April 5, the National Guard was taking an oath with neighboring regions to protect the constitution.[153]

The effort of Strasbourg to cling to its privileges is not surprising. It had been under the control of France for just over a century and had been given more autonomy than other areas of France. An imperial free city for more than four centuries, its sense of civic identity as a self-ruling urban center was greater than its sense of attachment to France. One notable aspect of the insubordination of Strasbourg was that the Assembly never menaced or coerced the city. Convinced of the validity of its new ideals, the Assembly proceeded calmly and confidently and did not at any point resort to threats or intimidation. Its composure in the face of obstinate behavior strengthened the legitimacy of its new ideals and facilitated their acceptance.

Indeed, the administrative transformation of Strasbourg culminated in the summer of 1790 and produced a communication that was remarkable in view of the situation in the city seven months earlier. In late July 1790, after the formation of departments, the administrators of the Department of Bas-Rhin, based in Strasbourg, wrote to administrators of other departments. Hailing the new structure established by the Assembly, they began by observing that in the past, provinces, isolated from each other, effectively comprised different nations, with different mores, customs, languages and forms of administration, all of which served to divide them and make them indifferent to one another. They then declared:

> Today everything is different. Our rights, our duties, our interests are the same; the privileges that divided [us] no longer exist. We are all brothers, all equal, all free—in a word, we are all French and that is the most cherished designation. Reciprocally imbued with this new spirit, without which particular prosperity cannot exist, we have all sworn to uphold the Revolution, to carry out the laws and decrees of the representatives of the nation [with] the respect and obedience that is their due, ready to offer aid and mutual assistance against the enemies of the public good.

It concluded that only by working closely together could they fulfill all their duties as citizens and as administrators and establish unity of principles.[154]

The Forgotten Constitution: The Origins, Realization, and Legacy of the French Constitution of 1791.
Michael P. Fitzsimmons, Oxford University Press. © Oxford University Press 2025.
DOI: 10.1093/9780197793978.003.0009

9
The Completion and Consolidation of the Constitution

The prolonged resistance of Strasbourg to the constitutional project indicates that the success of the Assembly in giving France a constitution was by no means assured. Although other difficult periods would follow, there was deep unease in the fall of 1789—in late 1789 one deputy expressed his fear of insurrection in the provinces.[1] In early 1790 deputies of Nantes wrote to their constituents to encourage them, reassuring them that the year that had just concluded was one of troubles, inquietude, and calamities but it was from these very troubles that public happiness would be born.[2] Deputies were firm in their resolve to realize the constitution despite discontent and opposition.[3]

When it was drafting the August decrees the Assembly had announced that it would create the constitution and then establish institutions that would harmonize with it. Following the determination of the length of the suspensive veto, however, Rabaut de Saint-Etienne, speaking for the Committee on the Constitution, sought to defer work on the constitution, specifically citing conditions in cities and towns.[4] He contended that working toward a constitution would be in vain if each municipality established its own structure, which would lead to a multitude of bodies that would be disconnected from each other as well as any larger structure.[5] The Assembly accepted his argument that the establishment of provincial and municipal administration was the most pressing task and began to reshape institutions at the same time that it drafted the constitution. The Committee on the Constitution offered its report on the new administrative structure of the kingdom on September 29 and the first component of it to be put in place was municipal administration.[6]

In preparation for municipal elections, in early 1790 the Assembly set the requirements necessary to be an active citizen, the key component of which was the local value of a day of unskilled labor. The Assembly did not set a minimum but it did set a ceiling—the sum of a day of unskilled labor could not exceed twenty *sous*. According to a contemporary observer, this was guided by the principle of the Assembly to exclude the fewest number of citizens possible from participating in governance, directly or indirectly.[7]

The effect of the legislation, however, was to require municipalities to give up the certainty of centuries-old governing structures for a new and untested framework of municipal government.[8] However deficient or unsatisfactory any number of municipal governments may have been, they were at least familiar. Aix-en-Provence offers an illustration of how an area receptive to the August decrees became unnerved by the transition to a new system of municipal government. During the municipal assembly held on September 4 to renounce the privileges of the city, an official had hailed the meeting of the night of August 4 as one of the most beneficial since the foundation of the French monarchy and declared that it would become as celebrated in France as the year 1689 was in England.[9]

By early January 1790, however, as municipal elections were approaching, another municipal official reminded his colleagues that at the September 4 meeting he had opined against renouncing the regime and constitution of the city. Professing the desire to be joined to the rest of the kingdom for the common good, he nevertheless asserted that Provence should not be despoiled of its rights and constitution. He reminded his audience that the first instruction given to its deputies at the Estates General had been to preserve the rights of the Provençal constitution and contended that they were not authorized to renounce it.

The Assembly had deemed it appropriate to establish one constitution and one uniform regime for the entire kingdom and deputies had given their consent to the decree that sacrificed the privileges of the province and had asked their constituents to ratify the act. They had solicited the convening of village assemblies to offer adhesion, but, he asked, could these isolated municipalities offer a legal consent? He asserted that they had been pressured to give up rights that the province itself could not surrender. The city of Aix had unfortunately followed this example, offering its ratification and he reminded attendees that the approval had not been unanimous.[10]

As municipal elections were underway or about to begin, Louis visited the Assembly in an informal fashion on February 4. The Assembly fell into complete silence before rising when the monarch entered, which gave more weight to his words in view of the tensions that were present.[11] He told deputies that the time had come for him, in the interest of the state, to associate himself more clearly and explicitly with the work of the Assembly.

He promised to defend and maintain the constitution, the principles of which were sanctioned by the will of the nation and himself.[12]

The Assembly responded enthusiastically, leading the deputy Guillaume François Charles Goupil de Préfelne to propose that members of the Assembly emulate the monarch and swear loyalty to the constitution. His motion quickly passed and each deputy took an oath to be faithful to the nation, the law, and the monarchy and to uphold the constitution with all of his power. The process was compelling and after it was completed alternate deputies and spectators in the Assembly asked to take it as well.[13]

Although a British observer wrote that some were reluctant to swear fidelity to a constitution that was not yet in existence, he acknowledged that the visit would produce a favorable impression in the nation, inspire confidence in the Revolution and strengthen the project of the constitution.[14] Indeed, the visit erased doubts that a Parisian barrister had been having about Louis and, in conversations he was having with neighbors in its aftermath, some were elevating Louis above Henri IV as the greatest king in French history.[15] Deputies were elated—Jean-Antoine Huguet wrote to his constituents that it was no longer possible to doubt the consent that the monarch was giving to the constitution and professed his happiness that Louis's visit to the Assembly would hasten work on it. Similarly, Ménard de la Groye expressed his satisfaction that Louis's visit should dispel the hopes of those opposed to the constitution that they might be able to overturn it.[16]

The Assembly, seeking to make known the new unity between the king and itself, sent an address to the French nation prepared by the Committee on the Constitution exhorting it to come together in a spirit of common purpose and assuring it that it had nothing to fear.[17] The text of the address was to be posted on city walls, read from the pulpit in all parishes and, as needed, explained by *curés*.[18]

A few days later, on February 10, Aix-en-Provence began conducting its municipal elections, which concluded on February 20. On the first day of the elections each electoral assembly heard a reading of Louis's speech, which inspired confidence.[19] The city elected a mayor and eleven municipal officers who took office on February 21. According to the minutes, the city reverberated with applause and cries of joy. The deputy Verdolin attended and praised the elections as the first benefit of the new constitution.[20]

After the formation of the municipal structure in Aix, the new officials sent a message to the Assembly in which they pronounced that one of their first duties was to express their gratitude to it and to pledge full adhesion to its decrees. A new political order, they declared, had succeeded the old one as easily as if it was an ordinary continuation or based on the same principles.[21] The officials pledged to help the Assembly achieve its goals and also sent a warm message to the king praising him for his visit to the Assembly. They declared him "head of the Revolution" for announcing his acceptance of the constitution and promising to rear his son in accordance with its principles.[22]

As the example of Aix makes clear, Louis's visit did much to alleviate apprehension in the kingdom as the first major transition brought about by the new vision of the Assembly occurred. Its beneficial effect was also evident in Nevers. On February 6 voting was about to begin but was interrupted for the day. All sections in which voting was taking place went to the *Hôtel de Ville* where electors heard a reading of the king's speech. The next day the speech was read again, a *Te Deum* was chanted "with emotion," artillery was fired, military and religious music was played in the town square and church and that evening there was a general illumination.[23]

Following the formation of its new municipal government, the town of Saint-Jean-de-Losne wrote to the Assembly. After observing that it had been, through its deputy, the first to speak in the Assembly to renounce privileges won through the bravery and blood of its ancestors, it praised the constitution. It declared itself irrevocably attached to the principles the Assembly had established and to all of its decrees and hailed the deputies of the Assembly as the fathers of the fatherland and the restorers of French liberty.[24]

The municipal elections, which proceeded without difficulties, were, as Verdolin noted, the first tangible result of the Revolution and fulfilled the ideals that emerged from the night of August 4. Article seven of the August decrees had proclaimed the end of venality in municipal and judicial offices and article eleven had stated that all citizens could be admitted, without distinction of birth, to all civil, ecclesiastical, and military offices. The municipal elections were the first application of these principles and the first realization of the concept of uniform government.[25] Their success inspired great confidence in the constitutional project.[26]

After its legislation on municipalities, the Assembly enacted the division of France into departments, which in turn were subdivided into districts.[27] In eradicating provinces deputies sought to disassociate geography and privilege—the Assembly mandated that no department could use the name of its former province in its name. Each was to be named after its most prominent geographical feature.[28] Elections for departmental and district officials were held in subsequent months, followed by judicial elections.

Just as contemporaries were unnerved by the prospect of the transformation of municipal government, so, too, the division of provinces with centuries-old identities into distinct departments was unsettling.[29] Once again Provence is illustrative. The municipal official in Aix who said that he had warned the city in September not to renounce its privileges so readily also lamented the end of the province. After more than two thousand years of an aggregation to which it owed its good fortune, Provence was going to be divided into three departments, which, he argued, meant three *pays* with separate governments that would have nothing in common. Provence vainly sought to resist the division of the province and may have been aided in its effort by the deputy Bouche.[30] Similar misgivings occurred in Brittany, which unsuccessfully sought to maintain a central provincial assembly.[31]

In another region of France, the reaction went beyond unease to overt direct opposition. In November 1789, as the Assembly was discussing the reorganization of municipal government and Strasbourg was resisting changes in its municipal structure, the Intermediate Commission of the small province of Cambrésis, added to the kingdom by Louis XIV in 1675 and perceived by some deputies to be under strong clerical and noble influence, challenged the authority of the Assembly.[32] The commission convened and declared that the Assembly was ruining the kingdom with its decrees and, asserting that it was attached to France only by the faith of its capitulation, called for the revocation of the powers of the deputies from the province.[33]

Although other bodies had gathered to denounce the Assembly or its decrees, this was the first time that a province sought to recall its deputies. It was a significant challenge because the Assembly had determined that deputies of any province had tacitly renounced its privileges from the time that they had taken their seat. Whatever protest deputies might make or receive, the Assembly asserted, their presence in the Assembly comprised an assent to all that the Assembly would enact.[34] It was for this reason that the Intermediate Commission sought to recall its deputies, hoping to undermine the Assembly.

The undertaking angered the Assembly.[35] It took up the matter on November 17 and influential deputies demanded strong action. Le Chapelier wanted the members of the commission taken before the *Châtelet* and Barnave proposed that they be suspended from office. A week later, however, on November 24, the Assembly resolved it by declaring that the Intermediate Commission did not represent the inhabitants of the province and that its deliberations were invalid, damaging to the sovereignty of the nation and to the rights of citizens. It voted to ask the king to recall the members of the commission to their duties and to carry out the decrees of the Assembly in the province.[36]

The Assembly faced challenges elsewhere as well, including Dauphiné and Languedoc, which sought to reconvene its provincial Estates, again indicating that the success of the Assembly in enacting a constitution was by no means assured.[37] Whenever it was confronted with opposition, however, the Assembly refrained from resorting to force or coercion and its calm and equanimity not only strengthened the moral force of its vision but also increased its stature and that of the constitution that it produced.[38]

After the smooth transition of municipal government, by the spring of 1790 the new ideals of the Assembly had gained the confidence of much of the kingdom. In late May 1790 the electors of the Department of Côte d'Or gathered to elect departmental administrators and began by sending a message to the Assembly. The electors expressed their admiration and gratitude for the enormity and wisdom of its work and hailed the Assembly for regenerating the kingdom without civil conflict through public opinion and reason.

The electors denounced partisans of the old regime who accused the Assembly of exceeding its mandates. Throughout the kingdom, a cry had gone out asking for a constitution and deputies had given inhabitants reason for admiration and made France the envy of all the peoples of Europe. Deputies, they asserted, may have surpassed expectations but they had not exceeded their powers. The electors endorsed the abolition of the privileges of their former province as beneficial and praised the new administrative structure as a bulwark of liberty.[39] The establishment of departments and districts went smoothly throughout France, as did the elections for a new judiciary in the fall.[40]

In the confident and optimistic atmosphere that prevailed after the formation of new municipal governments, a time in which the completion of the constitution seemed imminent to many, Saint-Jean-de-Losne sought to assert a central place for itself. The village sent a message to the Assembly in April 1790 recalling that it was the first to give up its privileges and suggesting that its action had been the inspiration for the subsequent renunciations on August 4 that had served to redefine the kingdom. It also created a large, ornate document to commemorate its renunciation, the night of August 4 and the inclusion of its message in the *procès-verbal* of the Assembly in April.[41]

1790: The Zenith and Nadir for the New Ideals

The zenith of unity in the Revolution came with the *Fête de la Fédération* held at the Champ de Mars on July 14, 1790.[42] Paris was the site of the primary festival but there was an analogue in each department. The simultaneous celebrations were a metaphor for the new ideal of the Assembly—just as its members had come together in a single moment to repudiate privilege, all of the newly-formed departments of France, previously provinces divided from one another by privilege, would join together to support the new civic values through an oath.[43] Indeed, one Breton deputy characterized the *Fête de la Fédération* as the expression of the pact of association forged during the night of August 4.[44] The disparate ceremonies were timed in a manner that enabled the entire kingdom to take the oath at the same moment. In Paris, before an immense crowd, Louis swore to maintain the constitution.[45]

The summer of 1790 represented the apogee of the Revolution but also saw the enactment of two measures that the Assembly thought of as largely ancillary but would become solvents of the consensus forming around the constitution. In June 1790 the Assembly abolished nobility. It had previously suppressed distinction of orders and the deputy who proposed it claimed to be seeking to destroy titles that were in conflict with the principle of equality that was one of the bases of the constitution. Some prominent nobles, including Lafayette, supported the proposal, with Lafayette offering a motion comprised of five articles that banned all titles. Lafayette declared that the motion so clearly conformed to the constitution that he believed it did not require a long debate and that he supported it wholeheartedly.

Opponents sought to use the constitutional component against the motion, with Louis, marquis de Foucauld de Lardimalie contending that because the issue, which was being discussed in an evening session, was constitutional, it should be examined in a morning meeting of the Assembly. Lafayette replied that the articles were not constitutional in nature but "necessary consequences" of the constitution. After a spirited and sometimes contentious debate, the motion, with an additional provision barring the display of coats of arms, passed.[46]

In the view of many deputies, the suppression of nobility was logical and non-controversial, but it alienated a considerable portion of the nobility from the Revolution. Many among them believed that the nobility had led the way in renouncing their fiscal privileges and had acquiesced to legal and fiscal equality, so the abolition of nobility after its members had accepted civic equality seemed gratuitous and excessive.[47]

In this respect, the reaction of the marquis de Ferrières is illustrative. He had been effusive after the meeting of August 4, despite having entered the Assembly only on June 27. Years later, in his memoirs, he wrote that the nobility had patiently tolerated all that the Revolution had done against it, an allusion to the loss of its privileges. The majority of the nobility in the provinces, he asserted, had observed the drafting of the constitution without concern but the abolition of nobility made much of the nobility irreconcilable enemies of the Revolution.[48]

Again, for deputies the rationale for the action was logical and even incidental. As Lafayette had stated, it was a necessary consequence of the constitution and did not seem to require debate, an interpretation also shared by Thomas Jefferson, who considered the action as complementing the meeting of the night of August 4.[49] In the final analysis, however, it produced a significant erosion of support for the constitution among a small but influential group that might otherwise have supported it.

The following month, in July 1790, the Assembly inadvertently provoked a dispute with the Catholic Church when it enacted the Civil Constitution of the Clergy, ultimately alienating many among the clergy and the faithful. Once again, however, in the view of deputies, the legislation was almost incidental, an alignment of an institution with the new administrative structure that the Assembly had created.[50]

Under the old regime there had been 135 bishops in France, but the Assembly, having organized the kingdom into eighty-three departments, determined that dioceses would be in accordance with departments, meaning there would be one bishop for each department. Deputies viewed the action not only as reasonable but also, because the Church was to be supported by the state after the appropriation of its property in November 1789, fiscally responsible. Fiscal considerations also led it to consolidate local parishes. With perhaps the exception of its treatment of monasteries, scholars generally agree that the Assembly, through its Ecclesiastical Committee, undertook a good-faith effort to reform the Church.[51]

Indeed, the legislation itself was less the cause of the schism that resulted than was the refusal of a substantial part of the clergy to accept any regulation of the Church. The reaction of the clergy surprised the Assembly. The kingdom had accepted the reorganization of municipal and provincial government—indeed, in numerous rural villages *curés* had organized municipal elections and some had been elected as municipal officers.[52] That experience almost certainly led members of the Assembly to believe that the Civil Constitution of the Clergy would also be well received. It was not, which led the Assembly to take a fateful action that widened the breach and eroded support for the constitution. In November 1790 the Assembly required all clergy to take an oath of loyalty to the Civil Constitution of the Clergy. For deputies it was a question of obedience to the law.[53]

Whereas deputies would have seen negotiation with the Papacy as compromising national sovereignty, many in the clergy viewed the matter differently. They perceived it in terms of reorganizing the Church without consulting the clergy. Although French kings had chosen bishops since the sixteenth century and the Assembly inferred that it could transfer that prerogative to the new sovereign power, the people, through elections, some saw the election of bishops as contrary to Church doctrine and the omission of the Papacy in the reform effort as unacceptable.[54] For its part, the Assembly believed that it was not interfering in doctrinal, sacramental, or spiritual matters but simply harmonizing the Church with the new administrative structure of the kingdom.[55] Ultimately, the requirement of the oath precipitated a schism that led to a distinction between constitutional and refractory clergy, forcing lay Catholics to make a choice.[56] The condemnation of the Civil Constitution of the Clergy by the pope in 1791 forced yet another choice and the break with the Church weakened the constitution.

During the summer and fall of 1790 the Assembly undertook a restructuring of the judiciary, again resorting to the elective principle for the selection of judges. In the winter and spring of 1791, it debated the requirements and eligibility for the legislature. One of the measures it enacted in this respect also had an unanticipated influence on the constitution.

In May 1791, as a gesture of good faith as it neared completion of the constitution, the Assembly, in an act known as the Self-Denying Ordinance, disqualified its entire membership from election to the next legislature.

In doing so, deputies were forcing themselves to enter the society that they had created, but the measure also deprived the kingdom of its only experienced legislators in a country with no legislative tradition.[57] All continuity at the legislative level would be lost as an entirely new group of men came to interact with the king.

Buoyed by Louis's visit to the Assembly and by the *Fête de la Fédération*, deputies were optimistic as the year 1790 came to a close.[58] Indeed, the contrast in outlook in the Assembly between the end of 1789 and the end of 1790 was striking. At the end of 1789 one deputy had written of his fear of insurrection in the provinces. Toward the end of 1790 a different deputy expressed his complete sense of hopefulness, writing that the monarch was entirely in favor of the Revolution and how fortunate France was to have a king who was a friend of laws and the constitution.[59]

The Constitution Takes Hold

From the moment the Assembly had declared its intention to produce a constitution, the undertaking had captured the attention of much of the public.[60] In early 1790, on the eve of municipal elections, a newspaper reported that the mayor of Gap had introduced the practice of reading the proceedings of the Assembly aloud at the *Hôtel de Ville*. Citizens heard the sound of a bell and hurried to learn about their true interests, leading them to become more capable of participating in public administration and more devoted to the constitution.[61]

There were other methods of engagement as well. A number of "catechisms," pamphlets or short books, appeared that offered the traditional question and answer format of religious catechisms to explain the constitution. Instead of religion or religious doctrine, the instruction was to be in the meaning and ideals of the constitution as an integral component of civic education.[62]

Often the catechisms were rudimentary and specifically directed toward rural inhabitants. One of them, for example, began with the question "What is a constitution?" and provided an answer that drew an invidious comparison with the old regime.[63] Another asked "What needs to be done to give harmony and lasting stability to a political society?" to which the answer was "it is necessary to determine the constitution."[64] The Jacobin Club, the formal name of which was the Society of Friends of the Constitution, issued a "patriotic instruction" that was subtitled "catechism of the constitution."[65] The constitution was also an object of song and poetry.[66]

Deputies were favorably disposed toward the civic catechisms. Rabaut de Saint-Etienne praised the format for reducing two hundred decrees to a few pages. He wrote that if deputies had wanted to explain the seven volumes of decrees that currently existed, beginning with the first, it would take more than ten years to accomplish, but a man who knew the catechism well would know the constitution. He also underscored the central place of the constitution, calling it the moral foundation of the state and asserting that there was only one moral foundation.[67]

There were more extensive and sophisticated efforts as well. Jean Joseph Regnault published a two-volume exposition of the constitution intended for a wide audience, especially students but also others, including parents and political clubs. One question posed in his work was whether there had previously been a constitution. The answer was that there had not been one because all powers were combined and resided in the hands of one individual, whereas the constitution represented the division and distribution of powers. Regnault used a footnote to dispute the notion that France previously had a constitution.[68]

There was also a work of hundreds of pages that appeared as a dictionary, which was a popular format early in the Revolution. The *Dictionnaire de la constitution* by P. M. Gautier initially appeared in 1791 and had a second printing in 1792 after the completion of the constitution. Gautier contended that the right to establish a constitution belonged to the people and only the people. Any constitution that the people itself did not make or if one was given to them was flawed and invalid. Previously, Gautier wrote, France had not had a constitution. The people obeyed laws they had not made, sovereignty was shared between the monarch and aristocratic bodies, powers were confused, the rights of citizens consistently violated because they were misunderstood, and those of the nation were forgotten.

In the edition published after the completion of the constitution, Gautier acknowledged that it had some deficiencies, which he attributed to the inexperience of its authors, something they had admitted. Time, he wrote, would repair the flaws and he declared it to be the most perfect of all then in existence, providing a large number of examples to support his judgment. Equality of rights, he stated, was the base of the French constitution.[69]

It would be difficult to overstate the degree of attachment felt by much of the French populace for the constitution. The most tangible manifestation was the establishment of an extraordinary number of chapters of the Society of Friends of the Constitution across France after the founding of the original chapter in Paris, known as the Jacobin Club because it met in a Dominican monastery—in Paris the Dominicans were called Jacobins. Although there was a tradition of social organizations such as salons, academies, literary societies, and the like, the clubs founded during the Revolution were new entities, demarcated from the previous bodies by their focus on politics. According to the most comprehensive study of them, they were "spontaneous creations of local patriots."[70] In a sign of the hope generated by the municipal elections, the network of clubs began to expand from the original Paris club in 1790. Approximately a year later, in March 1791, they numbered in the hundreds, with clubs in sixty-eight departments.[71]

The esteem and affection that developed within the kingdom for the constitution was extraordinary.[72] Indeed, in early 1791, as the constitution seemed to be nearing completion, the administrators of the Department of Creuse suggested to the eighty-two other departments that each of them send two administrators to the Assembly and the king to express their gratitude for the blessing of the constitution.[73]

The King Repudiates the Constitution

As the constitution took hold in the kingdom, Louis was immensely popular because of his linkage with it.[74] Although he had professed to bind himself to the work of the Assembly on multiple occasions—his acceptance of the title of Restorer of French liberties in August 1789, his visit to the Assembly on February 4, 1790, and especially the *Fête de la Fédération* on July 14, 1790, at which, in the presence of tens of thousands, he had taken an oath to uphold the constitution—as the constitution neared completion Louis concluded that he did not wish to be associated with it.

On the night of June 21 the monarch and his family surreptitiously left the Tuileries palace and headed toward eastern France.[75] Only days before it had been publicly reported that Louis had written an urgent letter to Condé urging him to return to France and submit himself to the national will. Reports also circulated that the comte d'Artois was paying all his debts in Paris and was preparing to return before July 14 in order to attend the *Fête de la Fédération*.[76] It was because of such accounts that the news of Louis's departure precipitated the profound shock and disbelief that it did.[77]

The king left behind a letter presenting a long list of grievances that began with a denunciation of the constitution that he had solemnly sworn before the Assembly and the nation to uphold. Condemnation of the constitution pervaded the document, which he had spent six months preparing.[78] Louis criticized the new judiciary and objected that the new administrative structure enacted by the Assembly vested too much power in departments, districts, and municipalities. He complained that the officials of those bodies were elected and stated that he did not believe it was possible to govern the country through the structure established by the Assembly. He asked whether the French had sent representatives to the Assembly to see their king insulted and deprived of his freedom as he devoted himself to the establishment of theirs.[79]

Hardman argued that Louis wished to modify rather than reject the constitution, but ultimately it made no difference.[80] His demonstrable insincerity and the acrimonious tone of his criticisms established a binary choice between himself and the constitution. He effectively admitted to creating such a choice in the opening paragraph that criticized the constitution, declaring that he was presenting to Frenchmen and the universe an account of his conduct and that of the government that had established itself in the kingdom. Underscoring the choice that the king had instigated, the deputies of the Department of Côte d'Or wrote letters to the administrators and electors of their department in which they characterized Louis's departure as an attack on the constitution and assured their constituents that far from demoralizing deputies, the crisis had instead given them new courage and vigor.[81] Similarly, a message from the Jacobin Club to its affiliates, which was read at the *Hôtel de Ville* of Paris, called for citizens to view the Assembly as their guide and the constitution as their rallying cry.[82]

Louis's decision to force a choice between himself or the constitution was a mistake of catastrophic proportions. The king and his party were detained in the small town of Varennes in eastern France. After initially promising Louis, who had told some of the townspeople that he would not leave the kingdom, that they would accompany him to his destination, Montmédy, they later told him that his residence was in Paris and that he must return to it. Unaware of the existence of the letter Louis had left behind, of course, the citizens of Varennes had to make a direct choice between their loyalty to the king and their loyalty to the Assembly and the constitution. They unreservedly chose the latter.[83] It was a choice replicated all over France.

Indeed, from Paris one deputy wrote a private letter, apparently to his brother and sister, telling them that the Assembly was greatly venerated in Paris and that people in the street cried out that they no longer had a king and that the Assembly was their monarch.[84] One contemporary was struck by the complete calm in Paris and the unity of the Assembly. Describing Louis as traitorous and useless, he declared that the king was no longer desired.[85] Pocket portraits of Louis carried by citizens were discarded and his name removed from signs. The word "national" quickly replaced that of "royal" nearly everywhere.[86]

It was not just in Paris or a small eastern town that the meaning of Louis's departure from Paris was understood. Citizens in distant rural departments also comprehended the clear choice thrust upon them by the king. In its aftermath, the directory of the Department of Cantal wrote to the Assembly to express its unqualified support. The directory lamented that the chief administrator of the state had abandoned the position assigned to him by law. It speculated that the king undoubtedly believed that all powers were going to dissolve, the constitution would self-destruct and despotism would hover over its ruins. The administrators assured deputies that the Assembly was the center of all authority, had never ceased to enjoy the full confidence of the nation and that the French would rally around it. They pledged to reinforce the efforts of the Assembly, to support the nation and the law and die if necessary because of their unwavering zeal for the constitution decreed by the Assembly.[87] The messages of support for the constitution encouraged deputies.[88]

There is not one recorded instance of any demonstration or activity in favor of the king anywhere.[89] To the contrary, Louis's standing eroded considerably once the contents of his letter became known. When he returned to Paris on June 25 he was not jeered but met instead with utter silence and upon his arrival at the Tuileries palace a group of spectators shouted *vive la loi, vive la nation*.[90]

As addresses of support for the Assembly poured in from all over the kingdom, one deputy wrote to his constituents that there was only one desire in France and that no human power could resist it.[91] At the same time, however, Louis's departure from Paris dealt a blow to the constitution. His faithlessness with respect to the constitution led to the emergence of a republican movement in Paris after his return to the city. The development unsettled deputies, who believed that the proclamation of a republic would upend their two years of work on the constitution. These concerns culminated with the Assembly's debate on the fate of the king in July 1791.

Resolving the Dilemma of an Unwilling King

Deputies now had to confront the role of the king in a constitutional structure that he had renounced. Under questioning from three deputies named by the Assembly to examine his conduct, Louis claimed that during his trip back to Paris he had become aware that the public heavily supported the constitution and that he was prepared to make personal sacrifices for the happiness of his people. He made a similar remark privately to Lafayette soon after his return to Paris.[92]

On July 13 several committees jointly charged with making a report on Louis's flight submitted their findings. The committees had to navigate the Assembly's earlier declaration of the inviolability of the king with his action, but did not lift the suspension imposed after his return to Paris. The report declared that Louis was free to refuse acceptance of the constitution but that if he did it would be put into effect without him—a statement that he would lose his throne.[93]

Under extraordinary security precautions, the Assembly debated the report for three days.[94] On the third day of debate Barnave gave a speech that began with the statement that he was leaving aside the constitution to speak about the Revolution. Ignoring the question of royal inviolability, he drew attention to the grandeur of the Revolution and asked if the Assembly defied the constitution once, at what point would it or its successors stop? He argued that any further change would be disastrous and asked the Assembly if it was going to conclude the Revolution or begin it again? Declaring that the night of August 4 had given greater strength to the Revolution than any of the Assembly's constitutional decrees, he asked deputies what night of August 4 remained to be done, except against property?

Barnave urged his colleagues to recognize that the common interest required that the Revolution be concluded. The Assembly had already demonstrated its ability to establish beneficial institutions and he urged his colleagues to prove that they had the strength and wisdom to protect and maintain them. Alluding to the expressions of support the Assembly had received after Louis's flight for being courageous and powerful, he asserted that it should now be wise and moderate.[95] Barnave's speech, which followed two other powerful ones by Adrien Jean François Duport and Jean Baptiste Salle, concluded the debate.[96] The Assembly voted to close discussion and print the three speeches, which were to be sent to all departments. Deputies approved the report and the proposed articles of the committee and the following day, July 16, it confirmed Louis's suspension until the constitution was completed and could be presented to him in its entirety for acceptance or rejection.[97]

The decision was unpopular, but the Assembly was more fearful of politicized popular elements in Paris overturning its ideals than it was of a king whom deputies hoped had been chastened and would embrace the constitution.[98] The Assembly's decision to retain Louis angered republicans and led to the formulation of a petition at the Cordeliers Club that asked the Assembly to annul its decree, consider the monarch as having abdicated and create a new executive power. The petition also asked that the decision by the Assembly to retain Louis be the object of a plebiscite in the departments, a request that could only have angered the Assembly. Confident in the ideals that emerged from the night of August 4, the Assembly had never submitted any of its actions to a plebiscite. Moreover, they feared that such an action could provoke a civil war. To gain signatures, the petition was placed on the Altar of the Fatherland used days earlier at the *Fête de la Fédération*.

After two men found under the Altar of the Fatherland were murdered, Parisian authorities responded forcefully. They declared martial law and, after the crowd failed to obey an order to disperse, the National Guard opened fire, leading to a significant loss of life.[99] Although they deplored the bloodshed, most in the Assembly believed the incident validated the decision to allow Louis to retain the throne if he accepted the constitution. The episode seemed to indicate the danger of violence and civil war if it abandoned its course.

A letter by the deputy Duquesnoy provides insight into the outlook of many in the Assembly. When he sent his constituents a copy of the three speeches, Duquesnoy wrote that he wanted to add some details to the information contained in them. From the time the king had left Paris, he wrote, malevolent or ill-informed men had attacked the constitution and attempted to intimidate the Assembly. Moreover, in seeking to have Louis dethroned and tried, they had advocated principles contrary to those established by the Assembly.

Duquesnoy claimed that republicans had not given thought to how the king should be replaced and asked how one could replace an institution sanctioned by the national will? However mistaken their view may have been, republicans had the right to espouse it, but only until the promulgation of the law. After that, their activity was an act of rebellion against the law, especially when it was underpinned by a mob that jeopardized the freedom of the Assembly to deliberate.

Asserting that representatives of the people should not suffer such affronts against national sovereignty, Duquesnoy concluded by declaring that the Assembly was firmly determined to have the sovereign will of the nation, of which it was the organ and interpreter, respected and executed. The patriot deputies of the Assembly, having been divided among themselves for too long on various issues, had joined together on the important question of the monarch and any effort to divide them would fail.[100]

Another deputy explained the decision to his constituents with the observation that in the constitution of a monarchical state it was difficult not to acknowledge the necessity of a monarch. One could not criticize the decree without undertaking the overturning of the constitution and without establishing a different form of government. The worst outcome would be to replace a soon to be completed constitution founded on important principles with a state of affairs subversive of all order and to reopen a new revolution.[101]

Concern about popular agitation also led the Assembly to revise the constitution in a manner that made it less democratic than it had originally been. It left the requirements to qualify as an active citizen unchanged, which somewhat disguised its intent, but raised considerably the qualification to be an elector in electoral assemblies. Prior to the revision, the qualification to be an elector had been that one had to pay a sum in direct taxes equal to the value of ten days wages for unskilled labor. The revised requirement to qualify as an elector was that one had to own property valued at the sum of 200 days of unskilled labor or, if one rented a residence, to pay in taxes a sum equivalent to 150 days of unskilled labor. In smaller towns, with 6,000 or fewer inhabitants, the requirements were 150 and 100 days respectively. In rural areas one had to own property valued at the sum of 100 days of unskilled labor or to be a sharecropper with property valued at 400 days of unskilled labor. In one respect, the revisions are meaningless because the elections to the successor body of the National Assembly, the Legislative Assembly, had already occurred under the original criteria, meaning that the revised requirements were never utilized. The revisions, however, represented a retreat by deputies from their earlier, more democratic, impulse.[102]

The Completion of the Constitution

On August 5 the Committee on the Constitution began the presentation of the constitution, which had been drafted piecemeal, to the Assembly for final deliberations. Its spokesman, Jacques Guillaume Thouret, noted that the previous day had been the anniversary of the night when many abuses had been eradicated and had laid the foundations for the significant edifice that was nearing completion.[103]

The Assembly began discussion on August 8. Thouret, speaking for the Committee on the Constitution and the Committee on Revision, which had separated statutory laws from constitutional ones to prepare the document for consideration, told deputies that they had not established a constitution for a new people or a virgin land, but for a country that had been weighed down for centuries by institutions that were not compatible with a true constitution. The Assembly began to examine it clause by clause and the task continued until the end of the month.

The process provoked disagreements between the committees and the Assembly. The tension was evident in a letter one deputy wrote to his constituents in mid-August in which he asked who was more infallible than the pope and the Committees on the Constitution and Revision?[104] Jean-Marie Roland de la Platière, a close observer who had been sent by the city of Lyon as its liaison to the Assembly, wrote to a municipal official in Lyon of the great anger directed toward the Committee on the Constitution, which Roland believed had distorted the constitution.[105]

The dissension abated after Thouret made a conciliatory speech acknowledging that the constitution was a common responsibility and that the committees were not seeking to impose their view. He asked his colleagues to consider the common good rather than compromise the Revolution out of resentment toward the committees.[106]

The disagreement should not be overestimated. One of those opposed to the revisions, Bertand Barère, provided details on the group and its efforts. He claimed that there was a majority of deputies in the Assembly, about seven hundred in number, who were working to complete the constitution and that there were approximately thirty-five deputies opposed to the revisions of the committees. If one accepts Barère's statement that there were thirty-five dissidents—and being one of them he was unlikely to understate their number—and his number of seven hundred deputies working to complete the constitution, then those opposed to the revisions comprised only 5 percent of those engaged in its completion. Barère wrote that by their resistance the thirty-five who fought the committees were able to attain much of what they wanted.[107] The completion, however, took longer than anticipated.[108]

The numbers indicate that although the constitution may have been regarded as imperfect, it was nonetheless an object of consensus, backed by 95 percent of the seven hundred deputies dedicated to its completion. Barére, in fact, vigorously defended and fulsomely praised the work of the Assembly in his memoirs, hailing its establishment of a constitution that guaranteed rights and freedoms and lauding the Assembly for founding national unity.[109] Deputies were proud of the document they had created.[110]

The Assembly completed its review at the end of the month and on September 2 Thouret began a final reading of the constitution to the Assembly, which he completed the next day. At 9:00 p.m. on September 3 sixty deputies of the Assembly, with Thouret as their spokesman, went to the Tuileries to present it to the monarch. As a gesture of goodwill and a symbol of the hope for a new beginning, the Assembly ordered the removal of Louis's guards.

The day after the delegation presented the constitution to the king, a Sunday, the gates to the Tuileries Gardens, which had been locked, were opened and the public streamed in in large numbers. They went to the chapel and royal apartments, where Louis made an appearance. The crowd erupted with cheers of "vive la nation! vive la constitution! vive la liberté! vive le roi!" What was especially noticeable, however, according to one report, was a new acclamation: "Vive le premier roi constitutionnel des François!"[111]

Expectations were high—the hope was that the benevolence of the constitution and the sincerity of the king in accepting the principles of the Revolution would lead to his quick acceptance of it, which would subsume all differences.[112] Louis, however, waited ten days before giving his assent. His initial acceptance was by letter, but he appeared personally in the Assembly the next day to sign it in the presence of deputies.[113]

Despite the delay, Louis's acceptance was warmly greeted and regarded as a new beginning.[114] The administrators of the Department of Eure sent a letter to the king telling him that he had just sealed a "treaty of alliance" between himself and the French people by accepting the constitution. They expressed the hope that the oath of fidelity he had taken would be the guarantor of a reciprocal confidence.[115] There were effusive celebrations in Paris, with one deputy comparing the intensity of the celebration in Paris to the *Fête de la Fédération* in 1790.[116] Louis appeared in many places throughout Paris and his participation in public joy was seen as evidence of his sincerity. There were similar reactions in the departments.[117]

Amid the joy, however, there were troubling undercurrents. On August 31, as the constitution neared completion, a number of conservative deputies, overwhelmingly former nobles along with a few clergy, had denounced the work of the preceding two years and declared that they would never cease to be enemies of the new constitution.[118] On September 15 a group of conservative deputies criticized the monarch's acceptance of the constitution, claiming that it was not done freely.[119] Although they represented only a minority of the Assembly, the declaration signified that there was a cohort in the Assembly, as well as in the kingdom, that was unwilling to accept the constitution even after the king had.

Nevertheless, the exuberance driving the celebrations is easy to understand—for many weeks the kingdom had endured a state of unprecedented and perilous uncertainty, far greater than the paralysis that had initially led to the demand for a constitution in 1788–89. Never before had an unimpaired hereditary monarch been suspended from the throne with his fate in the hands of a body legitimized only by the force of public opinion, which in both July 1789 and June 1791 had overwhelmingly rallied to it rather than the king.

Louis's acceptance of the constitution seemed to mark the end of a period of unprecedented irregularity, unpredictability, and confusion.[120] For the majority of the populace that supported it, the constitution, fully in force for the first time, represented the best hope for regular, stable, and fixed government, which had been absent since at least 1788.[121] The sense of relief and accomplishment is evident in a speech by a priest during scheduled celebrations across the kingdom on September 25. He asked if the passage of the Red Sea was any more miraculous than that from the old regime to the new and praised the constitution as the work of God for the happiness of men.[122]

The Assembly wanted to integrate the principles of the Revolution into the educational system through a reorganization of it.[123] It was only after the constitution had been presented to the king, however, that Talleyrand brought forward a plan. His report highlighted the importance of the constitution and declared that the constitution would be incomplete if it did not address public instruction. With the constitution completed, and exhausted after twenty-eight months without respite, the Assembly decided to defer the task to its successor, the Legislative Assembly.[124]

The day after the Assembly delegated the reorganization of national education to the succeeding legislature, it voted to preserve all currently existing institutions. It did enact one change, however. In an effort to instill the principles of the constitution, the Assembly mandated that every law school in the kingdom designate a professor to teach a course on the French constitution to law students, effective the following month.[125]

Seeking to make the constitution a rallying point for the entire kingdom, the Assembly declared a general amnesty for all offenses arising from the Revolution.[126] It freed both those who had been accused of colluding in Louis's flight from Paris in June as well as those who had been implicated in disturbances in the aftermath of the killings at the *Champ de Mars*.

Days after his term as a deputy in the Assembly ended and as he prepared to return to Le Mans, Ménard de la Groye wrote to his wife that he blessed the revolution in which he had had the good fortune to take part. He declared that he loved the constitution with all of his heart because it seemed to be founded on lasting principles and was wisely conceived in all of its components. It met the standard of good government, about which he claimed to have been thinking for thirty years, and one could not advocate the principles of freedom and equality excessively nor teach men too much about respect for laws.[127] Another deputy, calling it "imposing and sublime," hoped that the benevolence of the constitution and the certitude that the king would accept the Revolution would make differences disappear and ensure a happy future.[128]

On September 30, its last day, Louis once again appeared in the Assembly and pledged to maintain the constitution.[129] All deliberations ended at 2:30 p.m., after which a "mournful silence" descended on the chamber as deputies realized that the existence of the National Assembly was about to end.[130] They had shared an experience infinitely larger than any of them had anticipated. In this somber moment of inactivity and, for some, reflection, the full weight of what they had accomplished settled on them as they prepared to enter the society that they had created.

The Forgotten Constitution: The Origins, Realization, and Legacy of the French Constitution of 1791.
Michael P. Fitzsimmons, Oxford University Press. © Oxford University Press 2025.
DOI: 10.1093/9780197793978.003.0010

Conclusion

It would be difficult to overstate the significance of the promulgation of the Constitution of 1791. After nearly two centuries of monarchy-centered government, by the late 1780s the desire for a constitution had taken hold among the subjects of the French king. The concept was inchoate and its form uncertain, but the driving force of the demand was fear of despotism, with the idea of a constitution linked to the rule of law. The expectation when the Estates General opened was that the body would impart order and regularity to French government by stipulating the duties of Crown and *parlement* and integrate the Estates General into the political structure through convocations at fixed intervals, the periodicity of which was to be determined.

After the night of August 4, however, the constitution evolved to a much larger project, ultimately bestowing civil and natural rights on a sovereign citizenry. The proclamation of the constitution marked the end of a mode of government that the people of France no longer believed represented its interests or met its needs. The change from monarchy-centered government to constitutional monarchy came about through the willful actions of elected representatives of the French people and led to the transformation of a traditionally consultative body into a legislature that became the organ of the sovereign people.

Legacy

The Constitution of 1791 also inspired and set the standard for constitutionalism on a global scale. At a time when the United States Constitution accepted and institutionalized slavery, making it a weapon of control, the Constitution of 1791 conferred rights on all citizens through legal equality, making it an instrument of liberation and rights.[1] In this manner, it became the aspirational model for Europe and the world.

The Constitution of 1791 also proclaimed the idea of natural rights. It opened with the Declaration of the Rights of Man and Citizen, which had originally been intended to serve as the preamble but was instead proclaimed independently in August, 1789. The first sentence of the first article declared "The Constitution guarantees as natural and civil rights" and enumerated them. The Declaration of the Rights of Man and Citizen was a primary inspiration for the Universal Declaration of Human Rights promulgated by the United Nations in 1948.

In addition to conferring civil and natural rights on citizens, the Constitution of 1791 enacted the broadest franchise in Europe and the Atlantic world, replacing the factional Court politics of monarchy-centered government with participatory citizen politics. One historian noted that "the electoral principle became the battering-ram of the new regime against the old, and elections its most striking constitutional innovation."[2] Another wrote that elections became the source of political legitimacy and that the French Revolution brushed aside the political governing class of the old regime and gave birth to electoral democracy.[3] It did not establish universal manhood suffrage but instead created the categories of active and passive citizens. Active citizens had rights and responsibilities whereas passive citizens had rights.[4] The Assembly set the threshold of tax payment required to be an active citizen low, seeking to expand the number of active citizens as much as possible.[5] Between 60 and 70 percent of the eligible male population, numbering in the millions, met the requirement for participation in elections.[6]

The primary assemblies that became the cornerstone of the electoral system further reinforced the ideals of equality and fraternity proclaimed by the Assembly. The transformation wrought was particularly striking in Rennes, where in January 1789, members of the nobility had used servants and lackeys to unleash a violent assault on the Third Estate that led to fatalities for contesting the dominant position of the clergy and nobility in the Estates of Brittany.[7] The *parlement* of Rennes refused to undertake an investigation in its aftermath. Fewer than eighteen months later, tanners, a carpenter, and a fish seller—an illustration of how far down the social scale the quality of active citizen extended—mingled as equals with a former magistrate of the *parlement* of Rennes in a primary assembly to determine their future together.[8] It was a situation that would have been inconceivable in the hierarchical and polarized Brittany of 1788 and most of 1789.

Despite its legacy of leading the way on fundamental values of the modern world, the Constitution of 1791 has received little recognition or acknowledgment outside of France. A noted American legal scholar, for example, in an admirable work on Revolutionary constitutions, never mentioned the Constitution of 1791, the template for Revolutionary constitutions.[9] Similarly, a distinguished historian produced an impressive history of the emergence of written constitutions in the modern world in which she argued that constitutions emerged largely from "patterns of war and violence." Much of her focus, however, is after the Constitution of 1791, which is scarcely mentioned. Moreover, the impetus for the Constitution of 1791 was organic, arising from within the kingdom through a crisis partially generated by the costs of French participation in the War of American Independence, to be sure, but it was not a product of war or violence, again underscoring its distinctive character.[10]

The Constitution of 1791 became emblematic of the bond between a people and its government, rendering a constitution a symbol of legitimacy. One contemporary who authored an extensive dictionary on the Constitution of 1791 declared that the purpose of a good constitution was to ensure that all citizens enjoyed the full and free exercise of their natural rights. He also asserted that the right to establish a constitution belonged only to the people.[11] This understanding of a constitution gave it a central place in French political life and the conquests of the French republic spread the idea of a constitution across Europe.

The Directory created satellite or "sister" republics in the Netherlands, Switzerland, and Italy and put constitutions in place in all of them, although that in the Netherlands proved contentious.[12] After internal divisions in Switzerland, France invaded the country in 1798, leading to the collapse of the Swiss Confederation. The French supported the creation of the Helvetic Republic, which came into existence in April 1798, with a constitution modeled after the French Constitution of the Year III.[13] Napoleon Bonaparte, who had given the Cisalpine Republic in Italy a constitution in 1797, continued the practice of implanting constitutions after he came to power in France in 1799, which ultimately spread constitutions from Spain to Poland.[14] It proved to have a strong attraction to other peoples—by 1820, fifty constitutions were in existence in continental Europe.[15]

After the defeat of Bonaparte, the Prussian monarch, Frederick William III, promised to establish constitutional government and several south German states promulgated constitutions. The reactionary Carlsbad Decrees in 1819, however, dealt a severe blow to constitutional efforts. Frederick William III reneged on his plan for a constitution in Prussia and northern German states gave up constitutional projects that they had been considering. Although the southern state of Hesse-Darmstadt enacted a constitution in 1820, in many respects the constitutional ideal and other reforms effectively ended in 1819. Similar repression took place in Spain and Italy.

Decade's later economic hardship and political discontent produced a reemergence of constitutionalism in the Revolutions of 1848. A primary impetus of the Revolutions of 1848 was nationalism, but embedded within the nationalistic impulse was a sense of national self-determination, symbolized by a constitution that defined the relationship between monarch and people, as the Constitution of 1791 had.

The catalyst for the Revolutions of 1848 was the February Revolution in France, and a critical moment in the February Revolution occurred when the leader of the opposition movement in Paris invoked a right enumerated in the Constitution of 1791, which was not the constitution then in force, that guaranteed citizens the right to assemble peacefully, a component of what has been called "a reverence for particular constitutions."[16] A recent study of the Revolutions of 1848 declared that "1848 was the year of constitutions," noting that every state that experienced a revolution promulgated a constitution of some kind. Even in countries that did not experience a revolution, significant changes came through a constitution.[17] Constitutions became a new tactic in political struggle, leading to the promulgation of multiple constitutions, each with a different purpose, leading one scholar to classify constitutions as "preventive, revolutionary and counter-revolutionary."[18]

The same scholar, in his sweeping treatment of the Revolutions of 1848, acknowledged that he had barely begun to scratch the surface of what he termed a "prodigious European effort at constitution-making."[19] He cataloged some of the governmental and societal changes that the constitutions brought about, which included religious freedom and Jewish emancipation, legal equality, abolition of seigneurial obligations, termination of monarchy-centered government, and an expansion of the franchise.[20] All of these accomplishments had been achieved by the Constitution of 1791 more than half a century earlier, indicating the degree to which it was consciously or perhaps even subconsciously a model.

The Constitution of 1791 proclaimed legal equality and natural rights for all and brought into existence the greatest degree of popular sovereignty in the world.[21] Its spirit is captured in a letter written by one of its primary architects, Rabaut de Saint-Etienne, a member of the Committee on the Constitution, who wrote that the constitution was the moral foundation of the state.[22] It was this ethos that made the Constitution of 1791 the model and inspiration for the wave of constitution-making that spread across Europe in the early and mid-nineteenth century and later across the world. It replaced the will of monarchs with law and legalism codified in a written constitution as the governing principle of the state.

The Constitution of 1791 opened with the Declaration of the Rights of Man and Citizen, its original preamble, which was followed by a new preamble. After declaring its adherence to the Declaration of Rights as the basis for the constitution, the new preamble proclaimed the irrevocable abolition of all institutions injurious to liberty and equality of rights and enumerated many of them. It further declared that privilege had been abolished and that there was no exception to laws common to all French. The preamble was the incarnation of a larger principle that comprised the fundamental meaning of the French Revolution—the right of a people to break with its past and to create new institutions that it believed best expressed its needs and values.

The Constitution of 1791 is critical to understanding the significance and legacy of the French Revolution. Constitutionalism became a central component of the Revolution. The National Convention, the body that assumed power after the negation of the Constitution of 1791, produced two constitutions, although the first of them was never put in force. Recognizing the attachment of the French people to the constitution, after the *coup* of Brumaire, which terminated the constitution established by the Convention, Bonaparte sought to legitimize his seizure of power by promulgating a constitution. Moreover, he sought to cover each accretion of power with legitimacy through a new constitution.

A decisive development occurred with the return of the Bourbon dynasty in 1814. A defining principle of the Counter-Revolution, a longtime leading source of support for Louis XVIII, was refusal to accept a constitution.[23] Louis XVIII acquiesced to this outlook by calling the document he issued a charter rather than a constitution. It was rhetorical legerdemain to obscure the fact that the Charter of 1814 ratified the acceptance by the Bourbon dynasty of most of the changes achieved by the Revolution, beginning with, despite its nomenclature, a constitution.[24] The Charter of 1814 opened with a declaration of rights that proclaimed equality before the law and stipulated that the legislature had power over taxation, to which all were subject. It created a constitutional monarchy and, with the exception of the issue of censorship, brought into existence a more liberal state than the contemporary England of Liverpool and Castlereagh.[25]

The centrality of constitutionalism as a focal point for legitimacy and loyalty became apparent only months later when Bonaparte escaped from Elba and returned to France. As Bonaparte approached Paris, Louis XVIII, in a bid to retain support, went before a joint session of the chambers and strongly affirmed his allegiance to the Charter.[26] It was in vain as Louis fled Paris a few days later and Bonaparte retook power. Bonaparte quickly formed a committee to draft a constitution, with the liberal Benjamin Constant a leading member. The document it produced was called the Additional Act to the Constitutions of the Empire, signifying that it did not replace Bonaparte's earlier texts, which would be revised at a later time. It was a mistake because the secretive nature of the drafting generated suspicion. The prevailing ideal favored the calling of a constitutional assembly, similar to what had happened in 1789.[27] The Additional Act was put to a plebiscite for approval but only a small percentage of those eligible to vote did so. Bonaparte, once the strong man of Europe, intuitively understood the need for a constitution to gain acceptance, although he did not believe in constitutionalism.[28]

It was precisely to avoid this outcome—the need for a constitution for a ruler to gain acceptance—that the monarchy-centered governments of Europe cracked down on burgeoning constitutional undertakings and other liberal ideals in 1819. Nevertheless, they, particularly constitutionalism, would burst forth again in 1848.

The progenitor of the drive toward constitutionalism was the Constitution of 1791. Apart from being the first constitution to endow citizens with civil and human rights and to inaugurate electoral democracy, the Constitution of 1791 has an additional transcendent legacy. With its enumeration in its preamble of the principles and institutions that had been eradicated, the Constitution of 1791—and the French Revolution—were a proclamation of the right to change. The legitimation of that right has continued to inspire down to the present.

Aftermath

A major paradox of the Constitution of 1791 is that it was arguably the most significant of French constitutions but also the shortest lived. On one hand, it not only inaugurated a constitutional tradition in France, Europe, and the world that continues to the present but it was also a progenitor of the concept of human rights. On the other hand, it was in force for just over ten months, negated by the overthrow of the monarchy on August 10, 1792. Its end was the result of the cumulative effect of discrete events, some already treated in this study, as well as royal behavior.

The enactment of the suspensive veto in September 1789 represented a compromise between an absolute veto and no veto power whatsoever. An absolute veto would potentially have enabled the monarch to compromise or even overturn the constitution to be produced by the Assembly. To deny him a veto would have rendered him a figurehead, an affront to dynastic tradition and a personal insult to Louis XVI. The structure of the suspensive veto, which was the linchpin of a "defensive constitution," preserved the ultimate sovereignty of the nation but also left the monarch with genuine power.

Under the terms of the suspensive veto, the king could veto a legislative act. The veto would hold for the remainder of the current legislative session and would have to be overridden by two successive legislatures, with each legislative session having a duration of two years. This meant that it would take years for a veto to be resolved. The lingering uncertainty inherent in the suspensive veto could disturb or inflame the body politic for years, as it quickly did.

In early November 1791, only weeks after beginning its duties, the Legislative Assembly passed a decree mandating that *émigrés* return to France by January 1, 1792. If they did not, they would be considered counterrevolutionary suspects, in which case they could have their lands sequestered and they could be sentenced to death if captured. At the end of the month, it also passed punitive legislation against refractory clergy, requiring them to take an oath of loyalty to the Constitution of 1791 within one week. Louis vetoed both measures, which gave the appearance, months after his involuntary return from Varennes, of being sympathetic to *émigrés* and refractory clergy and exacerbated residual distrust of him among the citizenry.[29] The vetoes could not have been resolved until October 1795 at the earliest, and were a source of tension.

The transfer of the king and his family from Versailles to Paris in early October 1789 was also a factor. The intent of the move to Versailles by Louis XIV in the seventeenth century had been to insulate the monarch from popular influence after the Fronde. After October 1789, however, Louis XVI was once again subject to pressure from the Parisian populace, which would ultimately lead to his overthrow.

Two other actions that vitiated support for the constitution among key constituencies during the summer of 1790 should be reiterated. In June 1790 the Assembly abolished nobility, which embittered members of an influential group whose support would have improved prospects for the constitution. Having agreed to give up fiscal privileges and accept legal equality, many within the nobility, which no longer had tangible privileges, saw its suppression as gratuitous. It alienated much of a group that might otherwise have been supportive of the constitution.

The following month, July 1790, the Assembly approved the Civil Constitution of the Clergy, a reorganization of the Church necessitated by the appropriation of Church lands in November 1789. To the Assembly, the Civil Constitution of the Clergy was a means to harmonize the Church with the new administrative structure of the kingdom that the Assembly had created. It was also necessary to provide financial support for the Church, particularly the clergy, because it had been stripped of its lands and property.

To many in the kingdom, however, the Church was a sacred and cherished religious institution, self-governed through the Papacy and bishops. What the Assembly saw as the exercise of sovereign authority in reorganizing civil society, many among the faithful saw as an unwarranted intrusion into the affairs of the Church, particularly because the Papacy was not consulted. In their view, the Assembly was making decisions that they believed could be made only by a General Council of the Church. The Assembly believed that it had acted in good faith through its Ecclesiastical Committee and the reaction against the Civil Constitution of the Clergy came as a surprise.

The reaction of deputies soon evolved into anger at what the Assembly came to view as disrespect for its authority and disloyalty to civic ideals. In late November 1790 it mandated that all clerical officeholders had to take an oath of loyalty to the Civil Constitution of the Clergy. The requirement created a divide that became even more bitter in 1791 after the Papacy refused to countenance the Civil Constitution of the Clergy. It forced a choice not only among clergy but also among parishioners and faithful who had to decide whether to follow their priest or bishop in whichever choice he made.[30] The Civil Constitution of the Clergy democratized the counter-revolution, extending it into every department and parish and effectively splitting France in two.

The Self-Denying Ordinance also played a role in undermining the constitution. By the spring of 1791 the entire new administrative and judicial structure of society was in place. As a gesture of good faith and accountability, in May 1791 the Assembly passed the Self-Denying Ordinance, which disqualified its members from election to its successor body, the Legislative Assembly, thereby depriving the kingdom of its only experienced legislators. As a result of the Self-Denying Ordinance, the Legislative Assembly consisted of an entirely new group of men. It began with no continuity, no institutional memory among its membership and no history of having worked with the monarch. The men of the Legislative Assembly did not have the degree of emotional investment in the constitution as their predecessors, for whom it had been, for the most part at least until June 1791, a unifying force.[31]

In June 1791, equally aware that the new administrative and judicial structure of the polity was in place and that the completion of the constitution, which was imminent, would cement it, the king made a crucial choice. Deeming the new constitution unacceptable, Louis secretly left Paris, moving toward the eastern frontier only to be detained at Varennes. He left behind a letter that castigated the constitution in the most scathing terms, alleging that the monarchy had been destroyed and that the constitution was unable to remedy any of the many ills of the kingdom, including violation of property, the endangerment of personal safety, unpunished crimes and complete anarchy. He contended that he had complained about all of these matters during what he called his captivity.

He denounced the judicial system and objected that he had no role in the making of laws but only the right to "obstruct" until the meeting of the third legislature.[32] He also lamented that justice was rendered in the name of the king but that it was in form only. He cast aspersions on the administrative reorganization, complaining that it vested too much authority with the municipalities, districts, and departments and protesting that the members of these bodies were elected. He disparaged them as possessing little influence and gaining little respect.

The letter cited finances as another area of disaffection and characterized the form of government as vicious, warning that it was becoming worse as the Assembly exceeded its authority. Indeed, he asserted that the Assembly was despotic and more barbarous and insufferable than any body in history. Louis declared that he could not govern through the system established by the Assembly in its current state and called its members rebels.

Far from rallying the populace to his side, as Louis clearly anticipated, the kingdom turned strongly against him. There was no backing for him in the Assembly and no demonstration of support for him anywhere in France. His harsh comments on the state of the kingdom and his denunciation of the constitution and the Assembly were jarring. Most regarded the king as dishonest and insincere and lost trust in him. His return to Paris met with sullen silence and the Assembly made his acceptance of the constitution a condition for regaining the throne.

All of these independent aspects and events, particularly the last, combined to destroy the Constitution of 1791. The Legislative Assembly convened on October 1, 1791, with many of its members having previously held positions in municipal, district, or departmental administration, which Louis had disparaged. In addition, whereas the king had been respected and liked at the opening of the Estates General, he was distrusted when the Legislative Assembly convened.

A number of deputies came to believe that the Holy Roman emperor was preparing to intervene in favor of the French royal family, although this does not appear to have been the case. France, however, began a drift toward war, with different political factions, both in the Legislative Assembly and at Court, believing war would serve its interests. The Brissotins saw war as a means to gain power and also believed that war would force Louis to reveal his true loyalties. For its part, the Crown believed that a victorious war would strengthen the monarch. Conversely, if France lost, he could regain powers and roll back much of the Revolutionary program. The hidden agendas of different constituencies drove France toward war.

In April 1792, in its single most significant act, the Legislative Assembly declared war on Austria. After initial success, the tide turned against France. As foreign troops approached Paris and with widespread suspicion about secret communications with the enemy by the royal family, strengthened by the dismissal of the war ministry, hostility toward the monarchy grew. In late July 1792 the Austrian military commander issued a manifesto threatening Paris with severe retribution if any harm came to the royal family.

The statement provoked both fear and hatred, and on August 10, 1792, a crowd of approximately 80,000 surrounded the Tuileries, almost certainly intending to kill Louis and proclaim a republic. Their effort failed when Louis made his way to the Legislative Assembly and received its protection, but deputies left his fate to the National Convention, which was to be elected through universal male suffrage. Technically, the constitution was still in effect, but with the king, a critical component of it, "suspended," in reality it was null and void.

Decades after the event, a close observer, the adult son of a deputy to the Assembly, noted that when the Constitution of 1791 was proclaimed the joy at the occasion was both widespread and sincere, rooted in the belief that the Revolution was over. The Assembly, he wrote, had declared it as if it had been in its power to do so.[33] Ultimately, however, among the essential conditions necessary for the success of the constitution were that it become firmly established, that all concerned abide by it peaceably in good faith and that there be no significant enemies within France or outside of its borders. None of these conditions were obtained. The Constitution of 1791 fell victim to a conflagration of its own shortcomings, duplicity, suspicion, and blind ambition.

During the time when study of the French Revolution was more ideologically oriented, historians who favored the Revolution asserted that the march on the Tuileries was emblematic of the sentiment of much of France and demonstrated that "the people" risked their lives to save France and to establish a republic. Georges Lefebvre cited the expressions of approval that arrived from provincial cities but these came from only a minority of the departments. In addition, the messages came from towns, which contained less than 10 percent of the population and even in the towns it was revolutionary radical minorities that formulated and sent declarations of support.

The insurrection of August 10, itself the product of a siege mentality in Paris generated by the Brunswick manifesto and not reflective of the sentiments of the kingdom as a whole, was the action of a minority of 80,000 in a city of 660,000 that was approved by radical minorities in urban centers of the kingdom. The small element that approved of the overthrow of the monarchy also explains the membership of the Convention that was elected in early September 1792, with only approximately 10–20 percent of eligible adult males participating, was drawn overwhelmingly from the urban middle class.[34] Participation generally declined even though the National Convention significantly enlarged the electorate—many who did not countenance the overthrow of the king stayed away from the assemblies.

In the final analysis, the National Convention was chosen by a small minority, which meant in turn that the republic was established by a minority. Under these circumstances, the Convention from its beginning had to govern a hostile or indifferent majority. It is not surprising that coercion, violence, and conflict followed. The years after the overthrow of the Constitution of 1791 were remembered with fear and loathing.

The period of the National Assembly seemed remarkable in contrast. It had ended the conflict between Crown and *parlement* and successfully introduced extraordinary change in the kingdom peacefully. A constitution became associated with good order and sanctioned authority, particularly because the Terror occurred during a period when no constitution was in force. It is illustrative of both the political disorder unleashed by the overthrow of the Constitution of 1791 and the sense of legitimacy conferred by a constitution that every successive regime has drafted one—since the negation of the Constitution of 1791 in August 1792 France has had eleven constitutions, although that of the Year II was never put into force. The brevity of the Constitution of 1791 in no way diminishes its significance.

The Forgotten Constitution: The Origins, Realization, and Legacy of the French Constitution of 1791.
Michael P. Fitzsimmons, Oxford University Press. © Oxford University Press 2025.
DOI: 10.1093/9780197793978.003.0011

Notes

Notes to Introduction

1. *Memoirs of the Duchess de Tourzel, governess of the children of France during the years 1789, 1790, 1791, 1792, 1793, and 1795*, François Joseph de Pérusse, duc de Cars, ed., 2 vols. (London: Remington, 1886), 2: 1–2.
2. Richard Bonney, "Was There a Bourbon Style of Government?" in *From Valois to Bourbon: Dynasty, State & Society in Early Modern France*, Keith Cameron, ed. (Exeter: University of Exeter, 1989), pp. 161–77, which used the province of Béarn as a case study of the particular Bourbon manner of governance.
3. Andrew Lossky, "The Absolutism of Louis XIV: Reality or Myth?" *Canadian Journal of History* 19 (1984): 1–15; Richard Bonney, "Absolutism: What's in a Name?" *French History* 1 (1987): 93–117; Nicholas Henshall, *The Myth of Absolutism: Change and Continuity in Early Modern European Monarchy* (London: Longman, 1992).
4. See, for example, William Beik, *Absolutism and Society in Seventeenth-Century France: State Power and Provincial Aristocracy in Languedoc* (Cambridge: Cambridge University Press, 1985).
5. For brief but incisive overviews, see William Doyle, "The Parlements," in *The French Revolution and the Creation of Modern Political Culture: The Political Culture of the Old Regime*, Keith Michael Baker, ed. (Oxford: Pergamon Press, 1987), pp. 157–67; Julian Swann, "Parlements and Provincial Estates," in *The Oxford Handbook of the Ancien Régime*, William Doyle, ed. (Oxford: Oxford University Press, 2012), pp. 93–108.
6. Peter R. Campbell, "Absolute Monarchy," in *The Oxford Handbook of the Ancien Régime*, William Doyle, ed. (Oxford: Oxford University Press, 2012), p. 17; Donna Bohanan, *Crown and Nobility in Early Modern France* (New York: Palgrave Macmillan, 2001), p. 3.
7. The term "absolutism" was not contemporaneous but arose in nineteenth-century France and Britain. In France, it was used as an invidious comparison with the reforms of the Revolution that redefined the monarchy. In Britain, it was a pejorative intended to create a contrast with the British constitutional monarchy.
8. David Bien, "The *Secrétaires du Roi*: Absolutism, Corps and Privilege under the Ancien Régime," in *Vom Ancien Régime zur Französischen Revolution*," Ernst Hinrichs, Eberhard Schmitt, and Rudolph Vierhaus, eds. (Göttingen: Vandenhoeck & Ruprecht, 1978), pp. 153–68, with the characterization on p. 159. For an earlier, somewhat less specific assertion of linkage between privilege and the constitution, particularly during the eighteenth century, Lester B. Mason, *The French Constitution and the Social Question in the Old Regime 1700–1789* (Bonn: Trapp, 1954), especially pp. 12–64. See also Michael P. Fitzsimmons, "Privilege and the Polity in France, 1786–1791," *The American Historical Review* 92 (1987): 269–95, especially pp. 270–71.
9. Linda Colley, "Empires of Writing: Britain, America and Constitutions, 1776–1848," *Law and History Review* 32 (2014): 257–58, 262–63.
10. Poland promulgated a constitution on May 3, 1791, before the French Constitution of 1791, but it was drafted by the king and put into force using coercive methods that are sometimes compared to a coup.
11. Eric Foner, *The Second Founding: How the Civil War and Reconstruction Remade the Constitution* (New York: W. W. Norton, 2019), pp. 1–2.
12. Michael A. Belleisles, *Inventing Equality: Reconstructing the Constitution in the Aftermath of the Civil War* (New York: St. Martin's Press, 2020), p. 3.
13. Melvin Edelstein, *The French Revolution and the Birth of Electoral Democracy* (Burlington, VT: Ashgate, 2014).

14. Linda Colley, "Writing Constitutions and Writing World History," in *The Prospect of Global History*, James Belich, John Darwin, Margaret Frenz, Chris Wickham, eds. (Oxford: Oxford University Press, 2016), p. 160.
15. Indeed, during the process of extricating the United Kingdom from the European Union, especially in 2019 as confusion reigned and norms were tested after Boris Johnson sought to suspend the Parliament, several British commentators lamented the lack of a written constitution. See, for example, Rebecca Jones, "Author Hilary Mantel Says UK Needs Written Constitution," *BBC News*, May 21, 2021 (accessed December 7, 2022); Benjamin Mueller, "Britain's Unwritten Constitution Looks Fragile under Johnson," *New York Times*, September 1, 2019.

Notes to Chapter 1

1. Richard A. Jackson, *Vive le Roi! A History of the French Coronation from Charles V to Charles X* (Chapel Hill: University of North Carolina Press, 1984), pp. 45–46.
2. Useful biographies of Henri IV are Jean-Pierre Babelon, *Henri IV* (Paris: Fayard, 1982); David Buisseret, *Henri IV: King of France* (London: Unwin Hyman: 1984).
3. Michel Pernot, *Les Guerres de religion en France, 1559–1598* (Paris: Sedes, 1987), pp. 337–63. On the fiscal effects, Richard Bonney, *The King's Debts: Finance and Politics in France, 1589–1661* (Oxford: Clarendon Press, 1981), pp. 23–58. For a regional perspective on the impact of the wars, James B. Collins, *Classes, Estates and Order in Early Modern Brittany* (Cambridge: Cambridge University Press, 1994), pp. 126–35.
4. David Parker, *The Making of French Absolute Monarchy* (New York: St. Martin's Press, 1983), p. 1; Howell Lloyd, *The State, France and the Sixteenth Century* (London: George Allen & Unwin, 1983), xv.
5. It is the case that the princes of the blood revolted against Marie de Medici and were the driving force of the second Fronde, but thereafter the Crown maintained control over them.
6. On Sully, David Buisseret, *Sully and the Growth of Centralized Government in France 1598–1610* (London: Eyre & Spottiswoode, 1968); Bernard Barbiche and Ségolène de Dainville-Barbiche, *Sully: L'homme et ses fidèles* (Paris: Fayard, 1997); Babelon, *Henri IV*, pp. 731–67.
7. Raymond Kierstead, *Pomponne de Bellièvre: A Study of the King's Men in the Age of Henry IV* (Evanston: Northwestern University Press, 1968); Olivier Poncet, *Pomponne de Bellièvre (1529–1607): un homme d'état au temps des guerres de religion* (Paris: École des Chartes, 1998).
8. Françoise Hildesheimer, *Richelieu* (Paris: Flammarion, 2021), pp. 145–56; Buisseret, *Henry IV*, pp. 111–14; Babelon, *Henri IV*, pp. 887–96.
9. Richard Bonney, "Was There a Bourbon Style of Government?" p. 173. Also on the transformation of the royal council under Henri IV, Kierstead, *Pomponne de Bellièvre*, pp. 5–6.
10. Roland Mousnier, *The Assassination of Henry IV* (New York: Charles Scribner's Sons, 1973), pp. 36–37.
11. Ibid., p. 251.
12. Françoise Hildesheimer, *La double mort du roi Louis XIII* (Paris: Flammarion, 2007), pp. 41–42.
13. Barbiche and Dainville-Barbiche, *Sully*, pp. 327–31.
14. J. Michael Hayden defended the 1614 meeting by arguing that deputies had never encountered "overbearing absolutism" and were unable to assert themselves against a government that was unwilling to accept what Hayden contended was a reasonable reform program. J. Michael Hayden, *France and the Estates General of 1614* (Cambridge: Cambridge University Press, 1974), p. 216.
15. Mousnier, *The Assassination of Henry IV*, p. 280.
16. G. R. R. Treasure, *Cardinal Richelieu and the Development of Absolutism* (London: Adam & Charles Black, 1972), p. 159.
17. Ibid., pp. 159–61; Hildesheimer, *La double mort de Louis XIII*, pp. 41–42.
18. Treasure, *Cardinal Richelieu*, pp. 161–62.
19. On Burgundy passing under French rule, Mack P. Holt, "Burgundians into Frenchmen: Catholic Identity in Sixteenth-Century Burgundy," in *Changing Identities in Early Modern France*, Michael Wolfe, ed. (Durham: Duke University Press, 1997), pp. 345–70.
20. Holt, "Burgundians into Frenchmen," pp. 352, 360. Not only was Burgundy a League stronghold, but the governor of Burgundy was a brother of the two slain Guise brothers.

21. The following account is based on Philippe Dhetel, *Annales Historiques de la ville de Saint-Jean-de-Losne, Côte d'Or et ancien duché de Bourgogne depuis ses origines jusqu'en 1789...*, 2 vols. (Paris: Champion, 1908–10), 1: 507–666, and the more concise Charles Méraud, *Étude sur l'invasion allemande en Bourgogne et le siége de Saint-Jean-de-Losne* (Dijon: Carré, 1886).
22. Méraud, *Étude sur l'invasion allemande*, p. 49.
23. Noted by Hildesheimer, *Richelieu*, p. 393. For his part, Gallas remained disconsolate at having been checked by a "shanty" and for many years afterward the phrase "unhappy as Gallas" was a part of regional parlance. Méraud, *Étude sur l'invasion allemande*, p. 57.
24. Méraud, *Étude sur l'invasion allemande*, pp. 53–54; AD Côte d'Or C 2987[6*], letter of Saint-Jean-de-Losne to Estates of Burgundy, November 19, 1787.
25. Apart from the general situation of Burgundy as a former League stronghold, it will be recalled that in the fifteenth century Saint-Jean-de-Losne had been a leader in rallying to Mary of Burgundy and resisting French annexation.
26. The theme of Hildesheimer, *La double mort du roi Louis XIII.*
27. Joël Cornette, *La mort de Louis XIV: apogée et crépuscule de la royauté* (Paris: Gallimard, 2015), pp. 88–91.
28. Thierry Sarmant, *Louis XIV: homme et roi* (Paris: Tallandier, 2012), p. 73.
29. On the Frondes, A. Lloyd Moote, *The Revolt of the Judges: The Parlement of Paris and the Fronde 1643–1652* (Princeton: Princeton University Press, 1971); Orest Ranum, *The Fronde: A French Revolution* (New York: W. W. Norton, 1993); Michel Pernot, *La Fronde 1648–1653* (Paris: Tallandier, 2012).
30. Moote, *The Revolt of the Judges*, p. 156.
31. Ibid., pp. 189–90.
32. On the siege of Paris, ibid., pp. 192–210.
33. Moote considered the treaty largely a victory for the body because it retained most of its authority and generally represented a reversion to the *status quo ante*, although that reversion also included Mazarin staying in power. Ibid., pp. 212–14.
34. *Louis XIV and the Craft of Kingship*, John C. Rule, ed. (Columbus: Ohio State University Press, 1969), p. 17, described the arrests as "tantamount to a *coup d'état*."
35. Geoffrey Treasure, *Mazarin: The Crisis of Absolutism in France* (London: Routledge, 1995), p. 176.
36. For a description, Sarmant, *Louis XIV*, pp. 83–85.
37. Moote, *The Revolt of the Judges*, p. 317.
38. Condéan forces alienated subjects with their conduct, including establishing their own "intendants," seizing royal funds or making royal military forces a part of the Condéan army. To those Frenchmen who endured them, the actions of the Condéans seemed high-handed and arbitrary. Ibid., pp. 321–23.
39. Sarmant characterized it as a major mistake. Sarmant, *Louis XIV*, p. 87.
40. Moote, *The Revolt of the Judges*, pp. 345, 347.
41. Sarmant claimed that that an agreement by Mazarin to go into exile tipped the balance in favor of the Crown. Sarmant, *Louis XIV*, p. 87.
42. Moote, *The Revolt of the Judges*, p. 351.
43. Treasure, *Mazarin*, p. 202.
44. On the suffering, Pernot, *La Fronde*, pp. 388–89.
45. Moote, *The Revolt of the Judges*, p. 234.
46. Treasure, *Mazarin*, pp. 228–29; Pernot, *La Fronde*, p. 387.
47. Moote, *The Revolt of the Judges*, pp. 335, 345.
48. Treasure, *Mazarin*, p. 140.
49. Pernot, *La Fronde*, pp. 390, 396.
50. Cornette stated that Louis XIV was the only victor in the Frondes. Cornette, *La mort de Louis XIV*, p. 101.
51. Pernot, *La Fronde*, pp. 368–69.
52. Treasure, *Mazarin*, p. 309.
53. Thierry Sarmant and Mathieu Stoll, *Régner et gouverner: Louis XIV et ses ministres* (Paris: Perrin, 2010), pp. 61–64; Cornette, *La mort de Louis XIV*, p. 110.
54. Richard Bonney, *Political Change in France under Richelieu and Mazarin 1624–1661* (Oxford: Oxford University Press, 1978), p. 441.

55. On this phenomenon, Franklin L. Ford, *Robe and Sword: The Regrouping of the French Aristocracy after Louis XIV* (Cambridge, MA: Harvard University Press, 1953); on the idea of the compromise state, Campbell, "Absolutism," p. 17.
56. A point on which Bonney was also in agreement. Bonney, *Political Change in France*, pp. 448–49.
57. Treasure, *Mazarin*, p. 210. Bonney similarly noted that the changes introduced by Richelieu and Mazarin had developed the power of the Crown to its natural limits but it entailed the continuation of privilege and the existing social structure. Bonney, *Political Change in France*, p. 450. See also Beik, *Absolutism and Society in Seventeenth-Century France*, pp. 335–36.
58. On Crown policy with respect to privilege in conquered lands, Olivier Chaline, *Le règne de Louis XIV*, 2 vols. (Paris: Flammarion, 2009), 1: 745–49.
59. Alain Lottin, "Louis XIV and Flanders," in *Conquest and Coalescence: The Shaping of the State in Eaarly Modern Europe*(London: Edward Arnold, 1991), pp. 84–93. Similarly, Julian Swann asserted that recent scholarship suggests that skillful use of patronage and vigilant oversight of the nobility appear to be more significant factors in the increase of royal power than the centralizing drive of an "absolutist bureaucracy." Rather than casting Louis XIV as the progenitor of "absolutism," Swann contended that the distinguishing feature of his reign was instead the "ability to make old methods of rule function more effectively and the restoration of order was the result." Julian Swann, *Provincial Power and Absolute Monarchy: The Estates General of Burgundy 1661–1790* (Cambridge: Cambridge University Press, 2003), pp. 15, 19, with the quotation from the latter. Privilege was a critical component of the "old methods of rule" to which Swann alluded.
60. *Mémoire de droit public sur la ville de Strasbourg et d'Alsace en général* (Strasbourg: Dannbach, 1789), pp. 14–34; Franklin L. Ford, *Strasbourg in Transition 1648–1789* (Cambridge, MA: Harvard University Press, 1958), pp. 10–15.
61. Ford, *Strasbourg in Transition*, pp. 93, 98 with the quotation from the latter. The status of the area was so singular that in 1789, when its privileges were threatened, Strasbourg and Alsace claimed that they had made an agreement with the monarch in a manner "absolutely different" from the other provinces of the kingdom, so much so that it had not been fully incorporated into the French nation. *Mémoire de droit public*, p. 15.
62. Gail Bossenga, "City and State: An Urban Perspective on the Origins of the French Revolution," in *The French Revolution and the Creation of Modern Political Culture: The Political Culture of the Old Regime*, Keith Michael Baker, ed. (Oxford: Pergamon Press, 1987), pp. 115–40.
63. Ibid. See also Chaline, *Le règne de Louis XIV*, 2: 263–77.
64. David Bien, "Offices, Corps, and a System of State Credit: The Uses of Privilege under the Ancien Régime," in ibid., p. 92.
65. Although it was an agency of the Crown, Philip Mansel believed that the *parlement* saw itself as the equivalent of the Roman Senate. Philip Mansel, *King of the World: The Life of Louis XIV* (Chicago: University of Chicago Press, 2019), p. 28.
66. On these developments, John J. Hurt, *Louis XIV and the Parlements* (Manchester: Manchester University Press, 2002), pp. 24–25, 27.
67. Bonney, *Political Change in France*, p. 420; Andrew Lossky, *Louis XIV and the French Monarchy* (New Brunswick: Rutgers University Press, 1994), p. 111; and, less strongly, Hurt, *Louis XIV and the Parlements*, p. 54.
68. Cornette asserted that Louis believed the role of the *parlement* had been too great during his minority and had been dangerous to the kingdom and that he believed it necessary to reduce its standing. Cornette, *La mort de Louis XIV*, pp. 107–8.
69. After 1665, in fact, Louis referred to the *parlements* as superior courts rather than sovereign courts.
70. Hurt, *Louis XIV and the Parlements*, p. 32. See also Albert Hamscher, *The Parlement of Paris after the Fronde 1653–1673* (Pittsburgh: University of Pittsburgh Press, 1976), p. 145, in which he notes that Louis wished to exclude the court from affairs of state. On earlier efforts by Louis to assert his dominance over the *parlement*, Mansel, *King of the World*, pp. 60, 67.
71. Matthew D'Auria, *The Shaping of French National Identity: Narrating the Nation's Past, 1715–1830* (Cambridge: Cambridge University Press, 2020), pp. 48–49.
72. Swann, *Provincial Power and Absolute Monarchy*, pp. 8–9, 19.
73. Dismay at the prospect of French hegemony in Europe and Louis's interest in restoring James II to power after his overthrow in 1688 persuaded England and Scotland to join the League in 1689, after which the League renamed itself the Grand Alliance.

74. In a remarkable claim, which he advanced hesitantly, Marcel Lachiver argued that the demographic effects of the famine were four times more severe than those of World War I. After 1694, he asserted, nothing was ever the same as before. Marcel Lachiver, *Les Années de misère: la famine au temps du Grand Roi* (Paris: Fayard, 1991), pp. 197, 205–6, 209, 454. See also Cornette, *La mort de Louis XIV*, pp. 202–3.
75. His personal health declined during the war as well. Sarmant, *Louis XIV*, p. 377. On the desire for peace, ibid., p. 437. In 1698, a year after the Nine Years War ended, he said of war that one knows when it begins but not when it will end and that the only certainty was that it would bring misfortunes and suffering to the people. Lossky, *Louis XIV and the French Monarchy*, p. 263.
76. Lossky asserted that the intent of the *lettres-patentes* was to assure that Philippe and his descendants would retain the right to assume the French throne after giving up the Spanish crown. Ibid., p. 262.
77. Lachiver, *Les Années de misère*, p. 382.
78. W. Gregory Monahan, *Year of Sorrows: The Great Famine of 1709 in Lyon* (Columbus: Ohio State University Press, 1993), p. 178; Cornette, *La Mort de Louis XIV*, pp. 203–5, with the quotation from the former.
79. On the letter, Mansel, *King of the World*, p. 404.
80. Joseph Klaits, *Printed Propaganda under Louis XIV: Absolute Monarchy and Public Opinion* (Princeton: Princeton University Press, 1976), pp. 208, 217, 219. Sarmant viewed the letter as a precursor to possible limited monarchy if military defeats continued. Sarmant, *Louis XIV*, p. 557.
81. On the precipitous decline in the prospects of dynastic succession, Sarmant, *Louis XIV*, pp. 477–92.
82. Lossky, *Louis XIV and the French Monarchy*, p. 295. See also, Sarmant, *Louis XIV*, pp. 498–500.
83. Michel Antoine, *Le Conseil du roi sous le règne de Louis XV* (Geneva: Droz, 1970), p. 77.
84. Cornette, *La mort de Louis XIV*, p. 88.

Notes to Chapter 2

1. J. H. Shennan, *Philippe, Duke of Orléans* (London: Thames and Hudson, 1979), pp. 30–31. Antoine noted a remark by Orléans on the right of remonstrance but made no mention of a prior agreement. Antoine clarified that the *parlement* did not invalidate Louis's will but ignored its awkward provisions. Antoine, *Le conseil du roi*, p. 78.
2. Shennan, *Philippe, Duke of Orléans*, pp. 31–33.
3. *Remonstrances du Parlement de Paris au XVIIIe siècle*, Jules Flammermont and Maurice Tourneux, eds., 3 vols. (Paris: Imprimerie nationale, 1888–1898), 1: xxxvii.
4. Ellen Zwicker Curtin, "Constitutional Monarchy versus Absolutism: The Remonstrances of the Parlement of Paris 1716–1771." M.A. thesis, University of North Carolina at Chapel Hill, 1975, pp. 4, 28.
5. James D. Hardy, Jr., *Judicial Politics in the Old Regime: The Parlement of Paris during the Regency* (Baton Rouge: Louisiana State University Press, 1967), pp. 74–89.
6. Ibid., pp. 94–98, 110–15.
7. Ibid., p. 120.
8. Ibid., pp. 130–41.
9. Curtin, "Constitutional Monarchy versus Absolutism," pp. 13, 63, 74.
10. Indeed, Jean Egret asserted that there were few committed Jansenists in the *parlement* in the first half of the eighteenth century—they were more Gallican. Jean Egret, *Louis XV et l'opposition parlementaire* (Paris: Armand Colin, 1970), p. 18.
11. Ibid., pp. 25–33. See also Peter R. Campbell, *Power and Politics in Old Regime France 1720–1745* (London: Routledge, 1996), pp. 47–48 on the settlement, pp. 82–86 on it being undermined.
12. J. H. Shennan, "The Political Role of the Parlement of Paris under Cardinal Fleury," *English Historical Review* 81 (1966): especially 539–40, 542.
13. Campbell contended that Jansenism was primarily religious in nature and that its political dimension was a strategy rather than a motive. Campbell, *Power and Politics*, pp. 197, 211–13.
14. Keith Michael Baker, "Memory and Practice: Politics and the Representation of the Past in Eighteenth-Century France," in *Inventing the French Revolution: Essays on French Political Culture in the Eighteenth Century*, Keith Michael Baker, ed. (Cambridge: Cambridge University Press, 1990), p. 33; Dale Van Kley, *The Religious Origins of the French Revolution: From Calvin to the Civil Constitution, 1560–1791* (New Haven: Yale University Press, 1996), especially p. 77.

15. Michael Kwass, *Privilege and the Politics of Taxation in Eighteenth-Century France: Liberté, Egalité, Fiscalité* (New York: Cambridge University Press, 2000), pp. 172–73. Some, however, despite the Crown's best efforts, were leaked to printers.
16. Baker, "Memory and Practice," pp. 36–37.
17. Van Kley, *The Religious Origins of the French Revolution*, pp. 203–15.
18. J. H. Shennan, *The Bourbons: The History of a Dynasty* (London: Hambledon, 2007), p. 145.
19. Ibid., p. 149.
20. Egret, *Louis XV et l'opposition parlementaire*, p. 33.
21. John Rogister, *Louis XV and the Parlement of Paris*, 1737–1755 (Cambridge: Cambridge University Press, 1995), p. 49.
22. Egret, *Louis XV et l'opposition parlementaire*, pp. 56–58.
23. *Remonstrances du Parlement de Paris au XVIIIe siècle*, 1: 508–609.
24. William Church, *Constitutional Thought in Sixteenth-Century France: A Study in the Evolution of Ideas*, reprint ed. (New York: Octagon Books, 1969), pp. 116–17, 236–37, 308, 311, 325–26, 333.
25. The remonstrance of April 1753 is regarded as a landmark. Rogister stated that it made a major contribution to the renewal of the debate on the nature of the monarchy as well as fundamental laws. He further contended that it encapsulated a strong argument about the nature and force of law in French society and in the political configuration of the *ancien régime*. Rogister, *Louis XV and the Parlement of Paris*, pp. 176–77.
26. Herbert H. Rowen, *The King's State: Proprietary Dynasticism in Early Modern France* (New Brunswick: Rutgers University Press, 1980), pp. 49–92, with the quotation from p. 53. Indeed, Rowen argued that Louis held a "property view of kingship at its most extreme while remaining within the traditions of Western thought and practice." Ibid., pp. 75–76.
27. To be sure, there was the potential for considerable disagreement within even those agreed upon principles, including the role of the *parlement* itself.
28. Egret, *Louis XV et l'opposition parlementaire*, p. 61.
29. Rogister, *Louis XV and the Parlement of Paris*, pp. 176–78. Indeed, many thousands of copies were sold and pirated copies would have added to the large numbers. *Remonstrances du Parlement de Paris au XVIIIe siècle*, 1: 609–10.
30. Shennan, *The Parlement of Paris*, p. 308; Shennan, *The Bourbons*, pp. 151–53, with the quotation from p. 152. Baker, however, asserts that Le Paige's *Lettres historiques* was the foundation for the constitutional doctrine of the *parlement* of Paris. Baker, "Memory and Practice," p. 37.
31. Curtin, "Constitutional Monarchy versus Absolutism," p. 75.
32. Baker, "Memory and Practice," pp. 33–34.
33. William Doyle, "The Parlements," in *The French Revolution and the Creation of Modern Political Culture: The Political Culture of the Old Regime*, Keith Michael Baker, ed. (Oxford: Pergamon Press, 1987), pp. 160–61, 163.
34. See Julian Swann, "Parlements, Politics and the Parti Janséniste: The Grand Conseil Affair, 1755–1756," *French History* 6 (1992): 435–61; Egret, *Louis XV et l'opposition parlementaire*, pp. 72–76.
35. Swann, "Parlement, Politics and the Parti Janséniste," pp. 446–47. His participation also enhanced the Jansenist influence on constitutional issues.
36. The *Conseil du roi* also had judicial authority. Antoine, *Le Conseil du roi*, pp. 512–42. Antoine said its jurisdiction was universal. Ibid., p. 540.
37. *Dictionnaire de l'Académie Françoise*, 4th ed., 2 vols. (Paris: Brunet, 1762), 1: 313; 2: 773.
38. Doyle, "The Parlements," p. 162.
39. Ibid.
40. Swann, "Parlements, Politics and the Parti Janséniste," p. 446. Curtin argued that the years 1753–56 marked a watershed as the *parlement* moved away from Church-related issues to a concern with consent to taxation and the right to reject legislation. Moreover, she notes that the vague references to "fundamental laws" early in Louis XV's reign were often replaced by allusions to a constitution. Curtin, "Constitutional Monarchy versus Absolutism," pp. 110–12.
41. *Remonstrances du Parlement de Paris au XVIIIe siècle*, 2: 92.
42. Julian Swann, *Politics and the Parlement of Paris under Louis XV, 1754–1774* (Cambridge: Cambridge University Press, 1995), pp. 122–55, offers a thorough treatment of this episode.
43. The progress of the concept was slow because of fear of a strong Crown response. Ibid., pp. 147, 163–65.
44. *Remonstrances du Parlement de Paris au XVIIIe siècle*, 2: 269–79. Also in 1760 a much stronger remonstrance came from the *parlement* of Rouen. It, too, argued for free registration and

asserted the autonomy of law. More notably, it used unprecedented language, including "despotism," "nation," and "citizen" to convey the sense of a kingdom on the verge of catastrophe. Kwass, *Privilege and the Politics of Taxation*, pp. 161–65. Kwass also notes the apparent influence of Montesquieu's *The Spirit of Laws* but asserts that the main source of inspiration was Jansenist. The loss of the Seven Years War also led to greater claims and criticism. Swann, *Politics and the Parlement of Paris*, p. 197. Indeed, Kwass declared that 1763 saw the "fiercest campaign of opposition to the Crown since the Fronde." Kwass, *Privilege and the Politics of Taxation*, p. 181.

45. Egret, *Louis XV et l'opposition parlementaire*, pp. 158–74.
46. It consisted of two anonymous letters that three handwriting experts said were written by him.
47. Swann, *Politics and the Parlement of Paris*, pp. 251–83, for a close examination.
48. *Remonstrances du Parlement de Paris au XVIIIe siècle*, 2: 501–26.
49. Ibid., 2: 534–38.
50. Ibid., 2: 541–51.
51. Louis also discussed the *parlement* of Pau, but it was that of Rennes that was the object of the greatest attention.
52. *Remonstrances du Parlement de Paris au XVIIIe siècle*, 2: 555–59.
53. J. H. Shennan, *The Parlement of Paris* (Ithaca: Cornell University Press, 1968), p. 316.
54. *Remonstrances du Parlement de Paris au XVIIIe siècle*, 2: 563–65. On the communication, Swann, *Politics and the Parlement of Paris*, pp. 273–74.
55. *Remonstrances du Parlement de Paris au XVIIIe siècle*, 2: 663–78.
56. Ibid., 2: 680–85.
57. Ibid., 2: 839–53.
58. Ibid., 2: 853–88.
59. Ibid., 2: 889–91.
60. Flammermont described its actions as a virtual revolt. Ibid., 2: 890.
61. Ibid., 2: 892–97.
62. Ibid., 2: 897–900.
63. On possible reasons for the action, Swann, *Politics and the Parlement of Paris*, pp. 281–82.
64. *Remonstrances du Parlement de Paris au XVIIIe siècle*, 3: 103–58.
65. Ibid., 3: 161–65.
66. Ibid., 3: 157, 164. The monarch had notified the *parlement* that he had had two judges in Rennes arrested because he was offended by their conduct and threatened others who acted like them. Swann, *Politics and the Parlement of Paris*, p. 335.
67. *Remonstrances du Parlement de Paris au XVIIIe siècle*, 3: 169–81. There were also ministerial politics involved in the action. See William Doyle, "The Parlements of France and the Breakdown of the Old Regime 1771–1788," *French Historical Studies* 6 (1970): 415–58, especially pp. 416–23.
68. On the ambiguous origins of Maupeou's actions, Doyle, "The Parlements of France," pp. 416–17.
69. Shennan, *Parlement of Paris*, p. 328.
70. Ibid., pp. 318–19. Swann contended that the *parlement* had acted as it had because magistrates were outraged by contradictory and provocative Crown policy. Swann, *Politics and the Parlement of Paris*, p. 347.
71. Egret observed that the existence of the *parlement* had been useful to the nation but it had been even more useful to the monarch because it afforded at least the illusion of a limited monarchy. Egret, *Louis XV et l'opposition parlementaire*, p. 217.
72. *Paris et Versailles: Journal anecdotique de 1762 à 1789*, Celestin Hippeau, ed. (Paris: A. Aubry, 1869), pp. 76–77, 78. Even within the realm of underground pornography, the issues of despotism and the destruction of the constitution arose. Robert Darnton, "The High Enlightenment and the Low-Life of Literature in Pre-Revolutionary France," *Past & Present* 51 (May 1971): 81–115, especially p. 110.
73. *Remonstrances du Parlement de Paris au XVIIIe siècle*, 1: 119.
74. Swann wrote that "it seemed as if the hour of despotism had arrived." Swann, *Politics and the Parlement of Paris*, p. 360.
75. Egret, *Louis XV et l'opposition parlementaire*, p. 222. Indeed, an often inchoate local or national opinion of greater or lesser intensity formed the basis of much parlementary action. Ibid., pp. 230–31.
76. Elie Carcassonne, *Montesquieu et le problème de la constitution française au XVIIIe siècle* (Paris: Presses universitaires de France, 1927), pp. 473–99, 526–27.

77. Ibid., pp. 500–501.
78. Egret, *Louis XV et l'opposition parlementaire*, p. 230.
79. Doyle, "The Parlements," p. 164.
80. *Paris et Versailles*, p. 85.

Notes to Chapter 3

1. John Hardman, *The Life of Louis XVI* (New Haven: Yale University Press, 2016), pp. 13–14. On Moreau, Keith Michael Baker, "Controlling French History: The Ideological Arsenal of Jacob-Nicolas Moreau," in *Inventing the French Revolution: Essays on French Political Culture in the Eighteenth Century*, Keith Michael Baker, ed. (Cambridge: Cambridge University Press, 1990), pp. 59–85, which notes the influence of the theory of parlementary unity in his thinking. Baker described a project directed by Moreau as devoted to the themes of the constitutional legitimacy and political necessity of strong monarchy.
2. Hardman, The *Life of Louis XVI*, pp. 13–15.
3. Egret, *Louis XV et l'opposition parlementaire*, p. 223.
4. Flammermont, *Remontrances*, 3: 233–37. Because Maupeou did not yield the title of chancellor, which was a lifetime appointment, after his dismissal, the session also saw the announcement of the creation of the office of *Garde des sceaux*.
5. Louis, however, was ambivalent about the action, especially encouraging subjects to revolt against a monarch. Hardman, *The Life of Louis XVI*, pp. 115–16.
6. Ibid., p. 111.
7. J. F. Bosher, *French Finances 1770–1795: From Business to Bureaucracy* (Cambridge: Cambridge University Press, 1970), pp. 148–65.
8. George V. Taylor, review of *Necker: Reform Statesman of the Ancien Régime* by Robert D. Harris, *Journal of Economic History* 40 (1980): 878.
9. Ibid., pp. 878–79.
10. Ibid., p. 879.
11. Ibid.
12. Peter Jones, *Reform and Revolution in France: The Politics of Transition, 1774–1791* (Cambridge: Cambridge University Press, 1995), p. 112.
13. Hardman, *Life of Louis XVI*, p. 162.
14. Évelyne Lever, *Louis XVI* (Paris: Fayard, 1985), pp. 368–69.
15. Ibid., pp. 395–96.
16. Ibid., pp. 396–97, with the quotation from p. 396; Jones, *Reform and Revolution*, pp. 121–22; Hardman, *Life of Louis XVI*, pp. 186–88.
17. William Doyle, "The Parlements of France and the Breakdown of the Old Regime 1771–1788," *French Historical Studies* 6 (1970): 445–46.
18. Olwen Hufton, *Europe: Privilege and Protest 1730–1789* (Ithaca: Cornell University Press, 1980), p. 341, presents a useful summary of the borrowing by each.
19. Hufton described Calonne as "a heavy borrower and a heavy spender, scrupulous in payment of interest, almost profligate in the field of public spending." Ibid., p. 343.
20. Flammermont, *Remontrances*, 3: 600–603.
21. Sarah Maza, *Private Lives and Public Affairs: The Causes Célèbres of Prerevolutionary France* (Berkeley: University of California Press, 1993), p. 185. See also Lever, *Louis XVI*, p. 433.
22. Maza, *Private Lives and Public Affairs*, pp. 186–87.
23. Ibid., p. 187; Lever, *Louis XVI*, p. 434.
24. As Hardman observed, it "shed a lurid light on almost every aspect of the *ancien régime* establishment." John Hardman, *Marie-Antoinette: The Making of a Queen* (New Haven: Yale University Press, 2019), p. 98. Maza argued that the Diamond Necklace Affair was a critical catalyst in the formation of an anti-female sentiment that expanded into a larger condemnation of female rule, epitomized by the Court, the epicenter of political life under the old regime, as "the worst, most corrupt form of power spawned by the Old Regime." She contended that aversion to perceived female influence at Court subsequently redounded to the benefit of the Estates General/National Assembly because of its all-male composition. The *parlement*, seen as a bulwark against excessive monarchy-centered government, also gained favorable standing, particularly as it began to present itself as the organ of the French nation. Maza, *Private Lives and Public Affairs*, pp. 207–8, 313, with the quotation from p. 208.
25. Hardman stated that the *parlement* had revealed itself to be "nakedly venal and political." Hardman, *Marie-Antoinette*, p. 98.

26. Lever, *Louis XVI*, p. 434; Hardman, *Life of Louis XVI*, p. 218.
27. Munro Price, *Preserving the Monarchy: The Comte de Vergennes 1774–1787* (Cambridge: Cambridge University Press, 1995), p. 185; Hardman, *Marie-Antoinette*, p. 98.
28. Flammermont, *Remontrances*, 3: 600–603.
29. Flammermont, *Remontrances*, 3: 640–49. Calonne also prepared a lengthy handwritten document refuting the concerns expressed by the *parlement*, chiding it for its reluctance to register the edict. He warned it that delay in securing authorization could harm state credit and that the loan request should be supported rather than opposed. He concluded by telling the magistrates that when the need for and utility of loans had been clearly demonstrated the *parlement* should be "the voice of the interests of the nation." He stated that the resistance of the *parlement* went against the public good and could produce a highly detrimental result. Charles Alexandre de Calonne, *Réponse de M. de Calonne aux observations du parlement sur le nouvel emprunt (Décembre 1785)* (BnF F-21215 (37)).
30. Joël Félix, *Louis XVI & Marie-Antoinette: un couple en politique* (Paris: Payot, 2006), pp. 360–61. Peter Jones observed that circumstances alone made Calonne a reformer. Jones, *Reform and Revolution*, p. 115.
31. Félix asserted that Calonne's presentation of the plan to Louis on August 20 placed France on the road to the French Revolution. Félix, *Louis XVI & Marie-Antoinette*, p. 359.
32. Ibid., p. 366.
33. Ibid., p. 364; Hardman, *Life of Louis XVI*, p. 235, with the quotation from the latter.
34. Charles Alexandre de Calonne, *Requête au Roi* (London: Spilsbury, 1787), p. 2.
35. Félix, *Louis XVI & Marie-Antoinette*, p. 369.
36. John Hardman, *Overture to Revolution: The 1787 Assembly of Notables and the Crisis of France's Old Regime* (Oxford: Oxford University Press, 2010), p. 44.
37. Ibid., p. 80.
38. AD Ille-et-Vilaine C 1799, letter of Bertrand to Calonne and Breuteuil, January 10, 1787.
39. *Procès-verbal de l'Assemblée de Notables, tenue à Versailles, en l'année deMDCCLXXXVII* (Paris: Imprimerie royale, 1788), p. 52.
40. A point well developed in Félix, *Louis XVI & Marie-Antoinette*, pp. 371–72.
41. *Procès-verbal de l'Assemblée de Notables*, pp. 56–81. See also *Discours prononcé de l'ordre du Roi et en sa présence par M. de Calonne, Contrôleur Général des Finances, dans l'Assemblée des Notables, tenue à Versailles, le 22 février 1787* (Versailles: Pierres, 1787).
42. *Correspondance secrète inédite sur Louis XVI, Marie-Antoinette, la cour et la ville de 1777 à 1792*, Adolphe de Lescure, ed., 2 vols. (Paris: Plon, 1866), 2: 110.
43. *Procès-verbal de l'Assemblée de Notables*, p. 134.
44. A Parisian barrister who followed public affairs was completely surprised at the convocation of the Assembly of Notables. Timothy Tackett, *The Glory and the Sorrow: A Parisian and His World in the Age of the French Revolution* (New York: Oxford University Press, 2021), p. 65.
45. *Correspondance secrète*, 2: 114–15, 118.
46. Ibid., 2: 113. See also Félix, *Louis XVI & Marie-Antoinette*, p. 386.
47. Hardman, *Overture to Revolution*, p. 80. It was possible because eleven votes within a committee constituted a majority and four committees comprised a majority out of seven. The Assembly met as a unified body only six times over three months, with the sixth being for its dismissal.
48. AD Ille-et-Vilaine C 1799, letter of Bertrand to Calonne and Breteuil, January 10, 1787; AD Ille-et-Vilaine C 3899, letter of commission of Estates of Brittany to bishop of Dol, February 2, 1787, letters of commissioners of Estates to deputies of Assembly of Notables, March 28, 1787, and April 3, 1787; AD Côte d'Or C 3476, *Cahier des deliberations de premier bureau présidé par M. Frère du Roi, Assemblée de Notables*, 1787; *Observations en forme d'avis sur les différens mémoires présentés à l'Assemblée des Notables en 1787, bureau de S.A.S. Mgr. Le Prince de Condé, M. l'abbé de la Fare. Observations conservatoires des droits et privilèges de la Province de Bourgogne* (undated but between March 7 and 23, 1787).
49. *Correspondance secrète*, 2:115–16.
50. *Procès-verbal de l'Assemblée de Notables*, pp. 137–40.
51. Ibid., pp. 136–226; *Correspondance secrète*, 2: 116–17, 119.
52. *Journal de Paris*, March 29, 1787; *Correspondance secrète*, 2: 125.
53. Charles-Alexandre Calonne, "Avertissement," *De l'état de la France, présent et à venir*, 5th ed. (London and Paris: Laurent, 1790), pp. 435–40.

54. When he learned of the agenda in mid-April, a Parisian barrister, Adrien Joseph Colson, favored the tax reform program and was shocked by the resistance of the Notables. Tackett, *The Glory and the Sorrow*, pp. 67–68. The timing at least suggests that Calonne's pamphlet may have influenced him.
55. Félix said that *Avertissement* had the effect of a bomb going off in Versailles. Félix, *Louis XVI & Marie-Antoinette*, p. 390. On the public reaction, *Correspondance secrète*, 2: 128.
56. AD Ille-et-Vilaine C 3899, letter of bishop of Dol, April 10, 1787.
57. *Observations présentées au roi par les bureaux de l'Assemblée des notables: sur les mémoires remis à l'Assemblée ouverte par le roi, à Versailles, le 23 février 1787* (Lyon: Imprimerie royale, 1787), pp. 35–46, 53–60. On the recognition by the Notables that Louis had met most of their objections, AN M 788, dossier 2^{17}, document 89.
58. *Procès-verbal de l'Assemblée de Notables*, pp. 263–69.
59. Félix, *Louis XVI & Marie-Antoinette*, pp. 397–98.
60. *Procès-verbal de l'Assemblée de Notables*, pp. 262, 289–90; *Correspondance secrète*, 2: 135, 138.
61. AN M 788, dossier 2^{17}, document 89; *Correspondance secrète*, 2: 132.
62. *Correspondance secrète*, 2: 139–40.
63. Ibid., 2: 132, 140, 142.
64. Albert Goodwin, "Calonne, the Assembly of French Notables of 1787 and the Origins of the Révolte Nobiliaire," *The English Historical Review* 6 (1946): 373.
65. *Correspondance secrète*, 2: 142.
66. *Procès-verbal de l'Assemblée de Notables*, pp. 291–92 for Louis's remarks; pp. 297–308, especially pp. 303–6, for those of Brienne.
67. Ibid., p. 316. On la Fare at the Assembly of Notables, Bernard de Brye, *Un évêque d'ancien régime a l'épreuve de la Révolution: le cardinal A. L. H. de la Fare (1752–1829)* (Paris: Publications de la Sorbonne, 1985), pp. 139–71.
68. See also Peter R. Campbell and John Hardman, "Malesherbes and the Crisis of 1787–8," *French History* 35 (2021): 174.
69. One observer wrote of his shock at learning of an extraordinary crisis and the sad state of the kingdom living day by day and subsisting by precarious and artificial means. He was hopeful, however, that the crisis could be addressed by an assembly that could be viewed as national. M. O. Monod, "Lettres de Guillaume-Benoît Couderc, bourgeois de Lyon, député à l'Assemblée Constituante, à son oncle M. Vernier-Dupan, à Genève (1781–1792)," *Revue d'histoire de Lyon: études, documents, bibliographie* 5 (1906): 413.
70. Indeed, the statement may have been a final effort by the Notables to forestall reform. Traditionally, it was the role of the Estates General to approve new taxes, but the Notables would have been well aware of the deep aversion the Crown had to calling an Estates General.
71. Hilarion du Puget de Barbantane, *Réflexions sur les causes et les événemens de la Révolution, par un député suppléant de Paris* (Paris: Desenne, 1790), pp. 4–5.
72. Stephen Miller, "Venal Offices, Provincial Assemblies and the French Revolution," *French History* 28 (2014): 343–65; Stephen Miller, "Provincial Assemblies, Fiscal Reform and the Language of Politics in the 1770s and 1780s," *French Historical Studies* 35 (2012): 441–75. Jones described the reform effort as "faltering" but also noted the favorable beginnings of the assembly in Auvergne. Like Miller, he asserted that the provincial assemblies expanded and nationalized the arena of public debate. Jones, *Reform and Revolution in France*, pp. 42–43, 142.
73. *Procès-verbal de l'Assemblée de Notables*, p. 303.
74. *Correspondance secrète*, 2: 145; Jean Sylvain Bailly, *Mémoires d'un témoin de la Révolution*, 3 vols. (Paris: Levrault, 1804), 1: 4.
75. BM Nantes Collection Dugast-Matifeux, vol. 12, p. 8.
76. Félix, *Louis XVI & Marie-Antoinette*, p. 382.
77. Ibid., p. 390.
78. Also on the Assembly of Notables ushering in a new kind of politics because of the increased importance of public opinion, Campbell and Hardman, "Malesherbes and the Crisis of 1787–8," pp. 168, 177.
79. Van Kley, *The Religious Origins of the French Revolution*, pp. 251, 281–90.
80. Campbell and Hardman, "Malesherbes and the Crisis of 1787–8," p. 190.
81. Orville T. Murphy, *The Diplomatic Retreat of France and Public Opinion on the Eve of the French Revolution, 1783–1789* (Washington, DC: Catholic University of America Press, 1998), especially pp. 72–73, 77–79, 90–91, 95. See also, Price, *Preserving the Monarchy*, pp. 190–92.
82. Campbell and Hardman, "Malesherbes and the Crisis of 1787–8," p. 175.

Notes to Chapter 4

1. *Remontrances*, 3: 663–75.
2. *Remontrances*, 3: 676.
3. *Remontrances*, 3: 676–81.
4. *Remontrances*, 3: 681–84.
5. *Remontrances*, 3: 684–87.
6. *Remontrances*, 3: 667–75.
7. *Remontrances*, 3: 663–66; *Journal de Paris*, August 12, 1787, August 13, 1787.
8. *Remontrances*, 3: 688–92.
9. *Remontrances*, 3: 693.
10. *Remontrances*, 1: 101.
11. Campbell and Hardman asserted that the *parlement* hoped that the Estates General would fail. Campbell and Hardman, "Malesherbes and the Crisis of 1787–8," p. 170.
12. Hardman has offered an alternative interpretation, which is that the *parlement* acted out of spite. By calling the Assembly of Notables, Louis had fundamentally altered the political architecture of the kingdom and given rise to doubt among the magistrates about the continuation of their political role. If Louis was willing to convene the Assembly of Notables, the *parlement* could raise the stakes by calling for the convocation of the Estates General. Hardman, *Life of Louis XVI*, p. 279.
13. Doyle, "The Parlements of France and the Breakdown of the Old Regime," pp. 451, 456, 458.
14. *Correspondance secrète*, 2: 169, 176.
15. *Remontrances*, 3: 693. On the negotiations, *Correspondance secrète*, 2: 182.
16. *Correspondance secrète*, 2: 174–75.
17. Ibid., 2: 184.
18. Ibid., 2: 174.
19. Ibid., 2: 170.
20. Ibid., 2: 200.
21. *Remontrances*, 3: 721–34.
22. Ibid., 3: 735–36.
23. Ibid., 3: 736–43.
24. *Correspondance secrète*, 2: 216.
25. Ibid., 2: 217.
26. Ibid., 2: 246–47.
27. Ibid., 2: 237, 238, 243, 249, 251.
28. Ibid., 2: 252, 253, 255; *Remontrances*, 3: 748.
29. *Remontrances*, 3: 747–50.
30. *Correspondance secrète*, 2: 253.
31. Doyle, "The Parlements," p. 165.
32. *Remontrances*, 3: 750–77.
33. William Doyle, *The Parlement of Bordeaux and the End of the Old Regime 1771–1790* (London: Ernest Benn, 1974), p. 278.
34. *Correspondance secrète*, 2: 260, 266.
35. Jean Egret, *Le Parlement de Dauphiné et les affaires publiques dans la deuxième moitié du XVIIIe siècle*, 2 vols. (Grenoble: B. Arthaud, 1942), offers the most thorough treatment. Grenoble was not alone. In Toulouse, where it had been reported that residents were pulling up paving stones, the *parlement* put forward a provocative statement, declaring that with the people no longer having a barrier between itself and the monarch it was left only with the sense of its own strength. *Correspondance secrète*, 2: 254, 260. Apart from the perception of despotism or other issues, in the cities and towns in which one was located, the *parlement* was a source of civic identity and pride. Any reduction in the status of the *parlement* was an affront that would galvanize the populace.
36. AD Côte d'Or E 642, no. 35, letter of July 2, 1788; *Correspondance secrète*, 2: 265–66, 271; *Paris et Versailles*, p. 350.
37. AD Côte d'Or E 642, no. 47, letter of August 11, 1788; *Correspondance secrète*, 2: 262, 266, 270. Indeed, in mid-June 1788, one observer characterized the situation as a conflict between justice and authority. AD Côte d'Or E 642, no. 33, letter of June 18, 1788.

38. From 1774 to 1786, 312 pamphlets had been published, an average of twenty-four per year. There were 217 pamphlets published in 1787 but the number nearly quadrupled to 819 in 1788. In 1789 that number more than quadrupled again with the appearance of 3305 pamphlets. Antoine de Baecque, "Pamphlets: Libel and Political Mythology," in *Revolution in Print: The Press in France 1775–1800*, Robert Darnton and Daniel Roche, eds. (Berkeley: University of California Press, 1989), p. 165. The impact the torrent of pamphlets had on the Parisian barrister Colson was considerable. Tackett, *The Glory and the Sorrow*, pp. 70–71.
39. Mitchell B. Garrett, *The Estates-General of 1789: The Problems of Composition and Organization* (New York: Appleton-Century, 1935), pp. 25–40. Given the opposition that the Lamoignon edicts had unleashed across France and the reluctance of the Crown, despite its promise, to convene the Estates General, the interpretation is plausible. A future deputy to the Estates General recalled that acquainting oneself with the history of the Estates General became "the mania of the moment." BM Nantes Collection Dugast-Matifeux, vol. 12, pp. 17–18.
40. *Correspondance secrète*, 2: 275–76.
41. On Brittany and Dauphiné as focal points, AD Côte d'Or E 642, no. 32, letter of June 12, 1788, no. 33, letter of June 18, 1788; Marc-Marie, marquis de Bombelles, *Journal de marquis de Bombelles*, Jean Grassion and Frans Durif, eds., 8 vols. (Geneva: Droz, 1978–2013), 2: 205; Adrien-Joseph Colson, *Lettres d'un bourgeois de Paris à un ami de province 1788–1793* (Saint-Cyr-sur-Loire: Christian Pirot, 1993), p. 21.
42. *Correspondance secrète*, 2: 278.
43. Jean Egret, "Les Origines de la Révolution en Bretagne (1788–1789)," *Revue historique* 113 (1955): 193–97.
44. *Déliberations de la ville de Grenoble, du samedi quatorze juin mil sept cent quatre-vingt-huit, à l'Hôtel de Ville de Grenoble, sur les dix heures du matin* (n.p., n.d.).
45. *Correspondance secrète*, 2: 275.
46. On the Estates, Jean Egret, *Les Dernier Etats de Dauphiné: Romans (septembre 1788–Janvier 1789* (Grenoble: Allier, 1942).
47. *Assemblée des trois-ordres de la province de Dauphiné* (n.p., n.d.). Although she acknowledged that it is difficult to determine how deeply rooted it was, Bohanan argued that there was an inchoate sense of national identity in seventeenth-century Dauphiné. The sentiment formed in opposition to the nobility by partnering with the king. Bohanan, *Crown and Nobility in Early Modern France*, pp. 111–12, 154–55. For a larger treatment of the issue, see David Bell, *The Cult of the Nation in France: Inventing Nationalism, 1680–1800* (Cambridge, MA: Harvard University Press, 2001).
48. *Correspondance secrète*, 2: 278; *Paris et Versailles*, p. 356.
49. *Correspondance secrète*, 2: 279, 281.
50. Even a leading minister, Malesherbes, was troubled by the authoritarian measures taken against the *parlement*, beginning with the exile to Troyes, which led him to make the difficult decision that he would resign. Campbell and Hardman, "Malesherbes and the Crisis of 1787–8," p. 178.
51. A point recognized by Doyle, *The Parlement of Bordeaux and the End of the Old Regime*, p. 278.
52. In August 1788, for example, it was rumored that Béarn had formed a military regiment for the defense of its privileges and franchises. *Correspondance secrète*, 2: 283. See also [François Marie Périchou de Keverseau and G. Clavelin], *Histoire de la Révolution de 1789, et de l'établissement d'une constitution en France*, 20 vols. (Paris: Clavelin, 1790–1803), 1: 113.
53. AD Calvados C 6348, memoir presented to monarch by barristers of bailliage of Avranches on next Estates General, December 1, 1788, in which the barristers lament that in the system of orders the two orders are consumed with their privileges and honors while the needs and interests of the nation are forgotten. See also AN AB^{XIX} 3494, dossier 13, February 2, 1789, in which the author of the letter complains that men of letters have portrayed fiscal exemptions as incompatible with the interests of the nation.
54. AN 284 AP 3, dossier 2, part 2 (August 1788).
55. (Emmanuel Joseph Sieyes) *Essai sur les privilèges* (n.p., n.d.).
56. *Correspondance secrète*, 2: 284.
57. AD Côte d'Or E. 642, no. 56, letter of September 12, 1788.
58. One observer wrote that when one saw the French pass from overwhelming distress to a state of hope and joy one could not deny Necker the moniker of "savior." *Correspondance secrète*, 2: 288, 289.

59. *Remontrances*, 3: 778–79.
60. One contemporary observed that demanding the protocols of 1614 took France back to a time when Cardinal Richelieu governed with an iron scepter. Ibid., 3: 779; *Correspondance secrète*, 2: 292.
61. Van Kley, "The Estates-General as Ecumenical Council," p. 47.
62. Doyle, "The Parlements of France and the Breakdown of the Old Regime," pp. 451, 458; Hardman, *Life of Louis XVI*, pp. 280, 304; Kenneth Margerison, *Pamphlets and Public Opinion: The Campaign for a Union of Orders in the Early French Revolution* (West Lafayette: Purdue University Press, 1998), p. 51.
63. *Correspondance secrète*, 2: 291, 292.
64. *Venise et la Révolution française: Les 470 dépêches des ambassadeurs de Venise au doge 1786–1795*, Alessandro Fontana, Francesco Furlan and Georges Saro, eds., (Paris: Robert Laffont, 1997), p. 256. See also Campbell and Hardman, "Malesherbes and the Crisis of 1787–8," p. 185, who concur with the ambassador's judgment.
65. *Venise et la Révolution*, p. 256.
66. *Procès-verbal de l'Assemblée de Notables, tenue à Versailles, en l'année M. DCCCLXXXVIII* (Paris: Imprimerie Royale, 1789), pp. 65–69.
67. Ibid., pp. 48–69.
68. *Correspondance secrète*, 2: 302; *Despatches from Paris, 1784–1790*, 2 vols., Oscar Browning and John Frederick Sackville Dorset, duke of, eds. (London: Offices of the Society, 1909–1910), 2: 112.
69. BnF Mss. Nouvelles acquisitions française (hereafter Nouv. acq. fr.) 17275, fols. 13v°, 15v°–16, 19.
70. Ibid., fol. 19.
71. *Correspondance secrète*, 2: 304.
72. Ibid., 2: 308; AM Arles AA 23, fol. 43.
73. *Remontrances*, 3: 779–82; BnF Mss. Nouv. Acq. fr. 17275, fol. 25.
74. *Remontrances*, 3: 782; *Correspondance secrète*, 2: 312; BHVP Ms. 713, fol. 206.
75. BnF Mss. Nouv. acq. fr. 17275, fol. 13.
76. [Jean-Joseph Mounier], *Lettre écrite au Roi par les trois orders de la province de Dauphiné, sur les Etats-Généraux* (n.p., n.d.). One contemporary praised it as a patriotic and very lucid letter and urged others to procure a copy of it. BnF Nouv. acq. fr. 17275, fols. 17–17v°.
77. *Procès-verbal de l'Assemblée de Notables, tenue à Versailles, en l'année M. DCCCLXXXVIII*, pp. 101, 108–9, 148, 149–51, 227–28, 231–32, 269, 330–32, 415, 425.
78. Fitzsimmons, "Privilege and the Polity in France, 1786–1791," *The American Historical Review* 92 (1987): 269–95; Félix, *Louis XVI & Marie-Antoinette*, p. 447.
79. [Joseph-Antoine-Joachim Cerutti], *A la mémoire auguste de feu de Monsieur le Dauphin* (n.p., n.d.), p. xi. On the discontent, see also AN B[a] 57, liasse 141, dossier 1, document 20; AN H[1] 207, dossier 1, documents 21–22; *Correspondance secrète*, 2: 312.
80. AD Côte d'Or C 3367, fol. 189 v°; AN H[1] 200[4], dossier 2, document 88.
81. AD Côte d'Or C 2987[6*], letter of Saint-Jean-de-Losne to Estates of Burgundy, November 19, 1787.
82. Ibid.; AD Côte d'Or C 3367, fol. 133v°.
83. AN H[1] 200[4], dossier 2, document 88.
84. AD Côte d'Or C 3367, fol. 189v°.
85. AD Côte d'Or C 3367, fol. 144v°.
86. AD Côte d'Or C 2987[6*], fols. 114v°–117v°; AD Côte d'Or C 3843, fols. 114v°–117v°. For the confirmation of the privileges of the province by Louis XVI, AD Côte d'Or C 2976, *lettres-patentes* of May 1777.
87. AN H[1] 200[4], dossier 2, documents 93, 94; AD Côte d'Or C 3843, fol. 165.
88. The comte de Provence and the duc d'Orléans refused to sign. BnF Nouv. Acq. fr. 17275, fol. 31.
89. *Mémoire des princes présenté au Roi* (n.p., n.d.).
90. Van Kley, *Religious Origins of the French Revolution*, pp. 323–24; Margerison, *Pamphlets and Public Opinion*, p. 44.
91. On the leading role of the princes at the second Assembly of Notables, Margerison, *Pamphlets and Public Opinion*, p. 44.
92. BnF Mss. Nouv. acq. fr. 6687, fols. 185, 188, 200. See also [Keverseau and Clavelin], *Histoire de la Révolution de 1789*, 1: 89.

93. One contemporary contemptuously dismissed their offer with the observation that "in your system we are at the mercy of the nobles." *Ultimatum d'un citoyen du tiers-état au Mémoire des princes présenté au roi, seconde édition* (n.p., 1789), p. 61. Another that gained notice used parody, inverting or amending sentences from the *Mémoire des princes*. It opened with the statement that the state was not in danger but that a revolution was underway in the assessment of taxes—the opening of the *Mémoire des princes* had declared that the state was in danger, angering many in the Third Estate. The implication of the statement was that the cause of the Third Estate was endangering the state and was therefore illegitimate. *Mémoire du tiers-état à présenter au Roi* (n.p., n.d.). On the attention it attracted, as well as an attribution of authorship, BnF Nouv. acq. fr. 17275, fols. 33v°–34. On the anger, *Correspondance secrète*, 2: 315.
94. Emmanuel-Joseph Sieyes, *Qu'est-ce que le Tiers-état?*, 3rd ed. (n.p., 1789), especially pp. 3, 135, 136, 155. On Sieyès, Murray Forsyth, *Reason and Revolution: The Political Thought of the Abbé Sieyès* (New York: Holmes & Meier, 1987); Jean-Denis Bredin, *Sieyés: la clé de la Révolution française* (Paris: Fallois, 1988); William H. Sewell, Jr., *A Rhetoric of Bourgeois Revolution: The Abbé Sieyès and What Is the Third Estate?* (Durham: Duke University Press, 1994).
95. Immediately upon reading it a British observer anticipated a hostile reaction. *Despatches from Paris*, 1784–1790, 2 vols., Oscar Browning, ed. (London: Offices of the Society, 1909–1910), 2: 127–128.
96. Carcassonne, *Montesquieu et le problème de la constitution*, pp. 591–92, 615. The perception led to the creation of the awkward phrase *sénati-clérico-aristocratique*. Ibid., pp. 612, 632.
97. Ibid., p. 592.
98. Ibid., pp. 615–16, 619–25.
99. BnF Mss. Nouv. acq. fr. 17275, fol. 41v°; *Correspondance secrète*, 2: 316.
100. *Despatches from Paris*, 2: 117, 119–20, 124.
101. Ibid., 2: 137; *Venise et la Révolution*, p. 256.
102. *Correspondance secrète*, 2: 316.
103. BnF Mss. Nouv. acq. fr. 17275, fol. 54, on the concern about fiscal privileges; *Correspondance secrète*, 2: 317, on the intensified debate on political privilege.

Notes to Chapter 5

1. AD Gironde 3 L 82, script letter of January 3, 1789, in a collection of handbills of news and opinion (*nouvelles à la main*). Some are handwritten whereas others are in a typescript. Indeed, at a much more elevated level than handbills, figures such as Le Paige, Mably, and others were debating French history to frame constitutional arguments or claims. Baker, "Memory and Practice," especially pp. 57–58. Also in January an observer asserted that in the last six months the nation had advanced by a century. *Correspondance secrète*, 2: 321.
2. *Correspondance secrète*, 2: 316, 318.
3. BnF Mss. Nouv. acq. fr. 17275, fol. 55, which described a pamphlet in response to it licentious and reprehensible.
4. BnF Mss. Nouv. acq. fr. 17275, fol. 92.
5. BnF Mss. Nouv. acq. fr. 17275, fol. 54. On taxation as an issue, Gilbert Shapiro and John Markoff, *Revolutionary Demands: A Content Analysis of the Cahiers de Doléances of 1789* (Stanford: Stanford University Press, 1998), pp. 277, 380.
6. AN H[1] 563, deliberation of town of Pontivy, November 11, 1788; deliberation of town of Rennes, instructions given to deputies, undated; AN H[1] 564, extract from registers of deliberations of town of Quimper, November 13, 1788.
7. *Correspondance secrète*, 2: 318.
8. On tensions in Brittany, BnF Mss. Nouv. acq. fr. 17275, fols. 69–69v°.
9. AD Ille-et-Vilaine C 1799, letter of Bertrand to Calonne and Breuteuil, January 10, 1787; letter of Bertrand to Fourqueux, April 21, 1787.
10. AN H[1] 409, dossier 4, document 186. The *procureur général syndic* of the Estates had written Necker in September 1788 to remind him of the promises contracted with the monarch and asking him to preserve all of the privileges of the province. AN H[1] 564, letter of Botheret to Necker, September 3, 1788.
11. AD Ille-et-Vilaine C 3898, *mémoire* to monarch from Intermediate Commission of Estates of Brittany, June 22, 1788.
12. AN H[1] 564, *mémoire* of city of Morlaix, December 1, 1788, and *passim*.

13. AN H[1] 409, dossier 4, document 131; AN H[1] 563, extract from registers of Rennes, November 3, 1788, deliberation of Rennes, instructions given to deputies, undated, letter of mayor and *procureur-syndic* of Vitré, November 5, 1788, and attached declaration of November 4, 1789, *passim.*
14. AN H[1] 563, letter of Dufaure to Necker (no addressee but internal evidence indicates Necker), January 14, 1789.
15. AN H[1] 419, circular of nobility of bishopric or Rennes to nobility of Brittany, undated; letter of Paysant Dubourg to Necker, December 30, 1788; letter of Thiard to Necker, December 30, 1788.
16. AN H[1] 419, letter of Thiard to Necker, December 30, 1788.
17. AN H[1] 419, minutes of Estates of Brittany, December 31, 1788, January 2, 1789, January 3, 1789, January 7, 1789; AD Ille-et-Vilaine C 1804, decree of *Conseil d'état*, January 3, 1789.
18. AN H[1] 419, letter of Paysant Dubourg to Necker, December 27, 1789.
19. They had pledged to the comte de Thiard that they would not attack members of the nobility. AN C 12[2], dossier Bretagne, document 17.
20. AN H[1] 419, letter of Dufaure Rochefort to Necker, December 30, 1788; AD Ille-et-Vilaine 1 F 1842, letter of men of Rennes to club at Nantes, January 4, 1789. The law students were led by future Revolutionary general and rival of Bonaparte, Jean Victor Moreau.
21. AN H[1] 419, minutes of Estates of Brittany, January 8, 1789. On the belief that the suspension represented an effort to abolish the Estates, AN H[1] 419, letter of Thiard to Necker, January 8, 1789. See also *Protestation de l'ordre de la noblesse de Bretagne* (n.p., n.d).
22. AN H[1] 419, minutes of Estates of Brittany, January 1789; BnF Mss. Nouv. acq. fr. 17275, fol. 57. One contemporary in Paris characterized events in Brittany as always in a state that made one almost despair at being able to reconcile the Third Estate with the nobility, the clergy and the magistracy. AN AB[XIX] 3494, dossier 13, January 26, 1789.
23. AN H[1] 419, letter of Thiard to Necker, January 29, 1789.
24. *Détail de ce qui s'est passé à Rennes le 26 janvier 1789* (n.p., n.d.); *Précis exact et historique des faits arrivées à Rennes, les 26 & 27 janvier & autres jours suivants* (n.p., n.d.). The Crown banned the former pamphlet. AD Ille-et-Vilaine 1 F 1184, extract of register of *Conseil d'état,* February 14, 1789.
25. *Relation de ce qui s'est passé à Rennes le 26, 27 & jours suivants du mois de janvier 1789* (n.p., 1789), p. 23. There was a celebration held in their honor in Nantes when they returned from Rennes. BnF Mss. Nouv. acq. fr. 17275, fol. 91.
26. *Relation de ce qui s'est passé à Rennes*, p. 24.
27. AD Maine-et-Loire 1 J 51, statement and decree of law students in town of Angers, February 3, 1789.
28. *Relation de ce qui s'est passé à Rennes*, pp. 12, 16, 21–22. The Crown suppressed one pamphlet because it contained vehement denunciations of the nobility and the *parlement.* The decree said that the pamphlet, *Détail de ce qui s'est passé à Rennes le 26 janvier 1789*, contained injurious and even outrageous expressions against the nobility. In the early reports, the number of fatalities was initially believed to be much higher and, although hyperbolic, the bitterness is evident in the comparison of it by one contemporary to the St. Bartholomew's Day massacre. BnF Mss. Nouv. acq. fr. 17275, fol. 75.
29. In Franche-Comté fifty to sixty nobles came together to protest the December 27 decision. BnF Mss. Nouv. acq. fr. 17275, fol. 69. See also *Venise et la Révolution*, p. 263.
30. AN H[1] 419, letter of Thiard to Necker, April 18, 1789.
31. AN H[1] 419, letter of Thiard to Necker, April 21, 1789. Also on the situation in Brittany, Margerison, *Pamphlets and Public Opinion*, pp. 79–83.
32. *Procès-verbal de l'assemblée générale des trois-ordres de la province de Dauphiné, tenue dans la ville de Romans, le 2 novembre 1788* (Grenoble: Cuchet, 1788), pp. 98–99.
33. AN B[A] 74[2], liasse 174, dossier 5, document 3, September 17–24, pp. 2–2v°.
34. *Procès-verbal de l'Assemblée générale*, p. 102.
35. *Procès-verbal de l'assemblée générale*, p. 21.
36. Ibid., pp. 60–62.
37. Ibid., pp. 68–72.
38. After receiving a copy of the minutes of the meeting at Romans, the Third Estate of Alès expressed its admiration and told the Dauphinois that they had become an example for the entire kingdom. AM Grenoble AA 41, letter of Giraudet la Laquière, undated. Because it is undated, it is not clear to which assembly they were responding.

39. AB^{XIX} 3494, dossier 13, January 22, 1789.
40. Guy-Marie Sallier, *Annales françaises, depuis le commencement du règne de Louis XVI jusqu'aux Etats-Généraux, 1774–1789* (Paris: Leriche & Thomine, 1813), p. 308. He said that they did so certain that they would not meet with the disapproval of the government.
41. AB^{XIX} 3494, dossier 13, January 22, 1789.
42. AN B^{A} 75^{A2}, liasse 175, dossier 8, document 1.
43. *Procès-verbal des États de Dauphiné, assemblés à Romans dans le mois de Décembre 1788* (Grenoble: Cuchet, 1788), pp. 118–21, 124–25; on its circulation, AN AB^{XIX} 3494, dossier 13, January 29, 1789.
44. AN B^{a} 74^{1}, liasse 174, dossier 3, document 9, letter of Caze de la Bove to *Garde des sceaux*, January 4, 1789. Elections would have been in progress when the letter was written.
45. AN B^{a} 75^{A1}, liasse 175, dossier 2, document 31, letter of Caze de la Bove to *Garde des sceaux*, January 9, 1789. See also AN B^{A} 75^{A1}, liasse 175, dossier 3, document 8, letter of archbishop of Vienne to Necker, January 10, 1789.
46. BM Grenoble Ms. R. 7109, fol. 34 (January 6, 1789).
47. AN B^{a} 75^{A1}, liasse 175, dossier 3, document 8, letter of archbishop of Vienne to Necker, January 10, 1789; AN B^{a} 75^{A1}, liasse 175, dossier 3, document 20, letter of Caze de la Bove to Necker, February 9, 1789; *Correspondance secrète*, 2: 323; *Procès-verbal des États de Dauphiné*, pp. 131–33.
48. AN AB^{XIX} 3494, dossier 13, February 19, 1789; AN H^{1} 670, document 1.
49. AN B^{a} 75^{A1}, liasse 175, dossier 2, document 56, letter of archbishop of Vienne to Necker, January 29, 1789.
50. *Correspondance secrète*, 2: 322.
51. *Lettre écrite par plusiers citoyens du clergé, de la noblesse & des communes de Dauphiné à Messieurs les Syndics-Généraux des Etats de Béarn* (n.p., n.d.). The pamphlet, credited to Mounier, had signatories. Similarly, in response to an effort by business interests to have their own deputies at the Estates General, businessmen in Grenoble declined to join it. They denounced the division of interests and argued that all parts of the kingdom should conclude an eternal alliance among themselves and with the monarch. They declared that they desired a France in which the least of the French had the same rights as the most illustrious of their fellow citizens. At the Estates General the business group members should not consider themselves as anything other than citizens and should guard against all prejudices rooted in corporate bodies or profession. They asserted that French businessmen should be aware of the injustice of exclusive privileges and devote themselves to the happiness of their fatherland. *Réponse des négociants de la ville de Grenoble, à MM. Les juges-consulaires de Montauban, Clermont-Ferrnad, Châlons, Orléans, Tours, Besançon, Dunkerque & Saint-Quentin, et à la Chambre de Commerce de Picardie, de St. Malo et de Lille en Flandres* (n.p., n.d.). It also had signatories. The curés of Dauphiné likewise appear to have written an anonymous pamphlet addressed to their colleagues in Brittany and other anonymous or pseudonymous pamphlets advanced the same themes. *Les curés de Dauphiné, à leurs confrères les recteurs de Bretagne* (n.p., 1789); *Lettre de Charles ROUX, habitant de Valgondemar, dans les montagnes de Dauphiné, a MM. Du Tiers-état de Bretagne* (n.p., n.d.).
52. The example of Dauphiné was invoked, for example, at a municipal council meeting in Alençon in December 1788. AN B^{a} 11, liasse 5, dossier 16, document 6.
53. *Réponse des négociants de la ville de Grenoble*, p. 3.
54. AN B^{a} 75^{A1}, liasse 175, dossier 2, document 56, letter of archbishop of Vienne to Necker, January 29, 1789.
55. AD Eure 5 F 63, fol. 22; BnF Mss. Nouv. acq. fr. 12938, fol. 3v°.
56. *Venise et la Révolution*, pp. 261, 263.
57. Margerison, *Pamphlets and Public Opinion*, pp. 35–40, 59.
58. Ibid., pp. 42, 70, 78.
59. On disappointment with the second Assembly of Notables, AM Arles, AA 23, fol. 43.
60. BnF Mss. Nouv. acq. fr. 17275, fol. 54.
61. BnF Mss. Nouv. acq. fr. 17275, fol. 92; *Venise et la Révolution*, p. 269. The Venetian ambassador also included the clergy in endorsement of the principle of equality of taxation, but consent was more prevalent among the nobility than the clergy. AN H^{1} 207, dossier 1, document 4, letter of Amelot to Necker, April 1, 1789.
62. Margerison, *Pamphlets and Public Opinion*, p. 123.
63. Ibid., pp. 110–11.

64. Margerison noted that a reader could draw from Necker's report numerous and contradictory conclusions about the course the government intended to follow. Ibid., p. 75.
65. Indeed, in late January, the nobility of Burgundy, which had played a major role in the renunciation of fiscal privileges, was viewed as posing an obstacle to the union of orders by protesting in advance any departure from vote by order at the Estates General. AN AB^{XIX} 3494, dossier 13, January 26, 1789. In some cases the renunciation was more cynical in nature. See Kwass, *Privilege and the Politics of Taxation*, pp. 294–95.
66. Guy Chaussinand-Nogaret, *La Noblesse au XVIIIe siècle: de la féodalité aux Lumières* (Paris: Hachette, 1976), pp. 201–26. See also Lever, *Louis XVI*, p. 459.
67. AD Côte d'Or C 3475, extract of deliberations of chamber of Third Estate of Bar-sur-Seine, March 17, 1789.
68. AN B^{a} 20, liasse 25, dossier 4, document 3.
69. Timothy Tackett, *Becoming a Revolutionary: The Deputies of the French National Assembly and the Emergence of a Revolutionary Culture (1789–1790)* (Princeton: Princeton University Press, 1996), pp. 90–94.
70. Colson, *Lettres*, p. 27.
71. AD Charente-Maritime 4 J 1574 (28), *cahier* of Third Estate of Saintonge seated at Saint-Jean d'Angély.
72. AN B^{a} 31, liasse 55, dossier 6, document 5, pp. 19–20.
73. AN H^{1} 207, dossier 1, documents 21–22.
74. *Protestation de la noblesse de Bourgogne, assemblée à Dijon* (n.p., n.d.).
75. Shapiro and Markoff, *Revolutionary Demands*, p. 258. To be sure, among the peasantry, there were many complaints about the recreational privileges of the nobility, which allowed them to ride through fields, damaging crops and agriculture. Seigneurial monopolies were also unpopular. Ibid., pp. 258, 260, 385. These grievances, however, substantial as they were, were less germane to the debate over the composition of the Estates General.
76. *Requête au Roi, et deliberation du Tiers-État de la ville de Dijon, du 18 janvier 1789* (Dijon: Capel, 1789), p. 20. Despite this assurance, tensions in Dijon continued. AN H^{1} 203, dossier 3, document 148.
77. AM Le Havre AA 49, address of thanks to king by municipal officers of Alençon. See also AD Bouches-du-Rhône C 101, fol. 8; AD Calvados C 6348, *mémoire* presented to king by mayor and municipal officers of town of Avranches, December 1, 1788. A close noble friend of the Parisian barrister Colson was supportive of the suppression of tax privileges but wanted honorific privileges to be preserved. Tackett, *The Glory and the Sorrow*, p. 73.
78. AN B^{a} 25^{1}, liasse 42, dossier 2, document 2.
79. AN B^{a} 26^{1}, liasse 170bis, dossier 4, document 7. The profession of respect may have been *pro forma*, but, even if it was, it is telling that the Bretons felt the need to include it.
80. Tackett, *The Glory and the Sorrow*, p. 73, for the arrival of the Parisian barrister Colson to this firm position in March 1789.
81. See, for example, *Déliberation de la ville et communauté d'Agen, dans l'intérêt de ladite Ville et de toute la province d'Agenois. Du 25 décembre 1788* (Agen, n.d.); *Essai du patriotism, dédié, adressé et présenté à la Nation assemblée à Versailles, par un jeune citoyen philosophique* (n.p., 1789).
82. *Lettre écrite par plusiers citoyens du Clergé, de la Noblesse et des communes de Dauphiné*, p. 6.
83. *Procès-verbal des Etats de Dauphiné*, p. 121.
84. Shapiro and Markoff, *Revolutionary Demands*, p. 258.
85. Ibid., p. 294.
86. Ibid., p. 129.
87. BnF Mss. Nouv. acq. fr. 17275, fol. 92; *Venise et la Révolution*, p. 279; *Correspondance secrète*, 2: 332. For a survey of the elections to the Estates General, Edelstein, *The French Revolution and the Birth of Electoral Democracy*, pp. 11–42.
88. Beatrice Fry Hyslop, *French Nationalism in 1789 According to the General Cahiers*, reprint ed. (New York: Octagon, 1968), p. 6. According to Hyslop, 615 general *cahiers*, a number that omits colonial *cahiers*, were drawn up for the Estates General and of that number 523 are preserved in some form. Beatrice Fry Hyslop, *A Guide to the General Cahiers of 1789* (New York: Columbia University Press, 1936), pp. 45–46.
89. Hyslop, *French Nationalism in 1789*, pp. 67–68.
90. There were other motives for imperative mandates, including preventing deputies from being corrupted by the influence of the royal Court or to assure reform. Hyslop, *Guide to General Cahiers of 1789*, p. 100. There can be little doubt, however, that vote by order was the primary motivation.

91. [Guy-Jean-Baptiste Target], *II*[e] *Suite de l'écrit intitulé: les Etats-Généraux convoqués par Louis XVI* (n.p., n.d.), p. 22.
92. In its *cahier*, for example, the Third Estate of Le Havre had requested that the Estates General establish permanent and lasting order in all parts of the administration. AM Le Havre AA 46, *cahier* of Third Estate of Le Havre, March 5, 1789.
93. Shapiro and Markoff, *Revolutionary Demands*, pp. 277, 375–76.
94. AN H^1 148, dossier 2, documents 40, 41.
95. *Cahiers de doléances du Tiers État du bailliage de Rouen pour les États généraux de 1789*, Marc Bouloiseau, ed., 2 vols. (Paris and Rouen: Presses universitaires de France and Imprimerie administrative de la Seine-Maritime, 1957–60), 1: 229–31 (Rouen); 2: 73 (Duclair).
96. A British observer mentioned that the British constitution was viewed as a model in France, although he found the notion problematic. To the degree that its customary nature was the primary quality of the British constitution, it suggests that a customary constitution was the leading idea in France. *Despatches from Paris*, 2: 32–33.
97. Hyslop, *Guide to the General Cahiers of 1789*, pp. 97–98; BnF Mss. Nouv. acq. fr. 17275, fol. 114v°.
98. A point also made by Shapiro and Markoff, *Revolutionary Demands*, pp. 128–29.
99. BnF Mss. Nouv. acq. fr. 17275, fols. 112–112v°, 123–123v°; *Venise et la Révolution*, p. 279; Bombelles, *Journal*, 2: 295; *Correspondance secrète*, 2: 339.
100. Emile Queruau-Lamerie, "Lettres de Michel René Maupetit, député à l'Assemblée nationale constituante (1789–1791)," *Bulletin de la Commission historique et archéologique de la Mayenne* 17 (1901): 309, 312, 314.
101. AN B^a 12, liasse 7, dossier 11, document 1.
102. See, for example, AN B^a 20, liasse 26, dossier 4, document 1; AN AB^{XIX} 3258, *cahier* decreed by general assembly of nobility of Quercy, p. 3; AN AB^{XIX} 3258 *cahier* of order of nobility of *sénéchaussée* of Condom, p. 6; AN AB^{XIX} 3258, *cahier* of order of nobility of *bailliage* of Alençon, pp. 10–11; AN AB^{XIX} 3258, *cahier* and powers of nobility of *sénéchaussée* of Lannes, p. 3.
103. AN B^a 57, liasse 139, dossier 3, document 5; AN AB^{XIX} 3258, *cahier* of powers and instructions of deputy of order of nobility of *bailliage* of Nemours.
104. AN B^a 14, liasse 10, dossier 4, document 2. See also *Archives de l'Ouest: recueil de documents concernant la Révolution, 1789–1800*, Antonin Proust, ed., 3 vols. (Paris: Lacroix, Verboeckhoven et Cie, 1867–69), 2: 81–82.
105. AN AB^{XIX} 3258, *cahier* of order of nobility of *bailliage* of Troyes, pp. 5–6.
106. AN B^a 20^2, liasse 28, dossier 6, document 3; BnF Mss. Nouv. acq. fr. 17275, fol. 114v°.
107. AN B^a 38, liasse 78, dossier 3, document 5. More remarkably, perhaps influenced by the earlier actions of Dauphiné, they also offered a broader abandonment of provincial privileges.
108. Before the opening of the Estates General, the future deputy Maupetit wrote that the issue of vote by head or by order was the only issue that divided the nobility and the Third Estate, which were otherwise in accord. Queruau-Lamerie, "Lettres de Maupetit," 17 (1901), p. 312.
109. AN B^a 26, liasse 138, dossier 3, document 5.
110. Chaussinand-Nogaret found that half of noble *cahiers* asked for a constitution or a charter of the rights of the nation. Chausssinand-Nogaret, *La Noblesse au XVIII*[e] *siècle*, p. 208.
111. AN B^a 30, liasse 52, dossier 5, document 2. Its demand for vote by order came in the sixth article of the *cahier*.
112. AN H^1 149, dossier 1, document 7. The nobility of Berry and Cambrai and Cambrésis made similar requests. AN H^1 149, dossier 1, document 8 (Berry); AN H^1 149, dossier 1, document 11 (Cambrai and Cambrésis). Again, on the overlapping interests of nobles and Third Estate, Shapiro and Markoff, *Revolutionary Demands*, p. 294.
113. AN B^a 33, liasse 66, dossier 9, document 7.
114. *Dictionnaire de l'Académie française*, 4th ed., 1: 378.
115. AN H^1 148, dossier 2, document 40.
116. Hardman contended that removing the judiciary from politics through the creation of the *cour plenière* was more radical than the Maupeou action because Maupeou had simply changed the personnel of the *parlement*. Hardman, *Life of Louis XVI*, p. 284. The demand to have basic political tenets registered in courts throughout the land endorsed oversight but rejected the *parlement* as the body to undertake it and vested it more broadly with the nation.

117. On norms and order being associated with the concept of a constitution, Paolo Comanducci, "Ordre ou norme? Quelques idées de constitution du XVIIIe siècle," in *1789 et l'invention de la constitution*, Michel Troper and Lucien Jaume, eds. (Paris: Librairie Générale de Droit et de Jurisprudence, 1994), p. 25.
118. Kwass, *Privilege and the Politics of Taxation*, p. 281.
119. Sallier, *Annales françaises*, pp. 191–92.
120. AN AB[XIX] 3259, *cahier* of Third Estate of *bailliage* of Château-Thierry, pp. 12–13.
121. Because of its size, Paris was under a separate set of electoral regulations.
122. *Correspondance secrète*, 2: 350.
123. Ibid., 2: 347–48, 349.
124. *Venise et la Révolution française*, pp. 281–82.
125. *Correspondance secrète*, 2: 352.
126. Campbell and Hardman, "Malesherbes and the Crisis of 1787–8," p. 173; Hardman, *Life of Louis XVI*, pp. 281–87.
127. *Correspondance secrète*, 2: 349.

Notes to Chapter 6

1. *Ouverture des Etats-Généraux, faite à Versailles le 5 mai 1789* (Paris: Imprimerie royale, 1789), p. 3; *Correspondance secrète*, 2: 353.
2. *Ouverture des Etats-Généraux*, pp. 3–6; *Journal d'Adrien Duquesnoy, député du Tiers état de Bar-le-Duc, sur l'Assemblée constituante: 3 mai 1789–3 avril 1790*, Robert de Crèvecoeur, ed., 2 vols. (Paris: Picard, 1894), 1: 6.
3. *Ouverture des Etats-Généraux*, pp. 23–126, with the mention of separation on p. 110. *Procès-verbal de l'Assemblée nationale de France, précedé du Récit des séances des députés des communes; depuis le 5 mai 1789, jusqu'au 12 juin suivant, époque à laquelle la rédaction des procès-verbaux a commencé*, 73 vols. (Paris: Baudouin, 1789–91), 1: 6–7; *Archives parlementaires de 1787 à 1860. Recueil complet des débats législatifs et politiques des Chambres françaises*. M. J. Mavidal and M. E. Laurent, eds., 1st series, 1787–99, 82 vols. (Paris: Dupont, 1862–1913), 8: 1–27, with the reference to meeting separately on p. 24. See also BnF Mss. Nouv. acq. fr. 12938, fol. 2v°.
4. AD Oise J 136, document 1, May 5, 1789.
5. AD Côte d'Or 4 F 2, document 53. According to the Spanish ambassador, Necker had characterized the fiscal privileges that the clergy and nobility were to renounce as a long-time insult to the Third Estate, but the remark was excised from the printed version of his speech. Bombelles, *Journal*, 2: 308.
6. *Correspondance secrète*, 2: 348, 353; Duquesnoy, *Journal*, 1: 8.
7. AN H[1] 148, dossier 2, documents 40, 45, 55, 60.
8. Robert H. Blackman, *1789: The French Revolution Begins* (Cambridge: Cambridge University Press, 2019), p. 42.
9. Duquesnoy, *Journal*, 1: 6.
10. The *cahier* of the nobility of Saint-Quentin, for example, called for publicizing new constitutional principles of the monarchy, implying a restatement rather than creating a definitive, comprehensive document. *Cahier des remonntrances et doléances de l'ordre de la noblesse du bailliage de Saint-Quentin, le 10 mars 1789* (n.p., 1789).
11. Etienne Dumont, *Souvenirs sur Mirabeau et les deux premières assemblées legislatives*, J. Bénétruy, ed. (Paris: Presses universitaires de France, 1951), p. 45.
12. Blackman, *1789: The French Revolution Begins*, pp. 46, 70.
13. Dumont, *Souvenirs sur Mirabeau*, p. 47.
14. BM La Rochelle Ms. 21, May 6, 1789; *Procès-verbal des séances de la chambre de l'ordre de la noblesse aux Etats-Généraux, tenues à Versailles en mil sept cent quatre-vingt-neuf* (Paris: Imprimerie Nationale, 1792), pp. 1–5.
15. *Procès-verbal des séances de la chambre de l'ordre de la noblesse*, pp. 31–32.
16. Ibid., pp. 5–6.
17. Ibid., pp. 32–35. The numbers given in favor and against the motion are from AN KK 641, entry of May 11, 1789. BM La Rochelle Ms. 21, entry of May 11, 1789, gives a figure of 193 in favor, three voting for provisionally constituted, two as nothing to deliberate and thirty-one as not constituted on the motion to constitute itself as an order.
18. AN KK 641, entry of May 6, 1789.

19. *Procès-verbal des séances de la chambre de l'ordre de la noblesse*, p. 45.
20. AD Oise J 136, document 5. Similarly, the clergy, which had not renounced its fiscal privileges prior to the opening of the Estates General, repeatedly voted down motions to yield them after it opened. D. Marié, "Trois lettres inédites de l'abbé Jallet: Membre de l'Assemblée Constituante," *Annales historiques de la Révolution française* 22 (1950): 341–43.
21. *Procès-verbal des séances de la chambre de l'ordre de la noblesse*, pp. 67–68.
22. Ibid., pp. 85–102; BM La Rochelle Ms. 21, May 22, May 23, 1789; BHVP Ms. N.A. 22, fols. 1–2; BnF Mss. Nouv. acq. fr. 4121, fols. 16–17.
23. The deputy Maupetit mentions consensus use of the term on May 8, even before the Third Estate had organized itself, suggesting that deputies had discussed it among themselves before the opening of the Estates General. Queruau-Lamerie, "Lettres de Maupetit," 17 (1901), p. 443. The term had been used in electoral assemblies prior to the opening of the Estates General. The assembly in the parish of Saint Augustin had referred to itself in its *cahier* as the commons. AD Maine-et-Loire 1 B 61, dossier 2, p. 6.
24. *Procès-verbal de l'Assemblée nationale de France, précedé du Récit des séances des députés des communes*, 1: 8–9.
25. Ibid., 1: 9–11.
26. The "*récit des séances*" was the account of the sessions of the commons that predated the official minutes recorded in the "*procès-verbaux*."
27. BnF Mss. Fonds Français 13713, fol. 6. The chamber of the clergy was also disorganized and unproductive in its proceedings. Marié, "Trois lettres inédites de l'abbé Jallet," p. 339.
28. Urbain Réné Pilastre de la Brardière and J. B. Leclerc, *Correspondance de MM. Les députés des communes de la province d'Anjou avec leur commetants relativement aux Etats-Généraux…*, 10 vols. (Angers: Pavie, 1789–91), 1: 23. See also Francisque Mège, *Gaultier de Biauzat: sa vie et sa correspondance*, 2 vols. (Paris: Lechevalier, 1890), 2: 38; Queruau-Lamerie, "Lettres de Maupetit," 17 (1901), pp. 442–43.
29. BnF Mss. Nouv. acq. fr. 12938, fols. 6, 7v°.
30. Later the same day a deputation from the clergy arrived. They were escorted to the area reserved for the clergy at the opening of the Estates General. Pilastre de la Brardière and Leclerc, *Correspondance de MM. Les députés des communes de la province d'Anjou*, 1: 23. See also Mège, *Gaultier de Biauzat*, 2: 38; Queruau-Lamerie, "Lettres de Maupetit," 17 (1901), p. 443.
31. AD Gironde 3 L 82, letter of May 19, 1789.
32. BnF Mss. Nouv. acq. fr. 12938, fols. 9–9v°; AD Eure 5 F 63, fol. 22.
33. *Procès-verbal de l'Assemblée nationale de France, précedé du Récit des séances des députés des communes*, 1: 26–35; BnF Mss. Nouv. acq. fr. 12938, fols. 9v°–14.
34. AD Oise J 136, documents 20, 22; *Procès-verbal des séances de la chambre de l'ordre de la noblesse*, pp. 59–62; BnF Mss. Nouv. acq. fr. 4121, fol. 13.
35. BnF Mss. Nouv. acq. fr. 4121, fols. 16–17; *Procès-verbal des séances de la chambre de l'ordre de la noblesse*, p. 85.
36. On the wariness of the nobility on the issue, AN AB^{XIX} 3562, dossier 1, document 1.
37. AD Gironde 3 L 82, letter of May 26, 1789.
38. The word was meant to raise their status from that of deputies but the Estates General was not, of course, a legislative body.
39. *Procès-verbal des conférences sur la vérification des pouvoirs, tenues par MM. Les Commissaires du Clergé, de la Noblesse & des Communes, tant en la Salle du Comité des Etats-Géneraux, qu'en présence de MM. Les Commissaires du Roi, conformément au desir de Sa Majesté* (Paris: Baudouin, 1789), pp. 4–27; *Procès-verbal des séances de la chambre de l'ordre de la noblesse*, pp. 103–9; BnF Mss. Nouv. acq. fr. 12938, fols. 17v°–20; AD Oise J 136, documents 35–36.
40. *Procès-verbal des séances de la chambre de l'ordre de la noblesse*, p. 108; BnF Mss. Nouv. acq. fr. 12938, fol. 20; AD Nièvre 1 L 165, letter of June 4, 1789; BM Nantes Collection Dugast-Matifeux, vol. 98, letter of June 1, 1789.
41. *Procès-verbal des conférences sur la vérification des pouvoirs*, pp. 27–36.
42. AD Oise J 136, document 42.
43. *Procès-verbal de l'Assemblée nationale de France, précedé du Récit des séances des députés des communes*, 1: 50–54; *Procès-verbal des séances de la chambre de l'ordre de la noblesse*, pp. 111–16; AD Oise J 136, document 43; AD Eure 5 F 63, fol. 29.
44. *Lettres et bulletins de Barentin à Louis XVI*, Alphonse Aulard, ed. (Paris: Société de l'histoire de la Révolution française, 1915), pp. 3–12.

45. *Procès-verbal des conférences sur la vérification des pouvoirs*, pp. 38–39; *Procès-verbal de l'Assemblée nationale de France*, 1: 59–60; *Procès-verbal des séances de la chambre de l'ordre de la noblesse*, pp. 119–20.
46. AN AB^{XIX} 3359, dossier 4, document 3.
47. The vote had been overwhelming, passing by a margin of 207–38. AN KK 641, May 28, 1789.
48. *Procès-verbal de l'Assemblée nationale de France, précedé du Récit des séances des députés des communes*, 1: 57–69.
49. *Procès-verbal des conférences sur la vérification des pouvoirs*, pp. 41–99.
50. See BnF Mss. Nouv. acq. fr. 4121, fol. 29; AN KK 641, June 3, 1789; AD Oise J 136, document 56. On the basis of the objection, AD Nièvre 1 L 165, letter of May 23, 1789.
51. See *Résultat du Conseil d'État du Roi, tenu à Versailles le 27 décembre* (Paris: Imprimerie royale, 1788), especially pp. 10, 12, 13, 14, 18.
52. Bailly believed that the nobility and the clergy objected to the term because it seemed synonymous with the nation. *Mémoires de Bailly*, Saint-Albin Berville and François Barrière, eds., 3 vols. (Paris: Baudouin, 1821–23), 1: 95.
53. BnF Mss. Nouv. acq. fr. 4121, fol. 29.
54. *Procès-verbal des conférences sur la vérification des pouvoirs*, pp. 100–56.
55. Ibid., pp. 157–63.
56. The term had been discussed and criticized the day before in the chamber of the nobility. AN KK 641, June 5, 1789.
57. *Procès-verbal des conférences sur la vérification des pouvoirs*, pp. 168–212.
58. Ibid., pp. 213–16. See also AN AB^{XIX} 3359, dossier 4, document 6.
59. See, for example, AN AA 49, dossier 1391, document 52.
60. BnF Mss. Nouv. acq. fr. 17275, fol. 151.
61. Monod, "Lettres de… Couderc," pp. 418–19.
62. A deputy from Provence said that the commons could not, without exposing itself to great danger, remain divided and that he had been informed that a member of the Paris deputation had a motion of great importance to propose. The chamber expressed its desire to hear him, and it was in this manner that Sieyes was given the floor.
63. BnF Mss. Nouv. acq. fr. 12938, fol. 32v°. Also on the perceived imperiousness of the Bretons, AM Strasbourg AA 2003, fol. 41; Emile Queruau-Lamerie, "Lettres de Michel René Maupetit," *Bulletin de la Commission historique et archéologique de la Mayenne* 18 (1902), p. 151.
64. *Procès-verbal de l'Assemblée nationale de France, précedé du Récit des séances des députés des communes*, 1: 145–59. A noble deputy characterized Sieyès's motion as incendiary and stated that the nobility was determined not to accept the demand of the Third. AD Oise J 136, document 77.
65. By this time, the rigid stance of the nobility on vote by order was becoming an object of parody. BnF Mss. Nouv. acq. fr. 17275, fol. 157–157v°.
66. *Procès-verbal des séances de la chambre de l'ordre de la noblesse*, pp. 214–28; *Procès-verbal de l'Assemblée nationale de France, précedé du Récit des séances des députés des communes*, 1: 89–94; BnF Mss. Nouv. acq. fr. 17275, fol. 159.
67. *Procès-verbal de l'Assemblée nationale de France, précedé du Récit des séances des députés des communes*, 1: 48; BnF Mss. Nouv. acq. fr. 17275, fol. 159.
68. *Procès-verbal des séances des députés des communes, depuis le 12 juin 1789 jusqu'au 17 juin, jour de sa constitution en Assemblée Nationale* (Paris: Baudouin, 1789), pp. 28–29, 80–82. The idea of entering the chamber of the commons had been contemplated for weeks. Marié, "Trois lettres inédites de l'abbé Jallet," p. 341.
69. Also on the lack of cohesion among the nobility, Shapiro and Markoff, *Revolutionary Demands*, p. 285.
70. Some noble deputies had demanded greater transparency for its meetings. *Procès-verbal des séances de la chambre de l'ordre de la noblesse*, p. 239; AN KK 641, June 16, 1789; BHVP Ms. N.A. 108, fol. 133.
71. *Procès-verbal des séances de la chambre de l'ordre de la noblesse*, pp. 244, 245. There had also been a third unspecified motion offered.
72. *Procès-verbal des séances de la chambre de l'ordre de la noblesse*, pp. 244–46.
73. *Procès-verbal de l'Assemblée nationale de France, précedé du Récit des séances des députés des communes*, 1: 84.
74. BnF Mss. Nouv. acq. fr. 12938, fol. 42; Queruau-Lamerie, "Lettres de Maupetit," 18 (1902), p. 161.

75. Mounier, for example, proposed "The Legitimate Assembly of the Representatives of the Largest Portion of the Nation Acting in the Absence of the Smaller Portion," the length of which produced confusion. On the debate, see Robert Blackman, "What's in a Name? Possible Names for a Legislative Body and the Birth of National Sovereignty during the French Revolution, 15–16 June 1789," *French History* 21 (2007): 22–43. See also BHVP Ms. N.A. 108, fols. 133, 137; Barentin, *Lettres et bulletins*, pp. 30–31. Both the term National Assembly and the idea of the Third Estate unilaterally declaring itself the National Assembly were present at the time the Estates General opened. BnF Mss. Nouv. acq. fr. 12938, fol. 6v°.
76. BnF Mss. Nouv. acq. fr. 12938, fols. 43–43v°; *Le Point du Jour*, June 19, 1789. Sieyès acknowledged that the term was not new and traced it back to Voltaire. AN 294 AP 4, dossier 1.
77. *Procès-verbal de l'Assemblée nationale de France, précedé du Récit des séances des députés des communes*, 1: 100–101.
78. Ibid., 1: 104.
79. *Le Point du Jour*, June 19, 1789. The number closely corresponds with that of Barentin, in which he states that the vote was 490–90. *Lettres et bulletins de Barentin*, p. 37.
80. Its use by the Crown may have been Marolles's source for the term.
81. *Procès-verbal des séances de la chambre de l'ordre de la noblesse*, p. 252.
82. *Procès-verbal de l'Assemblée nationale*, no. 1 (June 17, 1789), pp. 2–4.
83. Ibid., pp. 11–14.
84. Ibid., pp. 14–15.
85. *Lettres et bulletins de Barentin*, pp. 32–33. The discussion is omitted from the records of the commons. *Procès-verbal de l'Assemblée nationale de France, précedé du Récit des séances des députés des communes*, 1: 83–96.
86. Carl Heinrich Christophelsmeier, "The First Revolutionary Step (June 17, 1789)," *University Studies of the University of Nebraska* 9 (1909): 1–87.
87. Blackman, "What's in a Name?"; Blackman, *1789: The French Revolution Begins*, p. 73.
88. Pilastre de la Brardière and Leclerc, *Correspondance de MM. Les députés des communes de la province d'Anjou*, 1: 205–6.
89. Maurice Hutt, "The Role of the Curés in the Estates General of 1789," *Journal of Ecclesiastical History* 6 (1955): 205–14.
90. Hardman, *Life of Louis XVI*, p. 313.
91. One deputy who had been discouraged by the lack of progress during the prolonged stalemate believed on June 20 that the Assembly was on the verge of breaking out of the restraints brought about previously by its wisdom and prudence. AN W 306, dossier 377, fols. 20, 39.
92. The only deputy who did not support the decree was Joseph Martin-Dauch, who stated that he could not carry out any decision that did not have the sanction of the monarch and signed "opposed" next to his signature, which led to an uproar in the Assembly. He resisted arguments of the president that the Assembly was in accord with his sentiments and the Assembly decided to leave his signature on the decree in order to demonstrate the freedom of opinions in the Assembly. *Le Point du Jour*, June 22, 1789.
93. *Procès-verbal de l'Assemblée nationale*, no. 3 (June 20, 1789).
94. The concern of the Assembly about a potential rump body was apparent in a phrase that it deleted from printed examples of its motion declaring itself the National Assembly. The passage declared that no other chamber of deputies could, through its deliberations, represent the nation. *Le Point du Jour*, June 20, 1789.

Notes to Chapter 7

1. *Procès-verbal des séances de la chambre de l'ordre de la noblesse*, pp. 251–54.
2. Blackman observed that the decision to meet on June 22 was more radical than the meeting of June 20, which had been previously scheduled. Blackman, *1789: The French Revolution Begins*, pp. 123–24.
3. AD Eure 5 F 63, fol. 90. See also *Lettres et bulletins de Barentin*, p. 41.
4. *Procès-verbal de l'Assemblée nationale*, no. 4 (June 22, 1789); Pilastre de la Brardière and Leclerc, *Correspondance de MM. Les députés des communes de la province d'Anjou*, 1: 204–6.
5. *Le Point du Jour ou résultat de ce qui c'est passé la veille à l'Assemblée Nationale* [Newberry Library Case FRC 6922]; *Le Point du Jour*, June 23, 1789. The former appears to be a specially printed supplement that circulated and contains information not included in the newspaper account. The royal session opened at 11:00 a.m. on June 23, although the deputies of the

National Assembly had arrived at 9:00 a.m., the time at which deputies had been told to arrive. The royal session had been scheduled to open at 10:00 a.m. Stories of the humiliation of the commons dismayed the Parisian barrister Colson. Tackett, *The Glory and the Sorrow*, p. 83.

6. The deputy Maupetit thought that the royal session might be the final meeting of the Estates General. Queurau-Lamerie, "Lettres de Maupetit," 18 (1902), p. 324. Also on the attempt to intimidate the commons, Joachim Heinrich Campe, *Été 89: lettres d'un Allemand à Paris* (Paris: 1989), p. 90.
7. *Journal des Etats-Généraux*, 1: 201.
8. Louis's tone was so imperious that even some in the nobility were offended. Hardman, *Life of Louis XVI*, p. 318.
9. *Journal des Etats-Généraux*, 1: 197–206. The meeting is treated in a notably abbreviated fashion in the minutes of the National Assembly. *Procès-verbal de l'Assemblée nationale*, no. 5 (June 23, 1789).
10. BnF Mss. Nouv. acq. fr. 12938, fol. 61v°. Félix characterized the meeting as the last *lit de justice* of the monarchy. Félix, *Louis XVI & Marie-Antoinette*, p. 468.
11. As an illustration of public reaction, Louis's conduct and pronouncements at the session enraged the Parisian barrister Colson. Tackett, *The Glory and the Sorrow*, p. 85.
12. BnF Mss. Nouv. acq. fr. 12938, fol. 53.
13. Ibid., fols. 53–53v°; *Procès-verbal de l'Assemblée nationale*, no. 6 (June 24, 1789), p. 2.
14. BnF Mss. Nouv. acq. fr. 12938, fols. 53v°–54. The guards had blocked all communications between the commons and the other two orders. Duquesnoy, *Journal*, 1: 124.
15. AN K 164, no. 4[3], June 24, 1789; AN KK 641, entry of June 24, 1789.
16. BnF Mss. Nouv. acq. fr. 12938, fols. 55–56; *Procès-verbal de l'Assemblée nationale*, no. 7 (June 25, 1789), pp. 18–19.
17. *Lettres et bulletins de Barentin*, pp. 49–51.
18. *Procès-verbal de l'Assemblée nationale*, no. 8 (June 26, 1789).
19. *Procès-verbal des séances de la chambre de l'ordre de la noblesse*, p. 305.
20. Ibid., pp. 302–3.
21. *Procès-verbal de l'Assemblée nationale*, no. 8 (June 26, 1789), pp. 4–6, 20–24.
22. BnF Mss. Nouv. acq. fr. 12938, fol. 57v°.
23. *Procès-verbal de l'Assemblée nationale*, no. 9 (June 27, 1789), pp. 1–2.
24. AN K 164, no. 4[3], June 27, 1789; *Procès-verbal des séances de la chambre de l'ordre de la noblesse*, pp. 307–8.
25. BnF Mss. Nouv. acq. fr. 12938, fols. 60v°–61; BnF Mss. Nouv. acq. fr. 17275, fol. 167. Moreover, in an apparent effort to prepare public opinion the Crown had sent copies of the monarch's June 23 speech to intendants and asked them to print it, post it and circulate it in both towns and the countryside. AD Calvados C 6347, letter of Barentin to intendant at Caen, June 24, 1789; letter of Villedueil to intendant at Caen, June 24, 1789.
26. Some members of the Assembly believed that the letter had been solicited from the monarch by the clergy and nobility in order to save face at their capitulation. BnF Mss. Nouv. acq. fr. 12938, fol. 59v°; *Lettres de l'Abbé Barbotin*, p. 27. See also *Lettres et bulletins de Barentin*, p. 51. One of the recalcitrant noble deputies entering the chamber thought that the entry meant that the nobility had been abolished. AD Ain 1 Mi 1, fol. 103, letter of June 27, 1789.
27. Ibid. See also AD Pyrénées-Orientales C 2119, no. 10, letter of June 27, 1789.
28. Duquesnoy, *Journal*, 1: 137–38; AN B[a] 73, liasse 172, dossier 6, document 18.
29. *Procès-verbal de l'Assemblée nationale*, no. 9 (June 27, 1789), pp. 6–8. Indeed, on the night of June 27 the streets of Versailles were illuminated and there were fireworks. BnF Mss. Nouv. acq. fr. 12938, fols. 60–60v°; BnF Mss. Nouv. acq. fr. 17275, fol. 167. Far from Paris also the arrival of the news became a celebratory occasion. AM Aix BB 5, fols. 134–36; AM Aurillac II 7, no. 15, fol. 1v°.
30. A fact of which deputies were well aware. See *Lettres de l'Abbé Barbotin*, pp. 28–29, although he was still elated that the "Estates General" was now complete. See also AN T* 1562/1, fol. 25.
31. BHVP Ms. N.A. 22, fols. 3–5.
32. BnF Mss. Nouv. acq. fr. 4121, fol. 50; AN KK 641, June 30, 1789.
33. AN AA 49, dossier 1395–97, document 102; AN AA 48, dossier 1388–90, document 87; which is dated even earlier, June 25, which makes it difficult to trace the origins of the effort.
34. An M 856, dossier 6[9], letter of Barentin to Louis XVI, June 28, 1789; *Lettres et bulletins de Barentin*, p. 56.

35. AN K 164, no. 4³, June 30, 1789.
36. BnF Mss. Nouv. acq. fr. 12938, fol. 61. Although the duc de Luxembourg did not seek the presidency, one of the issues that concerned the nobility was that they be under their president. AM Bayonne AA 51, unnumbered letter, June 30, 1789.
37. *Le Point du Jour*, July 1, 1789.
38. AN K 164, no. 4³, June 30, 1789; AM Lorient BB 12, no. 27, letter of June 30, 1789.
39. BnF Mss. Nouv. acq. fr. 12938, fol. 61; *Procès-verbal de l'Assemblée nationale*, no. 10, June 30, 1789, p. 4.
40. BnF Mss. Nouv. acq. fr. 4121, fol. 51; AM Bayonne AA 51, unnumbered, letter of June 30, 1789. The latter document states that the nobility also did not want to be presided over by the president of the Assembly.
41. AD Eure 5 F 63, fol. 99; AD Gironde 3 L 82, letter of June 30, 1789, at 5:00 p.m.; François Ménard de la Groye, *Correspondance (1789–1791)*, Florence Mirouse, ed. (n.p., Conseil général de la Sarthe, 1989), p. 55. One deputy wrote in his diary that the newly-arrived deputies were not directly challenging the principle of vote by head, which meant the issue had been resolved in favor of the commons and that it was a consolation for the time it had taken to achieve it. BnF Mss. Nouv. acq. fr. 12938, fols. 61–61v°.
42. Duquesnoy, *Journal*, 1: 141–44.
43. AD Pyrénées-Orientales C 2119, no. 17, letter of July 6, 1789.
44. *Procès-verbal des séances de la chambre de l'ordre de la noblesse*, p. 349.
45. Ibid., p. 348.
46. AM Le Havre, D³ 38, no. 5, letter of June 30, 1789.
47. BnF Mss. Nouv. acq. fr. 12938, fol. 61v°.
48. Bombelles, *Journal*, 2: 339, in which he wrote that the recalcitrant deputies were offended at all they had seen and heard.
49. AD Pyrénées-Orientales C 2119, no. 17, letter of July 6, 1789.
50. *Procès-verbal des séances de la chambre de l'ordre de la noblesse*, pp. 313, 317, 342, 344, 346.
51. *Procès-verbal de l'Assemblée nationale*, no. 11 (July 1, 1789), pp. 18, 20–21; BM La Rochelle Ms. 21, July 2, 1789.
52. AD Eure 5 F 63, fols. 102–4.
53. *Procès-verbal de l'Assemblée nationale*, no. 12 (July 2, 1789, pp. 3–4; BnF Mss. Nouv. acq. fr. 4121, fols. 54v°–55; *Lettres et bulletins de Barentin*, p. 57. Whether it was the archbishop of Aix or another member of the clergy is not clear, but during the discussion one also advanced the claim that the king had the authority to conduct a *lit de justice* in the meeting room of what he called the "Estates General." BnF Mss. Nouv. acq. fr. 12938, fols. 63–63v°.
54. *Suite des Nouvelles de Versailles*, July 3, 1789.
55. *Procès-verbal de l'Assemblée nationale*, no. 12 (July 2, 1789), p. 4; BnF Mss. Nouv. acq. fr. 12938, fol. 63v°.
56. BnF Mss. Nouv. acq. fr. 4121, fols. 55v°–56; BM La Rochelle Ms. 21, July 3, 1789, at 7:00 p.m.; Louis Henry Charles, baron de Gauville, *Journal du baron de Gauville, député de l'ordre de la noblesse au États généraux depuis le 4 mars, 1789 jusqu'au 1 juillet, 1790* (Paris: Lainé et Havard, 1864), p. 9.
57. *Procès-verbal des séances de la chambre de l'ordre de la noblesse*, pp. 316, 326–27. Furthermore, there was also a perception that the nobility was using charters and privileges to act against the public good. BnF Mss. Nouv. acq. fr. 17275, fol. 164v°.
58. BnF Mss. Nouv. acq. fr. 12938, fols. 64v°–65; *Procès-verbal de l'Assemblée nationale*, no. 14 (July 3, 1789), pp. 1–2; *Lettres et bulletins de Barentin*, pp. 58–59.
59. The nobility kept minutes, which suggested that such meetings were to continue.
60. AD Pyrénées-Orientales C 2119, no. 16, letter of July 4, 1789; no. 17, letter of July 6, 1789; *Procès-verbal des séances de la chambre de l'ordre de la noblesse*, pp. 359–60.
61. BnF Mss. Nouv. acq. fr. 4121, fol. 57; AM Le Havre D³ 38, no. 6, letter of July 8, 1789.
62. AN Bª 41, liasse 87, dossier 6, document 4. See also AD Pyrénées-Orientales C 2119, no. 17, letter of July 6, 1789, for a similar pronouncement.
63. AD Ain 1 Mi 1, fol. 115, letter of July 2, 1789; fol. 120, letter of July 7, 1789.
64. AD Pyrénées-Orientales C 2119, no. 17, letter of July 6, 1789.
65. AD Calvados F. 780, copy of letter of duc de Coigny, August 1, 1789. Indeed, correspondence between officials in Normandy, completely apart from any communication with deputies, reflects the general sense of chagrin over the unwillingness to compromise that the stalemate at

the Estates General had revealed. In early June 1789 Norman provincial officials wrote to municipal officers at Pont l'Evêque about an administrative problem and in the letter expressed the hope "…that a new order of things will stop all of these conflicts of which you so rightly complain and that there will come a day when in order to do good it will suffice to want to do it." AD Seine-Maritime C 2152, letter of *procureurs-syndics* to *bureau* of Pont l'Evêque, June 6, 1789. Coigny's statement to the Assembly drew the attention of deputies. See Pilastre de la Brardière and Leclerc, *Correspondance de MM. Les députés des communes de la province d'Anjou*, 2: 34.

66. AN B^{a} 41, liasse 87, dossier 6, document 2.
67. AN B^{a} 41, liasse 87, dossier 6, documents 9–10.
68. AN K 164, no. 4^{3}, June 27, 1789.
69. The nobility of many *bailliages* were sending annulments of imperative mandates to their deputies and vesting them with new powers to cooperate with the Assembly. Pilastre de la Brardière and Leclerc, *Correspondance de MM. Les députés des communes de la province d'Anjou*, 2: 36.
70. AN B^{a} 20, liasse 25, dossier 4, document 1.
71. AN B^{a} 33, liasse 68, dossier 5, document 6.
72. *Archives de l'Ouest*, 2: 174–75. The attendees also ordered that its deliberation be printed and posted throughout the city and distributed in the province.
73. AN B^{a} 77^{A}, liasse 181, dossier 5, document 6; AN B^{a} 29, liasse 49, dossier 11, document 9; AN B^{a} 47^{B2}, liasse 111, dossier 6, document 15; AN B^{a} 49^{2}, liasse 115; dossier 6, document 9; AN C 32^{1}, dossier 268, document 1.
74. AN B^{a} 77^{A}, liasse 181, dossier 4, document 6; AN AA 50, dossier 1424–27, document 50.
75. AN B^{a} 77^{A}, liasse 181, dossier 4, document 4. At the royal session on June 23, Louis had ordered deputies seeking new powers to remain in the Estates General so the departure of noble deputies from Versailles was highly irregular.
76. AN B^{a} 77^{A}, liasse 181, dossier 4, document 3. Indeed, the deputies, on March 22, had been granted full powers to address any unforeseen circumstances. AN B^{a} 77^{A}, liasse 181, dossier 4, document 1. A bit more gently, the nobility of Alençon, declaring that it sought the general happiness of the kingdom, calm in the fatherland and confidence in the wisdom and patriotism of the National Assembly, gave its deputy unlimited powers and instructed him to return to the Assembly and once there to work for the common good. It expressed its love for the general and particular good of all citizens. AN B^{a} 11, liasse 5, dossier 8, document 2. Similar instructions and injunctions from other noble assemblies in France include AN B^{a} 14, liasse 11, dossier 3, document 3; AN B^{a} 16, liasse 16, dossier 4, document 2; AN B^{a} 49, liasse 114, dossier 7, document 8; AN B^{a} 49^{2}, liasse 115, dossier 6, document 7; AN B^{a} 53, liasse 124, dossier 4, document 6; AN B^{a} 53, liasse 127, dossier 5, document 5. See also *Le Point du Jour*, July 29, 1789.
77. Tackett, *Becoming a Revolutionary*, pp. 32–35.
78. Stephen Miller, *Feudalism, Venality and Revolution: French Provincial Assemblies and the Late Ancien Régime* (Manchester: Manchester University Press, 2020), p. 179.
79. Ibid., pp. 157, 179.
80. BnF Mss. Nouv. acq. fr. 12938, fol. 66v°.
81. BnF Mss. Nouv. acq. fr. 4816, fol. 168.
82. BnF Mss. Nouv. acq. fr. 12938, fols. 67–67v°; *Procès-verbal de l'Assemblée nationale*, no. 18 (July 6, 1789), p. 3; Duquesnoy, *Journal*, 1: 166–67; Ménard de la Groye, *Correspondance*, p. 57; BnF Mss. Nouv. acq. fr. 4816, fol. 169.
83. It was not always merely a convenient fiction. The *cahier* was widely regarded as more significant than a deputy's individual judgment. See Shapiro and Markoff, *Revolutionary Demands*, pp. 128–29.
84. *Lettres et bulletins de Barentin*, p. 64.
85. AN B^{a} 23, liasse 38, dossier 5, document 8.
86. AN B^{a} 23, liasse 38, dossier 5, documents 9, 11.
87. AN B^{a} 23, liasse 38, dossier 5, document 11.
88. AD Ain 1 Mi 1, fols. 54–55, letter of May 30, 1789.
89. AD Ain 1 Mi 1, fol. 114, letter of July 2, 1789; fol. 120, letter of July 7, 1789.
90. AD Ain 1 Mi 1, fol. 114, letter of July 2, 1789.
91. AN B^{a} 23, liasse 38, dossier 5, document 15.

92. BnF Mss. Nouv. acq. fr. 12938, fols. 64v°–65; *Procès-verbal de l'Assemblée nationale*, no. 14 (July 3, 1789), pp. 1–2.
93. BnF Mss. Nouv. acq. fr. 12938, fols. 67v°–69. On the debate, *Le Point du Jour*, 1: 129–34.
94. BnF Mss. Nouv. acq. fr. 12938, fol. 69v°; *Procès-verbal de l'Assemblée nationale*, no. 18 (July 8, 1789), p. 2; *Le Point du Jour*, 1: 139–40.
95. BnF Mss. Nouv. acq. fr. 4121, fol. 64; BnF Mss. Fonds Fr. 10883, fol. 65v°; Duquesnoy, *Journal*, 1: 173–74. The discussion had originally begun with a proposal to affirm that all mandates that prevented deputies from voting in the Assembly be invalidated. It appears that those who wished to retain them believed that a resolution that there was "nothing to debate" meant that the mandates remained valid rather than that the question was already settled.
96. René Puaux, "Lettres inédites de Boissy d'Anglas sur la Révolution française," *Bulletin de la société de l'histoire du Protestantisme Français* 75 (1926): 285.
97. *Procès-verbal des séances de la chambre de l'ordre de la noblesse*, pp. 360–66.
98. AD Côte d'Or C 2987[6*], fols. 114 v°–117v°.
99. *Procès-verbal de l'Assemblée nationale*, no. 17 (July 7, 1789): 3–6; *Journal des Débats et des décrets*, 1: 111; *Journal des Etats-Généraux*, 1: 381; *Bulletin de l'Assemblée Nationale*, July 7, 1789.
100. Indeed, in the immediate aftermath of the renunciations made during the meeting of August 4, Hernoux suggested that the abandonment of privileges by Saint-Jean-de-Losne had prepared the way for the renunciations made during that meeting. BM Dijon Ms. 3917, fols. 35–36. I would like to thank the Bibliothèque Municipale of Dijon for making a digital copy of this document for me.
101. Puaux, "Lettres inédites de Boissy d'Anglas," pp. 285–86.
102. BnF Mss. Nouv. acq. fr. 12938, fols. 71–71v°; *Procès-verbal de l'Assemblée nationale*, no. 19 (July 9, 1789), pp. 1–2. The movement of troops, as Félix noted, was designed to protect the royal family but also to regain control of events. Félix, *Louis XVI & Marie-Antoinette*, p. 482.
103. Mège, *Gaultier de Biauzat*, 2: 156; see also p. 167. Also on the importance of the use of the term National Assembly, see Duquesnoy, *Journal*, 1: 234; *Lettres et bulletins de Barentin*, p. 60.
104. BnF Mss. Nouv. acq. fr. 12938, fols. 71–71v°; *Procès-verbal de l'Assemblée nationale*, no. 19 (July 9, 1789), pp. 4–5.
105. Lever, *Louis XVI*, p. 508; Munro Price, "The Ministry of the Hundred Hours: A Reappraisal," *French History* 4 (1990): 333. Lever argued that if the Assembly did not accept, it would be dissolved, whereas Price questioned whether the use of force was the preferred course of the Crown.
106. Mège, *Gaultier de Biauzat*, 2: 169.
107. On the hostility of the nobility to the project, BnF Mss. Nouv. acq. fr. 4121, fol. 66; *Procès-verbal des séances de la chambre de l'ordre de la noblesse*, pp. 371–72.
108. AM Brest 2 D 18 (formerly LL 44, fol. 30v°; LL 46, no. 29, July 9, 1789).
109. *Procès-verbal de l'Assemblée nationale*, no. 19 (July 9, 1789): 3–4; *Journal des débats et des décrets*, 1: 134. See also AN B[a] 9, liasse 2, dossier 6, document 7.
110. Clearly encouraged, the deputy Pierre Nicolas de Fontenay mentioned it in a letter to his wife. Pierre Nicolas de Fontenay, *Lettres à Babeth: chronique de l'Assemblée nationale par un Normand, 1789–1791*, Anne Mezin and Hugues de Boissien, eds. (Paris: SPM, 2015), p. 124.
111. *Le Point du Jour*, July 10, 1789.
112. AM Strasbourg AA 2003, fol. 76, in which the deputies from Strasbourg informed their constituents that the Assembly had decreed that nothing could interrupt work on the constitution.
113. On the uncertain sense of a constitution in the kingdom, AN B[a] 33, liasse 66, dossier 9, document 7. In its *cahier*, the nobility of Cambrai and Cambrésis requested that constitutional laws be immutably recorded in a "national register." AN H[1] 149, dossier 1, document 11.
114. In early June, one deputy, after weeks of stalemate, had written that he was firmly convinced that the Estates General had been called more to establish than to maintain the constitution and it was almost certainly in the sense of establishing a precise form of government to which he was alluding. AN W 306, dossier 377, fol. 25.
115. *Rapport du comité chargé du travail sur la constitution par M. Mounier* (Paris: Baudouin, 1789). BnF Mss. Nouv. acq. fr. 12938, fols. 71v°–72v°; *Journal des Etats-Généraux*, 1: 443–46; *Le Point du Jour*, July 10, 1789.
116. Duquesnoy, *Journal*, 1: 181; Mège, *Gaultier de Biauzat*, 2: 169; Ménard de la Groye, *Correspondance*, pp. 60–61; Puaux, "Lettres inédites de Boissy d'Anglas," p. 286.

117. BnF Mss. Nouv. acq. fr. 12938, fol. 72.
118. BnF Mss. Nouv. acq. fr. 12938, fols. 74–75.
119. BnF Mss. Nouv. acq. fr. 12938, fol. 57v°; René Puaux, "Lettres inédites de Boissy d'Anglas," p. 292.
120. Ménard de la Groye, *Correspondance*, pp. 59–60. Indeed, lending support to Ménard de la Groye's view, a message from Marseille stated that inhabitants from Marseille to Lyon had taken up arms to defend the constitution. *Journal des Etats-Généraux*, 2: 300.
121. Puaux, "Lettres inédites de Boissy d'Anglas," p. 289.
122. AM Bayonne AA 51, no. 19, letter of July 14, 1789; AM Lorient BB 12, no. 34, letter of July 14, 1789; AN KK 647, entry of July 17, 1789; BnF Mss. Fonds Fr. 10883, fols. 70–70v°; BnF Mss. Nouv. acq. fr. 4816, fol. 172.
123. AD Ain 1 Mi 1, fol. 151, letter of July 22, 1789.
124. AM Bayonne AA 51, no. 19, letter of July 14, 1789; BnF Mss. Nouv. acq. fr. 12938, fol. 78v°; *Le Point du Jour*, July 15, 1789.
125. Indeed, the Assembly had not learned of the fall of the Bastille until the day after it occurred. BnF Mss. Nouv. acq. fr. 12938, fol. 80.
126. BnF Mss. Nouv. acq. fr. 12938, fols. 81–82; *Procès-verbal de l'Assemblée nationale*, no. 24 (July 15, 1789), pp. 6–10; *Le Point du Jour*, July 16, 1789; *Journal des Etats-Généraux*, 2: 41–43.
127. *The Papers of Thomas Jefferson*, Julian Boyd and William H. Gaines, eds., 37 vols. (Princeton: Princeton University Press, 1950–2010), 15: 278, 279. Deputies were also aware of the position of strength that the Assembly now had. See AM Strasbourg AA 2003, fol. 92.
128. The royal bodyguard offered a detachment to accompany them but in yet another illustration of awareness of the loyalty the Assembly had inspired, the delegation declared that it would be better to enter the city without any military presence. BnF Mss. Nouv. acq. fr. 12938, fol. 82; *Journal des Etats-Généraux*, 2: 44–45. Clermont-Tonnerre noted that armed men surrounding deputies could be misinterpreted and exacerbate disorder.
129. On the festive atmosphere in Paris, Gandilhon, "Cinq lettres sur les événements parisiens," pp. 274–75.
130. *Le Point du Jour*, July 16, 1789.
131. *Despatches from Paris*, 2: 244–47. Also on the powerlessness of the monarch and his defeated demeanor, BM Lyon Ms. 5430, no. 8–8(2), letter of July 24, 1789; Puaux, "Lettres inédites de Boissy d'Anglas," p. 292; Gandilhon, "Cinq lettres sur les événements parisiens," pp. 274–75. Years later, he harbored bitter memories of the day and was in tears in the days after his return to Versailles. Hardman, *Life of Louis XVI*, pp. 330–31.
132. BM Dijon Ms. 2074, fol. 429. See also BnF Mss. Nouv. acq. fr. 4816, fol. 173; AD Pyrénées-Atlantiques C 2119, no. 23, letter of July 16, 1789.
133. BM La Rochelle Ms. 21, July 16, 1789.
134. *Suite des Nouvelles de Versailles*, July 16, 1789.
135. Gauville, *Journal*, pp. 8–9. Gauville described invitations to the meeting being passed almost surreptitiously through a small sheet of paper as deputies left the Assembly, so it was perhaps possible to try to continue them. See also AN KK 647, entry of July 17, 1789.
136. AN W 306, dossier 377, fol. 4; *Procès-verbal de l'Assemblée nationale*, no. 25 (July 16, 1789), pp. 4–6; *Le Point du Jour*, July 17, 1789; *Journal des Etats-Généraux*, 2: 49–50; BnF Mss. Nouv. acq. fr. 4816, fol. 173. On the unsuccessful attempt to continue them, AN KK 647, July 17, 1789. On the perceived insincerity of the minority of the clergy and the majority of the nobility at this time, AM Bergerac, fonds Faugère, Carton 1, no. 6, letter of July 17, 1789.
137. *Papers of Thomas Jefferson*, 15: 279.
138. AD Cantal 27 J 176, document 81, letter of July 31, 1789. See also AD Ain 1 Mi 1, fol. 156, letter of July 26, 1789.
139. AD Marne E supp. 4812* (formerly AM Châlons-sur-Marne BB 36), letter of mayor and municipal officials of Châlons-sur-Marne to National Assembly, July 22, 1789.

Notes to Chapter 8

1. On contrasting municipal revolutions, Lynn Avery Hunt, *Revolution and Urban Politics in Provincial France: Troyes and Reims, 1786–1790* (Stanford: Stanford University Press, 1978), pp. 68–91; Paul R. Hanson, *Provincial Politics in the French Revolution: Caen and Limoges, 1789–1794* (Baton Rouge: Louisiana State University Press, 1989), pp. 31–36, 53.

2. AN C 90, dossier 65, document 21. See also AD Ain 1 Mi 1, fol. 156, letter of July 26, 1789.
3. Duquesnoy, *Journal*, 1: 231–32.
4. AM Bergerac, fonds Faugère, Carton 1, no. 6, letter of July 17, 1789; Creuzé-Latouche, *Journal*, pp. 238–39. For an observation by a non-deputy of the lack of cohesion in the Assembly, Dumont, *Souvenirs sur Mirabeau*, pp. 131–32.
5. Creuzé-Latouche, *Journal*, p. 239. See also AD Ain 1 Mi 1, fols. 123–24, letter of July 10, 1789.
6. *Papers of Thomas Jefferson*, 15: 291. He, of course, had not been present at the Constitutional Convention but had been kept apprised of its proceedings.
7. *Journal des Etats-Généraux*, 2: 107.
8. *Le Point du Jour*, July 22, 1789. The minutes indicate only that the president of the Assembly ordered the committee to meet. *Procès-verbal de l'Assemblée nationale*, no. 29 (July 21, 1789): 5.
9. C. Leroux-Cesbron, "Lettres de Lofficial, député à l'Assemblée Constituante, sur la Révolution de 1789," *Nouvelle Revue Rétrospective* 7 (1897): 100.
10. For the impatience of the Assembly to move the constitution forward, AD Ain 1 Mi 1, fol. 151, letter of July 22, 1789; *Le Point du Jour*, July 22, 1789. In anticipation of beginning work on a constitution, on July 22 a noble deputy had suggested that the Assembly abandon seating by orders to facilitate communication among members of the same delegation. Pilastre de la Brardière and Leclerc, *Correspondance de MM. Les députés des communes de la province d'Anjou*, 2: 48–49.
11. *Procès-verbal de l'Assemblée nationale*, no. 31 (July 24, 1789): 12. BM La Rochelle Ms. 21, July 24. See also R. Herly, "Correspondance du lieutenant général du bailliage de Sarrelouis de la Salle, député de l'Assemblée Nationale, 1789–1791", *Bulletin de la Société des Amis des Pays de la Sarre* 4 (1927): 211–12; *Journal des Débats et des décrets*, 1: 253. Duquesnoy believed that internal division within the committee was slowing progress on the constitution. Duquesnoy, *Journal*, 1: 232–33.
12. According to one observer, when the president announced the forthcoming delivery of the report to the Assembly there was universal applause because the project had long been anticipated. *Le Point du Jour*, July 28, 1789.
13. Blackman, *1789: The French Revolution Begins*, pp. 45–50, 70.
14. See Caiani, *Louis XVI and the French Revolution*, pp. 204–5.
15. After those of Champion de Cicé and Clermont-Tonnerre, Mounier had also delivered a report for the committee. The Assembly also rotated the presidency of the body by order. Fontenay, *Lettres à Babeth*, p. 141.
16. Blackman, *1789: The French Revolution Begins*, p. 73.
17. They were a major issue in the noble and Third Estate *cahiers*. Shapiro and Markoff, *Revolutionary Demands*, pp. 277, 289.
18. *Procès-verbal des séances de la chambre de l'ordre de la noblesse*, pp. 124, 265.
19. Blackman, *1789: The French Revolution Begins*, p. 59.
20. George V. Taylor, "Revolutionary and Nonrevolutionary Content in the *Cahiers* of 1789: An Interim Report," *French Historical Studies* 7 (1972): 479–502, especially 494.
21. BM Dijon Ms. 2522, no. 3, letter of July 30, 1789; *Papers of Thomas Jefferson*, 15: 326. On the early caution of the Assembly see also BM Nantes Collection Dugast-Matifeux, vol. 12, p. 63. A news sheet passed hand to hand (*nouvelles à la main*) also emphasized that the report granted the monarch "the greatest authority and the most extensive powers. . . ." BHVP CP 6540, July 31, 1789. In the same vein, a deputy in the Assembly wrote to a correspondent after the report that executive power belongs to the monarch in full plentitude. Puaux, "Lettres inédites de Boissy d'Anglas," p. 298.
22. On the impatience, *Le Point du Jour*, August 1, 1789, August 2, 1789; on the excitement, *Journal des Etats-Généraux*, 2: 306–7.
23. The Breton deputy Laurent François Legendre appeared to allude to a plan when he wrote to his constituents of the motion and told them "we were all prepared." AM Brest 2 D 18 (formerly LL 46, no. 36). Bertrand Barère recounted being approached and told that it was essential that nobles make the renunciation. Bertrand Barère, *Mémoires de B. Barère*, 4 vols. (Paris: Labitte, 1842–44), 1: 268–70. See also AM Limoges AA 4, letter of August 5, 1789; Alexandre Lameth, *Histoire de l'Assemblée constituante*, 2 vols. (Paris: Moutardier, 1828), 1: 96. The plan, devised at the Breton Club, was undoubtedly facilitated by the fact that Le Chapelier had recently been elected president of the Assembly.
24. Barère, *Mémoires*, 1: 269.
25. One astonished observer described the renunciations as the product of "a kind of supernatural inspiration." BnF Fonds Français 13713, fol. 116v°.

26. The meeting is studied more fully in Michael P. Fitzsimmons, *The Night the Old Regime Ended: August 4, 1789, and the French Revolution* (University Park: Pennsylvania State University Press, 2003).
27. Lameth, *Histoire de l'Assemblée constituante*, 1: 98.
28. AM Strasbourg AA 2003, fols. 120–21; AM Lorient BB 12, no. 47, letter of August 5, 1789. See also *Journal de Versailles*, August 8, 1789.
29. AM Strasbourg AA 2003, fols. 120–21.
30. Ibid.
31. AD Meurthe-et-Moselle AC 527/187 (AM Toul JJ 7), fols. 103–106v°, especially fol. 105v°.
32. BnF Mss. Fonds Français 13713, fols. 115v°–116; AM Bordeaux D 220, no. 13, letter of August 5, 1789; AD Pyrénées-Atlantques C 1377, letter of August 7, 1789.
33. BnF Mss. Fonds Fr. 10883, fol. 84. Deputies who had not been in attendance the night before renounced the privileges of their provinces and towns the next day. AM Bayonne AA 51, no. 23, letter of August 5, 1789; AD Gironde 3 L 82, letter of August 7, 1789.
34. BM Angers Ms. 1888, pp. 161–62. See also Herly, "Correspondance," p. 219; Lameth, *Histoire de l'Assemblée Constituante*, 1: 194. Indeed, in the aftermath of the popular uprising in Paris one deputy had expressed concern that with the monarch rendered powerless the provinces would seek to consolidate and reinforce their privileges, leading to disunity. BM Lyon Ms. 5430, no. 8–8(2), letter of July 24, 1789. For a retrospective expression of the manner in which the Assembly had seemed to correct this situation, AD Côte d'Or L 151, dossier Yonne, letter of June 1790, with response June 20.
35. AD Bouches-du-Rhône C 1337, letter of Verdolin, August 7, 1789; AD Bouches-du-Rhône C 1380, fol. 248. See also Lameth, *Histoire de l'Assemblée Constituante*, 1: 97–98; Antoine-François Delandine, *De quelques changemens politiques, opérés ou projettés en France pendant les années 1789, 1790 et 1791, ou Discours sur divers points importans de la constitution et de la nouvelle législation du royaume* (Paris: Laurent, 1791), pp. 12–13. It was often considered of such significance that it was included in hasty summaries of the evening's accomplishments. See, for example, BHVP Ms. N.A. 198, fol. 193. On its centrality for the Assembly, *Le Point du Jour*, August 14, 1789.
36. BM La Rochelle Ms. 21, August 4, 1789. One Breton clerical deputy who was hostile to the new ideal forged on August 4 lamented that Brittany lost all of its rights, usages, and freedoms because one called them privileges, which, he claimed, one wanted to remove from the French vocabulary. BM Nantes Collection Dugast-Matifeux, vol. 12, p. 78. Another clerical deputy wrote in his diary that one could not think of this day without astonishment. Pierre Marie Rouph de Varicourt Ms. Journal, Brotherton Library, University of Leeds (BL Microfilm 0039), August 4, 1789.
37. AD Gironde 3 L 82, August 22, 1789.
38. *Journal de correspondence de Nantes*, 1: 249. Another noted that the interests, sentiments and passions that had driven members were rooted in virtue and patriotism. BHVP Ms. 736, fol. 30.
39. *Séance de la nuit du 4 au 5 août 1789, pour former la constitution* (Paris: Debray, n.d.); *Sommaire des articles convenus le 4 août 1789 pour former la constitution* (n.p., n.d.).
40. *Révolutions de Paris, dediées à la nation et du district des Petits Augustins*, August 2–8, 1789.
41. Campe, *Été 89*, pp. 51–52.
42. Although she ultimately judged the body to be unsuccessful, Mme. De Staël retrospectively reflected on the wide admiration that the Assembly won for having brought about so much good and overcoming so much that was odious. She added that in 1790 respect for the Assembly was so great that it seemed as if it was a century old rather than only a year. Anne Louise Germaine Staël-Holstein, *Considérations sur les principaux événemens de la Révolution française*, 3 vols. (London: Baldwin, Cradock and Joy, 1818), 1: 378–79, 381.
43. Charles-Elie, marquis de Ferrières, *Correspondance inédite, 1789, 1790, 1791*, Henri Carré, ed. (Paris: Armand Colin, 1932), p. 115. Similarly, François Chevallier, a clerical deputy who would resign from the Assembly on October 1, detested the meeting of the night of August 4 because it had been the source of the proclamation of religious freedom. Despite his antipathy for the meeting, he acknowledged unreservedly the generosity of spirit among those deputies present when the meeting concluded. BM Nantes Collection Dugast-Matifeux, vol. 12, fol. 69.
44. François de Saint-Just, *Chronique intime des Garnier d'Ardres, 1767–1824* (Paris: Clavreuil, 1973), p. 118. See also AD Bouches-du-Rhône C 1046, letter of Bouche, August 10, 1789.
45. H. Perrin de Boussac, *Charles Jean Marie Alquier: un témoin de la Révolution* (La Rochelle: Rumeur des âges, 1983), p. 8. The destruction of privilege eradicated many of the issues that had divided deputies of different orders or provinces and enabled them to come together in a

sense of common purpose. The deputy Dubois de Crancé wrote to a friend that for three months he had found himself in the middle of storms but after August 4 the Assembly had accomplished the first important fruits of its work. BHVP Ms. N.A. 152, fols. 58–59. See also AD Bouches-du-Rhône C 1046, letter of August 5, 1789, letter of August 10, 1789; AN KK 641, August 9, 1789; BM Albi Ms. 177, letter of August 8, 1789.

46. AN AP 29 102, fols. 68–69, 70–71. François Fournier de la Charmie, a deputy from Périgueux, wrote that "one wants to be French and nothing more." AD Dordogne O E DEP 5004, no. 5, letter of August 9, 1789. Indeed, the meeting led to the end of seating by orders in the Assembly—Fournier de la Charmie added that deputies were completely mingled and that at the meeting that morning he had been seated beside the duc d'Orléans. See also AD Bouches-du-Rhône C 1046, letter of Bouche, August 10, 1789.
47. Claude Klein, "Pourquoi écrit-on une Constitution?" in Troper and Jaume, *1789 et l'invention de la constitution*, pp. 89–99, especially pp. 89, 91.
48. AM Arles AA 23, fol. 634; Queurau-Lamerie, "Lettres de Maupetit," 19 (1903), p. 233.
49. BHVP Ms. 737, fol. 14. See also Journal de la Révolution de France en 1789 à Bourges, [Harvard University Houghton Library, GEN MS. FR. 515], fols. 288–89; Gallot, *Vues sur les bases de la Constitution, et la Déclaration des Droits de l'Homme et du Citoyen* (Versailles, n.d.); *Ce qu'on n'a jamais vu* (n.p., n.d.) [Newberry Library Case FRC 1678]; *Journal de la ville, par Jean-Pierre-Louis de Luchet*, September 8, 1789. On the general enthusiasm, *Observations d'un citoyen sur l'arrête du 4 août* (Versailles: Baudouin, n.d.).
50. AN AD XVIII^{c} 134, *Compte très succinct que rend à ses commettans Louis-Charles-Joseph Desclaibes, député de la noblesse du bailliage de Chaumont-en-Bresigny, aux états-généraux de 1789*, in which he recounts the innumerable times he had heard that said.
51. The pact of association is mentioned in J. Font-Réaulx, "Lettres de J. Bern: Colaud de la Salcette, chanoine de Die, député aux Etats-Généraux de 1789," *Bulletin de la Société d'Archéologie et de Statistique de la Drôme* 69 (1944): 149; Camille Looten, "Lettres de François-Joseph Bouchette, avocat à Bergues, member de l'Assemblée Nationale constituante," *Annales du Comité flamande de France* 29 (1908–9): 238; *Etats-Généraux. Bulletin de la correspondence de la deputation du tiers-état de la sénéchaussée de Brest* (Brest: n.p., 1789–91), p. 235; AM Lorient BB 12, no. 47, letter of August 5, 1789; AD Dordogne O E DEP 5004, no. 5, letter of August 9, 1789; AD Bouches-du-Rhône C 1337, letter of Verdolin, August 7, 1789. The idea of the pact of association appears to have originated with the Breton delegation. *Journal de Versailles*, August 8, 1789. Indeed, decades later one deputy viewed the pact of association as a weakness. The Constitution of 1791, he wrote, had been drafted with the purpose of ratifying the abolition of privileges and of preventing the monarch, the protector of privileges, from reestablishing them. The Assembly was more concerned with constructing the constitution in a manner that would enable it to counteract the monarch than it was with making it capable of sustaining itself. Pierre Louis Roederer, *L'Esprit de la Révolution de 1789* (Paris: n.p., 1831), p. 189.
52. When he yielded the presidency of the Assembly on August 17 Le Chapelier gave a brief speech in which he praised the meeting of August 4, noting that the Assembly had accomplished in one day what would have seemed to require a century. After mentioning the destruction of the feudal regime and systems of oppression, Le Chapelier invoked provinces united by the same bond, a great family compact that made all Frenchmen into brothers. *Assemblée nationale. Correspondance de Bretagne*, August 21, 1789; *Le Point du Jour*, August 18, 1789.
53. *Le Point du Jour*, August 14, 1789.
54. For a retrospective assessment of the August decrees as the foundation of the constitution, AN BB^{30} 21, dossier 4, state of constitutional decrees sent by *Garde des sceaux* to Camus, March 26, 1790, in which the first item is the August decrees. On the perception of observers that they formed the guidelines for the Assembly, AD Gironde C 4365, no. 44, letter of December 15, 1789.
55. François-Emmanuel Toulongeon, *Histoire de la France depuis la Révolution*, 7 vols. (Paris: Treuttel et Würtz, 1801–10), 1: 99.
56. *Procès-verbal de l'Assemblée nationale*, no. 47 (August 11, 1789), p. 9.
57. The appeal can be found in *Procès-verbal de l'Assemblée nationale*, no. 46 (August 10, 1789), pp. 1–5.
58. AN W 306, dossier 377, fols. 86–87.
59. AD Bouches-du-Rhône C 1046, letter of Bouche, August 17, 1789. The deputy Jean François Marie Goupilleau similarly expressed calm confidence in the Assembly and its vision despite

the unrest and agitation. BM Nantes Collection Dugast-Matifeux, vol. 98, letter of August 27, 1789. See also *Histoire philosophique et politique de l'Assemblée Nationale, par un député de communes de B****. Mois d'août* (Paris: Devaux et Gattey, 1789), pp. 6–7 [BHVP 959998].

60. Ménard de la Groye, *Correspondance*, pp. 88–89.
61. Edmond Louis Alexis Dubois-Crancé, *Analyse de la Révolution française depuis l'ouverture des Etats-Généraux jusqu'au 6 brumaire an IV de la république*, Théodore Iung, ed. (Paris: Charpentier, 1885), p. 71. Their spirit is further exemplified in the comment of the deputy Henri Quatrefages de Larouquette, another back-bencher from the commons who rarely took part in debates, in a letter to a relative in August 1791, a few weeks before the Assembly disbanded. He stated that his conscience had been his guide as a legislator and that although his voice had been weak it had been pure. François Rouvière, *Quatrefages de Larouquette Constituante du Gard, étude biographique pour servir à l'histoire de la Révolution française* (Paris: Charavay Frères, 1886), p. 89. See also, Leroux-Cesbron, "Lettres de Lofficial," p. 111, for a similar sentiment from another deputy in September 1789. The same idea was expressed even by a noble deputy who would be hostile to the Revolution but he placed the number of deputies at three hundred. *Mémoires du comte de Paroy, souvenirs d'un défenseur de la famille royalependant la Révolution (1789–1797)*, Etienne Charavay, ed. (Paris: Plon, 1895), p. 149. An example of one of the *curés* who would be in this category was Claude-Germain Rousselot. In April 1790, in a private letter to his nephew, he wrote that the Assembly took pride in following the guidelines of justice and reason rather than being influenced by individual deputies. *Correspondance de l'abbé Rousselot, constituant (1789–1795)*, Anne-Marie Malingrey, ed. (Besançon: Les Belles Lettres, 1992), p. 63. The deputy Maupetit more vaguely wrote of the faith he had in "the majority" that was driven by a desire to do good and see through the ideals of the Assembly. Emile Queruau-Lamerie, "Lettres de Michel René Maupetit," *Bulletin de la Commission historique et archéologique de la Mayenne* 22 (1906): 374. Earlier, he had estimated that more than two hundred of the "formerly privileged" had become staunch supporters of the Revolution. Emile Queruau-Lamerie, "Lettres de Michel René Maupetit," *Bulletin de la Commission historique et archéologique de la Mayenne* 21 (1905): 107.
62. AM Bergerac Fonds Faugère, carton 1, no. 14, letter of August 14, 1789; *Journal de Versailles*, August 18, 1789; *Le Point du Jour*, August 16, 1789; *Journal des Etats-Généraux*, 2: 532–33.
63. BnF Mss. Nouv. acq. fr. 12938, fol. 118v°. An astonished clerical deputy noted the changed circumstances of the king giving thanks to God in a *Te Deum* from his abject powerlessness only fifteen days earlier. Pierre Marie Rouph de Varicourt Ms. Journal, Brotherton Library, University of Leeds (BL Microfilm 0039), August 12, 1789 (misdated, should be August 13).
64. It was this belief that led a noble deputy to write that with the August decrees three-quarters of the bases of the constitution had been laid and that the Assembly could move quickly and complete the constitution in a month. AN AB^{XIX} 3562(1), no. 2, letter of August 14, 1789.
65. *Procès-verbal de l'Assemblée nationale*, no. 50 (August 14, 1789), p. 3; *Bulletin de l'Assemblée Nationale*, August 14, 1789.
66. On the deepening concern among deputies on the king's intentions, AM Arles AA 23, fol. 558; AN KK 642, August 28, 1789.
67. *Journal de la ville, par Jean-Pierre-Louis de Luchet*, September 9, 1789.
68. *Procès-verbal de l'Assemblée nationale*, no. 62 (August 29, 1789), pp. 1–2; AM Angoulême AA 19, no. 4, letter of August 31, 1789; AD Bouches-du-Rhône C 1046, letter of September 2, 1789.
69. One deputy felt that the time spent on the issue of the veto had delayed beginning work on the constitution. In his acknowledgement of its separate status from the constitution, his comment underscored the defensive nature of the veto. BM Douai Ms. 1035(1), letter of August 30, 1789.
70. Blackman, *1789: The French Revolution Begins*, p. 229.
71. On the anger and bitterness of the debate, AD Nièvre 1 L 165, letter of August 31, 1789.
72. AD Nièvre 1 L 165, letter of August 31, 1789; reply of municipal officers of Nevers to deputies of National Assembly, September 6, 1789; AM Strasbourg AA 2004, fol. 7; BHVP CP 6540, letter of September 4, 1789. Deputies believed that the effort to reclaim privileges by the clergy continued after the decision on the veto. See AD Nord L 10316, extract of letter of Merlin to Bertrant, September 22, 1789.
73. AM Strasbourg AA 2004, fols. 2–3.
74. D. Marié, "Trois lettres inédites de l'abbé Jallet: Membre de l'Assemblé Constituante," *Annales historiques de la Révolution française* 22 (1950): 346.
75. BnF Mss. Fonds Français 10883, fol. 141; BnF Mss. Fonds Français 13713, fol. 290. The resignations are omitted from the minutes of the National Assembly. On the election, AN C 31,

dossier 254, document 52; *Procès-verbal de l'Assemblée nationale*, no. 75 (September 15, 1789), p. 1. For insight into the fracture, which became complete for many after the removal of the royal family to Paris, Jean Egret, *La Révolution des Notables: Mounier et le monarchiens, 1789* (Paris: A. Colin, 1950); Robert Griffiths, *Le Centre perdu: Malouet et les "monarchiens" dans la Révolution française* (Grenoble: Presses universitaires de Grenoble, 1988), pp. 55–80.

76. Keith Michael Baker, "Fixing the French Constitution," in *Inventing the French Revolution: Essays on French Political Culture in the Eighteenth Century*, Keith Michael Baker, ed. (Cambridge: Cambridge University Press, 1990), p. 273.
77. Hardman, *Life of Louis XVI*, p. 332.
78. AD Pyrénées-Atlantiques C 1377, letter of September 21, 1789; AM Angoulême AA 19, no. 5, letter of September 4, 1789; AM Arles AA 23, fol. 558; *Journal d'Etat et du Citoyen*, September 10, 1789; *La Première année de la Révolution vue par un témoin: Les "Bulletins" de Poncet-Delpech, député de Quercy aux Etats-Généraux de 1789*, Daniel Ligou, ed. (Paris: Presses Universitaires de France, 1961), p. 82. On the origins of the concern, *Bulletin de l'Assemblée Nationale*, August 29, 1789.
79. One deputy wrote that if it had been anything other than a suspensive veto, the king would have become more despotic than ever. Leroux-Cesbron, "Lettres de Lofficial," p. 110. On its relationship to his resistance to the August decrees, Emile Queruau-Lamerie, "Lettres de Michel René Maupetit," *Bulletin de la Commission historique et archéologique de la Mayenne* 19 (1903): 247.
80. AM Bergerac Fonds Faugère, carton 1, no. 25, letter of September 14, 1789; BM Versailles F. 823, fol. 143.
81. AN KK 642, September 14, 1789; AM Le Havre D^3 38, no. 49, letter of September 18, 1789; AD Gironde 3 L 82, letter of September 18, 1789; AM Angoulême AA 19, no. 8, letter of September 14, 1789; BnF Mss. Nouv. Acq. fr 4121, fols. 153–55; AN C 31^1, dossier 256, document 49. See also *Procès-verbal de l'Assemblée nationale*, no. 74 (September 14, 1789), pp. 4–6. Despite a prohibition for those in the gallery to express signs of either approval or disapproval, those in attendance applauded vigorously at the outcome. *Journal du Citoyen*, September 14, 1789.
82. AC Forcalquier Series D, unclassified carton, letter of September 21, 1789; AD Nord L 10316, extract from letter written to Bertrand by Merlin, September 22, 1789; AD Seine-Maritime LP 8454, letter of September 19, 1789; See also *Journal d'Etat et du citoyen*, September 24, 1789; AM Lorient BB 13, no. 5, letter of September 20, 1789; AD Gironde 3 L 82, letter of September 19, 1789; Leroux-Cesbron, "Lettres de Lofficial," p. 112. Another deputy attributed the hesitation to the renunciation of privileges by provinces and cities that was leading the monarch to hesitate. S. Dardy, "Lettres de M. Grellet de Beauregard, député de la Haute Marche aux Etats-Généraux de 1789," *Mémoires de la Société des sciences naturelles et archéologiques de la Creuse*, 2nd series 7 (1899), p. 79. On the clergy asking the monarch not to approve the decrees, *Très-humbles et très-respectueuses supplications & représentations de la Chambre Ecclésiastique d'Auch, à Sa Majesté* (n.p., n.d.). One deputy of the commons questioned whether the nobility wanted a constitution. AD Ain 1 Mi 1, fol. 232, letter of August 30, 1789.
83. Lever, *Louis XVI*, p. 524. Unfortunately, she does not provide a citation for the letter.
84. Herly, "Correspondance…de la Salle," p. 221. Also on the sense of dismay in the Assembly, *Correspondance de l'abbé Rousselot*, pp. 45–46.
85. Journal de la Révolution de France en 1789. A Bourges 1789, fols. 387–88.
86. AM Bayonne AA 51, no. 29, letter of September 18, 1789; AM Angoulême AA 19, no. 9, letter of September 17, 1789; BnF Mss. Nouv. acq. fr. 12938, fols. 161v°–163; BnF Mss. Fonds Français 13713, fols. 311v°–315; Looten, "Lettres de Bouchette," p. 243; Thibaudeau, *Correspondance inédite*, p. 15; AD Seine-Maritime LP 8454, letters of Bourdon to president of commune of Dieppe, September 16, 1789, September 19, 1789; September 21, 1789. On Barnave's suspicions of the Crown's intentions during these weeks, AN W 12, no. 1, letter of October 4, 1789. See also AN W 423, dossier 958/3, document 42.
87. AM Lorient BB 13, no. 4, letter of September 18, 1789.
88. BM La Rochelle Ms. 21, fol. 90v°.
89. Journal de la Révolution de France en 1789. A Bourges 1789, fol. 390.
90. BnF Mss. Nouv. acq. fr. 4121, fols. 163–64; AD Gironde 3 L 82, letter of September 22, 1789; AD Pyrénées-Atlantiques C 1377, letter of September 21, 1789; BnF Mss. Nouv. acq. fr. 17275, fol. 218.
91. The dismissive attitude toward Louis's observations is apparent in Fontenay, *Lettres à Babeth*, p. 173.

92. Hardman, *Life of Louis XVI*, p. 339.
93. It had also worked on the Declaration of the Rights of Man and was eager to begin work on the constitution. AN W 13, no. 224, letter of September 5, 1789; AM Angoulême AA 19, no. 2, letter of August 22, 1789; AD Côtes d'Armor 1 L 389, letter of August 29, 1789.
94. AD Cantal 27 J 176, document 84, letter of August 20, 1789.
95. AD Gironde 3 L 82, script letter of September 22, 1789, letter of September 25, 1789. On the eagerness with which its work was anticipated, *Journal de la ville, par Jean-Pierre-Louis de Luchet*, September 23, 1789.
96. Fontenay, *Lettres à Babeth*, pp. 185–86. Fontenay referred to the sanction of the August decrees as whether the king accepted the constitution.
97. For a contemporary account, *Despatches from Paris*, 2: 263–64. See also Olwen Hufton, *Women and the Limits of Citizenship in the French Revolution* (Toronto: University of Toronto Press, 1992), pp. 7–12.
98. Blackman, *1789: The French Revolution Begins*, p. 231.
99. AN C 31[2], dossier 263, document 10. They are referred to as "constitutional articles." On the lingering uncertainty, AM Angoulême AA 19, no. 14, letter of October 5, 1789.
100. AD Dordogne O E DEP 5005 (formerly AM Perigueux AA 41), no. 1, act of union, August 23, 1789.
101. *Venise et la Révolution*, p. 332.
102. AM Arles AA 23, fols. 536–37, 540–41, 543, for the cautious approach taken by Provençal deputies with respect to the privileges of the province; Bohanan, *Crown and Nobility in Early Modern France*, pp. 77, 83, for the importance of privileges to provincial identity.
103. AD Bouches-du-Rhône C 1046, letter of Bouche, August 5, 1789. On the adherence to privilege in the province, *Droit constitutif, et privileges de la ville de Marseille* (n.p., n.d.) [Newberry Library Case 3575]. The privileges of the city were dealt with in a delicate fashion by deputies. See AC Marseille BB 361, no. 39. The identity of the city being tied to its privileges is apparent in a self-proclaimed title that the mayor and municipal officials took for themselves in April 1789, as "protectors and defenders of the privileges, franchises and liberties" of the city of Marseille. The occasion was making Mirabeau a citizen of the city and it stipulated that he had "all the rights, privileges, immunities and prerogatives" attached to the quality of citizen of Marseille. AM Marseille AA 70, fols. 81v°–82.
104. AD Bouches-du-Rhône C 1383, fols. 172–97; AM Arles AA 23, fols. 485–86.
105. AD Bouches-du-Rhône C 1337, letter of Verdolin, August 7, 1789.
106. AM Arles AA 23, fols. 544–45. Indeed, a Provençal deputy wrote that it was necessary to yield to necessity and to circumstances. AM Arles AA 23, fol. 547. For a similar situation in Sarrelouis, R. Herly, "Correspondance du lieutenant general du bailliage de Sarrelouis de la Salle, député de l'Assemblée nationale 1789–1790," *Bulletin de la Société des Amis des Pays de la Sarre* 4 (1927): 219.
107. One deputy told his constituents that if they chose to make a renunciation of their privileges it would only be symbolic because the decision had already been made by a majority of the Assembly that the privileges of provinces, cities, and individuals were to be suppressed. Herly, "Correspondance," p. 219.
108. Bouche also raised the example of Brittany in letters to constituents in Forcalquier. AC Forcalquier Series D, unclassified carton, undated letter of Bouche; letter of August 28, 1789. Brittany and Rennes were regarded as a benchmark because even within the commons the privileges of both had raised questions during the verification of credentials. AM Bayonne AA 51, no. 10, letter of June 14, 1789.
109. AD Bouches-du-Rhône C 1337, letter of Verdolin, August 16, 1789.
110. AD Bouches-du-Rhône C 1380, fol. 240.
111. AC Forcalquier Series D, unclassified carton, dossier August, 1789, circular of August 27, 1789; Newberry Library (Chicago) Case folio FRC 10160.
112. AD Bouches-du-Rhône C 1380, fols. 250–51; AD Bouches-du-Rhône C 1383, fols. 198v°–201. Deputies from Béarn also had to coax their constituents into accepting the new ideal. See AD Pyrénées-Atlantiques C 1377, letters of August 17, 1789; October 13, 1789; AD Pyrénées-Atlantiques C 1601, letter of Polverel to Estates of Béarn, August 7, 1789; extract from register of deputation of Third Estate of Navarre, August 10, 1789; September 11, 1789.
113. AN C 83, dossier 86, documents 16–25, dossier 87, documents 7–14, dossier 88, documents 6–7, dossier 89, docs. 36–62. An account of one such meeting is found in Thomas F. Sheppard, *Lourmarin in the Eighteenth Century: A Study of a French Village* (Baltimore: The Johns Hopkins Press, 1971), pp. 179–80.

114. AM Aix BB 114, fol. 58v°. The surrender of privileges also went easily in Sarrelouis. Herly, "Correspondance," p. 222.
115. AD Ille-et-Vilaine C 1812, declaration of the city of Rennes, September 7, 1789.
116. AM Nantes AA 82, docs. 15–69; AD Ille-et-Vilaine C 3842, entry of September 1, 1789; AN KK 1105, p. 4 (August 29, 1789).
117. AD Ille-et-Vilaine C 1807, copy of letter of deputies of sénéchaussée of Nantes to Bellabre, August 29, 1789; copy of letter of Bellabre to mayor and municipal officers of Nantes, September 7, 1789.
118. On the imperative mandate, see AM Brest 2 D 18 (formerly LL 44, fols. 29v°–30; LL 46, no. 24).
119. AM Nantes AA 82, document 70. A newspaper reported a gathering of nobility in Quimper that accepted all of the work of the Assembly, which the newspaper found remarkable because the Breton nobles had refused to send deputies to the Estates General. *Nouvelles de Versailles*, August 21, 1789.
120. AM Nantes BB 112, fols. 100–104.
121. AD Ille-et-Vilaine C 1807, copy of letter of Bellabre to unnamed addressee, October 4, 1789; *Journal de la correspondance de Nantes*, 2: 163–64, 250, 312.
122. AM Lorient BB 13, no. 20, letter of November 2, 1789.
123. AN W 13, no. 224, letter of January 2, 1789 (*sic*); BnF Mss. Nouv. acq. fr. 4121, fols. 226–27.
124. *Adresse au peuple breton des villes et campagnes: de la part de leurs députés a l'Assemblée nationale* (Paris: Imprimerie Nationale, 1789). It was signed by fifty-nine deputies from various towns. On its dissemination AD Loire-Atlantique L 176, no. 15, letter of December 16, 1789; BM Nantes Collection Dugast-Matifeux, vol. 98, letter of December 18, 1789. A Norman deputy admired the letter so much that he wished it would be circulated nationally. Fontenay, *Lettres à Babeth*, pp. 254, 257–58.
125. AD Ille-et-Vilaine C 3903, letter of Intermediate Commission of Brittany by other commissioners, January 2, 1790.
126. *Affiches d'Angers ou Journal national de la province d'Anjou*, February 9, 1790.
127. AD Ille-et-Vilaine 1 F 1842, letter of commissioners of young men of Rennes to Club of Nantes, January 4, 1790. One of the leaders was again the future Revolutionary general Moreau.
128. AD Ille-et-Vilaine L 337, extract from minutes for nomination of electors . . . in la Chapelle du Calvaire, May 17, 1790.
129. AM Strasbourg AA 2003, fol. 5.
130. *Procès-verbal de l'Assemblée nationale*, no. 40 bis (August 4, 1789), p. 32; a codified copy of the renunciation is found in *Mémoire de droit public sur la ville de Strasbourg et l'Alsace en général* (Strasbourg: Dannbach, 1789), unpaginated, but first appendix.
131. AM Strasbourg AA 2003, fols. 120–21.
132. The *cahier* for Strasbourg contained many stipulations that its privileges be preserved. AM Strasbourg AA 2002, fols. 1–5.
133. AM Strasbourg AA 2003, fol. 123.
134. AM Strasbourg AA 2003, fols. 122–23.
135. AM Strasbourg AA 2003, fols. 126–27.
136. AM Strasbourg 2004, fol. 11.
137. AN C 93, dossier 89, document 35; AN C 94, dossier 91, document 18. On reports of the hostile reception of the August decrees in Alsace and elsewhere, *Journal d'Etat et du citoyen*, September 24, 1789. See also AN F[1]c III Bas-Rhin 13, dossier 1, document 2; Pilastre de la Brardière and Leclerc, *Correspondance de MM. Les députés des communes de la province d'Anjou*, 2: 403.
138. AM Strasbourg AA 2004, fols. 11–13, 19. He advised the city to submit to laws common to all and save what they could afterward. AM Strasbourg AA 2004, fol. 21 shows Turckheim's dilemma between the night of August 4 and the demands of the province. See also AN AA 50, dossier 1435–38, document 93.
139. AM Strasbourg AA 2004, fol. 25. On the resistance of the clergy of Strasbourg and Alsace, AN C 93, liasse 82, documents 22–24; AN C 95, dossier 104, documents 19–26.
140. *Journal des débats et des décrets*, September 1, 1789, includes the city of Strasbourg among a number of locales accepting the August decrees.
141. AN B[a] 80, liasse 193, dossier 4, documents 4–5. It is published as *Mémoire de droit public sur la ville de Strasbourg et l'Alsace.*

142. AM Strasbourg AA 2004, fol. 70.
143. Jean de Turckheim, *Bericht an die Gemeinde von Strassburg über die Lage der National-Versammlung, in Monath October dieses Jahres, als ich dieselbe verliess von Johannes von Türckheim, chemahligen Abgeordneten der Stadt Strassburg an die General Staalen des französischen Reiches* (Strasbourg: Daunbach, 1789). See also Rodolphe Reuss, *L'Alsace pendant la Révolution française*, 2 vols. (Paris: Fischbacher, 1880–94), 1: 251.
144. AM Strasbourg AA 2004, fols. 49–50.
145. AM Strasbourg AA 2004, fols. 72, 74. Indeed, the dismissive comments of a deputy in his newspaper are reflective of the shift in outlook within the Assembly since late July, when the Committee on the Constitution had announced that it would be guided by the *cahiers*, and the manner in which the meeting of August 4 had transformed the scope of reform by obliterating prescriptive tradition. Noting the citing of its *cahier* as a reason to preserve its municipal government, he wrote that *cahiers* had long ago fallen into disfavor and that few speakers had invoked "this fragile authority" for some time. The *cahier* of patriots, he declared, was the greater good and it was necessary to adopt a uniform structure to prevent incoherence in governance. *Courier de Madon*, meeting of November 25, 1789.
146. AM Strasbourg AA 2004, fol. 75; *Questions d'état décisives resultants pour la province d'Alsace des décrets rendu par l'Assemblée nationale de France depuis le 4 août 1789 jusqu'au 13 février 1790 inclusivement* (n.p., 1790), p. 27.
147. AM Strasbourg AA 2005[a], fol. 12.
148. AM Strasbourg AA 2004, fol. 81.
149. AM Strasbourg AA 2004, fol. 85.
150. *Feuille Hébdomadaire Patriotique*, December 13, 1789. See also *Feuille Hébdomadaire Patriotique*, December 6, 1789, December 20, 1789. See also *Réflexions sur les inquiétudes auxquelles paroissent se livrer nombre de citoyens de cette ville* (Strasbourg: Dannbach, 1789); *Adresse à tous les bons citoyens de Strasbourg* (n.p., 1789).
151. *Discours prononcé le 2 janvier 1790 à l'assemblée de MM. les échevins représentans de la bourgeoisie de Strasbourg par M. le baron de Dietrich* (Strasbourg: Dannbach, n.d.). Schwendt had previously been in contact with Dietrich about the rumors that the city might form a confederation with German sovereign princes. AM Strasbourg AA 2005[a], fol. 7. See also AM Strasbourg AA 2005[a], fol. 36.
152. *Précis de ce qui s'est passé à l'élection du maire de Strasbourg* (n.p., n.d.). The election in Strasbourg had a high turnout. Edelstein, *The French Revolution and the Birth of Electoral Democracy*, p. 78.
153. *Feuille Hébdomadaire Patriotique*, April 21, 1790; *Patriotisches Wochenblatt*, April 21, 1790.
154. AD Aisne L 567, communication of president and members of administrative assembly of Department of Bas-Rhin, July 31, 1790.

Notes to Chapter 9

1. AN M 788, dossier 2[17], document 99. Another wrote in November 1789, that the Assembly was in an open war with the *parlements*. Emile Queruau-Lamerie, "Lettres de Michel René Maupetit," *Bulletin de la Commission hisorique et archéologique de la Mayenne* 20 (1904): 93. On unease and unrest in the fall of 1789, AC Marseille BB 361, no. 104; *Adresse au peuple breton des villes et campagnes* (Paris: Imprimerie Nationale, 1789); *Adresse à l'Assemblée Nationale, par le corps municipal et electoral de la ville de Rouen* (Rouen, n.d.); Herly, "Correspondance," p. 258. For expressions of calm and confidence by a deputy during this difficult period, BM Albi Ms. 177, letter of October 25, 1789, letter of November 28, 1789, December 24, 1789; Looten, "Lettres de Bouchette," pp. 276–77; Henri de Jessé, *Lettre de M. le baron de Jessé, député de la senéchaussée de Beziers, à ses commettans* (Paris: Gattey, 1790) [BHVP 954420].
2. *Journal de la correspondance de Nantes*, 3: 329–33. The deputy Couderc also felt optimistic at the end of 1789. Monod, "Lettres de…Couderc," pp. 420–22. Other letters from the same period, however, expressed discouragement. Font-Réaulx, "Lettres de Colaud de la Salcette," p. 156. Similarly, the deputy Goupilleau wrote privately to his cousin that posterity would benefit more from the beneficial effects of the constitution. BM Nantes Collection Dugast-Matifeux, vol. 98, letter of December 24, 1789.
3. Fontenay, *Lettres à Babeth*, p. 270.

4. The deputy Fontenay believed that the most crucial parts of the constitution had already been determined—the permanence of the legislature, its single-chamber structure and the suspensive veto. Ibid., p. 192.
5. *Journal de la correspondance de Nantes*, 2: 122; *Le Point du Jour*, September 23, 1789; *Procès-verbal de l'Assemblée nationale*, no. 82 (September 23, 1789), p. 7. For insight into the chaotic conditions in cities and towns, AD Seine-Maritime C 2, letter of Saint-Priest to intendant of Rouen, November 2, 1789. On the level of concern with the situation in urban centers, AN C 33[1], dossier 284, document 8.
6. BnF Mss. Fonds Français 13713, fol. 200; AM Bergerac, fonds Faugère, Carton 1, no. 45, letter of November 28, 1789. See also Fontenay, *Lettres à Babeth*, p. 182. On concern about the unstable situation in cities and towns, see AN AB^{XIX} 3562(1), letter of October 24, 1789. On the sense of urgency felt by the Assembly to establish new municipal administration, AD Morbihan 1 Mi 140, letter of November 27, 1789. On the intent of the Assembly in its establishment of the new administration, AD Seine-Maritime LP 8454, letter of Bourdon to municipal officers of Dieppe, February 28, 1790. On the hope for its enactment, Looten, "Lettres de Bouchette," pp. 298–99.
7. AD Seine-Maritime LP 8454, letter of Maizot to president of permanent committee of Dieppe, January 15, 1790. This was also affirmed by a deputy. Looten, "Lettres de Bouchette," p. 330. The liberality of the franchise initially unnerved some deputies. Fontenay, *Lettres à Babeth*, p. 250.
8. On the sense of unease in Dijon, for example, AN C 97, dossier 117, document 11.
9. AM Aix BB 114, fol. 58v°.
10. AM Aix BB 114, fols. 142–145v°.
11. AN C 37[1], dossier 310, document 6.
12. *Procès-verbal de l'Assemblée nationale*, no. 192 (February 4, 1790), pp. 18–19.
13. AN C 37[1], dossier 315, documents 4–8; BnF Mss. Nouv. acq. fr. 4121, fols. 425–26; *Procès-verbal de l'Assemblée nationale*, no. 192 (February 4, 1790), pp. 21, 23. On the ardor inspired by the visit among deputies, *Le Point du Jour*, February 6, 1790.
14. *Despatches from Paris*, 2: 290.
15. Tackett, *The Glory and the Sorrow*, p. 106.
16. AD Puy-de-Dôme 4 J 6, copy of letter of Huguet, February 6, 1790. Ménard de la Groye, *Correspondance*, p. 187. See also *Journal de la correspondance de Nantes*, 3: 469–70; BHVP CP 6540, letter of February 4, 1790; AN KK 643, February 4, 1790; BM Albi Ms. 177, letter of February 7, 1790; AM Bergerac, fonds Faugère, carton 1, no. 61, letter of February 6, 1790.
17. AN KK 643, February 10, 1790.
18. *L'Assemblée nationale aux François. Du onze février 1790* (Angers: Pavie, 1790). Indeed, the sense of common purpose that the meeting produced is apparent in the fact that the Crown sent out corrected copies of the address to some areas because a printing error had led to the word inseparable being printed as irreparable. AD Côte d'Or C 3359, no. 128, no. 130. For an illustration of its reception, Gabriel François Moreau, *Discours prononcé le Dimanche 14 février 1790, par M. l'Evêque de Mâcon, dans l'Eglise Cathédrale, avant la TE DEUM par lui ordonné relativement à la séance du Roi dans l'Assemblée nationale, le jeudi 4 du même mois*... (Macon: Goery, n.d.).
19. AN C 111, dossier 248, document 8.
20. AM Aix AA 55, fols. 322–28. On the establishment of municipal government in Aix, Christiane Derobert-Ratel, *Institutions et vie municipal à Aix en Provence sous la Révolution* (Millau: Edisud, 1981).
21. In a similar fashion, in Le Havre upon taking office the new municipal officials immediately complimented the former ones for all that they had done for the city. AM Le Havre BB 72, fol. 88.
22. AN C 111, dossier 248, document 8; AN F[1]c III Bouches-du-Rhône 8, letter of municipal officers of Aix to Louis XVI, March 9, 1790.
23. AM Nevers BB 46, fols. 143–143v°. There were similar reactions in Rouen and Toulon. AM Rouen Y 1, fols. 972–75, 978–82; AD Seine-Maritime C 3, letter of intendant to comte de Saint-Priest, February 9, 1790; AM Toulon L 94, dossier D[2] 1, fols. 283–283v°.
24. AN C 110, dossier 234, document 24.
25. On the favorable reception of them in Dijon, AN C 112, dossier 268, document 23; AD Côte d'Or L 210, speech of De Brois to electoral assembly of Department of Côte d'Or, May 10, 1790. On the first municipal elections, Edelstein, *The French Revolution and the Birth of Electoral Democracy*, pp. 75–81, 93–107.

26. AN C 111, dossier 246, document 10; AN C 114[A], dossier 298[4], document 7; AN C 114[A], dossier 300[3], document 4; AN C 116, dossier 316, document 18; AN C 117[1], dossier 325, document 3; AN F[1]c III Ain 7, minutes of municipal assembly of parish of Savigneux, May 9, 1790; AN F[1]c III Ardennes 1, dossier 1, document 5; AN F[1]c III Cher 1, address to Louis XVI voted by citizens of Bourges at installation of municipal officers and presented by general council of the commune, February 24, 1790; AN F[1]c III Gironde 11, address of citizens of Bordeaux to Louis XVI, February 16, 1791; *Adresses à l'Assemblée Nationale et au Roi, par le conseil-général de la commune de Grenoble. 24 février 1790* (Grenoble, n.d.); *Courier de Madon*, March 9, 1790. Melvin Edelstein claimed that the success of the Revolution depended on the establishment of municipalities. Edelstein, *The French Revolution and the Birth of Electoral Democracy*, pp. 105–6.
27. Marie-Vic Ozouf-Marignier, *La Formation des départements: la représentation du territoire français à la fin du 18e siècle* (Paris: Editions de l'Ecole des Hautes-Etudes en Sciences Sociales, 1989); Ted W. Margadant, *Urban Rivalries in the French Revolution* (Princeton: Princeton University Press, 1992).
28. [Keverseau and G. Clavelin], *Histoire de de la Révolution de 1789*, 3: 358, noted that the names of provinces were associated with privileges, inequality, and division. See also *Mémoires du comte de Paroy*, p. 139, who also emphasized that the division sought to destroy all privileges.
29. AD Haute-Garonne C 303, fols. 199–205. See also *Journal de la correspondance de Nantes*, 2: 417, 458.
30. AM Aix BB 114, fols. 143, 144v°–145.
31. AM Brest 2 D 18 (formerly LL 44, fol. 116; LL 46, no. 79 bis). On unease in other former *pays d'états* as well, AM Brest 2 D 18 (formerly LL 44, fol. 119, LL 46, no. 81).
32. *Le Point du Jour*, November 18, 1789.
33. *Extrait du Procès-verbal de l'Assemblée renforcé des Etats de Cambrai & du Cambrésis. Arrêté unanime de l'Assemblée du 9 novembre 1789* (n.p., n.d.); *Courier de Madon*, November 19, 1789.
34. AD Pyrénées-Atlantiques C 1601, register of decrees of committee of correspondence, August 4, 1789. AM Arles AA 23, fol. 544 also has deputies stating that the Assembly would not allow any protest about the abolition of privileges from individual deputies or groups of deputies.
35. Ménard de la Groye, a moderate, mild-mannered back-bencher, described the behavior of the Intermediate Commission as criminal and seditious. Ménard de la Groye, *Correspondance*, pp. 144, 146. See also BM Douai Ms. 1035(1), letter of November 30, 1789.
36. *Procès-verbal de l'Assemblée nationale*, no. 133 (November 24, 1789), pp. 15–19; AN KK 643, November 24, 1789; BnF Mss. Nouv. acq, fr. 4121, fols. 280, 284–85, 294; *Courier de Madon*, November 24, 1789.
37. There was alarm at the number of pamphlets opposed to Revolutionary reforms that were being circulated. *Annales Orléanoises*, December 26, 1789.
38. On the sense of equanimity in the Assembly amid the challenges, BM Lyon Ms. 5430, no. 16, letter of November 16, 1789; BM Nantes Collection Dugast-Matifeux, vol. 98, letter of (no date) September 1789; Monod, "Lettres de…Couderc, p. 420. See also *Lettre de M. de baron de Jessé, député de la senéchaussée de Beziers, à ses commettans* (Paris: Gattey, 1790), written in early January 1790, in which he urged his constituents not to become discouraged by a campaign against the work of the Assembly and assured them of its steadfastness. In early January 1790, one observer attributed the unrest of the fall to "the effect of an indigestion of privileges." He confidently hailed the society without rank, privilege or religious preference that the Assembly was seeking to create. AD Charente-Maritime 4 J 1523, letter of January 4, 1790.
39. AD Côte d'Or L 210, address of electors of Department of Côte d'Or to National Assembly, May 25, 1790.
40. On departmental and district elections, Edelstein, *The French Revolution and the Birth of Electoral Democracy*, pp. 109–33.
41. *Procès-verbal de l'Assemblée nationale*, no. 255 (April 10, 1790), p. 2. The ornate formal document has been digitized and can be foun,d at AD Côte d'Or 5 NUM 10.
42. On the *Fête de la Fédération* and other festivals, Mona Ozouf, *Festivals and the French Revolution* (Cambridge, MA: Harvard University Press, 1988). On the heightened emotions preceding the *Fête*, BHVP Ms. 805, fol. 154; on the emotional impact that the ceremonies had on participants and spectators, BM Albi Ms. 177, letter of July 17, 1790.
43. Staël-Holstein, *Considérations sur les principaux événemens*, 1: 379–80, in which she noted that although the constitution was not yet finished, all could swear an oath to it because its principles were universally accepted.

44. AM Lorient BB 13, letter of June 9, 1790. Similarly, in June 1790, in a letter to the electoral assembly of their department, two deputies wrote that the true spirit of the new French constitution was brotherhood (*fraternité*). AD Puy-de-Dôme L 481, letter of Gaultier de Biauzat and Huguet, June 15, 1790.
45. To give but one example of the confidence and sense of common purpose that the *Fête* inspired, AN F^{1}c III Var 9, letter of mayor and municipal officers of Toulon to Louis XVI, July 30, 1790. See also AM Marseille BB 360, fol. 101.
46. Fitzsimmons, *The Night the Old Regime Ended*, pp. 124–26. The definitive work on the topic is William Doyle *Aristocracy and Its Enemies in the Age of Revolution* (Oxford: Oxford University Press, 2009).
47. BHVP CP 6540, protest of marquis d'Argenteuil against decree suppressing nobility, June 21, 1790; François Louis, comte d'Escherny, *Tableau historique de la Révolution jusqu'à la fin de l'Assemblée constituante*, 2nd. ed., 2 vols. (Paris: Treuttel et Wurtz, 1815), 1: 169–70; 2: 101.
48. Charles Elie, marquis de Ferrières, *Mémoires*, 2 vols. (Paris: Baudouin, 1822), 2: 74.
49. *Papers of Thomas Jefferson*, 16: 571. For similar contemporary assessments, see *Assemblée Nationale, Commune de Paris et Corps Administratifs du Royaume*, June 21, 1790; *Annales Orléanoises*, June 22, 1789; *Courier de Madon*, June 19, 1790; *Journal de la correspondance de Nantes*, 5: 259–60.
50. AN 284 AP 4, dossier 9, folio 1.
51. John McManners characterized the legislation on monasteries as driven more by ideology than financial concerns, particularly in its rescinding of existing monastic vows as well as the suppression of mendicant and contemplative orders. It provisionally left educational and charitable orders in existence. John McManners, *The French Revolution and the Church* (New York: Harper & Row, 1969), p. 31. See also Rodney J. Dean. *L'Assemblée constituante et la réforme ecclésiastique, 1790* (Paris & London: Rodney Dean, 2014).
52. *Annales orléanoises*, February 13, 1790, February 20, 1790. Their election harmonized with the belief of deputies that the clergy had been returned to the common class of citizens rather than being a separate caste in the state. BM Albi Ms. 177, letter of November 28, 1789.
53. Ménard de la Groye, *Correspondance*, p. 305.
54. AN AA 62, dossier 1550, plaquette 3^{A}, document 2.
55. BM Douai Ms. 1035(1), letter of January 2, 1791.
56. See, for example, AD Calvados Caen 615 ED+ 586, letter of April 9, 1791.
57. Dubois-Crancé, *Analyse de la Révolution française*, pp. 68, 71–72. There were also internal political rivalries and calculations behind the measure. See Barry Shapiro, "Self-Sacrifice, Self-Interest or Self-Defense? The Constituent Assembly and the 'Self-Denying Ordinance' of May 1791," *French Historical Studies* 25 (2002): 625–56.
58. The tranquility of 1790, however, should not be overestimated. See Samuel F. Scott, "Problems of Law and Order during 1790, the 'Peaceful Year' of the French Revolution," *American Historical Review* 80 (1975): 859–88.
59. AD Puy-de-Dôme M 788, dossier 217, document 99 for the assessment at the end of 1789; AM Toulon L 104, dossier D^{4} 2, letter of Ricard to municipality of Toulon, December 3, 1790, for the optimistic one of 1790. The same optimism was present in the kingdom in late 1790. See AN F^{1}c III Nièvre 7, dossier 2, document 5.
60. See, for example, AN D XIV 5, dossier 47, letter of Gérard to president of National Assembly, August 30, 1789, in which he praised deputies as "creators of the French constitution."
61. *Annales orléanoises*, January 11, 1790.
62. On the catechisms, Adrian Velicu, *Civic Catechisms and Reason in the French Revolution* (Burlington, VT: Ashgate, 2010).
63. *Catéchisme de la constitution, à l'usage des habitans de la campagne* (Epinal: Vautrin, n.d.).
64. *Catéchisme du citoyen selon les principes de la nouvelle constitution. Par M. Terrasson…* (Clermont-Ferrand: Beaufils, 1790).
65. *Instruction patriotique* (n.p.: Imprimerie de la Société des amis de la constitution, 1790).
66. *La Constitution française, et les droits de l'homme. Chanson patriotique.* Troisième édition. (Paris: Simon, n.d.); *Chansonnier National, ou recueil de chansons choisies et patriotiques, sur la constitution française & les droits de l'homme* (Paris: Valleyre, 1790); Gabriel Bouquier, *Poème séculaire aux amis de la Constitution* (Brive: Robin, 1791).
67. François Rouvière, *Quatre lettres inédites de Rabaut de Saint-Etienne (1789–1791)* (Nîmes: A. Castélan, 1885), pp. 12–13.

68. Jean Joseph Regnault, *La Constitution française, mise à la portée de tout le monde*, 2 vols. (Bar-le-Duc: La Société typographique, 1791). See also *Catéchisme de la constitution, à l'usage des écoles, précédé de la Declaration des droits de l'homme, par M. Mirabeau* (Amiens: Caron-Berquier, 1791).
69. P. M. Gautier, *Dictionnaire de la constitution et du gouvernement français…*, 2nd ed. (Paris: Guillaume, 1792), pp. 97–101.
70. Michael L. Kennedy, *The Jacobin Clubs in the French Revolution: The First Years* (Princeton: Princeton University Press, 1982), pp. 10, 299, with the quotation from the latter.
71. Ibid., pp. 13–19, 21.
72. See the description of the elaborate ceremony for the proclamation of the constitution in the town of Vezelise. AN F^1c III Meurthe 9, meeting of general council of Vezelise, October 9, 1791.
73. AN F^1c III Seine-Inférieure 15, document 183.
74. AN F^1c III Aude 7, dossier 1, address of directory of Department of Aude to Louis XVI, April 30, 1791.
75. On Louis's flight, Timothy Tackett, *When the King Took Flight* (Cambridge, MA: Harvard University Press, 2003). See also Hardman, *Life of Louis XVI*, pp. 370–405.
76. *Journal de la correspondance de Nantes*, 9: 409.
77. On the shock felt at news of the departure, BHVP Ms. 805, fol. 162. See also *Journal des Décrets de l'Assemblée Nationale, pour les habitans des campagnes*, June 21, 1791.
78. Hardman, *Life of Louis XVI*, p. 382. A clerical deputy described the letter as "revoking all the approvals he had given to decrees." Rousselot, *Correspondance*, p. 132.
79. On the deep sense of betrayal felt at Louis's action and the manifesto, A.C. Thibaudeau, *Mémoires 1765–1792* (Paris: H. Champion, 1875), p. 138.
80. Hardman, *Life of Louis XVI*, p. 382. Lever said that the reading of the letter to the Assembly had the effect of a bomb. Lever, *Louis XVI*, p. 586.
81. AD Côte d'Or L 346^2, letter of deputies of Department of Côte d'Or to administrators of Department of Côte d'Or, June 22, 1791; letter of deputies of Department of Côte d'Or to electors of Department of Côte d'Or, June 22, 1791.
82. BHVP Ms. 805, fols. 182, 207.
83. Tackett, *When the King Took Flight*, pp. 20–24. AN F^1c III Cantal 2, decree of municipality of Aurillac, June 29, 1791.
84. AD Nord L 792, anonymous letter of June 22, 1791. On the confidence in and resolve of the Assembly AD Nord L 792, letter of deputies of Department of Nord to departmental administrators, June 22, 1791; Fontenay, *Lettres à Babeth*, p. 530.
85. AD Côte d'Or L 346^2, letter of Navier to administrators of Department of Côte d'Or, June 22, 1791. On the calm in Paris, see also Rousselot, *Correspondance*, p. 133.
86. *Journal de la correspondance de Nantes*, 9: 459. On the confusion surrounding the news of the monarch's departure from Paris and the preparations taken in Lille, AN AA 1, plaquette 2, document 13. See also Tackett, *The Glory and the Sorrow*, pp. 120–21.
87. AD Cantal L 76, entry no. 2234, address of directory of Department of Cantal to National Assembly, June 29, 1791. On the immediate rallying of another rural department to the constitution, AN BB^{30} 16, dossier 1, decree of directory of Department of Ardêche, June 24, 1791. On loyalty to the Assembly, see also AN F^1c III Ardennes 9, documents 481–85.
88. Queurau-Lamerie, "Lettres de Maupetit," 22 (1906), p. 476.
89. For a heartfelt expression of the sense of betrayal, see AN F^1c III Deux-Sèvres 8, letter of administrators of directory of Department of Deux-Sèvres to Louis XVI, June 28, 1791. It was read to Louis and elicited a response from him. AN F^1c III Deux-Sèvres 8, letter of Minister of the Interior to administrators of directory of Department of Deux-Sèvres, July 5, 1791.
90. In Pétion's account of the return trip to Paris, he wrote that in villages and towns there were expressions of joy, solidarity, and respect but never a cry of "vive le roi"—only "vive la nation," "vive l'Assemblée nationale." AN F^7 4385^1, dossier 5, account of Pétion de Villeneuve of trip from Varennes, p. 11.
91. AM Toulon L 338, dossier H^3 13, letter of June 28, 1791.
92. *Procès-verbal de l'Assemblée nationale*, no. 687 (June 27, 1791), pp. 32–35; Marie Joseph Paul Yves Roch Gilbert de Motier, marquis de Lafayette, *Mémoires, correspondance et manuscrits du général Lafayette, publiés par sa famille*, 6 vols. (Paris: Fournier, 1837–38), 3: 91–92. See also, Fontenay, *Lettres à Babeth*, p. 537.

93. *Procès-verbal de l'Assemblée nationale*, no. 703 (July 13, 1791), pp. 15–16, with the report annexed to the minutes.
94. On the unusual level of security, BnF Mss. Fonds Français 11697, fols. 267–68.
95. *Procès-verbal de l'Assemblée nationale*, no. 705 (July 15, 1791), p. 8, with the speech annexed to the minutes. The minutes mention that the speech was extemporaneous so versions differ somewhat.
96. AM Marseille 4 D 43, fol. 112v°; Queurau-Lamerie, "Lettres de Maupetit," 22 (1906), pp. 478–79; Fontenay, *Lettres à Babeth*, pp. 551–52.
97. *Procès-verbal de l'Assemblée nationale*, no. 706 (July 16, 1791), p. 28.
98. For one indication of the unfavorable reaction, Tackett, *The Glory and the Sorrow*, pp. 122–23.
99. The most useful study is David Andress, *Massacre at the Champ de Mars: Popular Dissent and Political Culture in the French Revolution* (Rochester, NY: Boydell & Brewer, 2000), especially pp. 157–90. The number of fatalities is unclear but one deputy wrote that there were nine killed. AM Marseille 4 D 43, fol. 114v°.
100. AD Meurthe-et-Moselle L 212, letter of Duquesnoy, July 19, 1791. See also AM Forcalquier, Series D, unclassified carton, letter of July 16, 1791.
101. AM Brest AM Brest 2 D 18 (formerly LL 46 (1791), no. 90, letter of July 24, 1791). The views of the active citizens of Albi were in complete accord with this view. AN F[1]c III Tarn 11, document 6. See also AD Bouches-du-Rhône L 56, fols. 202–202v°; AD Cantal L 76, entry 2440, July 30, 1791.
102. R. R. Palmer, *The Age of the Democratic Revolution: A Political History of Europe and America*, 2 vols. (Princeton: Princeton University Press, 1959–64), 1: 525.
103. *Procès-verbal de l'Assemblée nationale*, no. 726 (August 5, 1791), pp. 45–46; *Journal des Etats-Généraux*, 31: 159, 186.
104. AD Côtes d'Armor 1 L 389, letter of Poulain, August 15, 1791.
105. BnF Mss. Nouv. acq. fr. 6241, fol. 84°.
106. *Procès-verbal de l'Assemblée nationale*, no. 735 (August 14, 1791), p. 8; *Archives parlementaires*, 29: 429; *Journal des Etats-Généraux*, 31: 477–78.
107. Barère, *Mémoires*, 1: 286. A similar sense is found in the letter of Jean Poulain, the deputy who complained about the sense of infallibility of the committees. He wrote that he expected work on the constitution to be completed within a week, suggesting the gains made against many of the revisions. AD Côtes d'Armor 1 L 389, letter of Poulain, August 15, 1791.
108. AM Toulon L 104, dossier D[4] 2, letter of August 11, 1791.
109. Barère, *Mémoires*, 1: 291–94.
110. See, for example, AM Brest 2 D 18 (formerly AM Brest LL 46, 1791, no. 108, letter of September 5, 1791).
111. *Affiches d'Angers ou Journal national du département de Maine-et-Loire*, September 10, 1791.
112. Ibid. Also on the hope for a quick acceptance, Emile Queruau-Lamerie, "Lettres de Michel René Maupetit," *Bulletin de la Commission historique et archéologique de la Mayenne* 23 (1907): 103.
113. On his initial acceptance, AN C 77[2], dossier 769, document 22; on his visit to the Assembly, AN C 77[2], dossier 769, document 29.
114. AN AB[XIX] 3327, letter of Lindet, September 8, 1791. See also AD Rhône 1 L 371, address of administrators of Department of Rhône-et-Loire to citizens of department, September 17, 1791; AN F[1]c III Aude 8, document 147; AN F[1]c III Bouches-du-Rhône 8, undated letter of citizens of town of Saint-Chamas to Louis XVI; AN F[1]c III Meurthe 9, address of directory of Department of Meurthe to citizens, September 16, 1791; AN F[1]c III Nièvre 6, letter of directory of Department of Nièvre to Louis XVI, September 16, 1791; AN F[1]c III Vosges 10, document 10; AM Aix LL 75, fols. 152v°–153; AD Seine-Maritime L 225, document 128, letter of municipal officers of Le Havre to administrators of Department of Seine-Inférieure, September 16, 1791; AM Marseille AA 70, fols. 98–98v°.
115. AN F[1]c III Eure 9, letter of administrators of Department of Eure to Louis XVI, September 19, 1791. See also AN F[1]c III Aveyron 8, address of directory of Department of Aveyron to Louis XVI, September 26, 1791; AN F[1]c III Gironde 8, declaration of mayor and municipal officers of Bordeaux on acceptance of constitution by monarch, September 17, 1791, letter of mayor and municipal officers of Bordeaux to Minister of the Interior, September 20, 1791.
116. AM Brest 2 D 18 (formerly LL 46 (1791), no. 114, letter of September 19, 1791). In a subsequent letter he wrote of the explosion of public happiness in Paris. AM Brest 2 D 18 (formerly LL 46 (1791), no. 116, letter of September 24, 1791). On the reaction in Paris, see also AN AA 62, dossier 1550, plaquette 3[A], document 10; Queruau-Lamerie, "Lettres de Maupetit," 23 (1907), p. 109; *Spectateur National et le Modérateur*, September 16, 1791, September 18, 1791.

117. AM Brest AM Brest 2 D 18 (formerly LL 46 (1791), no. 117, letter of September 26, 1791); *Affiches d'Angers*, September 19, 1791, September 27, 1791; BM Dijon Ms. 1660, fol. 90.
118. *Déclaration d'une partie des députés aux Etats-Généraux, touchant l'acte constitutionnel et l'état du royaume* (Paris: n.p., 1791). The first signatory, and the one who almost certainly wrote the statement, was Duval d'Esprémesnil. Ferrières also signed it.
119. AN AD XVIII^{c} 132, *Declaration d'une partie des députés aux Etats-Généraux de France, sur l'acceptation donnée par le roi à l'acte constitutionnel. Du 15 septembre 1791.*
120. Rousselot, *Correspondance*, p. 156.
121. AN F^{1}c III Aude 8, document 147; AN F^{1}c III Charente 12, extract from registers of deliberations of directory of Department of Charente, September 16, 1791; AM Marseille AA 70, fols. 98–99v°. See also Thibaudeau, *Mémoires 1765–1792*, p. 139.
122. *Discours sur la Constitution française, par Charles Hervier, prêtre, prononcé le 25 septembre 1791 dans l'église métropolitaine et paroissale de Paris, avant le Te Deum, en action de graces de l'heureuse conclusion des travaux de l'Assemblée Nationale, 1791* (Paris: Didot, 1791), pp. 11, 32.
123. Adrian O'Connor, *In Pursuit of Politics: Education and Revolution in Eighteenth-Century France* (Manchester: Manchester University Press, 2017), especially pp. 97–159.
124. On the sense of exhaustion, AC Marseille 4 D 43, fol. 75.
125. *Procès-verbal de l'Assemblée nationale*, no. 778 (September 26, 1791), p. 4; AN C 78, dossier 776, document 6. It appears to have been appropriated from Talleyrand's report, which had proposed the creation of ten law schools, each of which would have a professor teaching the constitution. *Rapport sur l'instruction publique fait au nom du Comité de constitution le 10, 11 et 19 septembre 1791 par M. de Talleyrand-Périgord* (Paris: Baudouin, 1791), p. 163. See also Pilastre de la Brardière and Leclerc, *Correspondance de MM. Les députés des communes de la province d'Anjou*, 10: 469.
126. *Procès-verbal de l'Assemblée nationale*, no. 765 (September 13, 1791), pp. 12–20; AM Brest 2 D 18 (formerly LL 46 (1791), no. 108, letter of September 5, 1791). One contemporary observer asked what more noble use can one make of power than using it to calm passions while advocating forgetting the past? BM Angers Ms. 1888, p. 208.
127. Ménard de la Groye, *Correspondance*, p. 402.
128. AM Brest 2 D 18 (formerly LL 46 (1791), no. 108, letter of September 5, 1791), for the description of the constitution; AM Brest 2 D 18 (formerly LL 46 (1791), no. 107, letter of September 3, 1791), on the hopes for the future.
129. AN C 77^{1}, dossier 765, document 20.
130. *Affiches d'Angers ou Journal national du département de Maine-et-Loire*, October 6, 1791. Also conveying the solemnity of the meeting, AN C 78, dossier 780, document 4.

Conclusion

1. Again, the contrasting terms are drawn from Foner, *The Second Founding*, pp. 1–2.
2. P. M. Jones, *The Peasantry in the French Revolution* (Cambridge: Cambridge University Press, 1988), p. 168.
3. Edelstein, *The French Revolution and the Birth of Electoral Democracy*, pp. 333, 338.
4. Among the rights was the right to hold office. AN D IV* 2, p. 197.
5. The deputy Rousselot, in a letter to his nephew, who was making voter rolls, encouraged him not to be harsh and to exclude as few men as he could. *Correspondance de l'abbé Rousselot*, p. 67.
6. Palmer, *The Age of the Democratic Revolution*, 1: 523–27 arrived at a figure of 70 percent. Edelstein used a different population number than Palmer and estimated eligibility at 60 percent. Edelstein, *The French Revolution and the Birth of Electoral Democracy*, p. 69. The National Assembly calculated that there were 4,298,360 active citizens in France, based on a count of local returns. In England, by contrast, perhaps 4 percent of English males were eligible to vote. Jones, *Reform and Revolution in France*, p. 224. In the United States, where individual states set voting requirements, in many states property ownership was a requirement and some had religious restrictions. Neither of these held in France. Only the state constitution of Pennsylvania was more democratic than the Constitution of 1791. Palmer *The Age of the Democratic Revolution*, 1: 527.
7. The incident provides insight into the reason that that domestic servant was the sole occupational category relegated to the status of passive citizen. Deputies believed that they were dependent on their employer and could not be independent actors. The same reasoning applied to those who could not meet the requirement to pay a direct tax of three days of wages for an ordinary laborer. The Assembly judged their position might make them susceptible to vote-buying schemes in primary assemblies.

8. AD Ille-et-Vilaine L 337, extract from minutes of nomination of electors, fourth arrondissement, Rennes, May 18, 1790.
9. Bruce Ackerman, *Revolutionary Constitutions: Charismatic Leadership and the Rule of Law* (Cambridge, MA: Harvard University Press, 2019).
10. Linda Colley, *The Gun, the Ship, and the Pen: Warfare, Constitutions, and the Making of the Modern World* (New York: Liveright Publishing Corporation, 2021), with the quotation from p. 3.
11. Gautier, *Dictionnaire de la Constitution*, pp. 97–98.
12. Alexander Grab, *Napoleon and the Transformation of Europe* (New York: Palgrave Macmillan, 2003), pp. 63–64.
13. Ibid., p. 115. The new constitution, Grab declared, "laid the foundation of modern Switzerland."
14. Stuart Woolf, *Napoleon's Integration of Europe* (London: Routledge, 1991), pp. 125–27.
15. Linda Colley, "Writing Constitutions and Writing World History," in *The Prospect of Global History*, James Belich, John Darwin, Margaret Frenz, and Chris Wickham, eds. (Oxford: Oxford University Press, 2016), p. 160.
16. Christopher Clark, *Revolutionary Spring: Europe Aflame and the Fight for a New World, 1848–1849* (New York: Crown, 2023), p. 287.
17. Ibid., pp. 398–400.
18. Ibid., p. 403.
19. Ibid., p. 405.
20. Ibid., pp. 400, 402, 405, 710.
21. Patrice Higonnet wrote of the village of Pont-de-Montvert, as it prepared for municipal elections, that in Pont-de-Montvert, as well as the rest of France, "the franchise of 1789 was the widest in the world, not excluding any of the recently independent thirteen colonies." Patrice Higonnet, *Pont-de-Montvert: Social Structure and Politics in a French Village, 1700–1914* (Cambridge, MA: Harvard University Press, 1971), p. 84.
22. Rouvière, "Quatre lettres inédites de Rabaut de Saint-Etienne," p. 13.
23. Gérard Gengembre, "La Contre-Révolution et le refus de la constitution," in *1789 et l'invention de la constitution*, Michel Troper and Lucien Jaume, eds. (Paris: Bruylart and Librairie Générale de Droit et de Jurisprudence, 1994), especially p. 73.
24. On the significance of the Charter, Vincent W. Beach, *Charles X of France: His Life and Times* (Boulder, CO: Pruett Publishing Company, 1971), p. 139.
25. Philip Mansel, *Louis XVIII* (London: Blond & Briggs, 1981), pp. 185–86.
26. Beach, *Charles X*, p. 144; Mansell, *Louis XVIII*, pp. 223–24.
27. Michael Broers, *Napoleon: The Deline and Fall of an Empire: 1811–1821* (New York: Pegasus Books, 2022), p. 562.
28. Ibid.
29. Caiani notes that all goodwill from the acceptance of the constitution had evaporated by November. Caiani, *Louis XVI and the French Revolution*, p. 97.
30. For an example of the bitterness that it generated, AD Côte d'Or L 210, dossier 2, letter of bishop of Dijon to electors of Department of Côte d'Or, February 7, 1791.
31. Indeed, in late September, as the Assembly was preparing to disband, the deputy Grégoire gave an address through which he sought to instill in their successors the same spirit that had animated the National Assembly. Henri Grégoire, *Adresse aux députés de la seconde legislature* (Paris, n.d.). He had made the speech at the Jacobin Club in Paris and the club ordered it printed on September 26. In addition, some former deputies kept up a correspondence among themselves and occasionally criticized their successors. Louis de Noailles, for example, whose motion had unexpectedly set in motion the renunciations on the night of August 4, criticized the legislation against *émigrés*, especially the death penalty provision. He asserted that the royal veto had been welcomed by all friends of the constitution. Admitting that it was not perfect, they sought to defend the constitution against the excesses that had begun quickly after their departure. *Correspondance patriotique, entre les citoyens qui ont été membres de l'Assemblée Nationale constituante*, 4 vols. (Paris: Dupont de Nemours, 1791–99), 2: 70–79, 134–35, 334–41.
32. This admission almost certainly tainted his use of the veto under the Legislative Assembly.
33. Thibaudeau, *Mémoires 1765–1792*, p. 139.
34. Edelstein, *The French Revolution and the Birth of Electoral Democracy*, pp. 261–64, 276.

Bibliography

Archival Sources

Archives Nationales

Series AA: 1, 49, 62
Series AB^{XIX}: 3327, 3359, 3494, 3562
Series AP: 29 AP 102, 284 AP 3, 294 AP 4
AD XVIII^{c}: 132, 134
Series B^{a}: 11, 14, 16, 20^{2}, 25^{1}, 26^{1}, 30, 31, 38 49, 49^{2}, 53, 57, 77, 80
Series BB^{30}: 16, 21
Series C: 31, 32^{1}, 33^{1}, 37^{1}, 74^{1}, 74^{2}, 76^{A2}, 77^{1}, 78, 83, 90, 93, 94, 110, 111, 112, 114^{A}, 116, 117^{1}
Series F^{1}c III: Ain 7; Ardennes 1, 9; Aude 7, 8; Aveyron 8; Bas-Rhin 13; Bouches-du Rhône 8; Charente 12; Deux-Sèvres 8; Eure 9; Finistère 1; Gironde 8, 11; Hérault 10; Ille-et-Vilaine 9; Meurthe 9; Nièvre 6, 7; Seine-Inférieure 15; Var 9; Vosges 10
Series F^{7}: 4385^{1}
Series H^{1}: 207, 409, 563, 564
Series KK: 641, 642, 643, 647, 1105
Series M: 788
Series W: 13, 396, 423

Archives Départementales

Aisne: L 567
Bouches-du-Rhône: C 101, 1046, 1337, 1380, 1383; L 122
Calvados: C 6347, 6348; Caen ED+586; F. 780
Cantal: 27 J 176; L 76
Charente-Maritime: 4 J 1523, 1574
Côte d'Or: C 2975, 2976, 2987^{6*}, 3367, 3475, 3476, 3843; E 642; 4 F 2; L 210
Côtes d'Armor: 1 L 389
Dordogne: OE DEP 5005 (formerly AM Perigueux AA 41)
Eure: 5 F 63
Gironde: C 4364, 4365; 3 L 82
Haute-Garonne: C 303
Ille-et-Vilaine: C 1799, 1804, 1807, 1812, 3129, 3130, 3842, 3899, 3903; 1 F 1184, 1648, 1842; L 337
Maine-et-Loire: 1 B 61; 1 J 61
Marne: E. supp. 4812* (formerly AM Châlons-sur-Marne AA 36)
Meurthe-et-Moselle: AC 527/187 (formerly AM Toul JJ 7); L 212
Nièvre: 1 L 165
Nord: L 792, 10316
Oise: J 135, 136
Puy-de-Dôme: 4 J 6; L 481
Pyrénées Atlantiques: C 1377, 1601
Pyrénées Orientales: C 2119
Seine-Maritime: C 2; C 3; C 2152; L 225; LP 8454

Archives Municipales

Aix: AA 55, 114; BB 114
Angoulême: AA 19
Arles: AA 23
Bayonne: AA 51
Bergerac: Fonds Faugère Carton 1
Bordeaux: D 220
Brest: 2 D 18 (formerly LL 44, 45, 46)
Forcalquier: Series D, unclassified carton
Grenoble: AA 41
Le Havre: AA 49, 72; BB 72; D^3 38
Limoges: AA 4
Lorient: BB 13
Marseille: AA 70; BB 360, 361; 4 D 43
Nantes: AA 82; BB 112
Nevers: BB 46
Strasbourg: AA 2002, 2003, 2004, 2005^A
Toulon: L 94, 99, 104, 338

Bibliothèque Historique de la Ville de Paris

Ms. 805; Ms. CP 6540; Ms. N.A. 108

Bibliothèques Municipales

Albi: Ms. 177
Angers: Ms. 1888
Dijon: Ms. 1660, 2074, 2522
Douai: Ms. 1035
Grenoble: Ms. R. 7109
La Rochelle: Ms. 21
Lyon: Ms. 5430
Nantes: Collection Dugast-Matifeux, vols. 12, 98

Bibliothèque Nationale de France—Manuscrits

Collection Joly de Fleury: 1337
Fonds Français: 10883, 13713
Nouvelles acquisitions françaises: 307, 308, 4121, 4816, 6241, 6687, 12938, 17275

Harvard University

Houghton Library GEN MS. 515. Journal de la Révolution de France en 1789 à Bourges

University of Leeds

Brotherton Library, BL Microfilm 0039. Pierre Marie Rouph de Varicourt Ms. Journal

Published Primary Sources

Adresse à l'Assemblée Nationale et au Roi, par le conseil-général de la commune de Grenoble. 24 février 1790. Grenoble, n.d.

Adresse à l'Assemblée Nationale, par le corps municipal et electoral de la ville de Rouen. Rouen, n.d.

Adresse à tous les bons citoyens de Strasbourg. N.p., 1789.

Adresse au people Breton des villes et campagnes, de la part de leurs deputes à l'Assemblée Nationale. Paris: Imprimerie Nationale, 1789.

Archives d l'Ouest: Recueil de documents concernant la Révolution, 1789–1800, 3 vols. Antonin Proust, ed. Paris: Lacroix, Verboeckhoven et Cie, 1867–69.

Archives parlementaires de 1787 à 1860. Recueil complet des débats législatifs et politiques des Chambres françaises, 82 vols. M. J. Mavidal and M. E. Laurent, eds. 1st series, 1787–99. Paris: Dupont, 1862–1913.

Assemblée des trois-ordres de la province de Dauphiné. N.p., n.d.

Bailly, Jean Sylvain. *Mémoires d'un témoin de la Révolution*, 3 vols. Paris: Levrault, 1804.

Barère, Bertrand. *Mémoires de B. Barère*, 4 vols. Paris: Labitte, 1842–44.

Bombelles, Marc-Marie, marquis de. *Journal de marquis de Bombelles*, 8 vols. Jean Grassion and Frans Durif, eds. Geneva: Droz, 1978–2013.

Cahiers de doléances du Tiers État du bailliage de Rouen pour les États généraux de 1789, 2 vols. Marc Bouloiseau, ed. Paris and Rouen: Presses universitaires de France and Imprimerie administrative de la Seine-Maritime, 1957–60.

Calonne, Charles Alexandre de. *De l'état de la France, présent et à venir*, 5th ed. London and Paris: Laurent, 1790.

Calonne, Charles Alexandre de. *Réponse de M. de Calonne aux observations du parlement sur le nouvel emprunt (Décembre 1785).* (FRBNF31900258).

Calonne, Charles Alexandre de. *Requête au Roi.* London: Spilsbury, 1787.

Campe, Joachim Heinrich. *Été 89: Lettres d'un Allemand à Paris.* Paris: May, 1989.

Catéchisme de la constitution, à l'usage des écoles, précédé de la Declaration des droits de l'homme, par M. Mirabeau. Amiens: Caron-Berquier, 1791.

Catéchisme de la constitution, à l'usage des habitans de la campagne. Epinal: Vautrin, n.d.

Catéchisme du citoyen selon les principes de la nouvelle constitution. Par M. Terrasson.... Clermont-Ferrand: Beaufils, 1790.

Ce qu'on n'a jamais vu. N.p., n.d.

[Cerutti, Joseph-Antoine-Joachim] *A la mémoire auguste de feu de Monsieur le Dauphin.* N.p., n.d.

Colson, Adrien-Joseph. *Lettres d'un bourgeois de Paris à un ami de province.* Chantal Plantier-Sanson, ed. Saint-Cyr-sur-Loire: Christian Pirot, 1993.

Correspondance de l'abbé Rousselt, constituant (1789–1795). Anne-Marie Malingrey, ed. Besançon: Les Belles Lettres, 1992.

Correspondance secrète inédite sur Louis XVI, Marie-Antoinette, la cour et la ville de 1777 à 1792, 2 vols. Adolphe de Lescure, ed. Paris: Plon, 1866.

Delandine, Antoine-François. *De quelques changemens politiques, opérés ou projettés en France pendant les années 1789, 1790 et 1791, ou Discours sur divers points importans de la constitution et de la nouvelle legislation du royaume.* Paris: Laurent, 1791.

Déliberation de la ville et communauté d'Agen, dans l'intérêt de ladite Ville et de toute la province d'Agenois. Du 25 décembre 1788. Agen, n.d.

Déliberations de la ville de Grenoble, du samedi quatorze juin mil sept cent quatre-vingt-huit, à l'Hôtel de Ville de Grenoble, sur les dix heures du matin. N.p., n.d.

Despatches from Paris, 1784–1790, 2 vols. Oscar Browning, ed. London: Offices of the Society, 1909–10.

Détail de ce qui s'est passé à Rennes le 26 janvier 1789. N.p., n.d.

Dictionnaire de l'Académie Françoise, 4th ed. Paris: Brunet, 1762.

Discours prononcé de l'ordre du Roi et en sa présence par M. de Calonne, Contrôleur Général des Finances, dans l'Assemblée des Notables, tenue à Versailles, le 22 février 1787. Versailles: Pierres, 1787.

Discours prononcé le 2 janvier 1790 à l'assemblée de MM. les échevins représentans de la bourgeoisie de Strasbourg par M. le baron de Dietrich. Strasbourg: Dannbach, n.d.

Droit constitutif, et privileges de la ville de Marseille. N.p., n.d.

Dubois-Crancé, Edmond Louis Alexis. *Analyse de la Révolution française depuis l'ouverture des Etats-Généraux jusqu'au 6 brumaire an IV de la république.* Théodore Iung, ed. Paris: Charpentier, 1885.

Dumont, Etienne. *Souvenirs sur Mirabeau et les deux premières assemblées legislatives.* J. Bénétruy, ed. Paris: Presses universitaires de France, 1951.

Encyclopédie, ou Dictionnaire raisonné des sciences, des arts et des métiers, par une société des gens de lettres, 17 vols. Denis Diderot and Jean Lerond d'Alembert, eds. Paris: Briasson, 1751–65.

Essai du patriotism, dédié, adressé et présenté à la Nation assemble à Versailles, par un jeune citoyen philosophique. N.p., 1789.

Etats-Généraux, ou Récit de ce qui s'est passé aux Etats-Généraux, depuis le 17 juin 1789 jusqu'àu premier septembre de la même année. Paris: Imprimerie Nationale, 1791.

Extrait de procès-verbal des Etats de la province de Dauphiné, assemblées à Romans. N.p., n.d.

Extrait du Procès-verbal de l'Assemblée renforcé des Etats de Cambrai & du Cambrésis. Arrêté unanime de l'Assemblée du 9 novembre 1789. N.p., n.d.

Ferrières, Charles-Elie, marquis de. *Correspondance inédite, 1789, 1790, 1791.* Henri Carré, ed. Paris: Armand Colin, 1932.

Ferrières, Charles-Elie, marquis de. *Mémoires*, 2 vols. Paris: Baudouin, 1822.

Fontenay, Pierre Nicolas de. *Lettres à Babeth: chronique de l'Assemblée nationale par un Normand, 1789–1791.* Anne Mézin and Hugues de Boisseau, eds. Paris: SPM, 2015.

Font-Réaulx, Jacques de. "Lettres de J. Bern: Colaud de la Salcette, chanoine de Die, député aux Etats-Généraux de 1789." *Bulletin de la Société d'Archéologie et de Statistique de la Drôme* 69 (1944): 137–56.

Gallot. *Vues sur les bases de la Constitution, et la Déclaration des Droits de l'Homme et du Citoyen.* Versailles, n.d.

Gandilhon, René. "Cinq lettres sur les événements parisiens (30 août 1788–2 août 1789)." *Annales historiques de la Révolution française* 28 (1956): 267–78.

Gautier, P. N. *Dictionnaire de la constitution et du gouvernement français...*, 2nd ed. Paris: Guillaume, 1792.

Gauville, Louis Henri Charles. *Journal du Baron de Gauville, député de l'ordre de la noblesse aux Etats-Généraux depuis le 4 mars 1789 jusqu'au 1er juillet 1790.* Paris: Gay, 1864.

Herly R. "Correspondance du lieutenant général du bailliage de Sarrelouis de la Salle, député de l'Assemblée Nationale, 1789–1791." *Bulletin de la Société des Amis des Pays de la Sarre* 4 (1927): 195–323.

*Histoire philosophique et politique de l'Assemblée nationale, par un député de communes de B****. Mois d'août.* Paris: Devaux et Gattey, 1789.

Instruction patriotique. N.p.: Imprimerie de la Société des amis de la constitution, 1790.

Jessé, Henri de. *Lettre de M. le baron de Jessé, député de la senéchaussée de Beziers, à ses commettans.* Paris: Gattey, 1790.

Journal d'Adrien Duquesnoy, député du Tiers état de Bar-le-Duc, sur l'Assemblée constituante: 3 mai 1789–3 avril 1790, 2 vols. Robert de Crèvecoeur, ed. Paris: Picard, 1894.

[Keverseau, François Marie Périchou de and G. Clavelin]. *Histoire de la Révolution de 1789, et de l'établissement d'une constitution en France*, 20 vols. Paris: Clavelin, 1790–1803.

Lafayette, Marie Joseph Paul Yves Roch Gilbert de Motier, marquis de. *Mémoires, correspondance et manuscrits du général Lafayette, publiés par sa famille*, 6 vols. Paris: Fournier, 1837–38.

Lameth, Alexander. *Histoire de l'Assemblée constituante*, 2 vols. Paris: Moutardier, 1828.

La Première année de la Révolution vue par un témoin: Les "Bulletins" de Poncet-Delpech, député de Quercy aux Etats-Généraux de 1789. Daniel Ligou, ed. Paris: Presses Universitaires de France, 1961.

L'Assemblée nationale aux François. Du onze février 1790. Angers: Pavie, 1790.

Les curés de Dauphiné, à leurs confrères les recteurs de Bretagne. N.p., 1789.

Lettre de Charles ROUX, habitant de Valgondemar, dans les montagnes de Dauphiné, a MM. Du Tiers-état de Bretagne. N.p., n.d.

Lettre écrite par plusiers citoyens du clergé, de la noblesse & des communes de Dauphiné à Messieurs les Syndics-Généraux des Etats de Béarn. N.p., n.d.

Lettres et bulletins de Barentin à Louis XVI. Alphonse Aulard, ed. Paris: Société de l'histoire de la Révolution française, 1915.

Looten, Camille. "Lettres de François-Joseph Bouchette, avocat à Bergues, member de l'Assemblée Nationale constituante." *Annales du Comité flamande de France* 29 (1908–9): 219–645.

Marié, D. "Trois lettres inédites de l'abbé Jallet: Membre de l'Assemblée Constituante." *Annales historiques de la Révolution française* 22 (1950): 326–49.

Mège, Francisque. *Gaultier de Biauzat: Sa vie et sa correspondance*, 2 vols. Paris: Lechevalier, 1890.

Mémoire de droit public sur la ville de Strasbourg et d'Alsace en général. Strasbourg: Dannbach, 1789.

Mémoire des princes présenté au Roi. N.p., n.d.

Mémoires de Bailly, 3 vols. Saint-Albin Berville and François Barrière, eds. Paris: Baudouin, 1821–23.

Mémoires du comte de Paroy, souvenirs d'un défenseur de la famille royale pendant la Révolution (1789–1797). Etienne Charavay, ed. Paris: Plon, 1895.

Mémoire du tiers-état à présenter au Roi. N.p., n.d.

Ménard de la Groye, François. *Correspondance (1789–1791).* Florence Mirouse, ed. Mayenne: Conseil Général de la Sarthe, 1989.

Monod, M. O. "Lettres de Guillaume-Benoît Couderc, bourgeois de Lyon, député à l'Assemblée Constituante, à son oncle M. Vernet-Dupan, à Genève (1781–1792)." *Revue d'histoire de Lyon: études, documents, bibliographie* 5 (1906): 405–25.

[Mounier, Jean-Joseph]. *Lettre écrite au Roi par les trois orders de la province de Dauphiné, sur les Etats-Généraux.* N.p., n.d.

Observations présentées au roi par les bureaux de l'Assemblée des notables: sur les mémoires remis à l'Assemblée ouverte par le roi, à Versailles, le 23 février 1787. Lyon: Imprimerie royale, 1787.

Ouverture des Etats-Généraux, faite à Versailles le 5 mai 1789. Paris: Imprimerie royale, 1789.

Paris et Versailles: Journal anecdotique de 1762 à 1789. Celestin Hippeau, ed. Paris: A. Aubry, 1869.

Pilastre de la Brardière, Urbain-Réné and J. B. Leclerc. *Correspondance de MM. Les députés des communes de la province d'Anjou avec leur commettans relativement aux Etats-Généraux*, 10 vols. Angers: Pavie, 1789–91.

Précis de ce qui s'est passé à l'élection du maire de Strasbourg. N.p., n.d.

Précis exact et historique des faits arrivées à Rennes, les 26 & 27 janvier & autres jours suivants. N.p., n.d.

Procès-verbal de l'Assemblée de Notables, tenue à Versailles, en l'année de MDCCLXXXVII. Paris: Imprimerie royale, 1788.

Procès-verbal de l'Assemblée de Notables, tenue à Versailles, en l'année M. DCCCLXXXVIII. Paris: Imprimerie Royale, 1789.

Procès-verbal de l'Assemblée nationale de France, précedé du Récit des séances des députés des communes; depuis le 5 mai 1789, jusqu'au 12 juin suivant, époque à laquelle la rédaction des procès-verbaux a commencé, 73 vols. Paris: Baudouin, 1789–91.

Procès-verbal des conférences sur la vérification des pouvoirs, tenues par MM. Les Commissaires du Clergé, de la Noblesse & des Communes, tant en la Salle du Comité des Etats-Géneraux, qu'en présence de MM. Les Commissaires du Roi, conformément au desir de Sa Majesté. Paris: Baudouin, 1789.

Procès-verbal des séances de la chambre de l'ordre de la noblesse aux Etats-Généraux, tenues à Versailles en mil sept cent quatre-vingt-neuf. Paris: Imprimerie Nationale, 1792.

Procès-verbal des séances des députés des communes, depuis le 12 juin 1789 jusqu'au 17 juin, jour de sa constitution en Assemblée Nationale. Paris: Baudouin, 1789.

Protestation de la noblesse de Bourgogne, assemblée à Dijon. N.p., n.d.

Protestation de l'ordre de la noblesse de Bretagne. N.p., n.d.

Queurau-Lamerie, Emile. "Lettres de Michel René Maupetit, député à l'assemblée nationale constituante (1789–1791)." *Bulletin de la Commission historique et archéologique de la*

Mayenne 17 (1901): 302–27, 439–54; 18 (1902): 133–63, 321–33, 447–75; 19 (1903): 205–50, 348–78; 20 (1904): 88–125, 176–203, 358–77, 446–72; 21 (1905): 93–124, 204–23, 325–63, 465–88; 22 (1906): 67–95, 213–39, 349–84, 454–93; 23 (1907): 87–115.

Questions d'état décisives resultants pour la province d'Alsace des décrets rendu par l'Assemblée nationale de France depuis le 4 août 1789 jusqu'au 13 février 1790 inclusivement. N.p., 1790.

Rapport du comité chargé du travail sur la constitution par M. Mounier. Paris: Baudouin, 1789.

Récit des séances des députés des communes: depuis le 5 mai 1789 jusqu'au 12 juin suivant, époque à laquelle la redaction des procès-verbaux a commencé. N.p., n.d.

Réflexions sur les inquiétudes auxquelles paroissent se livrer nombre de citoyens de cette ville. Strasbourg: Dannbach, 1789.

Regnault, Jean Joseph. *La Constitution française, mise à la portée de tout le monde*, 2 vols. Bar-le-Duc: La Société typographique, 1791.

Relation de ce qui s'est passé à Rennes le 26, 27 & jours suivants du mois de janvier 1789. N.p., 1789.

Remontrances du Parlement de Paris au XVIIIe siècle, 3 vols. Jules Flammermont, ed. Paris: Imprimerie Nationale, 1888–98.

Réponse des négociants de la ville de Grenoble, à MM. Les juges-consulaires de Montauban, Clermont-Ferrnad, Châlons, Orléans, Tours, Besançon, Dunkerque & Saint-Quentin, et à la Chambre de Commerrce de Picardie, de St. Malo et de Lille en Flandres. N.p., n.d.

Requête au Roi, et délibération du Tiers-État de la ville de Dijon, du 18 janvier 1789. Dijon: Capel, 1789.

Résultat du Conseil d'État du Roi, tenu à Versailles le 27 décembre. Paris: Imprimerie royale, 1788.

Roederer, Pierre Louis. *L'Esprit de la Révolution de 1789.* Paris: N.p., 1831.

Rousselot, Claude-Germain. *Correspondance de l'abbé Rousselot, constituant (1789–1795).* Anne-Marie Malingrey, ed. Besançon: Université de Besançon, 1992.

Rouvière, François. *Quatre lettres inédites de Rabaut Saint-Etienne (1789–1791).* Nîmes: A. Catélan, 1885.

Sallier, Guy-Marie. *Annales françaises, depuis le commencement du règne de Louis XVI jusqu'aux Etats-Généraux, 1774–1789.* Paris: Leriche & Thomine, 1813.

Séance de la nuit du 4 au 5 août 1789, pour former la constitution. Paris: Debray, n.d.

Sieyès, Emmanuel Joseph. *Essai sur les privilèges.* N.p., n.d.

Sommaire des articles convenus le 4 août 1789 pour former la constitution. N.p., n.d.

Staël-Holstein, Anne Louise Germaine. *Considérations sur les principaux événemens de la Révolution française*, 3 vols. London: Baldwin, Cradock and Joy, 1818.

[Target, Guy-Jean-Baptiste]. *IIe Suite de l'écrit intitulé: Les Etats-Généraux convoqués par Louis XVI.* N.p., n.d.

Tempier, D. "Correspondance des députés des Cotes-du-Nord aux Etats-Généraux et à l'Assemblée Nationale Constituante." *Société d'émulation des Cotes-du-Nord, bulletins et mémoires* 26 (1888): 210–63.

Thibaudeau, A. C. *Mémoires 1765–1792.* Paris: H. Champion, 1875.

Toulongeon, François-Emmanuel. *Histoire de la France depuis la Révolution*, 7 vols. (Paris: Treuttel et Würtz, 1801–10).

Traité des droits, fonctions, franchises, exemptions, prérogatives et privilèges annexés en France à chaque dignité...ouvrage de plusieurs jurisconsultes et gens de lettres, 4 vols. Joseph-Nicolas Guyot and Philippe-Antoine Merlin, eds. Paris: Visse, 1786–88.

Ultimatum d'un citoyen du tiers-état au Mémoire des princes présenté au roi, seconde édition. N.p., 1789.

Newspapers

Affiches d'Angers ou Journal national de la province d'Anjou

Annales Orléanoises

Assemblée Nationale, Commune de Paris et Corps Administratifs du Royaume

Assemblée nationale. Correspondance de Bretagne
Bulletin de l'Assemblée Nationale
Courier de Madon
Etats-Généraux. Bulletin de la correspondence de la députation du tiers-état de la sénéchaussée de Brest
Feuille Hébdomadaire Patriotique
Journal d'Etat et du citoyen
Journal de correspondance de Nantes
Journal de la ville, par Jean-Pierre-Louis de Luchet
Journal de Paris
Journal des débats et des décrets
Journal des Décrets de l'Assemblée Nationale, pour les habitans des campagnes
Journal des Etats-Généraux
Le Point du Jour
Révolutions de Paris, dédiées à la nation et du district des Petits Augustins
Spectateur National et le Modérateur
Suite des Nouvelles de Versailles

Secondary Sources

Andress, David. *Massacre at the Champ de Mars: Popular Dissent and Political Culture in the French Revolution*. Rochester, NY: Boydell & Brewer, 2000.

Antoine, Michel. *Le Conseil du roi sous le règne de Louis XV*. Geneva: Droz, 1970.

Babelon, Jean-Pierre. *Henri IV*. Paris: Fayard, 1982.

Baker, Keith Michael. "Controlling French History: The Ideological Arsenal of Jacob-Nicolas Moreau." *Inventing the French Revolution: Essays on French Political Culture in the Eighteenth Century*. Cambridge: Cambridge University Press, 1990: 59–85.

Baker, Keith Michael. "Fixing the French Constitution." *Inventing the French Revolution: Essays on French Political Culture in the Eighteenth Century*. Cambridge: Cambridge University Press, 1990: 252–305.

Barbiche, Bernard and Ségolène de Dainville-Barbiche. *Sully: l'homme et ses fidèles*. Paris: Fayard, 1997.

Baecque, Antoine de. "Pamphlets: Libel and Political Mythology." *Revolution in Print: The Press in France 1775–1800*. Robert Darnton and Daniel Roche, eds. Berkeley: University of California Press, 1989: 165–76.

Beach, Vincent. *Charles X of France: His Life and Times*. Boulder, CO: Pruett Publishing Company, 1971.

Beik, William. *Absolutism and Society in Seventeenth-Century France: State Power and Provincial Aristocracy in Languedoc*. Cambridge: Cambridge University Press, 1985.

Bell, David A. *The Cult of the Nation in France: Inventing Nationalism, 1680–1800*. Cambridge, MA: Harvard University Press, 2001.

Bellesiles, Michael A. *Inventing Equality: Reconstructing the Constitution in the Aftermath of the Civil War*. New York: St. Martin's Press, 2020.

Bergin, Joseph. *The Rise of Richelieu*. New Haven: Yale University Press, 1991.

Bien, David. "Offices, Corps, and a System of State Credit: The Use of Privilege under the Ancien Régime." *The French Revolution and the Creation of Modern Political Culture: The Political Culture of the Old Regime*. Keith Michael Baker, ed. Oxford: Pergamon Press, 1987: 89–114.

Bien, David. "The Secrétaires du Roi: Absolutism, Corps and Privilege under the Ancien Regime." *Vom Ancien Régime zur Französischen Revolution*. Ernst Hinrichs, Eberhard Schmitt, and Rudolph Vierhaus, eds. Göttingen: Vandenhoeck & Ruprecht, 1978: 153–68.

Blackman, Robert H. *1789: The French Revolution Begins*. Cambridge: Cambridge University Press, 2019.

Blackman, Robert H. "What's in a Name? Possible Names for a Legislative Body and the Birth of National Sovereignty during the French Revolution, 15–16 June 1789." *French History* 21 (2007): 22–43.

Bohanan, Donna. *Crown and Nobility in Early Modern France.* New York: Palgrave Macmillan, 2001.

Bonney, Richard. "Absolutism: What's in a Name?" *French History* 1 (1987): 93–117.

Bonney, Richard. *The King's Debts: Finance and Politics in France, 1589–1661.* Oxford: Clarendon Press, 1981.

Bonney, Richard. *Political Change in France under Richelieu and Mazarin.* Oxford: Oxford University Press, 1978.

Bonney, Richard. "Was There a Bourbon Style of Government?" *From Valois to Bourbon: Dynasty, State & Society in Early Modern France.* Keith Cameron, ed. Exeter: University of Exeter Press, 1989: 161–77.

Bosher, J. F. *French Finances 1770–1795: From Business to Bureaucracy.* Cambridge: Cambridge University Press, 1970.

Bossenga, Gail. "City and State: An Urban Perspective on the Origins of the French Revolution." *The French Revolution and the Creation of Modern Political Culture: The Political Culture of the Old Regime.* Keith Michael Baker, ed. Oxford: Pergamon Press, 1987: 115–40.

Bredin, Jean-Denis. *Sieyès: La clé de la Révolution française.* Paris: Fallois, 1988.

Broers, Michael. *Napoleon: The Decline and Fall of an Empire: 1811–1821.* New York: Pegasus Books, 2022.

Brye, Bernard de. *Un évêque d'ancien régime a l'épreuve de la Révolution: Le cardinal A. L. H. de la Fare (1752–1829).* Paris: Publications de la Sorbonne, 1985.

Buisseret, David. *Henry IV King of France.* London: Unwin Hyman, 1984.

Buisseret, David. *Sully and the Growth of Centralized Government in France 1598–1610.* London: Eyre & Spottiswoode, 1968.

Caiani, Ambrogio A. *Louis XVI and the French Revolution, 1789–1792.* Cambridge: Cambridge University Press, 2012.

Campbell, Peter R. "Absolute Monarchy." *The Oxford Handbook of the Ancien Régime.* William Doyle, ed. Oxford: Oxford University Press, 2012: 11–38.

Campbell, Peter R. *Power and Politics in Old Regime France 1720–1745.* London: Routledge, 1996.

Campbell, Peter R. and John Hardman. "Malesherbes and the Crisis of 1787–8." *French History* 35 (2021): 167–91.

Carcassonne, Elie. *Montesquieu et le problème de la constitution française au XVIIIe siècle.* Paris: Presses universitaires de France, 1927.

Chaline, Olivier. *Le règne de Louis XIV*, 2 vols. Paris: Flammarion, 2009.

Chaussinand-Nogaret, Guy. *La Noblesse au XVIIIe siècle: De la féodalité aux Lumières.* Paris: Hachette, 1976.

Christophelsmeier, Carl Heinrich. "The First Revolutionary Step (June 17, 1789)." *University Studies of the University of Nebraska* 9 (1909): 1–87.

Church, William Farr. *Constitutional Thought in Sixteenth-Century France: A Study in the History of Ideas*, reprint ed. New York: Octagon Books, 1969.

Clark, Christopher. *Revolutionary Spring: Europe Aflame and the Fight for a New World, 1848–1849.* New York: Crown, 2023.

Colley, Linda. "Empires of Writing: Britain, America and Constitutions 1776–1848." *Law and History Review* 32 (2014): 237–66.

Colley, Linda. *The Gun, the Ship and the Pen: Warfare, Constitutions, and the Making of the Modern World.* London: Liveright Publishing, 2021.

Colley, Linda. "Writing Constitutions and Writing World History." *The Prospect of Global History.* James Belich, John Darwin, Margaret Frenz, and Chris Wickham, eds. Oxford: Oxford University Press, 2016: 160–77.

Collins, James B. *Classes, Estates and Order in Early Modern Brittany*. Cambridge: Cambridge University Press, 1994.

Cornette, Joël. *La mort de Louis XIV: apogée et crépuscule de la royauté*. Paris: Gallimard, 2015.

Cosandey, Fanny and Robert Descimon. *L'absolutisme en France: histoire et historiographie*. Paris: Seuil, 2002.

D'Auria, Matthew. *The Shaping of French National Identity: Narrating the Nation's Past, 1715–1830*. Cambridge: Cambridge University Press, 2020.

Darnton, Robert. "The High Enlightenment and the Low-Life of Literature in Pre-Revolutionary France." *Past & Present* 51 (May 1971): 83–115.

Dean, Rodney J. *L'Assemblée constituante et la réforme ecclésiastique, 1790*. Paris and London: Rodney Dean, 2014.

Derobert-Ratel, Christiane. *Institutions et vie municipal à Aix en Provence sous la Révolution*. Millau: Edisud, 1981.

Desplat, Christian. "Louis XIII and the Union of Béarn to France." *Conquest and Coalescence: The Shaping of the State in Early Modern Europe*. Mark Greengrass, ed. London: Edward Arnold, 1991: 63–83.

Dhetel, Philippe. *Annales Historiques de la ville de Saint-Jean-de-Losne, Côte d'Or et ancien duché de Bourgogne depuis ses origines jusqu'en 1789...*, 2 vols. Paris: Champion, 1908–10.

Doolin, Paul Rice. *The Fronde*. Cambridge, MA: Harvard University Press, 1935.

Doyle, William. *Jansenism: Catholic Resistance to Authority from the Reformation to the French Revolution*. New York: St. Martin's Press, 2000.

Doyle, William. *The Parlement of Bordeaux and the End of the Old Regime 1771–1790*. London: Ernest Benn, 1974.

Doyle, William. "The Parlements." *The French Revolution and the Creation of Modern Political Culture: The Political Culture of the Old Regime*. Keith Michael Baker, ed. Oxford: Pergamon Press, 1987: 157–67.

Doyle, William. "The Parlements of France and the Breakdown of the Old Regime 1771–1788." *French Historical Studies* 6 (1970): 415–58.

Edelstein, Melvin. *The French Revolution and the Birth of Electoral Democracy*. Burlington, VT: Ashgate, 2014.

Egret, Jean. *La Révolution des notables: Mounier et les monarchiens 1789*. Paris: A. Colin, 1950.

Egret, Jean. *Le Parlement de Dauphiné et les affaires publiques dans la deuxième moitié du XVIIIe siècle*, 2 vols. Grenoble: B. Arthaud, 1942.

Egret, Jean. "Les Origines de la Révolution en Bretagne (1788–1789)." *Revue historique* 213 (2) (1955): 189–215.

Egret, Jean. *Louis XV et l'opposition parlementaire*. Paris: Armand Colin, 1970.

Félix, Joël. *Louis XVI & Marie-Antoinette: un couple en politique*. Paris: Payot, 2006.

Fitzsimmons, Michael P. "Privilege and the Polity in France, 1786–1791." *American Historical Review* 92 (1987): 269–95.

Fitzsimmons, Michael P. *The Night the Old Regime Ended: August 4, 1789, and the French Revolution*. University Park: Pennsylvania State University Press, 2003.

Foner, Eric. *The Second Founding: How the Civil War and Reconstruction Remade the Constitution*. New York: W.W. Norton, 2019.

Ford, Franklin L. *Robe and Sword: The Regrouping of the French Aristocracy after Louis XIV*. Cambridge, MA: Harvard University Press, 1954.

Ford, Franklin L. *Strasbourg in Transition 1648–1789*. Cambridge, MA: Harvard University Press, 1958.

Forsyth, Murray. *Reason and Revolution: The Political Thought of the Abbé Sieyès*. New York: Holmes & Meier, 1987.

Gengembre, Gérard. "La Contre-Révolution et le refus de la constitution." *1789 et l'invention de la constitution*. Michel Troper and Lucien Jaume, eds. Paris: Bruylart and Librairie Générale de Droit et de Jurisprudence, 1994.

Goodwin, Albert. "Calonne, the Assembly of French Notables of 1787 and the Origins of the Révolte Nobiliaire." *English Historical Review* 6 (1946): 329–77.

Griffiths, Robert. *Le Centre perdu: Malouet et les "monarchiens" dans la Révolution française.* Grenoble: Presses universitaires de Grenoble, 1988.

Gruder, Vivian R. *The Notables and the Nation: The Political Schooling of the French, 1787–1788.* Cambridge, MA: Harvard University Press, 2008.

Hamscher, Albert. *The Parlement of Paris after the Fronde 1653–1673.* Pittsburgh: University of Pittsburgh Press, 1976.

Hanson, Paul R. *Provincial Politics in the French Revolution: Caen and Limoges, 1789–1794.* Baton Rouge: Louisiana State University Press, 1989.

Hardman, John. *Barnave: The Revolutionary Who Lost His Head for Marie-Antoinette.* New Haven: Yale University Press, 2023.

Hardman, John. *The Life of Louis XVI.* New Haven: Yale University Press, 2016.

Hardman, John. *Marie-Antoinette: The Making of a Queen.* New Haven: Yale University Press, 2019.

Hardman, John. *Overture to Revolution: The 1787 Assembly of Notables and the Crisis of France's Old Regime.* Oxford: Oxford University Press, 2010.

Hardy, Jr., James D. *Judicial Politics in the Old Regime: The Parlement of Paris during the Regency.* Baton Rouge: Louisiana State University Press, 1967.

Hayden, J. Michael. *France and the Estates General of 1614.* Cambridge: Cambridge University Press, 1974.

Higonnet, Patrice. *Pont-de-Montvert: Social Structure and Politics in a French Village, 1700–1914.* Cambridge, MA: Harvard University Press, 1971.

Hildesheimer, Françoise. *La double mort du roi Louis XIII.* Paris: Flammarion, 2011.

Hildesheimer, Françoise. *Richelieu.* Paris: Flammarion, 2021.

Holt, Mack P. "Burgundians into Frenchmen: Catholic Identity in Sixteenth-Century Burgundy." *Changing Identities in Early Modern France.* Michael Wolfe, ed. Durham: Duke University Press, 1997: 345–70.

Hufton, Olwen. *Europe: Privilege and Protest 1730–1789.* Ithaca: Cornell University Press, 1980.

Hufton, Olwen. *Women and the Limits of Citizenship in the French Revolution.* Toronto: University of Toronto Press, 1992.

Hunt, Lynn Avery. *Revolution and Urban Politics in Provincial France: Troyes and Reims, 1786–1790.* Stanford: Stanford University Press, 1978.

Hurt, John J. *Louis XIV and the Parlements.* Manchester: Manchester University Press, 2002.

Hutt, Maurice. "The Role of the Curés in the Estates-General of 1789." *Journal of Ecclesiastical History* 6 (1955): 205–14.

Hyslop, Beatrice Fry. *A Guide to the General Cahiers of 1789.* New York: Columbia University Press, 1936.

Hyslop, Beatrice Fry. *French Nationalism in 1789 According to the General Cahiers*, reprint ed. New York: Octagon, 1968.

Jackson, Richard A. *Vive le Roi! A History of the French Coronation from Charles V to Charles X.* Chapel Hill: University of North Carolina Press, 1984.

Jones, P. M. *Reform and Revolution in France: The Politics of Transition, 1774–1791.* Cambridge: Cambridge University Press, 1995.

Jourdan, Annie. "République française, Révolution batave: le moment constitutionnel." *Républiques soeurs: le Directoire et la Révolution atlantique.* Rennes: Presses Universitaires de Rennes, 2009: 301–14.

Kennedy, Michael L. *The Jacobin Clubs in the French Revolution: The First Years.* Princeton: Princeton University Press, 1982.

Kierstead, Raymond F. *Pomponne de Bellièvre: A Study of the King's Men in the Age of Henry IV.* Evanston: Northwestern University Press, 1968.

Klaits, Joseph. *Printed Propaganda under Louis XIV: Absolute Monarchy and Public Opinion.* Princeton: Princeton University Press, 1976.

Klein, Claude. "Pourquoi écrit-on une Constitution?" *1789 et l'invention de la constitution.* Michel Troper and Lucien Jaume, eds. Brussels: LGDJ-Bruylant, 1994: 89–99.

Kwass, Michael. *Privilege and the Politics of Taxation in Eighteenth-Century France: Liberté, Egalité, Fiscalité.* New York: Cambridge University Press, 2000.

Lachiver, Marcel. *Les Années de misère: la famine au temps du Grand Roi.* Paris: Fayard, 1991.

Lacorne, Denis. *L'Invention de la république: le modèle américain.* Paris: Hachette, 1991.

Le Gall, Yvon. "Sentiment régional et patriotisme en Bretagne (1788–1790)." *Aux origines provincials de la Révolution.* Robert Chagny, ed. Grenoble: Presses Universitaires de Grenoble, 1990: 403–14.

Lever, Évelyne. *Louis XVI.* Paris: Fayard, 1985.

Lloyd, Howell. *The State, France and the Sixteenth Century.* London: Allen & Unwin, 1983.

Lossky, Andrew. *Louis XIV and the French Monarchy.* New Brunswick: Rutgers University Press, 1994.

Lottin, Alain. "Louis XIV and Flanders." *Conquest and Coalescence: The Shaping of the State in Early Modern Europe.* Mark Greengrass, ed. London: Edward Arnold, 1991: 84–93.

Louis XIV and the Craft of Kingship. John C. Rule, ed. Columbus: Ohio State University Press, 1969.

Maire, Catherine. *De la cause de Dieu à la cause de la Nation: le Jansénisme au XVIIIe siècle.* Paris: Gallimard, 1998.

Mansel, Philip. *King of the World: The Life of Louis XIV.* Chicago: University of Chicago Press, 2019.

Mansel, Philip. *Louis XVIII.* London: Blond & Briggs, 1981.

Margadant, Ted W. *Urban Rivalries in the French Revolution.* Princeton: Princeton University Press, 1992.

Margerison, Kenneth. *Pamphlets and Public Opinion: The Campaign for a Union of Orders in the Early French Revolution.* West Lafayette, IN: Purdue University Press, 1998.

Mason, Lester B. *The French Constitution and the Social Question in the Old Regime 1700–1789.* Bonn: Trapp, 1954.

Maza, Sarah. *Private Lives and Public Affairs: The Causes Célèbres of Prerevolutionary France.* Berkeley: University of California Press, 1993.

McManners, John. *The French Revolution and the Church.* New York: Harper & Row, 1969.

Méraud, Charles. *Étude sur l'invasion allemande en Bourgogne et le siége de Saint-Jean-de-Losne.* Dijon: Carré, 1886.

Miller, Stephen. *Feudalism, Venality and Revolution: French Provincial Assemblies and the Late Ancien Régime.* Manchester: Manchester University Press, 2020.

Miller, Stephen. "Provincial Assemblies, Fiscal Reform and the Language of Politics in the 1770s and 1780s." *French Historical Studies* 35 (2012): 441–75.

Miller, Stephen. "Venal Offices, Provincial Assemblies and the French Revolution." *French History* 28 (2014): 343–65.

Monahan, W. Gregory. *Year of Sorrows: The Great Famine of 1709 in Lyon.* Columbus: Ohio State University Press, 1993.

Moote, A. Lloyd. *Louis XIII, the Just.* Berkeley: University of California Press, 1989.

Moote, A. Lloyd. *The Revolt of the Judges: The Parlement of Paris and the Fronde 1643–1652.* Princeton: Princeton University Press, 1971.

Mousnier, Roland. *La Venalité des offices sous Henri IV et Louis XIII*, 2nd ed. Paris: Presses universitaires de France, 1971.

Mousnier, Roland. *The Assassination of Henry IV.* New York: Charles Scribner's Sons, 1973.

Mousnier, Roland. *The Institutions of France under the Absolute Monarchy, 1598–1789*, 2 vols. Chicago: University of Chicago Press, 1979–84.

Murphy, Orville T. *The Diplomatic Retreat of France and Public Opinion on the Eve of the French Revolution, 1783–1789.* Washington, DC: Catholic University of America Press, 1998.

O'Connor, Adrian. *In Pursuit of Politics: Education and Revolution in Eighteenth-Century France.* Manchester: Manchester University Press, 2017.

Ozouf, Mona. *Festivals and the French Revolution*. Cambridge, MA: Harvard University Press, 1988.

Ozouf-Marignier, Marie-Vic. *La Formation des départments: la représentation du territoire français à la fin du 18e siècle*. Paris: Editions de l'Ecole des Hautes-Etudes en Sciences Sociales, 1989.

Palmer, R. R. *The Age of the Democratic Revolution: A Political History of Europe and America*, 2 vols. Princeton: Princeton University Press, 1959–64.

Parker, David. *The Making of Absolute Monarchy*. New York: St. Martin's Press, 1983.

Pernot, Michel. *La Fronde 1648–1653*. Paris: Tallandier, 2012.

Pernot, Michel. *Les Guerres de religion en France 1559–1598*. Paris: SEDES, 1987.

Poncet, Olivier. *Pomponne de Bellièvre (1529–1607): un homme d'état au temps des guerres de religion*. Paris: École des Chartes, 1998.

Price, Munro. *Preserving the Monarchy: The Comte de Vergennes 1774–1787*. Cambridge: Cambridge University Press, 1995.

Ranum, Orest. *Richelieu and the Councillors of Louis XIII: A Study of the Secretaries of State and Superintendents of Finance in the Ministry of Richelieu 1635–1642*. Oxford: Clarendon Press, 1963.

Ranum, Orest. *The Fronde: A French Revolution*. New York: W. W. Norton, 1993.

Renouvin, Pierre. *Les Assemblées provincials de 1787: origins, développement, résultats*. Paris: Picard, 1921.

Reuss, Rodolphe. *L'Alsace pendant la Révolution française*, 2 vols. Paris: Fischbacher, 1880–94.

Rogister, John. *Louis XV and the Parlement of Paris, 1737–1755*. Cambridge: Cambridge University Press, 1995.

Rowen, Herbert H. *The King's State: Proprietary Dynasticism in Early Modern France*. New Brunswick: Rutgers University Press, 1980.

Sarmant, Thierry. *Louis XIV: Homme et Roi*. Paris: Tallandier, 2012.

Sarmant, Thierry and Mathieu Stoll. *Régner et gouverner: Louis XIV et ses ministres*. Paris: Perrin, 2010.

Scott, Samuel F. "Problems of Law and Order during 1790, the 'Peaceful Year' of the French Revolution." *American Historical Review* 80 (1975): 859–88.

Sewell, Jr., William H. *A Rhetoric of Bourgeois Revolution: The Abbé Sieyès and What Is the Third Estate?* Durham: Duke University Press, 1994.

Shapiro, Gilbert and John Markoff. *Revolutionary Demands: A Content Analysis of the Cahiers de Doléances of 1789*. Stanford: Stanford University Press, 1998.

Shennan, J. H. *Philippe, Duke of Orléans*. London: Thames and Hudson, 1979.

Shennan, J. H. *The Bourbons: The History of a Dynasty*. London: Hambledon Continuum, 2007.

Shennan, J. H. "The Political Role of the Parlement of Paris under Cardinal Fleury." *English Historical Review* 81 (1966): 520–42.

Sheppard, Thomas F. *Lourmarin in the Eighteenth Century: A Study of a French Village*. Baltimore: Johns Hopkins University Press, 1971.

Swann, Julian. "Parlements and Provincial Estates." *The Oxford Handbook of the Ancien Régime*. William Doyle, ed. Oxford: Oxford University Press, 2012: 93–108.

Swann, Julian. *Politics and the Parlement of Paris under Louis XV, 1754–1774*. Cambridge: Cambridge University Press, 1995.

Swann, Julian. *Provincial Power and Absolute Monarchy: The Estates General of Burgundy 1661–1790*. Cambridge: Cambridge University Press, 2003.

Tackett, Timothy. *Becoming a Revolutionary: The Deputies of the French National Assembly and the Emergence of a Revolutionary Culture (1789–1790)*. Princeton: Princeton University Press, 1996.

Tackett, Timothy. *Religion, Revolution and Regional Culture in Eighteenth-Century France*. Princeton: Princeton University Press, 1986.

Tackett, Timothy. *The Glory and the Sorrow: A Parisian and His World in the Age of the French Revolution*. New York: Oxford University Press, 2021.

Tackett, Timothy. *When the King Took Flight*. Cambridge, MA: Harvard University Press, 2003.

Taylor, George V. Review of *Necker: Reform Statesman of the Ancien Régime* by Robert D. Harris. *Journal of Economic History* 49 (1980): 877–79.

Taylor, George V. "Revolutionary and Nonrevolutionary Content in the *Cahiers* of 1789: An Interim Report." *French Historical Studies* 7 (1972): 479–502.

Treasure, Geoffrey. *Cardinal Richelieu and the Development of Absolutism*. London: Adam & Charles Black, 1972.

Treasure, Geoffrey. *Mazarin: The Crisis of Absolutism in France*. London: Routledge, 1995.

Van Key, Dale K. "The Estates-General as Ecumenical Council: The Constitutionalism of Corporate Consensus and the 'Parliament's' Ruling of September 25, 1788." *Journal of Modern History* 61 (1989): 1–52.

Van Key, Dale K. *The Religious Origins of the French Revolution: From Calvin to the Civil Constitution, 1560–1791*. New Haven: Yale University Press, 1996.

Velicu, Adrian. *Civic Catechisms and Reason in the French Revolution*. Burlington, VT: Ashgate, 2010.

Wolfe, Michael. *The Conversion of Henri IV: Politics, Power and Religious Belief in Early Modern France*. Cambridge, MA: Harvard University Press, 1993.

Woolf, Stuart. *Napoleon's Integration of Europe*. London: Routledge, 1991.

Dissertations/Theses

Curtin, Ellen Zwicker. "Constitutional Monarchy versus Absolutism: The Remonstrances of the Parlement of Paris 1716–1771." M.A. thesis, University of North Carolina at Chapel Hill, 1975.

Index